DRAMATISTS
SOURCEBOOK

25TH EDITION

DRAMATISTS SOURCEBOOK

25TH EDITION

Complete opportunities for playwrights, translators, composers, lyricists and librettists

THEATRE COMMUNICATIONS GROUP

NEW YORK

2008

Published by Theatre Communications Group, Inc.
520 8th Ave, 24th Floor, New York, NY 10018-4156.

This publication is made possible in part with public funds from the New York State Council on the Arts, a State Agency.

TCG books are exclusively distributed to the book trade by Consortium Book Sales and Distribution.

Manufactured in the United States of America.

ISSN 0733-1606
ISBN 978-1-55936-336-5

CONTENTS

PREFACE

Welcome to the 25th edition of the *Dramatists Sourcebook*.

The *Sourcebook* was first published in 1981 and contained three hundred listings. Now, twenty-seven years later, it hosts nearly three times that many. This is good news.

Running a theatre or theatre-support organization is challenging work. The sustainability of the field is dependent on a fluctuating funding environment and the economy, in addition to other factors. For this reason, organizations often redefine their programs or eliminate them altogether. But because the theatre arts is a dynamic field with a regular infusion of new and creative people, additional programs and the theatres that run them are being created all the time. More than 850 opportunities for playwrights is something to get excited about!

Using the *Sourcebook*. Since the *Sourcebook* is published biennially, it is always important to confirm a deadline before submitting work; an organization's website is an excellent source for this. Years for annual deadlines are not included, since more than one deadline will pass before the next edition of the *Sourcebook* is printed. Always assume the deadline dates in this book refer to the day materials should arrive, not the postmark date, unless otherwise stated.

Study Tony Kushner's "A Simple Working Guide for Playwrights" (page ix, the Prologue). It offers great advice.

Select those listings your work is best suited for and follow the guidelines meticulously. The Special Interests Index is helpful in finding those listings that may be suited to your type of work. When instructed to write for guidelines, do so. This is a good idea in general, as dates and guidelines sometimes change after the *Sourcebook* is published. Most important is to **ALWAYS ENCLOSE AN SASE** with every mailed script, unless the entry specifies that scripts will not be returned. If a listing states that an organization accepts scripts, it should always be assumed that an SASE must be sent as well (we do not restate this for every listing).

"Full-length play" means just that—a full-length, original work for adult audiences, without a score or libretto. One-acts, musicals, adaptations, translations, plays for young audiences, solo pieces, performance art and screenplays are listed separately. "Young audiences" refers to audiences age 18 or younger, "young playwrights" refers to playwrights age 18 or younger, "students" refers to students in college or in an affiliated writing program.

Listings are alphabetized letter by letter (excluding "The" and "A"), for example, "A. D. Players" follows "Adirondack Theatre Festival." Entries are alphabetized by first word (excluding "The") even if they start with a person's name. So, for example, "John Drew Theater" is listed under "J." (In the index, you will find this theatre listed under "J" and "D.") Regardless of the way "theatre" is spelled in an organization's name, we alphabetize it as if it were spelled "re."

It is important to us that the *Sourcebook* continue to be a beneficial service to playwrights. With each edition, we take painstaking effort to ensure the accuracy of the listings and to make sure the book is clearly written and easy to navigate. Every organization listed in the *Sourcebook* has been contacted directly and the accuracy of their listing confirmed at press time. Because each edition of the *Sourcebook* is fully revised, it is important to always use the most recent edition.

We thank all of the organizations included here. It is through their support that the field stays strong. But, most of all, we thank you, the artists, for your great work and perseverance. We are honored to be of service. We wish you great success.

The Editors
September 2008

PROLOGUE

A Simple Working Guide for Playwrights
by Tony Kushner

A) Format: Most playwrights use a format in which character headings are placed centered above the line and capitalized:

LIONEL

I don't possess a mansion, a car, or a string of polo ponies...

Lines should be single-spaced. Stage directions should be indented and single-spaced. If a character's line is interrupted at the end of the page, its continuance on the following page should be marked as such:

LIONEL (CONT'D)

or a string of polo ponies...

There are denser, and thus more economical, formats; since Xeroxing is expensive, and heavy scripts cost more to ship, you may be tempted to use these, but a generously spaced format is much easier to read, and in these matters it doesn't pay to be parsimonious.

B) Typing and reproducing: Scripts should be typed neatly and reproduced clearly. Remember that everyone who reads your script will be reading many others additionally, and it will work to your serious disadvantage if the copy's sloppy, faded, or otherwise unappealing. If you use a computer printer, eschew old-fashioned dot-matrix and other robotic kinds of print. Also, I think it's best to avoid using incredibly fancy word-processing printing programs with eight different typefaces and decorative borders. Simple typescript, carefully done, is best. Check for typos. A playwright's punctuation may be idiosyncratic for purposes of expressiveness, but not too idiosyncratic, and spelling should be correct.

C) Sending the script:

1)   The script should have a title page with the title and your name, address and phone number, or that of your agent or representative. Scripts are now automatically copyrighted at the moment of creation, but simply writing © and the date on the title page can serve as a kind of scarecrow for thievish magpies.

2)   Never, never send an unbound script. Loose pages held together by a rubber band don't qualify as bound, nor do pages clamped together with a mega-paperclip. A heavy paper cover will protect the script as it passes from hand to hand.

3)   Always, always enclose a self-addressed stamped envelope (SASE) or you will never see your script again. You may enclose a note telling the theatre to dispose of the copy instead of returning it; but you must have the ultimate fate of the script planned for in the eventuality of its not being selected for production. Don't leave this up to the theatre! If you want receipt of the script acknowledged, include a self-addressed, stamped postcard (SASP).

D) Letter of inquiry and synopsis: If a theatre states, in its entry in the *Sourcebook*, that it does not accept unsolicited scripts, believe it. Don't call and ask if there are exceptions; there aren't. A well-written and concise letter of inquiry, however, accompanied by a synopsis possessed of similar virtues, can get you an invitation to submit your play. It's prudent, then, to spend time on both letter and synopsis. It is, admittedly, very hard for a writer to sum up his or her work in less than a page, but this kind of boiling-down can be of value beyond its necessity as a tool for marketing; use it to help clarify for yourself what's central and essential about your play. A good synopsis should briefly summarize the basic features of the plot without going into excessive detail; it should evoke both the style and the thematic substance of the play without recourse to clichéd description ("This play is about what happens when people lose their dreams..."); and it should convey essential information, such as cast size, gender breakdown, period, location, or anything else a literary manager deciding whether to send for the play might want to know. Make reference to other productions in your letter, but don't send thick packets of reviews and photos. And don't offer your opinion of the play's worth, which will be inferred as being positive from the fact that you are its parent.

E) Waiting: Theatres almost always take a long time to respond to playwrights about a specific play, frequently far in excess of the time given in their listings in the *Sourcebook*. This is due neither to spite nor indolence. Literary departments are usually understaffed and their workload is fearsome. Then, too, the process of selection invariably involves a host of people and considerations of all kinds. In my opinion you do yourself no good by repeatedly calling after the status of your script; you will become identified as a pest. It's terribly expensive to copy and mail scripts, but you must be prepared to shoulder the expense and keep making copies if they don't get returned. If, after a certain length of time past the deadline, you haven't heard from a theatre, send a letter inquiring politely about the play, reminding the appropriate people that you'd sent an SASE with the script; and then forget about it. In most cases, you will get a response and the script returned eventually.

One way to cut down on the expenses involved is to be selective about venues for submission. Reading *Sourcebook* entries and scrutinizing a copy of *Theatre Profiles* [available online at www.tcg.org; see the Useful Publications section of this book] will help you select the theatres most compatible with your work. If you've written a musical celebration of the life of Phyllis Schlafly, for example, you won't want to send it to theatres with an interest in radical feminist dramas. Or you won't necessarily want to send your play about the history of Western imperialism to a theatre that produces an annual season of musical comedy.

F) Produce yourself! In *Endgame*, Clov asks Hamm, "Do you believe in the life to come?" and Hamm responds, "Mine was always that." The condition of endless deferment is one that modern American playwrights share with Beckett's characters and other denizens of the postmodern world. Don't spend your life waiting. You may not be an actor, but that doesn't mean that action is forbidden you. Playwrights can, with very little expense, mount readings of their work; they can band together with other playwrights for readings and discussions; and they can, if they want to, produce their work themselves. Growth as a writer for the stage depends on seeing your work on stage, and if no one else will put it there, the job is up to you. At the very least, and above all else, while waiting, waiting, waiting for responses and offers, keep reading, thinking and writing.

Tony Kushner's plays include *Angels in America, Parts One and Two*; *A Bright Room Called Day*; *Caroline, or Change*; *Homebody/Kabul*; *Hydriotaphia* and *Slavs!* His adaptations include Corneille's *The Illusion*, Ansky's *The Dybbuk*, Brecht's *The Good Person of Szechuan*, Goethe's *Stella* and English-language libretti for two operas: Krása's *Brundibár* and Martinu's *Comedy on the Bridge*. In 2003, HBO presented a film version of *Angels in America*, directed by Mike Nichols. *Homebody/Kabul* is being adapted for film by Mira Nair. Recent books include *Brundibar*, a picture book for children, illustrated by Maurice Sendak; *The Art of Maurice Sendak, 1980–The Present* and *Wrestling with Zion: Progressive Jewish-American Responses to the Israeli-Palestinian Conflict*, co-edited with Alisa Solomon. Mr. Kushner is the recipient of numerous awards, including the Pulitzer Prize for Drama (*Angels in America, Part One*); two Tony Awards for Best Play (*Angels in America*, 1993 and 1994); three Obie Awards (*Slavs!*, *Homebody/Kabul* and *Caroline, or Change*); an Evening Standard Award (*Angels in America*); two Dramatists Guild/Hull-Warriner Awards (*Angels in America* and

Homebody/Kabul); an Arts Award from the American Academy of Arts and Letters; a Cultural Achievement Award from the National Foundation for Jewish Culture; the PEN/Laura Pels Award for Mid-Career Playwright; a Spirit of Justice Award from the Gay and Lesbian Advocates and Defenders; and the first Steinberg Distinguished Playwright Award, presented for the first time in 2008 by the Harold and Mimi Steinberg Charitable Trust. Mr. Kushner was born in Lake Charles, Louisiana, but he doesn't live there anymore.

PART 1
SCRIPT
OPPORTUNITIES

Production

Prizes

Publication

Development

PRODUCTION

What theatres are included in this section?

The overwhelming majority of the not-for-profit professional theatres throughout the U.S. that accept submissions is represented here. Theatres to which playwrights cannot submit work, even through an agent, are not included. (These are theatres that directly solicit playwrights only.) In order to be included, a theatre must meet professional standards of staffing, programming and budget; most have been operating for at least two years. Commercial and amateur producers are not included.

How should I go about deciding where to submit my play?

Don't send your play out indiscriminately. Take time to study the listings and select those theatres most likely to be receptive to your material. Find out all you can about each of the theatres you select. See the theatre's website. Read *American Theatre*'s "OnStage" section to see what plays the theatres are currently presenting and what their other activities are (see Useful Publications for more information). Whenever possible, see the theatre's work.

When I submit my play, what can I do to maximize its chances?

First, read carefully the Simple Working Guide for Playwrights in the Prologue of this *Sourcebook* for good advice on script submission. Then follow each theatre's guidelines meticulously. Pay particular attention to the Special Interests section: If a theatre specifies "gay and lesbian themes only," do not send them your heterosexual romantic comedy, however witty and well written it is. Also, bear in mind the following points about the various submission procedures:

3

1) "Accepts unsolicited scripts": Don't waste the theatre's time and yours by writing to ask permission to submit your play—just send it. If you want an acknowledgment of receipt, say so and enclose a self-addressed stamped postcard (SASP) for this purpose. **Always enclose a self-addressed stamped envelope (SASE) for the return of a script.**

2) "Synopsis and letter of inquiry": Never send an unsolicited script to these theatres. Prepare a clear, cogent and *brief* synopsis of your play and send it along with any other materials requested in the listing. The letter of inquiry is a cover note asking for permission to submit the script; if there is something about your play or about yourself as a writer that you think may spark the theatre's interest, by all means mention it, but keep the letter brief. We've asked theatres requiring letters and synopses to give us two response times—one for letters and one for scripts, should they ask to see one. All response times are approximate, and theatres may take longer to respond than stated. Always enclose an SASP for the theatre's response, unless the theatre specifies that it only responds if it wants to see the script.

3) "Professional recommendation": Send a script (not a letter of inquiry) accompanied by a letter of recommendation from a theatre professional. Wait until you have obtained such a letter before approaching these theatres.

4) "Agent submission": If you do not have an agent yet, do not submit to these theatres. Wait until you have had a production or two and have acquired a representative who can submit your script for you.

5) Do not email your submissions, unless specifically directed to do so. Email and web addresses are included for the purpose of general inquiries and, when noted, to obtain guidelines or applications.

6) Deadlines: Years for annual deadlines are not included since deadlines may occur over consecutive years. Some deadlines for special programs may fall outside the publication period of this book, which is biennial. All deadlines reflect the upcoming submission deadline for a theatre at press time. It is always best to confirm a deadline before submitting work (a theatre's website is an excellent resource for this).

ABOUT FACE THEATRE
(Founded 1995)

1222 West Wilson, 2nd Floor; Chicago, IL 60640; (773) 784-8565,
    FAX 784-8557; literary@aboutfacetheatre.com,
    www.aboutfacetheatre.com

Literary Department

Submission procedure: no unsolicited scripts; brief synopsis, bio and letter of inquiry. **Types of material:** full-length plays, literary adaptations, performance art. **Special interests:** queer artists and scripts about queer experience; material that challenges expectations and ideas about gender and sexuality in historical or contemporary contexts; work that explores urgent social justice issues through experimentation with dramatic form, structure, presentation and characters. **Facilities:** no permanent facility. **Best submission time:** year-round. **Response time:** 6 months. **Special programs:** writers' workshop; readings; rough stagings with audience response.

THE ACTING COMPANY
(Founded 1972)

Box 898; New York, NY 10108-0898; (212) 258-3111, FAX 258-3299;
    mail@theactingcompany.org, www.theactingcompany.org

Margot Harley, *Producing Director*

Submission procedure: no unsolicited scripts; professional recommendation. **Types of material:** full-length plays, translations, adaptations. **Special interests:** mainly classical repertory but occasionally produces new works suited to acting ensemble of approximately 8–12 performers; prefers works with poetic dimension and heightened language. **Facilities:** no permanent facility; touring company that plays in New York City for 1 or 2 weeks a year. **Production considerations:** productions tour in repertory; simple, transportable proscenium-stage set. **Best submission time:** year-round. **Response time:** varies.

ACTOR'S EXPRESS
(Founded 1988)

King Plow Arts Center, J-107; 887 West Marietta St NW; Atlanta, GA 30318;
    (404) 875-1606, FAX 875-2791; freddie@actorsexpress.com,
    www.actors-express.com

Freddie Ashley, *Artistic Director*

Submission procedure: no unsolicited scripts; 1-page synopsis and bio. **Types of material:** full-length plays, musicals. **Special interests:** contemporary, socially relevant material; gay themes; works with poetic dimension; multiethnic and minority works. **Facilities:** Actor's Express, 150 seats, black box. **Production considerations:** modest production demands; no fly space. **Best submission time:** Apr–Jul. **Response time:** 6 weeks letter; 6 months script.

ACTORS GUILD OF LEXINGTON

(Founded 1984)
141 East Main St; Lexington, KY 40507; (859) 233-7330, FAX 233-3773;
    actorsguild@qx.edu, www.actorsguildoflexington.org
Richard St. Peter, *Artistic Director*

Submission procedure: no unsolicited scripts; synopsis and letter of inquiry; prefers electronic submission. **Types of material:** full-length plays, solo pieces. **Facilities:** Main Stage, 200 seats, black box. **Production considerations:** cast limit of 6; no fly space; prefers single set. **Best submission time:** year-round. **Response time:** 1 month letter; 6 months script.

ACTORS THEATRE OF LOUISVILLE

(see Humana Festival of New American Plays in Development and National Ten-Minute Play Contest in Prizes)

ACTORS THEATRE OF PHOENIX

(Founded 1985)
Box 1924; Phoenix, AZ 85001-1924; (602) 253-6701, FAX 254-9577;
    info@actorstheatrephx.org, www.actorstheatrephx.org
Matthew Wiener, *Producing Artistic Director*

Submission procedure: no unsolicited scripts; professional recommendation. **Types of material:** full-length plays, translations, adaptations. **Special interests:** plays dealing with social and political issues. **Facilities:** Herberger Theater Center, Stage West, 300 seats, proscenium stage. **Production considerations:** cast limit of 8. **Best submission time:** year-round. **Response time:** 10 months.

ACT THEATRE

(Founded 1965)
Kreielsheimer Place, 700 Union St; Seattle, WA 98101-4037;
    (206) 292-7660, FAX 292-7670; www.acttheatre.org
Kurt Beattie, *Artistic Director*

Submission procedure: no unsolicited scripts; synopsis, 10-page dialogue sample and letter of inquiry from Northwest playwrights only. **Types of material:** full-length plays, translations, adaptations, musicals, solo pieces. **Special interests:** current social, political and psychological issues; plays theatrical in imagination and storytelling; multicultural themes; prefer no kitchen-sink realism or "message" plays. **Facilities:** The Allen, 387 seats, arena stage; The Falls, 381 seats, thrust stage; The Bullitt, 150 seats, cabaret. **Best submission time:** Sep–Apr. **Response time:** 6 months letter. **Special programs:** new play development workshops and commissions.

ACT II PLAYHOUSE

(Founded 1998)

Box 555, 56 E Butler Ave; Ambler, PA 19002; (215) 654-0200,
    FAX 654-9050; info@act2.org, www.act2.org

Steve Blumenthal, *Founding Artistic Director*

Submission procedure: accepts unsolicited scripts. **Types of material:** full-length plays, musicals, solo pieces. **Special interests:** no experimental plays; contemporary works. **Facilities:** Act II Playhouse, 130 seats. **Production considerations:** cast limit of 6; unit set, low ceiling, limited fly space. **Best submission time:** year-round. **Response time:** 1 month.

ADIRONDACK THEATRE FESTIVAL

(Founded 1995)

Box 3203; Glens Falls, NY 12801; (518) 798-7479, FAX 793-1334;
    atf@atfestival.org, www.atfestival.org

Mark Fleischer, *Producing Artistic Director*

Submission procedure: no unsolicited scripts; professional recommendation. **Types of material:** full-length plays, adaptations, musicals, cabaret/revues, solo pieces. **Special interests:** contemporary work. **Facilities:** Charles R. Wood Theater, 280 seats, flexible stage. **Production considerations:** prefers cast limit of 10; no fly space. **Best submission time:** Aug–Jan. **Response time:** 6 months letter; 6 months script.

A. D. PLAYERS

(Founded 1967)

2710 West Alabama St; Houston, TX 77098; (713) 526-2721,
    FAX 439-0905; lee@adplayers.org, www.adplayers.org

Literary Manager

Submission procedure: no unsolicited scripts; synopsis and dialogue sample. **Types of material:** full-length plays, adaptations, plays for young audiences, musicals. **Special interests:** plays for students grades K–8; "plays that uphold family values and support moral decisions"; children's plays that have strong role models; no "witchcraft, demons or ghosts." **Facilities:** Grace Theater, 220 seats, proscenium stage; Rotunda Theater, 148 seats, arena stage. **Production considerations:** for Grace Theater: cast limit of 10; very limited fly and wing space. For Rotunda Theater: cast limit of 6, shows no longer than 90 minutes; minimal scenery. **Best submission time:** year-round. **Response time:** 10 months.

AFRICAN CONTINUUM THEATRE CO. (ACTCO)

(Founded 1996)

3523 12th St NE, 2nd Floor; Washington, DC 20017; (202) 529-5763,
    FAX 529-5764; info@africancontinuumtheatre.com

Rubie G. Coles, *President, Board of Directors*

Submission procedure: accepts unsolicited scripts; prefers 2-page synopsis and 10-page dialogue sample. **Types of material:** full-length plays, translations, adaptations, musicals. **Special interests:** multicultural work, must be relevant to African-American community. **Facilities:** no permanent facility. **Production considerations:** small cast; unit set. **Best submission time:** year-round. **Response time:** 12 months. **Special programs:** Fresh Flavas New Works Program: reading series "designed to give a voice to writers on the fringe of an already marginalized community."

ALABAMA SHAKESPEARE FESTIVAL
(Founded 1972)
1 Festival Dr; Montgomery, AL 36117-4605; (334) 271-5300,
    FAX 271-5348; www.asf.net
Nancy Rominger, *Artistic Associate*

Submission procedure: accepts unsolicited scripts for Southern Writers' Project only (see below); agent submission for all other plays. **Types of material:** full-length plays, adaptations, plays for young audiences. **Special interests:** new plays with southern or African-American themes. **Facilities:** Festival Stage, 750 seats, modified thrust stage; Octagon, 225 seats, flexible stage. **Best submission time:** late spring. **Response time:** 12 months. **Special programs:** Southern Writers' Project: develops plays with southern and/or African-American themes; address submissions to Southern Writers' Project.

ALGONKUIN THEATRE COMPANY
(Founded 1993)
1231 Pulaski Blvd; Bellingham, MA 02019; algonkuintheatre@comcast.net,
    www.algonkuintheatre.org
Marty BlackEagle-Carl, *Artistic Director*

Submission procedure: no unsolicited scripts; letter of inquiry only. **Types of material:** full-length plays, one-acts, translations, adaptations. **Special interests:** Native American plays. **Facilities:** Algonkuin Theatre, 150 seats, black box. **Production Considerations:** unit set. **Best submission time:** summer. **Response time:** 1 day email; 1 month script. **Special programs:** Shakespeare-in-the-Park: Shakespearean-style play every summer; *deadline:* summer prior to production.

ALLEY THEATRE
(Founded 1947)
615 Texas Ave; Houston, TX 77002; (713) 228-9341; www.alleytheatre.org
Mark Bly, *Dramaturg*

Submission procedure: no unsolicited scripts; professional recommendation. **Types of material:** full-length plays, translations, adaptations, musicals. **Facilities:** Hubbard Stage, 824 seats, thrust stage; Neuhaus Stage, 310 seats, arena/thrust stage. **Best submission time:** year-round. **Response time:** 8 months.

ALLIANCE THEATRE

(Founded 1968)

1280 Peachtree St NE; Atlanta, GA 30309; FAX (404) 733-4625;
www.alliancetheatre.org

Literary Department

Submission procedure: no unsolicited scripts; agent submission; GA writers only may submit synopsis, maximum 10-page dialogue sample and letter of inquiry with SASE for response. **Types of material:** full-length plays, one-acts, plays for young audiences, musicals. **Special interests:** work that speaks to a culturally diverse community; plays with compelling stories and engaging characters told in adventurous ways. **Facilities:** Alliance Stage, 800 seats, proscenium stage; Hertz Stage, 200 seats, flexible stage. **Best submission time:** Mar–Sep. **Response time:** 2 months letter; 6 months script.

AMAS MUSICAL THEATRE, INC.

(Founded 1968)

115 West MacDougal St; New York, NY 10012; (212) 563-2565;
amas@amasmusical.org, www.amasmusical.org

Donna Trinkoff, *Producing Artistic Director*

Submission procedure: accepts unsolicited scripts. **Types of material:** musicals, cabaret/revues. **Special interests:** multicultural casts and themes. **Facilities:** no permanent facility; company performs in various proscenium or black box venues with 74–99 seats. **Production considerations:** cast limit of 10. **Best submission time:** summer, winter. **Response time:** 6 months. **Special programs:** Amas Mainstage Productions: 1-2 scripts per year receive 4-week Equity production. Amas Workshop: 1-2 scripts per year receive 2-3 weeks of rehearsal culminating in public staged reading. Amas Six O'Clock Musical Theatre Lab: 6-8 scripts per year receive minimal rehearsal culminating in public concert reading; writer must supply cast and musical director; Amas provides theatre and publicity.

AMERICAN CONSERVATORY THEATER

(Founded 1965)

30 Grant Ave, 6th Floor; San Francisco, CA 94108-5800;
FAX (415) 433-2711; www.act-sf.org

Literary Department

Submission procedure: no unsolicited scripts; synopsis, maximum 10-page dialogue sample and letter of inquiry; prefers agent submission or professional recommendation. **Types of material:** full-length plays, translations, adaptations. **Facilities:** American Conservatory Theater, 1000 seats, proscenium stage; Zeum Theater, 120 seats, black box. **Best submission time:** year-round. **Response time:** 12 months.

AMERICAN FOLKLORE THEATRE (AFT)

(Founded 1990)

Box 273; Fish Creek, WI 54212; (920) 854-6117, FAX 854-9106;
    aft@folkloretheatre.com, www.folkloretheatre.com

Jeffrey Herbst, *Artistic Director*

Submission procedure: no unsolicited scripts; synopsis and letter of inquiry; prefers electronic submission or send SASE for response. **Types of material:** full-length plays, one-acts, adaptations, plays for young audiences, musicals. **Special interests:** musicals appropriate for families. **Facilities:** summer: Peninsula State Park Theatre, 800 seats, modified proscenium stage; fall: various town halls, 125–200 seats. **Production considerations:** Summer show: cast limit of 10. Fall show: cast limit of 4; minimal set. **Best submission time:** year-round. **Response time:** 2 months letter; 6 months script. **Special programs:** workshops of new work; potential stipend and/or commission for development.

AMERICAN MUSIC THEATER FESTIVAL/
PRINCE MUSIC THEATER

(Founded 1984)

100 South Broad St, Suite 650; Philadelphia, PA 19110; (215) 972-1000,
    FAX 972-1020; www.princemusictheater.org

Submission procedure: no unsolicited scripts; synopsis, cassette and letter of inquiry. **Types of material:** music-theatre works including musical comedy, music drama, opera, experimental works, solo pieces. **Facilities:** Prince Music Theater, 450 seats, proscenium stage. **Best submission time:** year-round. **Response time:** 8 months.

AMERICAN REPERTORY THEATRE

(Founded 1979)

64 Brattle St; Cambridge, MA 02138; (617) 495-2668; www.amrep.org

Scott Zigler, *Artistic Coordinator, New Play Development*

Submission procedure: no unsolicited scripts; agent submission. **Types of material:** full-length plays, translations, adaptations, musicals, cabaret/revues. **Special interests:** prefers "nonrealistic material that lends itself to extremely theatrical staging." **Facilities:** Loeb Drama Center, 556 seats, flexible stage; Zero Arrow Street Theatre, 300 seats, flexible stage; Church Street Theatre, 200 seats, black box. **Best submission time:** Sep–Jan. **Response time:** 6 months.

AMERICAN THEATER COMPANY

(Founded 1985)

1909 West Byron St; Chicago, IL 60613; (773) 409-4125, FAX 929-5171;
    info@atcweb.org, www.atcweb.org

PJ Paparelli, *Artistic Director*

Submission procedure: no unsolicited scripts; synopsis, 10-page sample and letter of inquiry with SASP for response. **Types of material:** full-length plays, translations, adaptations, musicals. **Special interests:** prefers playwright familiar with theatre's mission statement and history (see website); distinctly American, language-oriented plays that utilize heightened theatrical reality; musicals; substantive comedies; social and political themes. **Facilities:** American Theater Company, 107 seats, modified thrust stage. **Production considerations:** prefers cast limit of 10; modest technical demands. **Best submission time:** year-round. **Response time:** 4 months letter; 12 months script.

AMERICAN THEATRE OF ACTORS, INC.

(Founded 1976)
314 West 54th St; New York, NY 10019; (212) 581-3044
James Jennings, *Artistic Director*

Submission procedure: accepts unsolicited scripts. **Types of material:** full-length plays, one-acts. **Special interests:** realistic plays dealing with contemporary social issues. **Facilities:** Chernuchin Theatre, 140 seats, proscenium stage; Sargent Theatre, 65 seats, proscenium stage; Beckmann Theatre, 35 seats, arena stage. **Production considerations:** cast limit of 8; minimal sets. **Best submission time:** year-round. **Response time:** 2 weeks.

THE AQUILA THEATRE COMPANY

(Founded 1991)
4 Washington Square N, Room 452; New York, NY 10003;
    aquila@aquilatheatre.com, www.aquilatheatre.com
Kimberly Donato, *Assistant Artistic Director*

Submission procedure: accepts unsolicited scripts. **Types of material:** translations only. **Facilities:** no permanent facility. **Best submission time:** year-round. **Response time:** 6 months. **Special Programs:** New Translations Reading Series.

ARDEN THEATRE COMPANY

(Founded 1988)
40 North 2nd St; Philadelphia, PA 19106; (215) 922-8900, FAX 922-7011;
    dsmeal@ardentheatre.org, www.ardentheatre.org
Dennis Smeal, *Literary Manager*

Submission procedure: no unsolicited scripts; 10-page dialogue sample, synopsis, character breakdown, play's developmental history, bio and letter of inquiry via email. **Types of material:** full-length plays, translations, adaptations, musicals. **Special interests:** new adaptations of literary works. **Facilities:** Haas Stage/mainstage, 400 seats, flexible stage; Arcadia Stage/studio theatre, 175 seats, flexible stage. **Best submission time:** year-round. **Response time:** 3 months letter; 6 months script.

ARENA STAGE

(Founded 1950)

1101 6th St SW; Washington, DC 20024; (202) 554-9066, FAX 488-4056;
    www.arenastage.org

Literary Manager

Submission procedure: no unsolicited scripts; 1-page synopsis, 10-page dialogue sample and bio. **Types of material:** full-length plays, translations, adaptations, musicals. **Special interests:** emphasis on American writers, history, culture and literary traditions. **Facilities:** Fichandler Stage, 827 seats, arena stage; The Kreeger Theater, 514 seats, modified thrust stage; The Cradle, 200 seats, black box stage. **Best submission time:** year-round. **Response time:** 1 week letter; 5 months script. **Special programs:** Downstairs Series: new play development initiative; scripts selected through theatre's normal submission procedure.

ARIZONA THEATRE COMPANY

(Founded 1966)

Box 1631; Tucson, AZ 85702-1631; (520) 884-8210;
    www.arizonatheatre.org

Jennifer Bazzell, *Literary Department*

Submission procedure: no unsolicited scripts; synopsis, 10-page dialogue sample, production history, resume and letter of inquiry. **Types of material:** full-length plays, translations, adaptations, musicals. **Facilities:** Herberger Theater Center (in Phoenix), 800 seats, proscenium stage; Temple of Music and Art (in Tucson), 600 seats, proscenium stage. **Best submission time:** spring–summer. **Response time:** 1 month letter; 6 months script. **Special programs:** National Latino Playwriting Award (see Prizes).

ARKANSAS ARTS CENTER CHILDREN'S THEATRE

(Founded 1979)

Box 2137; Little Rock, AR 72203; (501) 372-4000; banderson@arkarts.com,
    www.arkarts.com

Bradley Anderson, *Artistic Director*

Submission procedure: no unsolicited scripts; professional recommendation. **Types of material:** full-length plays, one-acts, adaptations, plays for young audiences, musicals. **Facilities:** Arkansas Arts Center, 348 seats, proscenium stage; studio, 150 seats, flexible stage. **Best submission time:** Nov–Dec. **Response time:** 4 months.

ARKANSAS REPERTORY THEATRE

(Founded 1976)

Box 110; Little Rock, AR 72203-0110; (501) 378-0445, FAX 378-0012

Leslie Golden, *Associate Producer*

Submission procedure: no unsolicited scripts; synopsis and letter of inquiry. **Types of material:** full-length plays, musicals, cabaret/revues, solo pieces. **Facilities:** Arkansas Repertory Theatre, 354 seats, proscenium stage; Second Stage, 99 seats, black box. **Production considerations:** prefers small cast. **Best submission time:** year-round. **Response time:** 3 months letter; 6 months script. **Special programs:** New Play Reading Series.

ARS NOVA

(Founded 2002)
511 West 54th St; New York, NY 10019; (212) 489-9800;
   artistic@arsnovanyc.com, www.arsnovanyc.com
Emily Shooltz, *Director of Artistic Development*

Submission procedure: no unsolicited scripts; synopsis, 10-page dialogue sample, resume and cover letter. **Types of material:** full-length plays, translations, adaptations, musicals, solo pieces. **Special interests:** emerging artists; "genre-bridging" work. **Facilities:** mainstage, 99 seats, proscenium stage. **Production considerations:** prefers small cast; no fly space, limited backstage. **Best submission time:** year-round. **Response time:** 6 months letter; 6 months script. **Special programs:** A.N.T. FEST: annual 6-week festival showcasing emerging writers/artists; 30 submissions receive 1-night performance and are part of artist-driven events throughout festival; submit 1-page description of performance idea, may also include script, CD, DVD or online materials; *deadline*: Aug (no submissions before 1 Apr); *notification*: late summer; *dates*: Oct–Nov. Out Loud: a biweekly play reading series for emerging playwrights. Tragedy Tomorrow: a showcase of alternative comedic storytelling and variety arts. Uncharted: monthly concert series featuring wide range of composers and songwriters. Play Group (see Development).

ARTISTS REPERTORY THEATRE

(Founded 1981)
1515 SW Alder St; Portland, OR 97205; (503) 241-9807,
   FAX 241-8268; smulligan@artistsrep.org, www.artistsrep.org
Stephanie Mulligan, *Literary Manager*

Submission procedure: no unsolicited scripts; synopsis and letter of inquiry. **Types of material:** full-length plays, adaptations. **Facilities:** Alder Street Theatre, 170 seats, black box; Morrison Street Theatre, 165 seats, black box. **Production considerations:** cast limit of 10. **Best submission time:** year-round. **Response time:** 2 months letter; 6 months script. **Special programs:** Play Lab: staged reading series.

ART STATION

(Founded 1986)
Box 1998; Stone Mountain, GA 30086; (770) 469-1105, FAX 469-0355;
   jon@artstation.org, www.artstation.org
Jon Goldstein, *Literary Manager*

Submission procedure: accepts unsolicited scripts; prefers synopsis and dialogue sample. **Types of material:** full-length plays, adaptations, musicals, solo pieces. **Special interests:** works not produced professionally; plays by southern playwrights, or that describe the southern experience. **Facilities:** ART Station Theatre, 108 seats, proscenium/thrust stage. **Production considerations:** cast limit of 6; unit set, no fly space. **Best submission time:** Jun–Dec. **Response time:** 8 months.

ARVADA CENTER FOR THE ARTS & HUMANITIES

(Founded 1976)
6901 Wadsworth Blvd; Arvada, CO 80003; (720) 898-7286, FAX 898-7217;
www.arvadacenter.org
Rod A. Lansberry, *Interim Performing Arts Director*

Submission procedure: no unsolicited scripts; synopsis and letter of inquiry. **Types of material:** plays for young audiences only. **Special interests:** plays for preschool-grade 6. **Facilities:** Arvada Center Amphitheater, 1200 seats, proscenium stage; Arvada Center Main Stage, 498 seats, thrust stage; Black Box, 200 seats. **Production considerations:** cast limit of 6–9; minimal set. **Best submission time:** Sep–Mar. **Response time:** 6 months letter; 8 months script.

ASIAN AMERICAN THEATER COMPANY

(Founded 1973)
55 Teresita Blvd; San Francisco, CA 94127; (415) 519-2920,
aatcspace@gmail.com, www.asianamericantheater.org
Darryl D. Chiang, *Executive Director*

Submission procedure: accepts unsolicited scripts with synopsis, character breakdown, resume and letter of inquiry; prefers electronic submission. **Types of material:** full-length plays, adaptations, comedy sketches. **Special interests:** innovative new voices reflecting America's Asian heritage; satire based on race and ethnicity; modern Asian American drama, including political pieces; romantic comedies. **Facilities:** venues rented based on production needs. **Best submission time:** year-round. **Response time:** 6 months. **Special programs:** NewWorks Incubator Project: developmental workshop for 8 new plays per year leading to potential staged reading or production; *deadline:* year-round; *notification:* 6 months.

ATLANTIC THEATER COMPANY

(Founded 1985)
76 9th Ave, Suite 537; New York, NY 10011; (646) 691-5919,
FAX (212) 645-8755; www.atlantictheater.org
Laura Savia, *Literary Associate*

Submission procedure: no unsolicited scripts; 10–20 page dialogue sample and letter of inquiry. **Types of material:** full-length plays, adaptations, musicals. **Facilities:** Atlantic Theater Mainstage, 180 seats, proscenium stage; second stage, 99 seats, thrust stage. **Production considerations:** small cast musicals. **Best submission time:** year-round. **Response time:** 6 months. **Special programs:** year-round play readings, workshops and productions in second stage space; emphasis on new American writers.

ATTIC THEATRE AND FILM CENTER

(Founded 1987)

5429 West Washington Blvd; Los Angeles, CA 90016; (323) 525-0600,
    FAX 525-0661; litmanager@attictheatre.org, www.attictheatre.org

James Carey, *Producing Artistic Director*

Submission procedure: no unsolicited scripts; synopsis, dialogue sample and letter of inquiry with SASE for response. **Types of material:** full-length plays, one-acts. **Facilities:** Attic Theatre and Film Center, 49 seats, flexible stage. **Production considerations:** simple sets; no fly or wing space. **Best submission time:** year-round. **Response time:** 3 months letter; 6 months script. **Special programs:** developmental workshops; reading series; Attic Theatre Ensemble's One-Act Marathon (see Prizes).

AURORA THEATRE COMPANY

(Founded 1992)

2081 Addison St; Berkeley, CA 94704; (510) 843-4042, FAX 843-4826;
    www.auroratheatre.org

Literary Manager

Submission procedure: no unsolicited scripts; synopsis and letter of inquiry. **Types of material:** full-length plays, adaptations. **Special interests:** plays emphasizing language and ideas. **Facilities:** Aurora Theatre, 150 seats, arena stage. **Production considerations:** cast limit of 8; minimal production demands. **Best submission time:** Aug–Dec. **Response time:** 6 months letter; 6 months script.

BARKSDALE THEATRE

(Founded 1953)

1601 Willow Lawn Dr, Suite 301E; Richmond, VA 23230; (804) 783-1688,
    FAX 288-6470; www.barksdalerichmond.org

Bruce Miller, *Artistic Director*

Submission procedure: no unsolicited scripts; synopsis and letter of inquiry. **Types of material:** full-length plays. **Facilities:** mainstage, 207 seats, thrust stage. **Production considerations:** small cast; no fly or wing space. **Best submission time:** year-round. **Response time:** 6 months letter; 12 months script.

BARRINGTON STAGE COMPANY

(Founded 1995)

30 Union St; Pittsfield, MA 01201; (413) 499-5446, FAX 499-5447;
    www.barringtonstageco.org

Julianne Boyd, *Artistic Director*

Submission procedure: no unsolicited scripts; 1-page synopsis, 10-page dialogue sample and letter of inquiry; include cassette or CD for musicals. **Types of material:** full-length plays, translations, adaptations, musicals, cabaret/revues, solo pieces. **Facilities:** mainstage, 550 seats, proscenium stage; Stage II, 125 seats, thrust stage. **Production considerations:** cast limit of 4–8 for plays, cast limit of 10–12 for musicals; modest set requirements. **Best submission time:** fall. **Response time:** 3 months letter; 6 months script. **Special programs:** The Musical Theatre Lab program for developing new musicals: selected scripts receive public readings, development contingent on funding.

THE BARROW GROUP

(Founded 1986)
312 West 36th St, #4W; New York, NY 10018; (212) 760-2615,
    FAX 760-2962; lit@barrowgroup.org, www.barrowgroup.org
Ron Piretti, *Literary Manager*

Submission Procedure: no unsolicited scripts; synopsis and letter of inquiry. **Types of material:** full-length plays, one-acts, translations, adaptations. **Facilities:** TBG Theatre, 99 seats, black box; studio, 40 seats, flexible stage. **Best submission time:** year-round. **Response time:** 1 month letter; 4 months script. **Special programs:** Short Stuff: short play festival.

BARTER THEATRE

(Founded 1933)
Box 867; Abingdon, VA 24212-0867; (276) 619-3344, FAX 619-3335;
    barterinfo@bartertheatre.com, www.bartertheatre.com
Richard Rose, *Producing Artistic Director*

Submission procedure: no unsolicited scripts; synopsis, dialogue sample and letter of inquiry; include cassette for musicals. **Types of material:** full-length plays, translations, adaptations, plays for young audiences, musicals. **Special interests:** social issues and current events; works that expand theatrical form; material exploring nonurban themes. **Facilities:** Barter Theatre, 508 seats, proscenium stage; Barter's Stage II, 167 seats, thrust stage. **Production considerations:** cast limit of 4-16. **Best submission time:** Mar, Sep. **Response time:** 9 months letter; 12 months script. **Special programs:** Barter's Early Stages: script development program. Appalachian Festival of Plays & Playwrights (see Prizes).

BERKELEY REPERTORY THEATRE

(Founded 1968)
2025 Addison St; Berkeley, CA 94704; (510) 647-2900, FAX 647-2910;
    madeleine@berkeleyrep.org, www.berkeleyrep.org
Madeleine Oldham, *Literary Manager/Dramaturg*

Submission procedure: accepts unsolicited scripts from Bay Area playwrights only; prefers double-sided submissions with SASE; recommendation from theatre professionals with whom there is an existing relationship or agent submission for all others. **Types of material:** full-length plays, translations, adaptations. **Facilities:** Roda Theatre, 600 seats, proscenium stage; Mark Taper Stage, 400 seats, thrust stage. **Best submission time:** year-round. **Response time:** 6 months.

BERKSHIRE THEATRE FESTIVAL

(Founded 1928)

Box 797; Stockbridge, MA 01262; (413) 298-5536, FAX 298-3368;
    info@berkshiretheatre.org, www.berkshiretheatre.org

Kate Maguire, *Artistic Director*

Submission procedure: no unsolicited scripts; agent submission. **Types of material:** full-length plays, musicals, solo pieces. **Facilities:** Playhouse, 408 seats, proscenium stage; Unicorn Theatre, 122 seats, thrust stage. **Production considerations:** small orchestra for musicals. **Best submission time:** Oct–Dec. **Response time:** 12 months.

THE BLACK REP

(Founded 1976)

1717 Olive St, 4th Floor; St. Louis, MO 63103; (314) 534-3807,
    FAX 534-4035; ronh@theblackrep.org, www.theblackrep.org

Ronald J. Himes, *Producing Director*

Submission procedure: no unsolicited scripts; synopsis, 3–5-page dialogue sample, resume and letter of inquiry. **Types of material:** full-length plays, plays for young audiences, musicals. **Special interests:** works by African-American and Third World playwrights. **Facilities:** Grandel Theatre, 470 seats, thrust stage. **Best submission time:** Jun–Aug. **Response time:** 2 months letter; 2 months script. **Special programs:** touring company presenting works for young audiences.

BLOOMINGTON PLAYWRIGHTS PROJECT

(Founded 1980)

107 West 9th St; Bloomington, IN 47404; (812) 334-1188;
    bppwrite@newplays.org, www.newplays.org

Sonja Johnson, *Literary Manager*

Submission procedure: accepts unsolicited scripts for Dark Alley Series only (see below). **Types of material:** one-acts. **Special interests:** short, "edgy" scripts, 10–45 minutes in length. **Facilities:** Timothy Wiles Mainstage Theater, 84-100 seats; Lora Shiner Studio Theater, 50 seats, black box. **Best submission time:** year-round. **Response time:** varies. **Special programs:** Dark Alley Series: late-night series of short plays; *deadline:* 15 Aug. Reva Shiner Full-Length Play Contest (see Prizes).

BLOOMSBURG THEATRE ENSEMBLE

(Founded 1978)

226 Center St; Bloomsburg, PA 17815; (570) 784-5530, FAX 784-4912;
    www.bte.org

Laurie McCants, *Ensemble Member*

Submission procedure: no unsolicited scripts; synopsis, dialogue sample, professional recommendation and letter of inquiry. **Types of material:** full-length plays, translations, adaptations. **Special interests:** new translations of classics; rural themes; plays suitable for small acting ensemble. **Facilities:** Alvina Krause Theatre, 350 seats, proscenium stage. **Production considerations:** small to mid-sized cast;

unit set. **Best submission time:** summer. **Response time:** 3 months letter; 6 months script.

BOARSHEAD THEATER

(Founded 1966)

425 South Grand Ave; Lansing, MI 48933; (517) 484-7800, FAX 484-2564; www.boarshead.org

Kristine Thatcher, *Artistic Director*

Submission procedure: no unsolicited scripts; synopsis, character breakdown, 6–10-page dialogue sample and letter of inquiry with SASP for response. **Types of material:** full-length plays, plays for young audiences. **Special interests:** one-act plays for young audiences and late-night theatre; social issues; comedies; plays that make use of theatrical conventions or create new ones. **Facilities:** Center for the Arts, 249 seats, thrust stage. **Best submission time:** year-round. **Response time:** 1 month letter; 6 months script. **Special programs:** staged readings of 4 new plays per year.

BORDERLANDS THEATER

(Founded 1986)

Box 2791; Tucson, AZ 85702; (520) 882-8607, FAX 884-4264; bltheater@aol.com

Submission procedure: no unsolicited scripts; synopsis and letter of inquiry. **Types of material:** full-length plays, translations, adaptations. **Special interests:** cultural diversity; race relations; "border" issues, including concerns of the geographical border region as well as the metaphorical borders of gender, class and race. **Facilities:** no permanent facility. **Production considerations:** cast limit of 7; minimal set. **Best submission time:** year-round. **Response time:** 1 month letter; 6 months script.

BRAT PRODUCTIONS

(Founded 1998)

56 South 2nd St; Philadelphia, PA 19107; (215) 627-2577, FAX 627-4304; info@bratproductions.org, www.bratproductions.org

Submission procedure: no unsolicited scripts; synopsis, dialogue sample and letter of inquiry. **Types of material:** full-length plays, translations, adaptations, musicals, solo pieces. **Special interests:** "material that connects with audiences in new and unique ways." **Facilities:** no permanent facility. **Production considerations:** cast limit of 5; prefers unit set. **Best submission time:** summer. **Response time:** 1 month letter; 6 months script.

BRAVA THEATER CENTER

(Founded 1986)

2781 24th Street; San Francisco, CA 94110; (415) 641-7657, FAX 641-7684; www.brava.org

Christine Mehr, *Literary Manager*

Submission procedure: accepts unsolicited scripts; see website for details. **Types of material:** full-length plays, translations, plays for young audiences, cabaret/revues. **Special interests:** works by women, people of color, cross-cultural pieces, gay and lesbian themes. **Facilities:** mainstage, 365 seats, proscenium stage; Studio Theatre, 100 seats, black box; Cabaret, 85 seats, cabaret stage. **Best submission time:** Nov–Mar. **Response time:** 3 months.

BRISTOL RIVERSIDE THEATRE

(Founded 1986)

Box 1250; Bristol, PA 19007; (215) 785-6664, FAX 785-2762; adam@brtstage.org, www.brtstage.org

Adam Goldstein, *Artistic Associate*

Submission procedure: no unsolicited scripts; agent submission; professional recommendation or submission via MFA program only. **Types of material:** full-length plays, one-acts, translations, adaptations, musicals, solo pieces. **Special interests:** cutting-edge works; plays that experiment with form; translations; musicals. **Facilities:** Bristol Riverside Theatre, 302 seats, flexible stage. **Production considerations:** cast limit of 10 for plays, 18 for musicals, 9 for orchestra; prefers smaller cast and orchestra; minimal production demands. **Best submission time:** spring. **Response time:** 6 months. **Special programs:** America Rising: Voices of Today: contemporary and new play staged reading series.

THE B STREET THEATRE

(Founded 1991)

2711 B St; Sacramento, CA 95816; (916) 443-5391, FAX 443-0874; rhellesen@bstreettheatre.org, www.bstreettheatre.org

Buck Busfield, *Artistic Director*

Submission procedure: no unsolicited scripts; agent submission. **Types of material:** full-length plays. **Special interests:** contemporary comedies and dramas. **Facilities:** The B Street Theatre, 196 seats, black box; B-2 Space, 112 seats, black box. **Production considerations:** cast limit of 6; modest production demands, no fly space. **Best submission time:** year-round. **Response time:** 6 months.

BURNING COAL THEATRE COMPANY

(Founded 1995)

Box 90904; Raleigh, NC 27675-0904; (919) 834-4001, FAX 834-4002;
    burning_coal@ipass.edu, www.burningcoal.org

Marc Williams, *Director of New Works*

Submission procedure: accepts unsolicited scripts from NC playwrights only; all others submit inquiry via email. **Types of material:** non-musical plays. **Special interests:** "plays about significant ideas and concerns"; works approximately 90 minutes in length only. **Facilities:** mainstage, 140 seats, flexible space. **Production considerations:** small cast; minimal set. **Best submission time:** Jun–Aug. **Response time:** varies.

THE CAPE COD THEATRE PROJECT

(Founded 1994)

Box 410; Falmouth, MA 02541; (508) 457-4242;
    info@capecodtheatreproject.org, www.capecodtheatreproject.org

Andrew Polk, *Artistic Director*

Submission procedure: no unsolicited scripts; synopsis only; prefers professional recommendation or agent submission. **Types of material:** full-length plays, musicals, solo pieces. **Special interests:** previously unproduced work; contemporary American plays. **Facilities:** Falmouth Academy, 160 seats, proscenium stage. **Production considerations:** minimal staging. **Best submission time:** Aug–Feb; *deadline:* 15 Mar annually. **Response time:** by 1 May.

CAPITAL REPERTORY THEATRE

(Founded 1981)

111 North Pearl St; Albany, NY 12207; (518) 462-4531, ext 201,
    FAX 465-0213

Maggie Mancinelli-Cahill, *Producing Artistic Director*

Submission procedure: no unsolicited scripts; agent submission. **Types of material:** full-length plays, translations, adaptations, musicals. **Special interests:** ethnically diverse works. **Facilities:** Capital Repertory Theatre, 299 seats, thrust stage. **Production considerations:** prefers small cast. **Best submission time:** late spring. **Response time:** 9 months.

CASA 0101

(Founded 2000)

2009 East First St; Los Angeles, CA 90033; info@casa0101.org,
    www.casa0101.org

José Casas, *Literary Manager*

Submission procedure: accepts unsolicited scripts. **Types of material:** full-length plays, one-acts, translations, adaptations, plays for young audiences, musicals, cabaret/revues, solo pieces. **Special interests:** plays by Chicano/Latino playwrights; plays dealing with Chicano/Latino culture. **Facilities:** mainstage, 50–60 seats, proscenium stage. **Production considerations:** cast limit of 10; modest production demands. **Best submission time:** year-round. **Response time:** 3 months. **Special programs:** The Josefina Lopez Playwriting Competition and The Josefina Lopez Youth Playwriting Competition (see Prizes).

CELEBRATION THEATRE
(Founded 1982)
7985 Santa Monica Blvd, Suite 109-1; West Hollywood, CA 90046;
    (323) 957-1884, FAX 957-1826; celebrationthtr@earthlink.net,
    www.celebrationtheatre.com
Celebrating: New Works Play Reading Series

Submission procedure: accepts unsolicited scripts. **Types of material:** full-length plays. **Special interests:** plays not previously produced that "provide a progressive gay and lesbian voice in contemporary theatre." **Facilities:** Celebration Theatre, 65 seats, thrust stage. **Best submission time:** year-round. **Response time:** 6 months. **Special programs:** Celebrating New Works: rehearsed readings of plays not previously produced, followed by audience discussion; all readings considered for future workshops and productions.

CENTERSTAGE
(Founded 1963)
700 North Calvert St; Baltimore, MD 21202-3686; (410) 986-4042,
    FAX 539-3912; dlichtenberg@centerstage.org
Drew Lichtenberg, *Associate Dramaturg*

Submission procedure: no unsolicited scripts; synopsis, dialogue sample and letter of inquiry with SASE for response. **Types of material:** full-length plays, translations, adaptations. **Special interests:** plays about the African-American experience. **Facilities:** Pearlstone Theater, 541 seats, modified thrust stage; Head Theater, 300–400 seats, flexible stage. **Best submission time:** Aug–Dec, Mar–May. **Response time:** 7 weeks letter; 6 months script.

CENTRE STAGE—SOUTH CAROLINA
(Founded 1983)
Box 8451; Greenville, SC 29604-8451; (864) 233-6733;
    information@centrestage.org, www.centrestage.org
Brian Haimbach, *Director, New Play Festival*

Submission procedure: accepts unsolicited scripts. **Types of material:** full-length plays. **Special interests:** works not previously produced. **Facilities:** mainstage, 292 seats, thrust stage. **Production considerations:** unit set, no fly space, limited wing space. **Best submission time:** Jan. **Response time:** 4 months. **Special programs:** Readers' Theatre: regularly scheduled rehearsed readings presented for public followed by audience discussion. New Playwrights Festival: 6 plays presented annually with winner receiving production in next season; *dates:* Jan.

CENTER THEATRE GROUP

(Founded 1967)

601 West Temple St; Los Angeles, CA 90012; (213) 972-8033;
    www.centertheatregroup.org

Pier Carlo Talenti, *Literary Manager*

Submission procedure: no unsolicited scripts; synopsis, 5–10-page dialogue sample and letter of inquiry with SASE for response; CD for musicals. **Types of material:** full-length plays, translations, adaptations, plays for young audiences, musicals, solo pieces. **Facilities:** Ahmanson Theatre, 1600–2000 seats, proscenium stage; Mark Taper Forum, 745 seats, thrust stage; Kirk Douglas Theatre, 317 seats, proscenium stage. **Best submission time:** year-round. **Response time:** 6 weeks letter; 4 months script.

CHARLESTON STAGE COMPANY

(Founded 1978)

Box 356; Charleston, SC 29402; (843) 577-5967, FAX 577-5422;
    email@charlestonstage.com, www.charlestonstage.com

Julian Wiles, *Producing Artistic Director*

Submission procedure: no unsolicited scripts; professional recommendation with SASE for response. **Types of material:** full-length plays. **Facilities:** The Historic Dock Street Theatre, 463 seats, proscenium stage. **Production considerations:** prefers small cast. **Best submission time:** year-round. **Response time:** 2 months.

CHERRY LANE THEATRE

(Founded 1997)

38 Commerce St; New York, NY 10014; (212) 989-2020, FAX 989-2867;
    company@cherrylanetheatre.org, www.cherrylanetheatre.org

Angela Scott, *Literary Associate*

Submission procedure: accepts unsolicited scripts for Mentor Project only (see below), submissions should be sent to nominating committee (see website). **Types of material:** full-length plays. **Facilities:** Cherry Lane Theatre, 178 seats, proscenium stage; Studio Theatre, 60 seats, black box. **Best submission time:** Mar–Jun. **Response time:** Oct. **Special programs:** Mentor Project: 3 writers work with master playwright for a season. Celebrating Women Playwrights and Celebrating Black Playwrights: plays chosen from Mentor Project submissions. Some semifinalists from Mentor Project will be considered for Tongues Play Reading Series.

THE CHILDREN'S THEATRE COMPANY

(Founded 1965)

2400 Third Ave S; Minneapolis, MN 55404-3597; (612) 874-0500,
    FAX 874-8119; eadams@childrenstheatre.org

Elissa Adams, *Director of New Play Development*

Submission procedure: no unsolicited scripts; agent submission. **Types of material:** plays for young audiences including full-length plays, adaptations, musicals. **Special interests:** work for preschoolers (ages 2–5) and teens; work samples from interested writers with no previous experience writing for children's theatre. **Facilities:** Children's Theatre Company, 745 seats, proscenium stage; Cargill Stage, black box, flexible seating. **Best submission time:** Jul-Feb. **Response time:** 6 months. **Special programs:** Threshold: 1-4 works for young audiences commissioned each year for development and production.

CHILDSPLAY
(Founded 1977)
Box 517; Tempe, AZ 85280; (480) 921-5700, FAX 921-5777;
    info@childsplayaz.org, www.childsplayaz.org
David Saar, *Artistic Director*

Submission procedure: no unsolicited scripts; synopsis, 10-page dialogue sample and letter of inquiry. **Types of material:** plays for young audiences including full-length plays, adaptations, musicals, performance art. **Special interests:** nontraditional plays; material that entertains and challenges both performers and audiences; 2nd and 3rd productions of unpublished work. **Facilities:** Scottsdale Center for the Arts, 800 seats, proscenium stage; Tempe Center for the Arts, 550 seats, proscenium stage; TCA Studio, 200 seats, flexible black box stage; also tours schools. **Production considerations:** some van-sized touring productions. **Best submission time:** Jun-Oct. **Response time:** 1 month letter; 3 months script. **Special programs:** commissioning program.

CINCINNATI PLAYHOUSE IN THE PARK
(Founded 1960)
Box 6537; Cincinnati, OH 45206-0537; (513) 345-2242; www.cincyplay.com
Edward Stern, *Producing Artistic Director*

Submission procedure: no unsolicited scripts; synopsis, character breakdown, 10-page dialogue sample, production history, bio or resume and letter of inquiry; agent submission of complete script; include CD or cassette for musicals. **Types of material:** full-length plays, translations, adaptations, musicals. **Special Interests:** previously unproduced works that take linguistic and/or stylistic risks. **Facilities:** Robert S. Marx Theatre, 626 seats, thrust stage; Thompson Shelterhouse, 225 seats, thrust stage. **Best submission time:** year-round. **Response time:** 4 months letter; 8 months script. **Special programs:** The Mickey Kaplan New American Play Prize (see Prizes).

CITY GARAGE
(Founded 1987)
Box 2016; Santa Monica, CA 90406; (310) 319-9939, FAX 396-1040;
    citygarage@earthlink.net, www.citygarage.org
Paul Rubenstein, *Literary Manager*

Submission procedure: no unsolicited scripts; synopsis and letter of inquiry. **Types of material:** full-length plays, translations, adaptations. **Special interests:** nonrealistic experimental work only; no family dramas, personal or confessional plays.

Facilities: City Garage, 48 seats, thrust stage. **Production considerations:** unit set. **Best submission time:** year-round. **Response time:** 2 weeks letter; 6 weeks script.

CITY THEATRE
(Founded 1996)
444 Brickell Ave, Suite 229; Miami, FL 33131; (305) 755-9401,
    FAX 755-9404; summershorts@citytheatre.org, www.citytheatre.org
Stephanie Norman, *Executive Director*

Submission procedure: accepts unsolicited scripts. **Types of material:** one-acts only. **Special interests:** one-acts that represent a diverse mix of subject matters, styles and genres including comedies, dramas, farces, monologues and musicals; bilingual plays, especially Spanish/English, encouraged for Summer Shorts Festival; one-act plays for young audiences (ages 10 and older) for Shorts 4 Kids. **Facilities:** Broward Center/Amaturo, 580 seats, proscenium stage; Arsht Center for the Performing Arts, 200 seats, proscenium/thrust; for Shorts 4 Kids, various school and community venues, 30-200 seats. **Production considerations:** For mainstage: cast limit of 8, plays performed by multicultural ensemble ages 20-60. For Shorts 4 Kids: cast limit of 4, plays performed by multicultural ensemble ages 20-40; prefers simple sets. **Best submission time:** year-round; scripts received by 1 Nov considered by City Theatre and Actors Theatre of Louisville for National Ten-Minute Play Contest (see Prizes). **Response time:** varies.

CITY THEATRE COMPANY
(Founded 1974)
1300 Bingham St; Pittsburgh, PA 15203; (412) 431-4400, FAX 431-5535;
    caquiline@citytheatrecompany.org, www.citytheatrecompany.org
Carlyn Aquiline, *Literary Manager/Dramaturg*

Submission procedure: no unsolicited scripts; synopsis, 10-page dialogue sample, character breakdown, resume, development/production history and letter of inquiry naming a professionl reference with SASE for response; include CD for musicals. **Types of material:** full-length plays, translations, adaptations, musicals, solo pieces. **Special interests:** "plays of ideas"; fresh use of language or form; plays by under-represented voices. **Facilities:** Mainstage, 272 seats, flexible stage; Hamburg Studio, 110 seats, thrust stage. **Production considerations:** cast limit of 10, prefers 6 or fewer. **Best submission time:** year-round. **Response time:** 2 months letter; 10 months script. **Special Programs:** Commissioning Program. Young Playwrights Festival: productions and readings by grades 7-12 in Western PA (see website). MOMENTUM-New Plays at Different Stages: annual new play festival of readings, workshops and productions.

CLASSICAL THEATRE OF HARLEM

(Founded 1999)

520 8th Ave, #313; New York, NY 10018; (212) 564-9983, FAX 564-9109; info@classicaltheatreofharlem.org, www.classicaltheatreofharlem.org

Alfred Preisser, *Artistic Director*

Submission procedure: no unsolicited scripts; agent submission. **Types of material:** full-length plays, translations, adaptations. **Special interests:** translations and adaptations of classic works. **Facilities:** Harlem Stage at The Gatehouse, 160 seats, flexible stage. **Best submission time:** year-round. **Response time:** varies. **Special Programs:** Future Classics Reading Series.

THE CLEVELAND PLAY HOUSE

(Founded 1916)

8500 Euclid Ave; Cleveland, OH 44106-0189; (216) 795-7000, FAX 795-7007

Seth Gordon, *Associate Artistic Director*

Submission procedure: no unsolicited scripts; synopsis, 10–page dialogue sample, resume and letter of inquiry with SASE for response. **Types of material:** full-length plays, adaptations, musicals. **Facilities:** Kenyon C. Bolton Theatre, 548 seats, proscenium stage; Francis E. Drury Theatre, 504 seats, proscenium stage; Baxter Stage, 300 seats, thrust stage. **Best submission time:** year-round. **Response time:** 2 months letter; 6 months script. **Special programs:** FusionFest (see Development).

THE COLONY THEATRE COMPANY

(Founded 1975)

555 North Third St; Burbank, CA 91502; (818) 558-7000, FAX 558-7110; michaelwadler@colonytheatre.org, www.colonytheatre.org

Michael David Wadler, *Literary Manager*

Submission procedure: no unsolicited scripts; synopsis, first 10 pages of dialogue, character breakdown, letter of inquiry and bio with SASE/SASP or email address for response. **Types of material:** full-length plays, adaptations. **Facilities:** Burbank Center Stage, 276 seats, thrust stage. **Production considerations:** cast limit of 4. **Best submission time:** year-round. **Response time:** 3 months letter; 12 months script.

COLUMBUS CHILDREN'S THEATRE

(Founded 1963)

372 West Nationwide Blvd; Columbus, OH 43215-2310; (614) 224-6673, FAX 224-8844; bgshows@aol.com, www.colschildrenstheatre.org

William Goldsmith, *Artistic Director*

Submission procedure: accepts unsolicited scripts. **Types of material:** one-acts, plays for young audiences. **Special interests:** social-issue one-acts suitable for audiences in grades K–5. **Facilities:** Columbus Children's Theatre, 170 seats, black box/thrust. **Production considerations:** cast limit of 4 for touring productions, maximum 50 minutes in length; prefers unit sets for mainstage season. **Best submission time:** Sep–Nov. **Response time:** 4 months.

COMMONWEAL THEATRE COMPANY

(Founded 1989)

Box 15; Lanesboro, MN 55949; (507) 467-2905, FAX 467-2468;
    hal@commonwealtheatre.org, www.commonwealtheatre.org

Hal Cropp, *Artistic Director*

Submission procedure: no unsolicited scripts; professional recommendation with work sample. **Types of material:** full-length plays, translations, adaptations. **Facilities:** Commonweal Theatre, 191 seats, thrust stage. **Production considerations:** prefers cast limit of 9; unit set, no wing space. **Best submission time:** Aug–Nov. **Response time:** 1 month. **Special programs:** Commonweal New Play Workshop: 4 playwrights contracted to work for 4 weeks each, culminating in public reading, 2 scripts then chosen for additional 1-week workshop, 1 play possibly chosen for full production in subsequent season; scripts selected through theatre's normal submission procedure; playwright receives housing during workshop.

CONTEMPORARY AMERICAN THEATRE COMPANY (CATCO)

(Founded 1984)

77 South High St; Columbus, OH 43215; (614) 461-1382, FAX 460-7216;
    jputnam@catco.org, www.catco.org

Jonathan Putnam, *Associate Artistic Director*

Submission procedure: no unsolicited scripts; 10-page dialogue sample and letter of inquiry. **Types of material:** full-length plays, adaptations, solo pieces. **Special interests:** OH and midwestern playwrights. **Facilities:** Capitol Theatre, 903 seats, proscenium stage; Studio One Theatre, 243 seats, proscenium stage. **Production considerations:** prefers cast limit of 8. **Best submission time:** year-round. **Response time:** 6-12 months. **Special programs:** The Shorts Festival: biennial festival of 10-15-minute plays with common setting; see website for details.

CORNERSTONE THEATER COMPANY

(Founded 1986)

708 Traction Ave; Los Angeles, CA 90013; (213) 613-1700, ext 16,
    FAX 613-1714; lwoolery@cornerstonetheater.org

Laurie Woolery, *Associate Artistic Director*

Submission procedure: no unsolicited scripts; letter of inquiry only. **Types of material:** full-length plays, adaptations, musicals. **Special interests:** collaborations with playwrights to develop new works or contemporary adaptations of classics, focusing on specific communities. **Facilities:** no permanent facility. **Best submission time:** year-round. **Response time:** 8 months.

THE COTERIE THEATRE

(Founded 1979)

2450 Grand Blvd, Suite 144; Kansas City, MO 64108; (816) 474-6785,
    FAX 474-7112; jchurch@coterietheatre.org, www.coterietheatre.org

Jeff Church, *Producing Artistic Director*

Submission procedure: no unsolicited scripts; synopsis, resume and letter of inquiry with SASE for response. **Types of material:** full-length plays, adaptations, musicals and solo pieces. **Special interests:** ground-breaking works for family audiences only; plays with culturally diverse casts or themes; social issues; adaptations of classic or contemporary literature; musicals. **Facilities:** The Coterie Theatre, 240 seats, flexible stage. **Production considerations:** cast limit of 12, prefers 5–7; no fly or wing space. **Best submission time:** year-round. **Response time:** 8 months letter; 8 months script.

COURT THEATRE

(Founded 1955)

5535 South Ellis Ave; Chicago, IL 60637; (773) 702-7005, FAX 834-1897

Submission procedure: no unsolicited scripts; synopsis, dialogue sample and letter of inquiry with email address for response. **Types of material:** translations and adaptations of classic texts only. **Special interests:** infrequently produced or "undiscovered" material. **Facilities:** Abelson Auditorium, 253 seats, thrust stage. **Production considerations:** limited fly space. **Best submission time:** summer. **Response time:** 6 weeks letter; 6 months script.

CREEDE REPERTORY THEATRE

(Founded 1966)

Box 269; Creede, CO 81130; (719) 658-2540, FAX 658-2343;
    litmgr@creederep.com, www.creederep.org

Frank Kuhn, *Literary Manager*

Submission procedure: no unsolicited scripts; synopsis, 10-page dialogue sample, resume, letter of inquiry; electronic submissions only. **Types of material:** full-length plays, translations, adaptations, musicals. **Special interests:** works by western playwrights; prefers plays dealing with western and rural culture and themes. **Facilities:** Mainstage, 235 seats, proscenium stage; Black Box, 175 seats, black box. **Production considerations:** cast limit 15; no fly space, minimal accompaniment for musicals. **Best submission time:** May–Oct. **Response time:** 6 months letter; 6 months script. **Special programs:** new play series, *dates:* fall.

CURIOUS THEATRE COMPANY

(Founded 1997)
1080 Acoma St; Denver, CO 80204; (303) 623-2349;
    www.curioustheatre.org
Chip Walton, *Artistic Director*

Submission procedure: agent submission only. **Types of material:** full-length plays, translations, adaptations, solo pieces. **Special interests:** plays with cultural, social and/or political emphasis; plays with challenging design elements. **Facilities:** Acoma Center, 199 seats, thrust stage. **Production considerations:** cast limit of 8; no fly space. **Best submission time:** year–round. **Response time:** 6 months. **Special programs:** informal developmental workshops; new play reading series; commissioning program.

CYRANO'S THEATRE COMPANY

(Founded 1992)
413 D St; Anchorage, AK 99501; (907) 274-2599, FAX 277-4698;
    cyrano@ak.edu, www.cyranos.org
Sandy Harper, *Producing Artistic Director*

Submission procedure: no unsolicited scripts; professional recommendation. **Types of material:** full-length plays, one-acts, adaptations, solo pieces. **Facilities:** Cyrano's Off Center Playhouse, 86 seats, black box. **Best submission time:** year-round. **Response time:** 8 months. **Special programs:** readings for works by Alaskan playwrights.

DAD'S GARAGE THEATRE COMPANY

(Founded 1995)
280 Elizabeth St, Suite C101; Atlanta, GA 30307; (404) 523-3141,
    FAX 688-6644; kate@dadsgarage.com, www.dadsgarage.com
Kate Warner, *Artistic Director*

Submission procedure: accepts unsolicited scripts. **Types of material:** full-length plays, translations, adaptations, musicals, solo pieces. **Special interests:** nontraditional plays, comedies. **Facilities:** Dad's Garage, 120 seats, proscenium stage; Top Shelf, 50 seats, flexible stage. **Best submission time:** year-round. **Response time:** 3 months letter; 3 months script.

DALLAS CHILDREN'S THEATER

(Founded 1984)
The Rosewood Center for Family Arts; 5938 Skillman; Dallas, TX 75231;
    www.dct.org
Artie Olaisen, *Artistic Associate*

Submission procedure: no unsolicited scripts; synopsis, character/set breakdown and letter of inquiry. **Types of material:** full-length plays, adaptations, plays for young audiences. **Special interests:** works for family audiences; adaptations of classics; historical plays; socially relevant works. **Facilities:** El Centro Theater, 500 seats, proscenium stage; Baker Theater, 400 seats, proscenium stage. **Best submission time:** year-round. **Response time:** 12 months.

DALLAS THEATER CENTER
(Founded 1959)
3636 Turtle Creek Blvd; Dallas, TX 75219-5598; (214) 526-8210,
    FAX 521-7666; www.dallastheatercenter.org
Lee Trull, *Associate Artist*

Submission procedure: no unsolicited scripts; professional recommendation. **Types of material:** full-length plays, musicals, adaptations, translations, solo pieces. **Special interests:** plays that "explore language or form"; material relating to the African-American or Hispanic experience. **Facilities:** Kalita Humphreys Theater, 466 seats, thrust stage. **Best submission time:** year-round. **Response time:** 12 months.

DELAWARE THEATRE COMPANY
(Founded 1978)
200 Water St; Wilmington, DE 19801-5030; (302) 594-1104, FAX 594-1107;
    dstradley@delawaretheatre.org, www.delawaretheatre.org
David Stradley, *Artistic Associate*

Submission procedure: no unsolicited scripts; agent submission. **Types of material:** full-length plays, translations, adaptations. **Facilities:** Delaware Theatre Company, 390 seats, modified thrust stage. **Production considerations:** cast limit of 10; prefers unit set. **Best submission time:** summer. **Response time:** 4 months.

THE DELL'ARTE COMPANY
(Founded 1971)
Box 816; Blue Lake, CA 95525; (707) 668-5663, FAX 668-5665;
    dellarte@aol.com, www.dellarte.com
Michael Fields, *Producing Artistic Director*

Submission procedure: no unsolicited scripts; synopsis and letter of inquiry. **Types of material:** full-length plays, adaptations, plays for young audiences. **Special interests:** physical theatre; new adaptations of classics; physical plays for young audiences. **Facilities:** 400 seats, outdoor amphitheatre; Dell'Arte Players, 100 seats, flexible stage. **Production considerations:** company of 3-4 actors; production demands adaptable to touring. **Best submission time:** Jan–Mar. **Response time:** 3 weeks letter; 6 weeks script.

DENVER CENTER THEATRE COMPANY
(Founded 1979)
1101 13th St; Denver, CO 80204; www.dcpa.org
Bruce K. Sevy, *Director of New Play Development*

Submission procedure: agent submission; residents of Rocky Mountain states only may submit a dialogue sample with SASE for response; limit 1 submission per year; no electronic submissions. **Types of material:** full-length plays. **Special interests:** works not produced professionally; plays by African-Americans, Latinos and women; no plays for young audiences. **Facilities:** The Stage, 642 seats, thrust stage; The Space, 450 seats, arena stage; The Ricketson, 250 seats, proscenium stage; The Source, 200 seats, thrust stage. **Best submission time:** year-round. **Response time:** 6 months. **Special programs:** Colorado New Play Summit: annual workshop festival.

DETROIT REPERTORY THEATRE
(Founded 1957)
13103 Woodrow Wilson St; Detroit, MI 48238-3686; (313) 868-1347,
    FAX 868-1705; detrepth@aol.com, www.detroitreptheatre.com
Barbara Busby, *Literary Manager*

Submission procedure: accepts unsolicited scripts with SASE for response; no electronic submissions. **Types of material:** full-length plays. **Special interests:** issue-oriented plays. **Facilities:** Detroit Repertory Theatre, 194 seats, proscenium stage. **Production considerations:** prefers cast limit of 7. **Best submission time:** Sep–Feb. **Response time:** 6 months.

DIVERSIONARY THEATRE
(Founded 1986)
4545 Park Blvd #101; San Diego, CA 92116;
    playsubmission@diversionary.org, www.diversionary.org

Submission procedure: no unsolicited scripts; first 10–15-pages and 2-page application (available from website); prefers electronic submission. **Types of material:** full-length plays. **Special interests:** plays about lesbian, gay, bisexual or transgendered people only; prefers cast limit of 6. **Facilities:** mainstage, 106 seats, modified thrust stage. **Best submission time:** year-round. **Response time:** 6 months. **Special programs:** Queer Theatre—Taking Center Stage: reading series of new plays by and for LGBT community.

EAST WEST PLAYERS
(Founded 1965)
120 North Judge John Aiso St; Los Angeles, CA 90012; (213) 625-7000,
    FAX 625-7111; info@eastwestplayers.org, www.eastwestplayers.org
Jeff Liu, *Literary Manager*

Submission procedure: accepts unsolicited scripts with SASE for response. **Types of material:** full-length plays, musicals. **Special interests:** plays by or about Asian-Pacific Americans. **Facilities:** The David Henry Hwang Theatre at Union Center for the

Arts, 240 seats, proscenium stage. **Production considerations:** minimal production demands. **Best submission time:** year-round. **Response time:** 9 months. (See David Henry Hwang Writers Institute in Development.)

EGYPTIAN THEATRE COMPANY

(Founded 1981)
Box 3119; Park City, UT 84060; (435) 645-0671, FAX 649-0446;
    dana@parkcityshows.com, www.parkcityshows.com
Terence Goodman, *Artistic Director*

Submission procedure: no unsolicited scripts; professional recommendation. **Types of material:** full-length plays, translations, adaptations, plays for young audiences, musicals, cabaret/revues, solo pieces. **Facilities:** Egyptian Theatre, 266 seats, proscenium stage. **Best submission time:** year-round. **Response time:** 6 months.

EL CENTRO SU TEATRO

(Founded 1971)
4725 High St; Denver, CO 80216; (303) 296-0219, FAX 296-4614;
    elcentro@suteatro.org, www.suteatro.org
Tony Garcia, *Artistic Director*

Submission procedure: accepts unsolicited scripts. **Types of material:** full-length plays, one-acts, translations, adaptations, plays for young audiences. **Special interests:** bilingual and/or Spanish-language plays; plays dealing with the Chicano/Latino cultural aesthetic and political experience. **Facilities:** mainstage, 107 seats, black box. **Production considerations:** cast limit of 6–8; minimal production requirements. **Best submission time:** Oct–Jan. **Response time:** 6 months.

ELECTRIC THEATRE COMPANY (ETC)

[formerly The Northeast Theatre (TNT)]
(Founded 1992)
Box 854; Scranton, PA 18501; (570) 558-1520;
    contact@thenortheasttheatre.us, www.electrictheatre.org
John Beck, *Literary Manager*

Submission procedure: no unsolicited scripts; synopsis and letter of inquiry. **Types of material:** full-length plays, solo pieces. **Facilities:** Performance Space at the Hotel Jermyn, 135–160 seats, flexible stage. **Production considerations:** cast limit of 6; minimal production demands. **Best submission time:** May–Aug. **Response time:** 3 months letter; 3 months script. **Special programs:** staged reading series.

THE ENSEMBLE THEATRE

(Founded 1976)

3535 Main St; Houston, TX 77002-9529; (713) 520-0055, FAX 520-1269;
www.ensemblehouston.com

Eileen J. Morris, *Artistic Director*

Submission procedure: accepts unsolicited scripts with professional recommendation and SASE; synopsis, sample scene, resume and letter of inquiry with SASE for all others; include cassette or CD for musicals. **Types of material:** full-length plays, adaptations, plays for young audiences, musicals. **Special interests:** plays portraying the African-American experience; imaginative plays for young audiences; plays suitable for touring by 5-person ensemble; contemporary plays or adaptations. **Facilities:** Performance Stage, 400 seats, flexible stage; Hawkins Stage, 199 seats, proscenium stage; Lawson Arena Stage, 80 seats, black box. **Production considerations:** prefers cast of 5-10; maximum of 2 sets, limited wing space. **Best submission time:** Jun–Oct. **Response time:** 5 months.

ENSEMBLE THEATRE OF CINCINNATI

(Founded 1986)

1127 Vine St; Cincinnati, OH 45202; (513) 421-3555, FAX 562-4104

D. Lynn Meyers, *Producing Artistic Director*

Submission procedure: no unsolicited scripts; synopsis, dialogue sample, resume and letter of inquiry. **Types of material:** full-length plays, adaptations, plays for young audiences. **Facilities:** Ensemble Theatre of Cincinnati, 191 seats, thrust stage. **Production considerations:** cast limit of 6, simple set. **Best submission time:** Sep. **Response time:** 3 months letter; 6 months script.

EVERYMAN THEATRE

(Founded 1990)

1727 North Charles St; Baltimore, MD 21201; (410) 752-2208,
FAX 752-5891; boxoffice@everymantheatre.org,
www.everymantheatre.org

Literary Department

Submission procedure: no unsolicited scripts; agent submission or professional recommendation. **Types of material:** full-length plays, translations, adaptations, musicals, cabaret/revues. **Facilities:** Everyman Theatre, 170 seats, flexible stage. **Production considerations:** cast limit of 6-10; no fly space, low grid. **Best submission time:** year-round. **Response time:** 3 months letter; 6 months script. **Special programs:** cabaret series.

EXPRESS CHILDREN'S THEATRE

(Founded 1991)

446 Northwest Mall; Houston, TX 77092; (713) 682-5044, FAX 682-5033;
    expresstheatre@sbcglobal.net, www.expresstheatre.com

Patricia Silver, *Executive Director*

Submission procedure: accepts unsolicited scripts; prefers synopsis and letter of inquiry. **Types of material:** plays for young audiences. **Special interests:** 40-minute plays; multicultural plays; bilingual plays. **Facilities:** mainstage, 90 seats, proscenium stage; touring company. **Production considerations:** cast limit of 3–4; portable minimal set. **Best submission time:** year-round. **Response time:** 2 weeks letter; 8 weeks script. **Special programs:** commissioning program; after-school education program.

THE 5TH AVENUE THEATRE

(Founded 1980)

1308 5th Ave; Seattle, WA 98101; (206) 625-1418, FAX 292-9610;
    admin@5thavenue.org, www.5thavenue.org

Bill Berry, *Associate Artistic Director*

Submission procedure: no unsolicited scripts; synopsis and letter of inquiry. **Types of material:** musicals. **Facilities:** 5th Avenue Theatre, 2115 seats, proscenium stage. **Best submission time:** year-round. **Response time:** 6 months. **Special programs:** Adventure Musical Theatre: year-round program that commissions original musicals performed for K–6 students; commissions range from $1000–$4000.

FIRST STAGE CHILDREN'S THEATER

(Founded 1987)

325 West Walnut St; Milwaukee, WI 53212; (414) 267-2929, FAX 267-2930;
    jfrank@firststage.org, www.firststage.org

Jeff Frank, *Artistic Director*

Submission procedure: no unsolicited scripts; synopsis, resume and letter of inquiry. **Types of material:** works for young audiences, including translations, adaptations and musicals. **Facilities:** Marcus Center for the Performing Arts's Todd Wehr Theater, 500 seats, thrust stage. **Best submission time:** spring–summer. **Response time:** 3 months letter; 6 months script.

FLEA THEATER

(Founded 1997)

41 White St; New York, NY 10013; (212) 226-0051; www.theflea.org

Literary Manager

Submission procedure: no unsolicited scripts; agent submission. **Types of material:** full-length plays. **Special interests:** political themes; language-driven plays. **Facilities:** mainstage, 70–99 seats, flexible stage; downstairs, 40 seats, fixed stage.

Production considerations: resident acting company composed primarily of 20–30-year-old actors. **Best submission time:** May–Sep. **Response time:** 12 months. **Special programs:** Pataphysics: workshops for writers led by master playwrights.

FLORIDA REPERTORY THEATRE
(Founded 1998)
Drawer 2483; Fort Myers, FL 33902-2483; (239) 332-4665, FAX 332-1808;
    robertcacioppo@floridarep.org, www.floridarep.org
Robert Cacioppo, *Producing Artistic Director*

Submission procedure: no unsolicited scripts; professional recommendation or agent submission. **Types of material:** full-length plays, translations, adaptations, plays for young audiences, musicals, cabaret/revues. **Facilities:** Arcade Theatre, 393 seats, proscenium stage. **Production considerations:** cast limit of 10; unit set, no fly space. **Best submission time:** Apr–May. **Response time:** 12 months.

FLORIDA STAGE
(Founded 1987)
262 South Ocean Blvd; Manalapan, FL 33462; (561) 585-3404,
    FAX 588-4708; info@floridastage.org, www.floridastage.org
Louis Tyrrell, *Producing Director*

Submission procedure: no unsolicited scripts; agent submission. **Types of material:** full-length plays, plays for young audiences. **Special interests:** contemporary issues and ideas. **Facilities:** Florida Stage, 250 seats, thrust stage. **Production considerations:** cast limit of 2-6, 1 set. **Best submission time:** year-round. **Response time:** 4 months. **Special programs:** reading series.

FOOTHILLS THEATRE COMPANY
(formerly Worcester Foothills Theatre Company)
(Founded 1974)
100 Front St, Suite 137; Worcester, MA 01608; (508) 754-3314,
    FAX 767-0676
Russell Garrett, Artistic Director

Submission procedure: no unsolicited scripts; synopsis and letter of inquiry. **Types of material:** full-length plays, translations, adaptations, plays for young audiences. **Facilities:** Foothills Theatre, 349 seats, proscenium stage. **Production considerations:** prefers cast limit of 10 (8 for children's theatre), simple set. **Best submission time:** Sep. **Response time:** 3 months letter; 4 months script.

THE FOOTHILL THEATRE COMPANY

(Founded 1977)

Box 1812; Nevada City, CA 95959; (530) 265-9320, FAX 265-9325;
    gary@foothilltheatre.org

Gary Wright, *Literary Manager*

Submission procedure: accepts unsolicited scripts. **Types of material:** full-length plays. **Special interests:** no 10-minute plays. **Facilities:** The Nevada Theatre, 243 seats, proscenium stage; also rents small spaces with 50–100 seats. **Production considerations:** cast limit of 7; very limited fly and wing space. **Best submission time:** year-round. **Response time:** 12 months. **Special programs:** New Voices of the Wild West: annual spring series that produces staged readings of 4 plays dealing with issues pertaining to rural American West; accepts submissions year-round.

FORD'S THEATRE

(Founded 1968)

511 Tenth St NW; Washington, DC 20004; (202) 638-2941, FAX 737-3017;
    www.fordstheatre.org

Mark Ramont, *Associate Producer/Artistic*

Submission procedure: no unsolicited scripts; synopsis, sample pages, demo CD and letter of inquiry. **Types of material:** full-length plays, musicals. **Special interests:** musicals and works celebrating the American experience from a historical perspective. **Facilities:** Ford's Theatre, 699 seats, proscenium stage. **Production considerations:** cast limit of 15. **Best submission time:** spring–summer. **Response time:** 3 months letter; 12 months script.

THE FOUNTAIN THEATRE

(Founded 1990)

5060 Fountain Ave; Los Angeles, CA 90029; (323) 663-2235, FAX 663-1629

Simon Levy, *Producing Director/Dramaturg*

Submission procedure: no unsolicited scripts; professional recommendation. **Types of material:** full-length plays, translations, adaptations. **Special interests:** lyrical dramas; social and political dramas; works with dance; adaptations of American literature. **Facilities:** Fountain Theatre Mainstage, 78 seats, thrust stage. **Production considerations:** cast limit of 12; unit set, no fly space, low ceiling. **Best submission time:** year-round. **Response time:** 3 months letter; 6 months script.

FREE STREET PROGRAMS

(Founded 1969)

1419 West Blackhawk St; Chicago, IL 60622; (773) 772-7248,
    FAX 772-7248; bryn@freestreet.org

Bryn Magnus, *Managing Director*

Submission procedure: no unsolicited scripts; send email with "a concept for the creation of a new performance with youth." **Types of material:** full-length works developed in ensemble process. **Special interests:** "ensemble-based creative processes that engage professional artists, emerging artists and youth artists to explore the form, language and essential meaning of theatre." **Facilities:** Studio Theater, 80 seats, proscenium stage; touring company of youth performers. **Production considerations:** limited technical support, youth production crew. **Best submission time:** year-round. **Response time:** 1 week.

GABLESTAGE

(Founded 1979)

1200 Anastasia Ave; Coral Gables, FL 33134; (305) 446-1116,
    FAX 445-8645; jadler@gablestage.org, www.gablestage.org
Joseph Adler, *Producing Artistic Director*

Submission procedure: no unsolicited scripts; synopsis with SASE for response. **Types of material:** full-length plays. **Facilities:** GableStage, 150 seats, proscenium stage. **Best submission time:** year-round. **Response time:** 3 months letter; 6 months script.

GALA HISPANIC THEATRE

(Founded 1976)

Box 43209; Washington, DC 20010; (202) 234-7174, FAX 332-1247;
    info@galatheatre.org, www.galatheatre.org
Hugo J. Medrano, *Producing/Artistic Director*

Submission procedure: accepts unsolicited scripts with synopsis/description of play and letter of inquiry with SASE for response. **Types of material:** full-length plays, plays for young audiences, musicals, solo pieces. **Special interests:** plays by Spanish, Latino or Hispanic-American writers in Spanish or English only; prefers Spanish-language works with accompanying English translation; works that reflect sociocultural realities of Hispanics in Latin America, the Caribbean or Spain, as well as the Hispanic-American experience. **Facilities:** GALA Hispanic Theatre, 270 seats, proscenium stage. **Production considerations:** no fly space. **Best submission time:** year-round. **Response time:** 1 month letter; 3 months script; scripts will not be returned. **Special programs:** poetry onstage.

GEFFEN PLAYHOUSE

(Founded 1995)

10886 LeConte Ave; Los Angeles, CA 90024; (310) 208-6500,
    FAX 208-0341; www.geffenplayhouse.com
Amy Levinson Millán, *Literary Manager/Dramaturge*

Submission procedure: no unsolicited scripts; agent submission. **Types of material:** full-length plays, adaptations, musicals. **Special interests:** new plays. **Facilities:** Geffen Playhouse, 504 seats, proscenium stage; Audrey Skirball Kenis Theater at the Geffen Playhouse, 117 seats, flexible stage. **Best submission time:** year-round. **Response time:** 6 months.

GEORGE STREET PLAYHOUSE

(Founded 1974)

9 Livingston Ave; New Brunswick, NJ 08901-1903; (732) 846-2895,
   FAX 247-9151; www.georgestplayhouse.org

Literary Manager

Submission procedure: no unsolicited scripts; agent submission. **Types of material:** full-length plays, one-act plays for young audiences. **Special interests:** comedies and dramas that present a fresh perspective on society; social issue one-acts suitable for touring to schools (not seeking any other kind of one-acts); "work that tells a compelling, personal, human story while entertaining, challenging and stretching the imagination." **Facilities:** mainstage, 367 seats, proscenium/thrust stage. **Production considerations:** prefers cast limit of 7. **Best submission time:** year-round. **Response time:** 12 months. **Special programs:** Next Stage Festival: annual developmental workshops of 3 new plays and musicals.

GERMINAL STAGE DENVER

(Founded 1974)

2450 West 44th Ave; Denver, CO 80211; (303) 455-7108;
   gsden@privatei.com, www.germinalstage.com

Ed Baierlein, *Director/Manager*

Submission procedure: no unsolicited scripts; synopsis, 5-page dialogue sample and letter of inquiry with SASP for response; no electronic submissions. **Types of material:** full-length plays, translations, adaptations. **Special interests:** adaptations that use both dialogue and narration. **Facilities:** Germinal Stage Denver, 100 seats, thrust stage. **Production considerations:** cast limit of 10; minimal production requirements. **Best submission time:** year-round. **Response time:** 2 weeks letter; 6 months script.

GEVA THEATRE CENTER

(Founded 1972)

75 Woodbury Blvd; Rochester, NY 14607-1717; (585) 232-1366

Marge Betley, *Literary Manager/Resident Dramaturg*

Submission procedure: no unsolicited scripts; synopsis, 10-page dialogue sample, production history, resume and letter of inquiry. **Types of material:** full-length plays, translations, adaptations. **Facilities:** Elaine P. Wilson Theatre, 552 seats, modified thrust stage; Ronald and Donna Fielding Nextstage, 180 seats, modified proscenium. **Best submission time:** year-round. **Response time:** 3 months letter; 6 months script. **Special programs:** American Voices New Play Reading Series. Hibernatus Interruptus Festival of New Plays: customized workshops of 3 plays. Regional Playwrights and Young Writers Festival.

GOODMAN THEATRE

(Founded 1925)

170 North Dearborn St; Chicago, IL 60601; (312) 443-3811,
    FAX 443-7448; www.goodmantheatre.org

Tanya Palmer, *Literary Manager*

Submission procedure: no unsolicited scripts; synopsis, professional recommendation and letter of inquiry. **Types of material:** full-length plays, translations, musicals. **Facilities:** Albert Ivar Goodman Theatre, 830 seats, proscenium stage; Owen Bruner Goodman Theatre, 200–400 seats, flexible stage. **Best submission time:** year-round. **Response time:** 3 months letter; 8 months script.

GOODSPEED MUSICALS

(Founded 1963)

Box A; East Haddam, CT 06423; (860) 873-8664, FAX 873-2329;
    info@goodspeed.org, www.goodspeed.org

Bob Alwine, *Associate Producer*

Submission procedure: no unsolicited scripts; letter of inquiry. **Types of material:** original musicals only. **Facilities:** Goodspeed Opera House, 400 seats, proscenium stage; The Norma Terris Theatre, 200 seats, proscenium stage. **Best submission time:** Jan-Feb. **Response time:** 3 months letter; 8 months script.

GREAT LAKES THEATER FESTIVAL

(Founded 1961)

1501 Euclid Ave, Suite 300; Cleveland, OH 44115; (216) 241-5490,
    FAX 241-6315; www.greatlakestheater.org

Artistic Department

Submission procedure: no unsolicited scripts; professional recommendation. **Types of material:** full-length plays, translations, adaptations. **Special interests:** translations and adaptations of classic plays, new works with specific relevance to classic repertoire. **Facilities:** Ohio Theatre, 1000 seats, proscenium stage; Hanna Theatre, 550 seats, thrust stage. **Best submission time:** year-round. **Response time:** 3 months.

GREENBRIER VALLEY THEATRE

(Founded 1966)

113 East Washington St; Lewisburg, WV 24901; FAX (304) 645-3818;
    cathey@gvtheatre.org, www.gvtheatre.org

Cathey Sawyer, *Artistic Director*

Submission procedure: no unsolicited scripts; synopsis and letter of inquiry. **Types of material:** full-length plays, one-acts, plays for young audiences, musicals. **Special interests:** regional plays. **Facilities:** Hollowell Theatre, 150–200 seats, black box; Studio, 25–35 seats, flexible stage. **Production considerations:** cast limit of 10 for plays; small or unit set preferred. **Best submission time:** late fall. **Response time:** 2 months letter; 6 months script.

GREENWAY ARTS ALLIANCE
(Founded 1992)
544 North Fairfax Ave; Los Angeles, CA 90036; (323) 655-7679,
    FAX 655-7906; wwgaa@aol.com, www.greenwayarts.org
Whitney Weston, *Co-Artistic Director*

Submission procedure: no unsolicited scripts; synopsis emailed or faxed. **Types of material:** full-length plays, one-acts, translations, adaptations. **Special interests:** large casts; current political themes/social relevance. **Facilities:** Greenway Court Theatre, 99 seats, flexible stage. **Best submission time:** year-round. **Response time:** 3 months letter; 2 months script.

THE GROWING STAGE—THE CHILDREN'S THEATRE OF NEW JERSEY
(Founded 1982)
Box 36; Netcong, NJ 07857; (973) 347-4946, FAX 691-7069;
    info@growingstage.com, www.growingstage.com
Stephen L. Fredericks, *Executive Director*

Submission procedure: accepts unsolicited scripts with production history and bio; include SASE for response. **Types of material:** plays for young audiences only, including full-length plays, translations, adaptations, musicals. **Special interests:** "intelligent theatre suitable for the entire family." **Facilities:** Palace Theatre, 250 seats, proscenium stage. **Production considerations:** cast limit of 3 for touring shows, mainstage work more flexible. **Best submission time:** Jun–Aug. **Response time:** 4 months.

THE GUTHRIE
(Founded 1963)
818 2nd St S; Minneapolis, MN 55415; (612) 225-6116;
    amyw@guthrietheater.org, www.guthrietheater.org
Michael Kinghorn, *Literary Manager*

Submission procedure: no unsolicited scripts; agent submission. **Types of material:** full-length plays, translations, adaptations. **Special interests:** "intelligent, imaginative, highly theatrical works of depth and significance"; rich language, humor, and complex ideas; political themes and contemporary issues. **Facilities:** Wurtele, 1100 seats, thrust stage; McGuire, 700 seats, proscenium stage; Dowling Studio, 250 seats, flexible stage. **Best submission time:** year-round. **Response time:** 6 months.

HANGAR THEATRE

(Founded 1974)

Box 205; Ithaca, NY 14851; (607) 273-8588, FAX 273-4516;
   literary@hangartheatre.org, www.hangartheatre.org

Robert Moss, *Interim Artistic Director*

Submission procedure: unsolicited scripts accepted only of one-act plays for young audiences; agent submission or invitation only for full-length plays. **Types of material:** full-length plays, one-acts for young audiences. **Facilities:** Mainstage, 359 seats, thrust stage. **Best submission time:** Sep–Jan. **Response time:** 9 months. **Special programs:** Lab Company Playwriting Residencies; see website or email for submission guidelines. School tour commissions, developmental readings and workshops.

HARWICH JUNIOR THEATRE

(Founded 1950)

Box 168; West Harwich, MA 02671; (508) 432-2002, ext 12, FAX 432-0726;
   hjt@capecod.edu, www.hjtcapecod.org

Nina K. Schuessler; *Producing Artistic Director*

Submission procedure: no unsolicited scripts; synopsis and dialogue sample. **Types of material:** full-length plays, one-acts, translations, adaptations, plays for young audiences, musicals, cabaret/revues, solo pieces. **Special interests:** intergenerational casts; plays for family audiences or with young adult themes. **Facilities:** Harwich Junior Theatre, 186 seats, thrust stage; Theatre In Corner, 60 seats, open space. **Production considerations:** prefers conceptual designs over literal settings; no fly space. **Best submission time:** early fall. **Response time:** 6 months letter; 6 months script.

HEDGEROW THEATRE

(Founded 1923)

64 Rose Valley Rd; Rose Valley, PA 19063; (610) 565-4211,
   FAX 565-1672; www.hedgerowtheatre.org

Penelope Reed, *Producing Artistic Director*

Submission procedure: no unsolicited scripts; synopsis and letter of inquiry. **Types of material:** full-length plays. **Special interests:** new plays by DE, NJ and PA playwrights; mysteries; comedies. **Facilities:** mainstage, 144 seats, proscenium stage. **Production considerations:** minimal production demands; small stage. **Best submission time:** year-round. **Response time:** 2 months letter; 4 months script. **Special programs:** play reading series, new play festival (see Hedgerow Horizons in Development).

HIP POCKET THEATRE

(Founded 1977)

Box 136758; Fort Worth, TX 76136; (817) 246-9775, FAX 246-5651;
    hippockettheatre@aol.com, www.hippocket.org

Johnny Simons, *Artistic Director*

Submission procedure: no unsolicited scripts; synopsis and dialogue sample; include cassette for musicals. **Types of material:** full-length plays, translations, adaptations, plays for young audiences, musicals, solo pieces, multimedia works. **Special interests:** well-crafted stories with poetic, mythic slant that incorporate ritual and ensemble; works utilizing masks, puppetry, music, dance, mime and strong visual elements. **Facilities:** mainstage, 130 seats (approx), outdoor amphitheatre. **Production considerations:** simple sets. **Best submission time:** Oct–Feb. **Response time:** 6 weeks letter; 6 months script.

THE HIPPODROME STATE THEATRE

(Founded 1973)

25 Southeast Second Pl; Gainesville, FL 32601-6596; (352) 373-5968,
    FAX 371-9130; www.thehipp.org

Tamerin Dygert, *Dramaturg*

Submission procedure: no unsolicited scripts; agent submission. **Types of material:** full-length plays, one-acts. **Special interests:** contemporary comedies and dramas. **Facilities:** Mainstage Theatre, 266 seats, thrust stage; Second Stage, 87 seats, flexible stage. **Production considerations:** cast limit of 6; unit set. **Best submission time:** Sep–Feb. **Response time:** 5 months. **Special programs:** informal play reading series: possibility of production at Second Stage.

HONOLULU THEATRE FOR YOUTH

(Founded 1955)

229 Queen Emma Square; Honolulu, HI 96813; (808) 839-9885,
    FAX 839-7018; executive@htyweb.org, www.htyweb.org

Eric Johnson, *Artistic Director*

Submission procedure: no unsolicited scripts; synopsis, resume and letter of inquiry. **Types of material:** plays for young audiences. **Special interests:** plays with contemporary themes for audiences from pre-school through high school; small-cast adaptations of classics; new works based on Pacific Rim cultures; plays with compelling language that are imaginative and socially relevant to young people in HI. **Facilities:** Tenney Theatre, 300 seats, proscenium stage; shows also tour to school theatres, gymnasiums and cafeterias. **Production considerations:** cast limit of 5. **Best submission time:** year-round. **Response time:** 1 month letter; 5 months script.

HORIZON THEATRE COMPANY
(Founded 1983)

Box 5376; Atlanta, GA 31107; (404) 523-1477, FAX 584-8815;
   literary@horizontheatre.com, www.horizontheatre.com

J. Caleb Boyd, *Literary Manager*

Submission procedure: no unsolicited scripts; synopsis, 10-page dialogue sample, resume and letter of inquiry. **Types of material:** full-length plays, translations, adaptations, musicals. **Special interests:** contemporary issues; plays by women and African-Americans; southern urban themes; comedies. **Facilities:** Horizon Theatre, 175 seats, modified thrust stage. **Production considerations:** cast limit of 8. **Best submission time:** year-round. **Response time:** 6 months letter; 12 months script. **Special programs:** New South Festival: annual festival of readings, workshops and full productions of plays by playwrights speaking from, for and about the South; *deadline:* 15 Mar; *notification:* 15 May; *dates:* Jun–Jul. New South Young Playwrights Festival: annual festival of new work by high school and college-age playwrights from the South or Southern schools; 5-day residency of classes and workshops for selected participants; one-acts and short plays preferred; see website for details.

THE HUMAN RACE THEATRE COMPANY
(Founded 1986)

126 North Main St, Suite 300; Dayton, OH 45402-1710; (937) 461-3823,
   FAX 461-7223; contact@humanracetheatre.org,
   www.humanracetheatre.org

Marsha Hanna, *Artistic Director (plays)*

Kevin Moore, *Executive Director (musicals)*

Submission procedure: no unsolicited scripts; professional recommendation. **Types of material:** full-length plays, musicals. **Special interests:** OH playwrights; contemporary issues; musicals in development for workshops. **Facilities:** The Loft Theatre, 219 seats, thrust stage. **Production considerations:** small cast. **Best submission time:** May–Oct. **Response time:** 6 months.

HUNTINGTON THEATRE COMPANY
(Founded 1981)

264 Huntington Ave; Boston MA 02115-4606; (617) 266-7900,
   FAX 353-8300; www.huntingtontheatre.org

Literary Manager

Submission procedure: accepts unsolicited scripts from Boston-area playwrights only; agent submission for others; include SASE for response. **Types of material:** full-length plays, translations, adaptations, musicals, solo pieces; include CD for musicals. **Facilities:** Boston University Theatre, 890 seats, proscenium stage; Virginia Wimberly Theatre, 360 seats, proscenium stage; Nancy and Edward Roberts Studio Theatre, 200 seats, flexible stage. **Best submission time:** year-round. **Response time:** 12 months. **Special programs:** Breaking Ground Festival of new play readings; Huntington Playwriting Fellows program; Calderwood Fund for New American Plays.

HYDE PARK THEATRE

(Founded 1992)

511 West 43rd St; Austin, TX 78751; (512) 479-7530, FAX 479-7531;
  inbox@hydeparktheatre.org, www.hydeparktheatre.org

Ken Webster, *Artistic Director*

Peck Phillips, Roger Topham, *Literary Managers*

Submission procedure: no unsolicited scripts; synopsis and letter of inquiry. **Types of material:** full-length plays, adaptations, solo pieces. **Facilities:** Hyde Park Theatre, 85 seats, flexible stage. **Best submission time:** year-round. **Response time:** 3 months letter; 6 months script. **Special programs:** Hyde Park Theatre Play Development Reading Series: annual reading series for developing new work.

HYPOTHETICAL THEATRE CO., INC.

(Founded 1992)

344 East 14th St; New York, NY 10003; (212) 780-0800, ext 254,
  FAX 780-0859; htc@hypotheticaltheatre.org,
  www.hypotheticaltheatre.org

Amy Feinberg, *Artistic Producing Director*

Submission procedure: no unsolicited scripts; agent submission only. **Types of material:** full-length plays. **Special interests:** contemporary, groundbreaking plays. **Facilities:** Hypothetical Theatre, 90 seats, proscenium stage. **Best submission time:** year-round. **Response time:** 6 months.

ILLINOIS THEATRE CENTER

(Founded 1976)

Box 397; Park Forest, IL 60466; (708) 481-3510, FAX 481-3693;
  ilthctr@bigplanet.com, www.ilthctr.org

Literary Manager

Submission procedure: no unsolicited scripts; synopsis and letter of inquiry with SASE for response. **Types of material:** full-length plays, musicals. **Facilities:** Illinois Theatre Center, 180 seats, proscenium/thrust stage. **Production considerations:** cast limit of 9 for plays, 14 for musicals. **Best submission time:** year-round. **Response time:** 1 month letter; 2 months script.

ILLUSION THEATER

(Founded 1974)

528 Hennepin Ave, Suite 704; Minneapolis, MN 55403; (612) 339-4944,
  FAX 337-8042; info@illusiontheater.org, www.illusiontheater.org

Michael Robins, *Executive Producing Director*

Submission procedure: no unsolicited scripts; synopsis and resume, or professional recommendation; electronic inquiry preferred. **Types of material:** full-length plays, one-acts, translations, adaptations, musicals, solo pieces. **Special interests:** emerging writers, women writers, "issue" plays. **Facilities:** Illusion Theater, 200 seats, proscenium stage. **Best submission time:** Sep–Jan. **Response time:** 18 months letter; script varies. **Special programs:** Fresh Ink Series: 5-6 plays presented with minimal set and costumes for 1 weekend; post-performance discussion with audience; scripts selected through theatre's normal submission procedure.

IMAGINATION STAGE
(Founded 1992)
4908 Auburn Ave; Bethesda, MD 20814; (301) 961-6060, FAX 718-9526;
    jstanford@imaginationstage.org, www.imaginationstage.org
Janet Stanford, *Artistic Director*

Submission procedure: no unsolicited scripts; dialogue sample and letter of inquiry. **Types of material:** plays and musicals for young audiences (ages 2–10). **Special interests:** 60–90-minute plays, "innovative treatment of children's classics," culturally diverse material. **Facilities:** Imagination Stage, 400 seats, thrust stage. **Production considerations:** cast size 4–10. **Best submission time:** year-round. **Response time:** 2 months letter; script varies.

INDIANA REPERTORY THEATRE
(Founded 1972)
140 West Washington St; Indianapolis, IN 46204-3465; (317) 635-5277,
    FAX 236-0767; rroberts@irtlive.com
Richard Roberts, *Resident Dramaturg*

Submission procedure: no unsolicited scripts; synopsis and resume. **Types of material:** full-length plays, translations, adaptations, solo pieces. **Special interests:** adaptations of classic literature; plays that explore cultural/ethnic issues "with a Midwestern voice." **Facilities:** mainstage, 600 seats, modified proscenium stage; Upperstage, 300 seats, thrust stage. **Production considerations:** cast limit of 6–8. **Best submission time:** year-round (season chosen by Jan each year). **Response time:** 6 months letter; 12 months script. **Special programs:** Discovery Series: presentation of plays for family audiences with focus on youth, culturally/ethnically diverse plays with emphasis on history and adaptations of literature; scripts selected through theatre's normal submission procedure.

INTAR HISPANIC AMERICAN ARTS CENTER
(Founded 1966)
Box 756; New York, NY 10108; (212) 695-6134, ext 19, FAX 268-0102
Literary Manager

Submission procedure: accepts unsolicited scripts. **Types of material:** full-length plays. **Special interests:** new plays by Hispanic-American writers and translations and adaptations of Hispanic works only. **Facilities:** INTAR 53, 74 seats, black box. **Production considerations:** small cast, modest production values. **Best submission time:** year-round (season chosen late summer–early fall). **Response time:** 3 months. **Special programs:** NewWorks Lab: workshop productions; reading series.

INTERACT THEATRE COMPANY

(Founded 1988)

2030 Sansom St; Philadelphia, PA 19103; (215) 568-8077, FAX 568-8095; bwright@interacttheatre.org, www.interacttheatre.org

Rebecca Wright, *Literary Director and Dramaturge*

Submission procedure: no unsolicited scripts; synopsis, bio and letter of inquiry with SASE for response. **Types of material:** full-length plays. **Special interests:** contemporary plays that theatrically explore issues of political, social and cultural significance. **Facilities:** The Adrienne, 106 seats, proscenium stage. **Production considerations:** cast limit of 10. **Best submission time:** year-round. **Response time:** 3 months letter; 12 months script.

INTERNATIONAL CITY THEATRE

(Founded 1986)

One World Trade Center, Suite 300; Box 32069; Long Beach, CA 90832; (562) 495-4595, FAX 436-7895; shashinict@earthlink.net, www.ictlongbeach.com

Shashin Desai, *Artistic Director/Producer*

Submission procedure: no unsolicited scripts; professional recommendation. **Types of material:** full-length plays, translations, adaptations, plays for young audiences, musicals, cabaret/revues, solo pieces. **Facilities:** ICT Center Theater, 349 seats, thrust stage. **Production considerations:** cast limit of 3-8; unit set, no fly space. **Best submission time:** year-round. **Response time:** 6 months.

IRISH CLASSICAL THEATRE COMPANY

(Founded 1990)

625 Main St; Buffalo, NY 14203; (716) 853-1380, FAX 853-0592; pezz@irishclassical.com, www.irishclassicaltheatre.com

Fortunato Pezzimenti, *Producing Director*

Submission procedure: no unsolicited scripts; professional recommendation. **Types of material:** full-length plays, one-acts, translations, adaptations, cabaret/revues, solo pieces. **Special interests:** plays by Irish or Irish-American writers, plays with Irish or Irish-American themes. **Facilities:** Irish Classical Theatre (Andrews Theatre), 200 seats, arena stage. **Production considerations:** unit set, fluid set changes, limited storage space. **Best submission time:** May–Jun. **Response time:** 1 month letter; 3 months script.

IRONDALE ENSEMBLE PROJECT

(Founded 1983)

Box 150604; Brooklyn, NY 11215; (718) 488-9233, FAX 788-0607; irondalert@aol.com, www.irondale.org

Jim Niesen, *Artistic Director*

Submission procedure: no unsolicited scripts; letter of inquiry from playwright interested in developing work with ensemble through ongoing workshop process. **Types of material:** full-length plays, adaptations, musicals. **Special interests:** works with political or social relevance. **Facilities:** Irondale Center for Theater, Education and Outreach, 200 seats, flexible stage. **Production considerations:** cast limit of 8–9. **Best submission time:** Apr–Sep. **Response time:** 3 months.

JEWISH ENSEMBLE THEATRE
(Founded 1989)
6600 West Maple Rd; West Bloomfield, MI 48322-3002; (248) 788-2900,
    FAX 788-5160; artisticdirector@jettheatre.org, www.jettheatre.org
Evelyn Orbach, *Artistic Director*

Submission procedure: accepts unsolicited scripts; no electronic submissions. **Types of material:** full-length plays, plays for young audiences. **Special interests:** works on Jewish themes and/or by Jewish writers; work not previously produced professionally. **Facilities:** Aaron DeRoy Theatre, 178 seats, thrust stage. **Production considerations:** no fly space. **Best submission time:** late spring–summer. **Response time:** 6 months. **Special programs:** Festival of New Plays in Staged Readings: 4 plays given readings, possibly leading to mainstage production; scripts selected through theatre's normal submission procedure; *deadline:* 15 Aug.

THE JEWISH THEATER OF NEW YORK
(Founded 1993)
Box 845; New York, NY 10108; (212) 494-0050; thejtny@aol.com,
    www.jewishtheater.org
Liz Lauren, *Dramaturg*

Submission procedure: no unsolicited scripts; letter of inquiry. **Types of material:** full-length plays, one-acts, translations, musicals. **Facilities:** The Triad, 140 seats, flexible stage. **Best submission time:** year-round. **Response time:** 3 months letter; 6 months script.

JOBSITE THEATER
(Founded 1998)
Box 7975; Tampa, FL 33673-7975; (813) 222-1092, FAX 222-1057;
    www.jobsitetheater.org
David Jenkins, *Artistic Director*

Submission procedure: accepts unsolicited scripts. **Types of material:** full-length plays, one-acts. **Special interests:** "topical, politically and socially relevant theatre; plays appealing to 20- and 30-somethings." **Facilities:** Shimberg Playhouse, 150 seats, black box. **Production considerations:** small cast, 1 set. **Best submission time:** spring. **Response time:** 3 months.

JOHN DREW THEATER

(Founded 1931)

158 Main St; East Hampton, NY 11937; (631) 324-0806, FAX 324-2722;
joshgladstone@guildhall.org, www.guildhall.org

Josh Gladstone, *Artistic Director*

Submission procedure: no unsolicited scripts; 1-page synopsis, character/set breakdown and letter of inquiry. **Types of material:** full-length plays, solo pieces. **Special interests:** comedies; plays with contemporary setting. **Facilities:** John Drew Theater, 382 seats, proscenium stage. **Production considerations:** unit set, no fly space. **Best submission time:** year-round. **Response time:** 6 months letter; 6 months script.

JUBILEE THEATRE

(Founded 1982)

506 Main Street; Fort Worth, TX 76102; (817) 338-4204, FAX 338-4206;
www.jubileetheatre.org

Benjamin Espino, *Managing Director*

Submission Procedure: accepts unsolicited scripts. **Types of material:** full-length plays, one-acts, plays for young audiences. **Special interests**: plays about the African-American experience. **Facilities:** Jubilee Theatre, 147 seats, proscenium stage. **Production considerations:** small cast; limited technical support, small stage. **Best submission time:** year-round. **Response time:** 6 months.

JUNGLE THEATER

(Founded 1991)

2951 South Lyndale Ave; Minneapolis, MN 55408; (612) 822-7063,
FAX 822-9408; info@jungletheater.com, www.jungletheater.com

Joel Sass, *Associate Artistic Director*

Submission procedure: no unsolicited scripts; synopsis, 10-page dialogue sample, resume and letter of inquiry; no electronic submissions. **Types of material:** full-length plays. **Facilities:** The Jungle Theater, 152 seats, proscenium stage. **Best submission time:** year-round. **Response time:** 3 months letter; 6 months script.

KANSAS CITY REPERTORY THEATRE

(Founded 1964)

4949 Cherry St; Kansas City, MO 64110-2263; (816) 235-2727,
FAX 235-6562; information@kcrep.org, www.kcrep.org

Eric Rosen, *Artistic Director*

Submission procedure: no unsolicited scripts; agent submission. **Types of material:** full-length plays, translations, adaptations. **Facilities:** Spencer Theatre, 645 seats, modified thrust stage; Copaken Stage, 320 seats, proscenium stage. **Best submission time:** year-round. **Response time:** varies.

THE KAVINOKY THEATRE

(Founded 1981)

320 Porter Ave; Buffalo, NY 14221; (716) 829-7652, FAX 829-7790;
    www.kavinokytheatre.com

David Lamb, *Artistic Director*

Submission procedure: no unsolicited scripts; professional recommendation. **Types of material:** full-length plays, adaptations, musicals. **Facilities:** Kavinoky Theatre, 260 seats, proscenium/thrust stage. **Production considerations:** prefers cast limit of 7; no fly and limited wing space. **Best submission time:** Jun–Aug. **Response time:** 1 month.

KENTUCKY REPERTORY THEATRE AT HORSE CAVE

(Founded 1977)

Box 215; Horse Cave, KY 42749; (270) 786-1200, FAX 786-5298;
    rbrock@kentuckyrep.org, www.kentuckyrep.org

Robert Brock, *Artistic Director*

Submission procedure: no unsolicited scripts; professional recommendation. **Types of material:** full-length plays. **Special interests:** KY-based plays by KY playwrights. **Facilities:** Kentucky Repertory Theatre at Horse Cave, 346 seats, thrust stage. **Production considerations:** cast limit of 10; unit set. **Best submission time:** Oct–Apr. **Response time:** varies.

KITCHEN DOG THEATER COMPANY

(Founded 1990)

3120 McKinney Ave; Dallas, TX 75204; (214) 953-2258, FAX 953-1873;
    tina@kitchendogtheater.org, www.kitchendogtheater.org

Christopher Carlos and Tina Parker, *Co-Artistic Directors*

Submission procedure: accepts unsolicited scripts. **Types of material:** full-length plays, translations, adaptations, solo pieces. **Special interests:** plays by TX and Southwest playwrights. **Facilities:** The McKinney Avenue Contemporary, 100–150 seats, thrust stage; Second Space, 75–100 seats, black box. **Production considerations:** cast limit of 5; moderate production demands, moderate set. **Best submission time:** year-round. **Response time:** 8 months; scripts will not be returned. **Special programs:** New Works Festival: annual presentation of new plays, including 1 full production, staged readings, mini workshops and artist residencies; submit script with SASP for response; *deadline:* 1 Feb; *notification:* 30 Apr; *dates:* Jun–Jul.

KUMU KAHUA THEATRE

(Founded 1971)

46 Merchant St; Honolulu, HI 96813; (808) 536-4222, FAX 536-4226;
    kumukahuatheatre@hawaiiantel.net, www.kumukahua.org

Harry Wong III, *Artistic Director*

Submission procedure: accepts unsolicited scripts with SASE for response. **Types of material:** full-length plays, one-acts, adaptations. **Special interests:** plays set in HI or dealing with the Hawai'i experience. **Facilities:** Kumu Kahua Theatre, 100 seats, black box. **Best submission time:** year-round. **Response time:** 4 months. **Special programs:** Kumu Kahua Theatre/UHM Theatre Department Playwriting Contest: includes the Hawai'i Prize, Pacific Rim Prize and Resident Prize (see Prizes).

LABYRINTH THEATER COMPANY

(Founded 1992)

307 West 38th St, Suite 1605; New York, NY 10018; (212) 513-1080,
    FAX 513-1123; literary@labtheater.org, www.labtheater.org

Literary Manager

Submission procedure: no unsolicited scripts; synopsis, 10-page dialogue sample, resume and letter of inquiry; no electronic submission. **Types of material:** full-length plays. **Special interests:** work not previously produced. **Facilities:** no permanent facility; in residence at The Public Theater (see listing this section). **Best submission time:** year-round. **Response time:** 8-12 months letter; 8-12 months script.

LA JOLLA PLAYHOUSE

(Founded 1947)

Box 12039; La Jolla, CA 92039; (858) 550-1070, FAX 550-1075;
    www.lajollaplayhouse.org

Gabriel Greene, *Literary Manager*

Submission procedure: no unsolicited scripts; 10-page sample from Southern California writers only; agent submission. **Types of material:** full-length plays, translations, adaptations, musicals, solo pieces. **Special interests:** world premieres, American premieres; innovative form and language, emphasis on ideas and theatricality. **Facilities:** Mandell Weiss Center for the Performing Arts, 500 seats, proscenium stage; Potiker Theatre, 450 seats, convertible black box; Weiss Forum, 400 seats, thrust stage. **Best submission time:** year-round. **Response time:** 1 month letter, 12 months script.

LA MAMA EXPERIMENTAL THEATRE CLUB

(Founded 1961)

74A East 4th St; New York, NY 10003; (212) 254-6468, FAX 254-7597;
    lamama@lamama.org, www.lamama.org

Ellen Stewart, *Artistic Director*

Submission procedure: no unsolicited scripts; professional recommendation. **Types of material:** full-length plays, one-acts, musicals, performance art. **Special interests:**

culturally diverse works with music, movement and media. **Facilities:** Annex Theater, 299 seats, flexible stage; The Club Theater, 99 seats, black box; First Floor Theater, 99 seats, black box. **Best submission time:** year-round. **Response time:** 6 months. **Special programs:** concert play reading series curated by George Ferencz; poetry series curated by William Electric Black; theatrical workshops and premiere productions involving collaboration among artists of varying geographic and ethnic origins that promote intercultural understanding and artistic exchange. La MaMa Umbria: summer artist's residency program and International Directors Symposium outside Spoleto in Umbria, Italy; contact theatre for more information.

L. A. THEATRE WORKS
(Founded 1974)
681 Venice Blvd; Venice, CA 90291; (310) 827-0808, FAX 827-4949; latw@latw.org
Susan Loewenberg, *Producing Director*

Submission procedure: no unsolicited scripts; agent submission. **Types of material:** full-length plays, adaptations. **Facilities:** Skirball Cultural Center, 330 seats, proscenium stage. **Best submission time:** year-round. **Response time:** 6 months.

LINCOLN CENTER THEATER
(Founded 1966)
150 West 65th St; New York, NY 10023; (212) 362-7600; www.lct.org
Anne Cattaneo, *Dramaturg*

Submission procedure: no unsolicited scripts; agent submission. **Types of material:** full-length plays, one-acts, translations, adaptations, musicals. **Facilities:** Vivian Beaumont, 1000 seats, thrust stage; Mitzi E. Newhouse, 300 seats, thrust stage. **Best submission time:** year-round. **Response time:** 4 months.

LONG WHARF THEATRE
(Founded 1965)
222 Sargent Dr; New Haven, CT 06511; (203) 787-4284, FAX 776-2287; april.donahower@longwharf.org, www.longwharf.org
April Donahower, *Dramaturg/Literary Manager*

Submission procedure: no unsolicited scripts; agent submission or professional recommendation. **Types of material:** full-length plays, translations, adaptations. **Special interests:** dramatic plays and comedies about human relationships, social concerns, ethical and moral dilemmas. **Facilities:** Newton Schenck Stage, 484 seats, thrust stage; Stage II, 199 seats, proscenium stage. **Best submission time:** year-round. **Response time:** 6 months.

LOST NATION THEATER

(Founded 1977)

39 Main St; City Hall; Montpelier, VT 05602; (802) 229-0492,
FAX 223-9608; info@lostnationtheater.org, www.lostnationtheater.org

Mr. Kim Bent, *Founding Artistic Director*

Submission procedure: no unsolicited scripts; synopsis, dialogue sample, resume and letter of inquiry. **Types of material:** full-length plays, translations, adaptations, plays for young audiences. **Special interests:** no "spectacles"; plays with music acceptable, but no musicals. **Facilities:** City Hall Auditorium, 100 seats, black box. **Production considerations:** cast limit of 10; unit set, no fly space. **Best submission time:** Nov. **Response time:** 3 months letter; 12 months script. **Special programs:** New Works Showcase: summer new play reading series on cabaret stage in theatre lobby, 1-2 rehearsals before reading in front of audience with post-reading feedback/discussion session; indicate interest in having reading only.

THE LYRIC STAGE COMPANY OF BOSTON

(Founded 1974)

140 Clarendon St; Boston, MA 02116; www.lyricstage.com

Spiro Veloudos, *Producing Artistic Director*

Submission procedure: no unsolicited scripts; 1-page synopsis, dialogue sample, character breakdown, set description and letter of inquiry; include cassette or CD for musicals. **Types of material:** full-length plays, musicals. **Special interests:** MA writers; women and minority writers; small-cast comedies and musicals; Boston themes. **Facilities:** mainstage, 240 seats, thrust stage. **Production considerations:** cast limit of 6 for plays, 9 for musicals; limited backstage space, prefers unit set. **Best submission time:** Jun-Jul. **Response time:** 2 months letter; 6 months script. **Special programs:** script development to production; commissioning program for MA writers.

MADISON REPERTORY THEATRE

(Founded 1969)

1 South Pinckney St, Suite 340; Madison, WI 53703; (608) 256-0029,
FAX 256-7433; postmaster@madisonrep.org, www.madisonrep.org

Trevin Gay, *Acting Artistic Director*

Submission procedure: no unsolicited scripts; agent submission. **Types of material:** full-length plays, translations, adaptations, musicals. **Facilities:** The Playhouse, 345 seats, thrust stage. **Production considerations:** cast limit of 15; no fly space. **Best submission time:** Jun-Aug. **Response time:** 6 months. **Special programs:** Madison New Play Festival: annual festival of readings and workshops for plays in development. Madison Young Playwrights Program and Festival.

MAGIC THEATRE

(Founded 1967)

Fort Mason Center, Bldg D; San Francisco, CA 94123; (415) 441-8001,
    FAX 771-5505; www.magictheatre.org

Erin Gilley, *Literary Manager*

Submission procedure: no unsolicited scripts; agent submission. **Types of material:** full-length plays. **Special interests:** world and American premieres; new plays with "a sense of urgency, original voice and wit." **Facilities:** Magic Theatre Northside, 160 seats, thrust stage; Sam Shepard Theatre, 160 seats, proscenium stage. **Best submission time:** Sep–May. **Response time:** 6 weeks letter; 8 months script.

MAIN STREET THEATER

(Founded 1975)

2540 Times Blvd; Houston, TX 77005-3225; (713) 524-3622,
    FAX 524-3977; rudden@mainstreettheater.com,
    www.mainstreettheater.com

Rebecca Greene Udden, *Artistic Director*

Submission procedure: no unsolicited scripts; synopsis, dialogue sample and letter of inquiry. **Types of material:** full-length plays, one-acts, translations, adaptations, plays for young audiences, musicals. **Special interests:** plays by women; plays dealing with multicultural issues. **Facilities:** MST-Chelsea Market, 250 seats, thrust stage; MST-Times Blvd, 99 seats, thrust stage. **Production considerations:** cast limit of 9. **Best submission time:** year-round. **Response time:** 1 month letter; 6 months script.

MANHATTAN THEATRE CLUB

(Founded 1972)

311 West 43rd St, 8th Floor; New York, NY 10036; (212) 399-3000,
    FAX 399-4329; www.manhattantheatreclub.com

Jerry Patch, *Director of Artistic Development*
Clifford Lee Johnson III, *Director of Musical Development*

Submission procedure: no unsolicited scripts; agent submission. **Types of material:** full-length plays, musicals. **Facilities:** Biltmore Theatre, 650 seats, proscenium stage; Stage I at City Center, 299 seats, proscenium stage; Stage II, 150 seats, thrust stage. **Production considerations:** prefers cast limit of 8; unit set. **Best submission time:** year-round. **Response time:** 6 months. **Special programs:** readings and workshop productions of new musicals; 7s@7: in-house, rehearsed readings of new plays.

MA–YI THEATER COMPANY
(Founded 1989)
520 8th Ave, Suite 309; New York, NY 10018; (212) 971-4862;
   info@ma-yitheatre.org, www.ma-yitheatre.org
Ralph Peña, *Artistic Director*

Submission procedure: no unsolicited scripts; synopsis and letter of inquiry. **Types of material:** full-length plays, one-acts, plays for young audiences, musicals, solo pieces. **Special interests:** works by Asian-American and non-Asian playwrights. **Facilities:** no permanent facility. **Best submission time:** Nov–Feb. **Response time:** 2 months letter; 6 months script.

McCARTER THEATRE CENTER
(Founded 1972)
91 University Place; Princeton, NJ 08540; (609) 258-6500, FAX 497-0369;
   literary@mccarter.org, www.mccarter.org
Carrie Hughes, *Literary Manager*

Submission procedure: no unsolicited scripts; agent submission or professional recommendation. **Types of material:** full-length plays, musicals. **Facilities:** Matthews Theatre, 1077 seats, proscenium stage; Berlind Theatre, 380 seats, proscenium stage. **Best submission time:** year-round. **Response time:** 4 months.

MCC THEATER
(Founded 1986)
311 West 43rd St, Suite 206; New York, NY 10036; (212) 727-7722,
   FAX 727-7780; www.mcctheater.com
Stephen Willems, *Literary Manager/Resident Dramaturg*

Submission procedure: no unsolicited scripts; synopsis, 10-page dialogue sample and letter of inquiry with SASE or SASP for response. **Types of material:** full-length plays, one-acts, translations, adaptations, musicals. **Facilities:** Lucille Lortel Theatre, 199 seats, proscenium stage. **Production considerations:** cast limit of 10. **Best submission time:** year-round. **Response time:** 2 weeks letter; 2 months script.

MEADOW BROOK THEATRE
(Founded 1967)
207 Wilson Hall; Rochester, MI 48309; (248) 370-3316, FAX 370-3344;
   cmarshall@mbtheatre.com, www.mbtheatre.com
Cheryl Marshall, *Acting Managing Director*

Submission procedure: no unsolicited scripts; professional recommendation. **Types of material:** full-length plays, adaptations. **Special interests:** plays with MI location or subject matter. **Facilities:** Meadow Brook Theatre, 584 seats, proscenium stage. **Production considerations:** no fly space. **Best submission time:** Sep–May. **Response time:** 2 months, if interested.

MERRIMACK REPERTORY THEATRE

(Founded 1979)

132 Warren St; Lowell, MA 01852; (978) 654-7550, FAX 654-7575;
www.merrimackrep.org

Charles Towers, *Artistic Director*

Submission procedure: no unsolicited scripts; agent submission. **Types of material:** full-length plays, translations, adaptations. **Special interests:** plays that reflect contemporary American experience. **Facilities:** Liberty Hall, 308 seats, proscenium stage. **Production considerations:** moderate cast size. **Best submission time:** year-round. **Response time:** 12 months.

MERRY-GO-ROUND PLAYHOUSE

(Founded 1958)

17 William St, 2nd Floor; Auburn, NY 13021; (315) 255-1305,
FAX 252-3815; youth@merry-go-round.com,
www.merry-go-round.com

Carole Estabrook, *Educational Theatre Coordinator*

Submission procedure: accepts unsolicited scripts. **Types of material:** plays for young audiences, including one-acts, translations, adaptations, musicals. **Special interests:** participatory plays for young audiences, plays for grades K–12; prefers familiarity with NY State learning standards and curriculum. **Facilities:** no permanent facility; touring company. **Production considerations:** cast limit of 4. **Best submission time:** Nov–Dec. **Response time:** 2 months.

METROSTAGE

(Founded 1984)

1201 North Royal St; Alexandria, VA 22314; (703) 548-9044,
FAX 548-9089; info@metrostage.org, www.metrostage.org

Carolyn Griffin, *Producing Artistic Director*

Submission procedure: no unsolicited scripts; synopsis, first 10 pages of dialogue, list of productions/readings and letter of inquiry. **Types of material:** full-length plays. **Facilities:** MetroStage, 130 seats, thrust stage. **Production considerations:** cast limit of 8, prefers 4; prefers unit set. **Best submission time:** year-round. **Response time:** 1 month letter; 1 month script. **Special programs:** First Stage: staged reading series Oct–May.

METRO THEATER COMPANY

(Founded 1973)

8308 Olive Blvd; St. Louis, MO 63132-2814; (314) 997-6777,
FAX 997-1811; carol@metrotheatrecompany.org,
www.metrotheatercompany.org

Carol North, *Artistic Director*

Submission procedure: no unsolicited scripts; professional recommendation. **Types**

of material: plays for young audiences. Special interests: works maximum 60 minutes in length; plays "not dramatically limited by traditional concepts of children's theatre." Facilities: no permanent facility; touring company. Best submission time: year-round. Response time: 3 months. Special programs: new play readings, commissioning program; interested writers send letter of inquiry with recommendations from theatres that have produced writer's work.

MILL MOUNTAIN THEATRE
(Founded 1964)
1 Market Square SE; Roanoke, VA 24011-1437; (540) 342-5730,
    FAX 342-5745; mmt@millmountain.org, www.millmountain.org
Literary Associate

Submission procedure: accepts unsolicited one-acts for CenterPieces reading series only; other scripts by agent submission. Types of material: full-length plays, one-acts, plays for young audiences, musicals, solo pieces. Facilities: Trinkle Main Stage, 360 seats, proscenium stage; Waldron Stage, 135 seats, flexible stage. Production considerations: cast limit of 15 for plays, 24 for musicals; unit set. Best submission time: year-round. Response time: 8 months. Special programs: CenterPieces: staged readings of unpublished one-acts 20–35 minutes in length (no 10-minute plays) suitable for general lunchtime audience. Mill Mountain Theatre's Norfolk Southern Festival of New Works (see Development).

MILWAUKEE CHAMBER THEATRE
(Founded 1975)
158 North Broadway; Milwaukee, WI 53202; (414) 276-8842,
    FAX 277-4477; michael@chamber-theatre.com
C. Michael Wright, *Producing Artistic Director*

Submission procedure: no unsolicited scripts; professional recommendation. Types of material: full-length plays, translations, adaptations. Special interests: strong, well-crafted plays. Facilities: Broadway Theatre Center: Cabot Theatre, 358 seats, proscenium stage; studio, 96 seats, black box. Production considerations: unit set. Best submission time: summer. Response time: 4 months.

MILWAUKEE REPERTORY THEATER
(Founded 1954)
108 East Wells St; Milwaukee, WI 53202; (414) 224-1761, FAX 224-9097;
    kcrouch@milwaukeerep.com, www.milwaukeerep.com
Kristin Crouch, *Literary Director*

Submission procedure: no unsolicited scripts; professional recommendation or agent submission. Types of material: full-length plays, translations, adaptations, cabaret/revues. Facilities: Quadracci Powerhouse Theatre, 720 seats, thrust stage; Stiemke Theatre, 200 seats, flexible stage; Stackner Cabaret, 100 seats, cabaret stage. Production considerations: For cabaret: maximum of 90 minutes in length. Best submission time: year-round. Response time: 4 months.

THE MIRACLE THEATRE GROUP
(Founded 1985)
425 Southeast Sixth Ave; Portland, OR 97214; (503) 236-7253,
   FAX 236-4174; mainstage@milagro.org, www.milagro.org
Olga Sanchez, *Artistic Director of Miracle Mainstage*

Submission procedure: accepts unsolicited scripts. **Types of material:** full-length plays, translations, adaptations. **Special interests:** Hispanic playwrights, plays that deal with the Hispanic experience. **Facilities:** El Centro Milagro, 120 seats, thrust stage. **Production considerations:** cast limit of 10; unit set, no fly space. **Best submission time:** year-round. **Response time:** 5 months.

MIXED BLOOD THEATRE COMPANY
(Founded 1976)
1501 South Fourth St; Minneapolis, MN 55454; (612) 338-0937;
   junior@mixedblood.com
Liz Engelman, *Resident Dramaturg*

Submission procedure: no unsolicited scripts; 1-page synopsis and letter of inquiry. **Types of material:** full-length plays, musicals, cabaret/revues. **Special interests:** political, issue-oriented comedies; contemporary plays set in U.S.; world theatre pieces; plays by and about people with disabilities. **Facilities:** Main Stage, 200 seats, flexible stage. **Best submission time:** Aug–Jan. **Response time:** varies, if interested.

THE MONTANA REPERTORY THEATRE
(Founded 1968)
Department of Drama and Dance; University of Montana;
   Missoula, MT 59812-8136; (406) 243-6809, FAX 243-5726;
   montana.rep@mso.umt.edu, www.montanarep.org
Greg Johnson, *Artistic Director*

Submission procedure: no unsolicited scripts; synopsis, resume and letter of inquiry. **Types of material:** full-length plays, one-acts, musicals. **Facilities:** no permanent facility; touring company. **Best submission time:** summer. **Response time:** 3 months letter; 6 months script.

MONTGOMERY THEATER
(Founded 1993)
Box 64033; Souderton, PA 18964; (215) 723-9984, FAX 723-1160;
   play@montgomerytheater.org, www.montgomerytheater.org
Tom Quinn, *Artistic Director*

Submission procedure: accepts unsolicited scripts. **Types of material:** full-length plays, plays for young audiences, musicals. **Facilities:** Mainstage, 122 seats, thrust stage; Project Stage, 70 seats, thrust stage. **Production considerations:** no fly space, limited wing space. **Best submission time:** year-round. **Response time:** varies.

MO`OLELO PERFORMING ARTS COMPANY
(Founded 2004)
Box 710564; San Diego, CA 92171-0564; (619) 342-7395, FAX 342-7395;
seema@moolelo.net, www.moolelo.net
Seema Sueko, *Artistic Director*

Submission procedure: accepts unsolicited scripts. **Types of material:** full-length plays, translations, adaptations. **Special interests:** "plays that explore political, social and cultural issues of our time; works that are female-centric." **Facilities:** Mainstage, 100 seats, black box. **Production considerations:** multicultural cast, cast limit of 5; unit set, no fly space. **Best submission time:** year-round. **Response time:** 6 months.

MU PERFORMING ARTS
(Founded 1992)
2700 Northeast Winter St, Suite 4; Minneapolis, MN 55413;
      (612) 824-4804, FAX 824-3396; info@muperformingarts.org,
      www.muperformingarts.org
Rick Shiomi, *Artistic Director*

Submission procedure: accepts unsolicited scripts. **Types of material:** full-length plays, one-acts, adaptations, musicals, plays for young audiences. **Special interests:** Asian-American plays; plays combining traditional Asian performance with Western theatre styles; short plays suitable for touring to schools. **Facilities:** no permanent facility; company performs in various proscenium venues with approximately 150 seats. **Production considerations:** cast limit of 10; simple sets. **Best submission time:** year-round. **Response time:** 3 months. **Special programs:** annual weekend staged reading series; touring and outreach programs.

NACL THEATRE
(Founded 1997)
110 Highland Lake Rd; Highland Lake, NY 12743; (845) 557-0694,
      FAX 557-0393; www.nacl.org
Brad Krumholz and Tannis Kowalchuk, *Artistic Directors*

Submission procedure: no unsolicited scripts; professional recommendation. **Types of material:** full-length plays, one-acts, translations, adaptations. **Special interests:** experimental, multidisciplinary performance works. **Facilities:** NACL Catskills, 150 seats, flexible stage. **Production considerations:** cast limit of 4–8; minimal set requirements. **Best submission time:** year-round. **Response time:** 3 months. **Special programs:** The NACL Catskill Festival of New Theatre: annual festival of new work; write for application and guidelines.

NATIONAL THEATRE OF THE DEAF

(Founded 1967)

139 North Main St; West Hartford, CT 06107; (860) 236-4193,
    FAX 236-4163; info@ntd.org, www.ntd.org

Aaron M. Kubey, *Executive Director*

Submission procedure: no unsolicited scripts; synopsis, character breakdown, sample pages and letter of inquiry with SASE for response. **Types of material:** full-length plays, adaptations, plays for young audiences. **Special interests:** work not produced professionally; deaf issues; culturally diverse plays. **Facilities:** no permanent facility; touring company. **Production considerations:** cast limit of 4; production must tour. **Best submission time:** year-round. **Response time:** 1 month letter; 6 months script.

NATIVE VOICES AT THE AUTRY

(Founded 1999)

4700 Western Heritage Way; Los Angeles, CA 90027-1462;
    (323) 667-2000, ext 299, FAX 660-5721;
    nativevoices@autrynationalcenter.org,
    www.nativevoicesattheautry.org

Carlene Lacosta, *Literary Associate*

Submission procedure: accepts unsolicited scripts. **Types of material:** full-length plays, adaptations, plays for young audiences, musicals, cabaret/revues, text-based solo pieces. **Special interests:** works by Native American writers only. **Facilities:** Wells Fargo Theatre, 199 seats, proscenium stage. **Best submission time:** year-round. **Response time:** 6 months. **Special programs:** Annual Playwrights Retreat and Festival of New Plays: selected playwrights participate in a week-long retreat to work with professional dramaturgs, directors, designers and actors; culminates in public reading; selected playwrights receive honorarium. First Look Series: public reading series that features a new play each month; selected playwrights receive honorarium and are teamed with professional directors and actors for an 8-hour workshop before the reading.

THE NEW CONSERVATORY THEATRE CENTER

(Founded 1981)

25 Van Ness, Lower Lobby; San Francisco, CA 94102; (415) 861-4914,
    FAX 861-6988; ed@nctcsf.org, www.nctcsf.org

Ed Decker, *Artistic/Executive Director*

Submission procedure: no unsolicited scripts; synopsis and letter of inquiry. **Types of material:** full-length plays, plays for young audiences, musicals. **Special interests:** gay plays for adult audiences. **Facilities:** Decker Theatre, 125 seats, proscenium stage; Walker Theatre, 65 seats, black box; City Theatre, 55 seats, black box. **Best submission time:** year-round. **Response time:** 3 months letter; 6 months script.

NEW FEDERAL THEATRE

(Founded 1970)

292 Henry St; New York, NY 10002; (212) 353-1176, FAX 353-1088; newfederal@aol.com, www.newfederaltheatre.org

Woodie King, Jr., *Producing Director*

Submission procedure: no unsolicited scripts; professional recommendation. **Types of material:** full-length plays. **Special interests:** social and political issues; family and community themes related to minorities and women. **Facilities:** Henry Street Settlement: Harry De Jur Playhouse, 300 seats, proscenium stage; Experimental Theatre, 143 seats, black box; Recital Hall, 99 seats, thrust stage. **Production considerations:** small cast; no more than 2 sets. **Best submission time:** year-round. **Response time:** 5 months.

NEW FREEDOM THEATRE

(Founded 1966)

1346 North Broad St; Philadelphia, PA 19121; (215) 765-2793, FAX 765-4191; www.freedomtheatre.org

Literary Department

Submission procedure: no unsolicited scripts; professional recommendation or agent submission. **Types of material:** full-length plays, musicals. **Special interests:** contemporary plays with African-American themes. **Facilities:** John E. Allen Theatre, 299 seats, proscenium stage; Freedom Black Box Theatre, 120 seats, flexible stage. **Best submission time:** year-round. **Response time:** 3 months.

NEW GEORGES

(Founded 1992)

109 West 27th St, Suite 9A; New York, NY 10001; (646) 336-8077, FAX 336-8077; info@newgeorges.org, www.newgeorges.org

Kara-Lynn Vaeni, *Literary Manager*

Submission procedure: accepts unsolicited scripts. **Types of material:** full-length plays. **Special interests:** plays by women only; works with "vigorous use of language and heightened perspectives on reality." **Facilities:** no permanent facility. **Best submission time:** year-round. **Response time:** 9 months.

THE NEW GROUP

(Founded 1991)

410 West 42nd St; New York, NY 10036; info@thenewgroup.org, www.thenewgroup.org

Ian Morgan, *Associate Artistic Director*

Submission procedure: no unsolicited scripts; 10–20-page dialogue sample, resume and letter of inquiry with SASE for response. **Types of material:** full-length plays. **Special interests:** works not previously produced in New York City; "challenging, risk-taking plays that explore character and emotion in a contemporary context." **Facilities:**

multiple 99–199 seat theatres. **Best submission time:** year-round. **Response time:** 9 months letter; 12 months script.

NEW JERSEY REPERTORY COMPANY

(Founded 1997)

179 Broadway; Long Branch, NJ 07740; (732) 229-3166;

njrep@njrep.org, www.njrep.org

SuzAnne Barabas, *Artistic Director*

Submission procedure: accepts unsolicited scripts with synopsis and character breakdown; electronic submission only. **Types of material:** full-length plays, musicals. **Special interests:** work not produced professionally; social, humanistic themes. **Facilities:** Main Stage, 72 seats, black box; Second Stage, 50 seats, flexible stage. **Production considerations:** cast limit of 5; unit set. **Best submission time:** year-round. **Response time:** 12 months. **Special programs:** Script-in-Hand: year-round reading series for more than 20 plays; of these, up to 7 selected for Main Stage production.

NEW REPERTORY THEATRE

(Founded 1985)

200 Dexter Ave; Watertown, MA 02472; (617) 923-7060, ext 204;

bridgetoleary@newrep.org, www.newrep.org

Rick Lombardo, *Producing Artistic Director*

Submission procedure: unsolicited scripts from local playwrights only; agent submission for all others. **Types of material:** full-length plays, translations, adaptations. **Special interests:** "plays of ideas that center around pressing issues of our time"; multicultural themes; intimate, interpersonal themes. **Facilities:** New Repertory Theatre, 340 seats, proscenium stage. **Production considerations:** cast limit of 10. **Best submission time:** May–Aug. **Response time:** 12 months.

NEW STAGE THEATRE

(Founded 1966)

1100 Carlisle St; Jackson, MS 39202; (601) 948-3533, FAX 948-3538;

www.newstagetheatre.com

Submission procedure: no unsolicited scripts; synopsis and letter of inquiry for previously produced plays. **Types of material:** full-length plays, musicals, plays for young audiences, solo pieces. **Facilities:** Meyer Crystal Auditorium, 364 seats, proscenium stage. **Production considerations:** cast limit of 12. **Best submission time:** summer/fall. **Response time:** 2 months letter; 6 months script. **Special programs:** Eudora Welty New Plays Series: 3 full-length, unproduced scripts receive staged reading in annual series; honorarium; submissions considered for production in theatre's regular season; workshop scripts accepted; see website for guidelines; *deadline:* 1 Dec.

NEW THEATRE

(Founded 1986)

4120 Laguna St; Coral Gables, FL 33146; (305) 443-5373, FAX 443-1642; rjmartinez@new-theatre.org, www.new-theatre.org

Ricky J. Martinez, *Artistic Director*

Submission procedure: no unsolicited scripts; synopsis, resume and letter of inquiry. **Types of material:** full-length plays, translations, adaptations. **Special interests:** new work and adaptations of classics; prefers theatrical, language-driven plays and plays with social/political themes. **Facilities:** New Theatre, 104 seats, endstage. **Production considerations:** cast limit of 7. **Best submission time:** year-round. **Response time:** 3 months letter; 6 months script.

NEW YORK STAGE AND FILM

(Founded 1984)

315 West 36th St, Suite 1006; New York, NY 10018; (212) 736-4240, FAX 736-4241; info@newyorkstageandfilm.org, www.newyorkstageandfilm.org

Johanna Pfaelzer, *Artistic Director*

Submission procedure: no unsolicited scripts; synopsis, resume and letter of inquiry. **Types of material:** full-length plays. **Special interests:** previously unproduced full-length plays for readings, workshops and full productions. **Facilities:** Martel Theatre, 325 seats, proscenium stage; Powerhouse Theatre, 135 seats, black box; Shiva Theatre, 135 seats, black box. **Best submission time:** 1 Sep–31 Oct only. **Response time:** 2 months letter; 3 months script.

NEW YORK STATE THEATRE INSTITUTE

(Founded 1974)

37 First St; Troy, NY 12180; (518) 274-3200, FAX 274-3815; pbs@capital.net, www.nysti.org

Patricia Di Benedetto Snyder, *Producing Artistic Director*

Submission procedure: no unsolicited scripts; synopsis, cast/scene breakdown and letter of inquiry. **Types of material:** full-length plays, adaptations, musicals. **Special interests:** works for family audiences only. **Facilities:** Schacht Fine Arts Center, 800 seats, proscenium stage. **Best submission time:** Mar–Sep. **Response time:** 2 months letter; 6 months script. **Special programs:** developmental workshops: playwrights receive staged reading or workshop production, negotiable remuneration, travel and housing.

NEW YORK THEATRE WORKSHOP

(Founded 1979)

83 East 4th St; New York, NY 10003; (212) 780-9037; www.nytw.org

Literary Department

Submission procedure: no unsolicited scripts; synopsis, 10-page dialogue sample, resume and letter of inquiry. **Types of material:** full-length plays, translations, musicals, solo pieces. **Special interests:** exploration of political and historical events and institutions that shape contemporary life. **Facilities:** 79 East 4th Street Theatre, 180 seats, proscenium stage; East 4th Street Theatre, 70 seats, proscenium stage. **Best submission time:** year-round. **Response time:** 8 months. **Special programs:** Mondays @ 3: in-house readings. Larson Lab: in-house developmental workshops. Summer Residencies Out-Of-Town: application by invitation only. New York Theatre Workshop Playwriting Fellowship for emerging and early-career writers of color (see Fellowships and Grants).

NEXT ACT THEATRE
(Founded 1990)
Box 394; Milwaukee, WI 53201; (414) 278-7780, FAX 278-5930
David Cecsarini, *Artistic Director/Producer*

Submission procedure: no unsolicited scripts; agent submission of synopsis, cast list, production requirements and letter of inquiry. **Types of material:** full-length plays, adaptations, solo pieces. **Facilities:** Studio Space, 99 seats, thrust stage. **Production considerations:** small cast size; minimal production demands. **Best submission time:** spring. **Response time:** 1 month letter; 6 months script.

A NOISE WITHIN
(Founded 1991)
234 South Brand Blvd; Glendale, CA 91204; (818) 240-0910, FAX 240-0826
Julia Rodriguez-Elliot & Geoff Elliot, *Founders/Artistic Directors*

Submission procedure: accepts unsolicited scripts. **Types of material:** translations, adaptations. **Special interests:** translations and adaptations of classical material only. **Facilities:** A Noise Within, 145 seats, thrust stage. **Best submission time:** fall. **Response time:** 8 months.

NORTH COAST REPERTORY THEATRE
(Founded 1982)
987D Lomas Santa Fe Dr; Solana Beach, CA 92075; (858) 481-2155,
        FAX 481-0530; ncrt@northcoastrep.org, www.northcoastrep.org
Stephen Elton, *Artistic Associate*
Submission procedure: no unsolicited scripts; synopsis, bio and letter of inquiry. **Types of material:** full-length plays, translations, adaptations, plays for young audiences, musicals, cabaret/revues. **Facilities:** NCRT, 194 seats, thrust stage. **Production considerations:** small cast size; limited space. **Best submission time:** year-round. **Response time:** 6 months letter; 6 months script.

THE NORTHEAST THEATRE (TNT)
[see Electric Theatre Company (ETC)]

NORTHERN STAGE

(Founded 1992)

Box 4287; White River Junction, VT 05001; (802) 291-9009,
FAX 291-9156; info@northernstage.org, www.northernstage.org

Brooke Ciardelli, *Artistic Director*

Submission procedure: no unsolicited scripts; professional recommendation. **Types of material:** full-length plays, musicals. **Special interests:** international playwrights; politically and socially themed plays. **Facilities:** Briggs Opera House, 245 seats, thrust stage. **Production considerations:** minimal production requirements. **Best submission time:** year-round. **Response time:** 8 months.

NORTHLIGHT THEATRE

(Founded 1975)

9501 North Skokie Blvd; Skokie, IL 60076; (847) 679-9501,
FAX 679-1879; www.northlight.org

Meghan Beals McCarthy, *Literary Manager*

Submission procedure: no unsolicited scripts; synopsis, 10-page dialogue sample, cast list and letter of inquiry with SASE for response. **Types of material:** full-length plays, chamber musicals. **Special interests:** the public world and public issues; "plays of ideas"; works that are "passionate and/or hilarious"; heightened realism, but nothing overtly experimental or absurdist. **Facilities:** Northlight Theatre, 345 seats, thrust stage. **Production considerations:** prefers cast limit of 2-6; unit or flexible set. **Best submission time:** year-round. **Response time:** 1 month letter; 8 months script. **Special programs:** public new play reading series.

NORTH SHORE MUSIC THEATRE

(Founded 1955)

Box 62; Beverly, MA 01915; (978) 232-7203, FAX 922-0768; www.nsmt.org

Courtney Adler, *Associate Producer*

Submission procedure: no unsolicited scripts; synopsis and letter of inquiry with SASE for response; include cassette or CD. **Types of material:** musicals, musicals for young audiences. **Facilities:** Main Stage, 1537 seats, arena stage; Workshop, 100 seats, flexible stage. **Production considerations:** prefers cast limit of 15. **Best submission time:** year-round. **Response time:** 1 month letter; 6 months script. **Special programs:** New Works Development Program: spring, fall and summer (with annual summer festival) workshop productions of new works with authors in residence; theatre pays and houses writers (rates vary); contact theatre for information.

NORTHWEST CHILDREN'S THEATER AND SCHOOL

(Founded 1993)

1819 Northwest Everett St, Suite 216; Portland, OR 97209; (503) 222-2190, FAX 222-4130; info@nwcts.org, www.nwcts.org

Sarah Jane Hardy, *Artistic Director*

Submission procedure: no unsolicited scripts; agent submission or professional recommendation. **Types of material:** full-length plays, one-acts, adaptations, plays for young audiences, musicals. **Facilities:** Northwest Neighborhood Cultural Center (NWNCC), 400 seats, proscenium stage. **Production considerations:** no fly space. **Best submission time:** Apr–Aug. **Response time:** 6 months.

ODYSSEY THEATRE ENSEMBLE

(Founded 1969)

2055 South Sepulveda Blvd; Los Angeles, CA 90025; (310) 477-2055; www.odysseytheatre.com

Sally Essex-Lopresti, *Director of Literary Programs*

Submission procedure: no unsolicited scripts; synopsis, 8–10-page dialogue sample, play's production history (if any), resume and letter of inquiry with SASE for response; include CD for musicals. **Types of material:** full-length plays, translations, adaptations, musicals. **Special interests:** culturally diverse works; works with innovative form or provocative subject matter; works exploring the enduring questions of human existence and the possibilities of the live theatre experience; works with political or sociological impact. **Facilities:** Odyssey 1, 99 seats, flexible stage; Odyssey 2, 99 seats, thrust stage; Odyssey 3, 99 seats, endstage. **Production considerations:** plays must be minimum 90 minutes in length. **Best submission time:** year-round. **Response time:** 1 month letter; 6 months script.

OLDCASTLE THEATRE COMPANY

(Founded 1972)

Box 1555; Bennington, VT 05201-1555; (802) 447-1267, FAX 442-3704

Eric Peterson, *Producing Artistic Director*

Submission procedure: accepts unsolicited scripts. **Types of material:** full-length plays, musicals. **Facilities:** Bennington Center for the Arts, 300 seats, modified proscenium stage. **Best submission time:** winter. **Response time:** 6 months.

THE OLD GLOBE

(Founded 1935)

Box 122171; San Diego, CA 92112-2171; (619) 231-1941

Kim Montelibano Heil, *Literary Associate*

Submission procedure: no unsolicited scripts; synopsis, 10-page dialogue sample and letter of inquiry with SASE for response. **Types of material:** full-length plays, translations, adaptations, musicals. **Special interests:** well-crafted, strongly theatrical material. **Facilities:** Lowell Davies Festival Stage, 620 seats, outdoor stage; Old Globe Theatre, 581 seats, modified thrust stage; Cassius Carter Centre Stage, 225 seats, arena stage. **Best submission time:** year-round. **Response time:** 3 months letter; 6 months script. **Special programs:** developmental program, includes commissions, readings and workshops, ideally toward full production; scripts selected through theatre's normal submission procedure and by invitation.

OLNEY THEATRE CENTER FOR THE ARTS
(Founded 1937)
2001 Olney-Sandy Spring Rd; Olney, MD 20832; (301) 924-4485,
     FAX 924-2654; www.olneytheatre.org
Jim Petosa, *Artistic Director*

Submission procedure: no unsolicited scripts; professional recommendation. **Types of material:** full-length plays, translations, adaptations, solo pieces. **Facilities:** mainstage, 500 seats, proscenium stage; The Lab Theatre, 200 seats, flexible stage. **Production considerations:** cast limit of 8. **Best submission time:** year-round. **Response time:** 6 months.

OMAHA THEATER COMPANY
(Founded 1949)
2001 Farnam St; Omaha, NE 68102; (402) 345-4852, FAX 344-7255;
     james1@rosetheater.org, www.rosetheater.org
James Larson, *Artistic Director*

Submission procedure: no unsolicited scripts; professional recommendation. **Types of material:** plays for young audiences. **Special interests:** 60-minute plays only; plays based on children's literature and contemporary issues. **Facilities:** Omaha Theater Company, 932 seats, proscenium stage; second stage, 175 seats, black box. **Production considerations:** cast limit of 10; prefers unit set. **Best submission time:** year-round. **Response time:** 6 months.

OPEN CIRCLE THEATER
(Founded 1992)
2222 2nd Ave, Suite 222; Seattle, WA 98121; (206) 382-4250;
     www.octheater.com
Ron Sandahl, *Artistic Director*

Submission procedure: no unsolicited scripts; synopsis, 10-page dialogue sample, resume and letter of inquiry. **Types of material:** full-length plays, one-acts, adaptations, musicals. **Special interests:** "new works and adaptations that speak to the human condition through fantasy and mythic storytelling"; plays suitable for site-specific staging; plays incorporating new music and dance or movement; no naturalism. **Facilities:** Open Circle Theater, 70 seats, flexible stage. **Best submission time:** year-round. **Response time:** 3 months letter; 6 months script.

THE OPEN EYE THEATER

(Founded 1972)

Box 959; Margaretville, NY 12455; (845) 586-1660, FAX 586-1660;
    openeye@catskill.net, www.theopeneye.org

Amie Brockway, *Producing Artistic Director*

Submission procedure: no unsolicited scripts; synopsis and letter of inquiry via email or with self-addressed envelope (no postage) for response. **Types of material:** full-length plays, one-acts, translations, adaptations, plays for young audiences. **Special interests:** plays for multigenerational audiences; plays with music; ensemble plays; plays 10 minutes or longer; Catskill Mountain–area writers. **Facilities:** 960 Main Street, 75 seats, modified proscenium stage. **Production considerations:** minimal set. **Best submission time:** Oct–Apr. **Response time:** 6 months letter; 12 months script. **Special programs:** workshop productions and readings.

OPENSTAGE THEATRE & COMPANY

(Founded 1973)

Box 617; Fort Collins, CO 80522; (970) 484-5237, FAX 482-0859;
    denisef@openstagetheatre.org, www.openstagetheatre.org

Denise Freestone, *Artistic Director*

Submission procedure: accepts unsolicited scripts with synopsis, cast list and dialogue sample consisting of first 2 pages, middle 2 pages and last 2 pages. **Types of material:** full-length plays; no musicals. **Facilities:** second-stage, 60 seats, black box. **Production considerations:** minimal technical capabilities; limited space. **Best submission time:** year–round. **Response time:** 12 months.

OREGON CHILDREN'S THEATRE

(Founded 1988)

600 Southwest 10th, Suite 313; Portland, OR 97205; (503) 228-9571,
    FAX 228-3545; stan@octc.org, www.octc.org

Stan Foote, *Artistic Director*

Submission procedure: accepts unsolicited scripts. **Types of material:** full-length plays, one-acts, adaptations, plays for young audiences, musicals. **Special interests:** plays based on works of literature. **Facilities:** Newmark, 880 seats, proscenium stage; Brunish, 206 seats, thrust stage. **Best submission time:** year-round. **Response time:** varies.

OREGON SHAKESPEARE FESTIVAL

(Founded 1935)

Box 158; Ashland, OR 97520; (541) 482-2111, FAX 482-0446;
    literary@osfashland.org

Lue Morgan Douthit, *Director of Literary Development/Dramaturgy*

Submission procedure: no unsolicited scripts; letter or email of inquiry. **Types of material:** full-length plays. **Special interests:** "plays of ideas"; language-oriented plays; works by women and minority writers. **Facilities:** Elizabethan Theatre, 1194 seats, outdoor Elizabethan stage; Angus Bowmer Theatre, 600 seats, thrust stage; New Theatre, 250–350 seats, flexible stage. **Best submission time:** fall. **Response time:** 6 months letter; 12 months script. **Special programs:** reading series; commissioning programs.

PAN ASIAN REPERTORY THEATRE
(Founded 1977)
520 Eighth Ave; New York, NY 10018; (212) 868-4030, FAX 868-4033; panasian@aol.com, www.panasianrep.org
Tisa Chang, *Artistic/Producing Director*

Submission procedure: no unsolicited scripts; synopsis and letter of inquiry. **Types of material:** full-length plays, translations, adaptations, musicals. **Special interests:** Asian or Asian-American themes only. **Facilities:** West End Theatre (in the church of St. Paul and St. Andrew), 99 seats, proscenium stage. **Production considerations:** prefers cast limit of 7. **Best submission time:** summer. **Response time:** 6 months letter; 9 months script. **Special programs:** staged readings and workshops. Diverse Voices Emerging Artist Forum. Master classes.

PANGEA WORLD THEATER
(Founded 1995)
711 West Lake St, Suite 102; Minneapolis, MN 55408; (612) 822-0015, FAX 821-1070; pangea@pangeaworldtheater.org, www.pangeaworldtheater.org
Meena Natarajan, *Executive & Literary Director*

Submission procedure: no unsolicited scripts; letter of inquiry. **Types of material:** full-length plays, translations, adaptations, solo pieces. **Special interests:** adaptations of international literature; multiethnic works. **Facilities:** no permanent facility. **Best submission time:** year-round. **Response time:** 6 months letter; 12 months script.

THE PASADENA PLAYHOUSE
(Founded 1917)
39 South El Molino Ave; Pasadena, CA 91101; (626) 737-2857, FAX 792-7343; patroninfo@pasadenaplayhouse.org, www.pasadenaplayhouse.org
Literary Department

Submission procedure: no unsolicited scripts; synopsis and letter of inquiry or agent submission; no electronic submissions. **Types of material:** full-length plays, musicals. **Facilities:** The Pasadena Playhouse, 650 seats, proscenium stage; Carrie Hamilton Theatre, 99 seats. **Best submission time:** year-round. **Response time:** 12 months letter; 18 months script. **Special programs:** play reading series.

PASSAGE THEATRE

(Founded 1985)

Box 967; Trenton, NJ 08605; (609) 392-0766, FAX 392-0318;
   info@passagetheatre.org, www.passagetheatre.org

Clare Drobot, *Literary Consultant*

Submission procedure: no unsolicited scripts; agent submission or professional recommendation. **Types of material:** full-length plays, solo pieces. **Special interests:** highly theatrical works; imaginative ensemble pieces; puppetry; African-American and multicultural works encouraged. **Facilities:** Mill Hill Playhouse, 115 seats, thrust stage. **Production considerations:** prefers cast limit of 8; very little wing space, no fly space. **Best submission time:** summer. **Response time:** 4 months.

THE PAUL MESNER PUPPETS

(Founded 1997)

1006 East Linwood Blvd; Kansas City, MO 64109; (816) 756-3500,
   FAX 756-3045; puppets@paulmesnerpuppets.org,
   www.paulmesnerpuppets.org

Diane Barker, *Executive Director*

Submission procedure: no unsolicited scripts; 10-page dialogue sample and letter of inquiry. **Types of material:** one-acts, translations, adaptations, plays for young audiences, solo pieces. **Special interests:** contemporary issues; plays for puppets and actors no more than 1 hour in length. **Facilities:** Unity Temple, 300 seats, endstage; PMP Studio, 200 seats, flexible stage. **Production considerations:** cast limit of 3, cast runs all technical effects; 1–3 movable sets. **Best submission time:** Jun–Sep. **Response time:** 3 months letter; 3 months script.

PCPA THEATERFEST

(Founded 1964)

800 South College Dr; Santa Maria, CA 93454-6399; (805) 928-7731,
   FAX 928-7506; literary@pcpa.org, www.pcpa.org

Patricia M. Troxel, *Literary Manager*

Submission procedure: no unsolicited scripts; agent submission of electronic inquiry only. **Types of material:** full-length plays, musicals. **Facilities:** Festival Theater, 708 seats, thrust stage; Marian Theatre, 448 seats, thrust stage; Severson Theater, 180 seats, flexible black box. **Production considerations:** cast limit of 6 for plays. **Best submission time:** Jun–Oct. **Response time:** 6 months. **Special programs:** InterPlay: The Stage Between: staged reading series.

THE PEARL THEATRE COMPANY, INC.

(Founded 1982)
80 Saint Marks Pl; New York, NY 10003; (212) 505-3401, FAX 505-3404;
    www.pearltheatre.org
Shepard Sobel, *Artistic Director*

Submission procedure: no unsolicited scripts; letter of inquiry. **Types of material:** translations. **Special interests:** translations (not adaptations) of classical plays. **Facilities:** Theatre 80, 160 seats, proscenium stage. **Best submission time:** year-round. **Response time:** 2 weeks letter; 3 months script.

PEGASUS PLAYERS

(Founded 1978)
1145 West Wilson; Chicago, IL 60640; (773) 878-9761, FAX 271-8057
Alex Levy, *Artistic Director*

Submission procedure: no unsolicited scripts; synopsis and letter of inquiry. **Types of material:** full-length plays, translations, adaptations, musicals, solo pieces. **Facilities:** The O'Rourke Center for the Performing Arts, 250 seats, proscenium stage. **Best submission time:** year-round. **Response time:** 1 month letter; 6 months script. **Special programs:** Chicago Young Playwrights Festival: annual Jan festival of plays by Chicago-area high school students; write for information.

PENDRAGON THEATRE

(Founded 1980)
15 Brandy Brook Ave; Saranac Lake, NY 12983; (518) 891-1854,
    FAX 891-7012; pdragon@northnet.org, www.pendragontheatre.com
Molly Pietz Walsh, *Literary Manager*

Submission procedure: no unsolicited scripts; synopsis, dialogue sample and letter of inquiry with SASP for response. **Types of material:** full-length plays, one-acts. **Facilities:** Pendragon Theatre, 132 seats, black box. **Production considerations:** unit set. **Best submission time:** year-round. **Response time:** 1 month letter; 3 months script. **Special programs:** New Directions Series: annual Mar series of play readings and developmental workshops.

PENINSULA PLAYERS THEATRE

(Founded 1935)
W4351 Peninsula Players Rd; Fish Creek, WI 54212; (920) 868-3287,
    FAX 868-2295; audra@peninsulaplayers.com,
    www.peninsulaplayers.com
Greg Vinkler, *Artistic Director*

Submission procedure: no unsolicited scripts; professional recommendation or agent submission. **Types of material:** full-length plays and musicals. **Facilities:** mainstage, 621 seats, proscenium stage. **Production considerations:** cast limit of 8. **Best submission time:** year-round. Response time: 10 months.

THE PENUMBRA THEATRE COMPANY

(Founded 1976)

The Martin Luther King Bldg; 270 North Kent St; St. Paul, MN 55102-1794;
  (651) 288-6795; dominic.taylor@penumbratheatre.org,
  www.penumbratheatre.org

Dominic Taylor, *Associate Artistic Director*

Submission procedure: no unsolicited scripts; electronic inquiry, see website prior to submitting. **Types of material:** full-length plays, one-acts, translations, adaptations, plays for young audiences, musicals. **Special interests:** works that address the African-American experience and the African diaspora. **Facilities:** Hallie Q. Brown Theatre, 260 seats, proscenium/thrust stage. **Best submission time:** year-round. **Response time:** 9 months. **Special programs:** Okra Playground: see website for details; *dates:* Jul–Aug.

THE PEOPLE'S LIGHT AND THEATRE COMPANY

(Founded 1974)

39 Conestoga Rd; Malvern, PA 19355-1798; (610) 647-1900;
  cortese@peopleslight.org, www.peopleslight.org

Alda Cortese, *Literary Manager*

Submission procedure: no unsolicited scripts; synopsis, 10-page dialogue sample, character breakdown and letter of inquiry. **Types of material:** full-length plays, translations, adaptations. **Special interests:** intelligent, original scripts for family audiences. **Facilities:** People's Light and Theatre, 350 seats, flexible stage; Steinbright Stage, 99–150 seats, flexible stage. **Production considerations:** unit set. **Best submission time:** year-round. **Response time:** 2 weeks letter; 10 months script.

PERFORMANCE NETWORK THEATRE

(Founded 1981)

120 East Huron; Ann Arbor, MI 48104; (734) 663-0696, FAX 663-7367;
  info@performancenetwork.org, www.performancenetwork.org

David Wolber, *Artistic Director*

Submission procedure: no unsolicited scripts; synopsis, 10-page dialogue sample and SASP. **Types of material:** full-length plays, musicals. **Facilities:** Performance Network, 139 seats, black box/thrust. **Production considerations:** prefers cast limit of 10; no fly space. **Best submission time:** year-round. **Response time:** 6 months.

PERSEVERANCE THEATRE

(Founded 1979)

914 3rd St; Douglas, AK 99824; (907) 364-2421, FAX 364-2603;
  info@perseverancetheatre.org, www.perseverancetheatre.org

Submission procedure: no unsolicited scripts; synopsis, dialogue sample and letter of inquiry from AK playwrights only. **Types of material:** full-length plays, one-acts, solo pieces, musicals. **Special interests:** AK playwrights; Native American playwrights and themes; ensemble-based pieces; documentary theatre. **Facilities:** mainstage, 150 seats, thrust stage; Phoenix, 50–75 seats, flexible stage. **Best submission time:** year-round. **Response time:** 1 month letter; 3 months script. **Special programs:** annual presentation of Native Alaskan work.

PHILADELPHIA THEATRE COMPANY
(Founded 1974)
230 South Broad St., Suite 1105; Philadelphia, PA 19102; (215) 985-1400, FAX 985-5800; www.philadelphiatheatrecompany.org

Submission procedure: accepts unsolicited scripts from local writers only; agent submission for all others. **Types of material:** full-length plays, musicals. **Special interests:** new American plays; social/humanistic themes; African-American plays; small-cast musicals; family and teen shows. **Facilities:** Suzanne Roberts Theater, 365 seats, proscenium stage. **Best submission time:** year-round. **Response time:** 6 months. **Special programs:** STAGES: program of staged readings.

PHOENIX ARTS ASSOCIATION THEATRE
(Founded 1985)
138 Carl St; San Francisco, CA 94117-3930; (415) 759-7696, lbaf23@aol.com, www.phoenixtheatresf.org
Linda Ayres-Frederick, *Executive Artistic Producing Director*

Submission procedure: no unsolicited scripts; synopsis and letter of inquiry. **Types of material:** full-length plays, one-acts, translations, adaptations, cabarets/revues, solo pieces. **Special interests:** plays about women, especially those dealing with mature women's issues; plays about contemporary and historical figures; plays in French and English. **Facilities:** Phoenix Theatre, 49–65 seats, thrust stage; Phoenix Annex, 49 seats, flexible proscenium. **Production considerations:** cast limit of 7; maximum 2 sets, unit set preferred, limited fly space. **Best submission time:** year-round. **Response time:** 6 weeks letter; 6 months script. **Special programs:** West Coast Playwrights Alliance; staged readings of new work.

PHOENIX THEATRE
(Founded 1920)
100 East McDowell Rd; Phoenix, AZ 85004; (602) 258-1974, FAX 889-5297; www.phoenixtheatre.com
Michael Barnard, *Artistic Director*

Submission procedure: no unsolicited scripts; synopsis, production history (if any) and letter of inquiry with SASE for response. **Types of material:** plays for young audiences, musicals, cabaret/revues. **Special interests:** plays with strong narratives suitable for a general audience. **Facilities:** mainstage, 373 seats, proscenium stage; Cookie Company, 150 seats, arena stage. **Best submission time:** Jun–Aug. **Response time:** 6 months letter; 6 months script.

THE PHOENIX THEATRE

(Founded 1983)

749 North Park Ave; Indianapolis, IN 46202; (317) 635-7529,
    FAX 635-0010; info@phoenixtheatre.org, www.phoenixtheatre.org

Scot Greenwell, *Literary Manager*

Submission procedure: no unsolicited scripts; 10-page dialogue sample, 2-page synopsis, cast and scene breakdown, bio and resume with SASE for response; include CD for musicals. **Types of material:** full-length plays, full-length musicals. **Facilities:** mainstage, 130 seats, proscenium stage; Frank and Katrina Basile Theatre, 75 seats, black box. **Production considerations:** prefers small cast; limited set. **Best submission time:** year-round. **Response time:** 1 month letter; 3 months script.

PILLSBURY HOUSE THEATRE

(Founded 1992)

3501 Chicago Ave S; Minneapolis, MN 55407; (612) 825-0459;
    www.pillsburyhousetheatre.org

Literary Manager

Submission procedure: no unsolicited scripts; letter of inquiry only. **Types of material:** full-length plays, solo pieces. **Facilities:** Pillsbury House Theatre, 100 seats, proscenium stage. **Best submission time:** year-round. **Response time:** 5 months letter; 6 months script.

PIONEER THEATRE COMPANY

(Founded 1962)

University of Utah, 300 South, 1400 East, Room 205;
    Salt Lake City, UT 84112-0660; (801) 581-6356, FAX 581-5472

Charles Morey, *Artistic Director*

Submission procedure: no unsolicited scripts; professional recommendation or agent submission. **Types of material:** full-length plays, translations, adaptations, musicals. **Facilities:** Simmons Pioneer Memorial Theatre, 932 seats, proscenium stage. **Best submission time:** fall. **Response time:** 6 months.

PITTSBURGH PUBLIC THEATER

(Founded 1975)

621 Penn Ave; Pittsburgh, PA 15222-3204; (412) 316-8200,
    FAX 316-8216; www.ppt.org

Heather Helinksy, *Resident Dramaturg*

Submission procedure: no unsolicited scripts; synopsis, dialogue sample and letter of inquiry with SASE for response. **Types of material:** full-length plays, translations, adaptations. **Facilities:** O'Reilly Theater, 650 seats, thrust stage. **Best submission time:** May–Oct. **Response time:** 2 months letter; 6 months script.

PLAYHOUSE ON THE SQUARE

(Founded 1969)
51 South Cooper St; Memphis, TN 38104; (901) 725-0776, FAX 272-7530
Jackie Nichols, *Executive Producer*

Submission procedure: accepts unsolicited scripts. **Types of material:** full-length plays, musicals. **Facilities:** Playhouse on the Square, 250 seats, proscenium stage; Circuit Playhouse, 136 seats, proscenium stage. **Best submission time:** year-round. **Response time:** 5 months. **Special programs:** Playhouse on the Square New Play Competition (see Prizes).

PLAYMAKERS REPERTORY COMPANY

(Founded 1976)
CB #3235, Center for Dramatic Art; Country Club Rd;
    Chapel Hill, NC 27599-3235; (919) 962-7005, FAX 962-4069
Joseph Haj, *Producing Artistic Director*

Submission procedure: no unsolicited scripts; agent submission. **Types of material:** full-length plays, translations, adaptations. **Facilities:** Paul Green Theatre, 498 seats, thrust stage; Elizabeth Price Kenan Theatre, 200 seats, flexible stage. **Best submission time:** Aug–May. **Response time:** 6 months.

PLAYWRIGHTS HORIZONS

(Founded 1971)
416 West 42nd St; New York, NY 10036-6896; (212) 564-1235,
    FAX 594-0296; www.playwrightshorizons.org
Christie Evangelisto, *Director of Musical Theater and Resident Dramaturg*
Adam Greenfield, *Literary Manager*

Submission procedure: accepts unsolicited scripts with bio and cover letter; for musicals, send script and CD (no synopses). **Types of material:** full-length plays, musicals. **Special interests:** works by American writers only; no adaptations, historical dramas, translations, one-acts or solo pieces. **Facilities:** mainstage, 198 seats, proscenium stage; studio theater, 98 seats, black box. **Best submission time:** year-round. **Response time:** 8 months.

PLAYWRIGHTS THEATRE OF NEW JERSEY

(Founded 1986)
Box 1295; Madison, NJ 07940; (973) 514-1787, ext 18, FAX 514-2060;
    phays@ptnj.org, www.ptnj.org
John Pietrowski, *Artistic Director*

Submission procedure: no unsolicited scripts; see website for submission guidelines. **Types of material:** full-length plays, one-acts. **Special interests:** "new American plays of substance and passion (comedies and dramas) that raise challenging questions about ourselves and our communities." **Facilities:** Playwrights Theatre of New Jersey, 99 seats, proscenium stage. **Production considerations:** prefers cast limit of 8; unit set, no fly space. **Best submission time:** year-round. **Response time:** 8 months letter; 12 months script. **Special programs:** Playwrights Theatre of New Jersey New Play Development Program (see Development).

PORCHLIGHT MUSIC THEATRE CHICAGO
(Founded 1995)
2814 North Lincoln; Chicago, IL 60657; (773) 325-9884; FAX 325-9883;
    porchlighttheatre@yahoo.com, www.porchlighttheatre.com
L. Walter Stearns, *Artistic Director*

Submission procedure: accepts unsolicited scripts with cassette or CD. **Types of material:** full-length and one-act musicals. **Facilities:** Theatre Building Chicago, 148 seats, black box. **Production considerations:** cast limit of 16. **Best submission time:** year-round. **Response time:** 6 months.

PORTLAND CENTER STAGE
(Founded 1988)
128 Northwest 11th Ave; Portland, OR 97209; (503) 445-3792;
    meadh@pcs.org, www.pcs.org
Mead Hunter, *Literary Director*

Submission procedure: no unsolicited scripts; 10-page dialogue sample, resume and letter of inquiry. **Types of material:** full-length plays. **Facilities:** Bob and Diana Gerding Theater, 599 seats, proscenium stage; Ellen Bye Studio, 270 seats, flexible black box. **Production considerations:** prefers cast limit of 12. **Best submission time:** year-round. **Response time:** 6 months letter; 12 months script. **Special programs:** JAW, A Playwrights Festival: best submission time Nov–Feb; see website for submission guidelines.

PORTLAND STAGE COMPANY
(Founded 1974)
Box 1458; Portland, ME 04104; (207) 774-1043, FAX 774-0576;
    dburson@portlandstage.com, www.portlandstage.com
Daniel Burson, *Literary Manager*

Submission procedure: no unsolicited scripts; synopsis, 10-page dialogue sample and cast breakdown. **Types of material:** full-length plays. **Facilities:** Portland Stage Company, 286 seats, proscenium stage; Portland Stage Studio, 70 seats, black box. **Best submission time:** May–Dec. **Response time:** 1 month letter; 6 months script. **Special programs:** The Little Festival of the Unexpected: script development process each spring with playwrights in residence for 1 week of rehearsals and staged readings; scripts selected through theatre's normal submission procedure (see Development).

PRIMARY STAGES

(Founded 1983)

307 West 38th St, Suite 1510; New York, NY 10018; (212) 840-9705,
      FAX 840-9725; www.primarystages.com

Michelle Bossy, *Associate Artistic Director*

Submission procedure: no unsolicited scripts; synopsis, description of play style; include CD for musicals; see website for guidelines. **Types of material:** full-length plays, musicals. **Special interests:** plays not previously produced in New York City; highly theatrical works by American playwrights for American or New York City premiere; plays by women and minorities. **Facilities:** Primary Stages Theatre at 59E59 Theaters, 199 seats, proscenium stage. **Production considerations:** small cast; unit set or simple set changes, no fly or wing space. **Best submission time:** Sep–Jun. **Response time:** 12 months. **Special programs:** The Dorothy Strelsin New American Writers Group. The Dorothy Strelsin Fresh Ink Reading Series. Prime Time Reading Series. The Primary Stages School of Theatre; see website for details.

THE PUBLIC THEATER

(Founded 1954)

The Joseph Papp Public Theater; 425 Lafayette St; New York, NY 10003;
      (212) 539-8530, FAX 539-8505; www.publictheater.org

Elizabeth Frankel, *Literary Associate*

Submission procedure: no unsolicited scripts; synopsis, 10-page dialogue sample and letter of inquiry; include CD of 3–5 songs for musicals. **Types of material:** full-length plays, translations, adaptations, musicals, solo pieces. **Facilities:** Newman Theater, 299 seats, proscenium stage; Anspacher Theater, 275 seats, thrust stage; Martinson Hall, 200 seats, proscenium stage; LuEsther Hall, 150 seats, flexible stage; Shiva Theater, 100 seats, flexible stage. **Best submission time:** year-round. **Response time:** 1 month letter; 6 months script. **Special programs:** Emerging Writers Group (see Development).

THE PURPLE ROSE THEATRE COMPANY

(Founded 1991)

Box 220; Chelsea, MI 48118; (734) 433-7782, FAX 475-0802;
      info@purplerosetheatre.org, www.purplerosetheatre.org

Guy Sanville, *Artistic Director*

Submission procedure: no unsolicited scripts; synopsis, 10-page dialogue sample, character breakdown and letter of inquiry. **Types of material:** full-length plays. **Special interests:** plays that speak to a "middle-American audience." **Facilities:** mainstage, 168 seats, thrust stage. **Production considerations:** cast limit of 10; no fly or wing space. **Best submission time:** year-round. **Response time:** 2 months letter; 9 months script.

QUEENS THEATRE IN THE PARK

(Founded 1993)

Box 520069; Flushing, NY 11352; (718) 760-0686,
    FAX 760-1972; urbinati@aol.com, www.queenstheatre.org

Rob Urbinati, *Director of New Play Development*

Submission procedure: no unsolicited scripts; synopsis, character breakdown, resume and letter of inquiry via email only. **Types of material:** full-length plays and musicals suitable for special programs only (see below). **Facilities:** Claire Shulman Playhouse, 464 seats, proscenium stage; Studio Theatre, 99 seats, black box. **Production considerations:** prefers cast limit of 8. **Best submission time:** year-round. **Response time:** 1 month letter; 6 months script. **Special programs:** Immigrant Voices Project: year-round project that seeks new plays reflecting the diverse demographics of the borough of Queens for play reading series, developmental workshops and full productions. Plays a Mother Would Love Series: year-round project that seeks new, mainstream comedies, musicals and thrillers with cast limit of 8 for play reading series, developmental workshops and full productions.

RED BARN THEATRE

(Founded 1981)

Box 707; Key West, FL 33040; (305) 296-9911, FAX 293-3035;
    hawkinswells@comcast.net

Joy Hawkins, *Artistic Director*

Submission procedure: no unsolicited scripts; synopsis and letter of inquiry with professional recommendation. **Types of material:** full-length plays, musicals, cabaret/revues. **Facilities:** Red Barn Theatre, 88 seats, proscenium stage. **Production considerations:** cast limit of 8, small band for musicals; no fly space, limited wing space. **Best submission time:** Mar–Jul. **Response time:** 6 months letter, if interested; 6 months script.

REPERTORIO ESPAÑOL

(Founded 1968)

138 East 27th St; New York, NY 10016; info@repertorio.org,
    www.repertorio.org

Robert Weber Federico, *Executive Director*

Submission procedure: no unsolicited scripts; synopsis and letter of inquiry. **Types of material:** full-length plays, adaptations, plays for young audiences. **Special interests:** plays dealing with Hispanic themes; comedies. **Facilities:** Gramercy Arts Theatre, 140 seats, proscenium stage. **Production considerations:** small cast. **Best submission time:** summer. **Response time:** 6 months letter; 12 months script. **Special programs:** Met Life Foundation Nuestras Voces National Playwriting Competition (see Prizes).

THE REPERTORY THEATRE OF ST. LOUIS
(Founded 1966)
130 Edgar Rd; Box 191730; St. Louis, MO 63119; (314) 968-7340;
    sgregg@repstl.org
Susan Gregg, *Associate Artistic Director*

Submission procedure: no unsolicited scripts; synopsis, character breakdown, technical requirements and letter of inquiry; prefers electronic submission. **Types of material:** full-length plays. **Special interests:** nonnaturalistic plays; contemporary social and political issues. **Facilities:** Main Stage, 750 seats, thrust stage; Studio Theatre, 130 seats, black box. **Production considerations:** small cast; modest production demands. **Best submission time:** year-round. **Response time:** 4 months letter; 24 months script.

RIVERLIGHT AND COMPANY
(Founded 1981)
75 Wendell St; Battle Creek, MI 49017-3821; (269) 962-2453,
    FAX 441-2707; riverlightbe@yahoo.com,
    www.willard.lib.mi.us/npa/rlight
J. Kline Hobbs, *Project Director*

Submission procedure: no unsolicited scripts; letter of inquiry. **Types of material:** documentary-based plays for young audiences. **Special interests:** stage documentaries about artists and scientists intended for grades 7–12; American history, literature and social issues. **Facilities:** no permanent facility; company tours to high school auditoriums. **Production considerations:** cast limit of 5, variable performance spaces. **Best submission time:** year-round. **Response time:** 2 weeks letter; 1 month script.

RIVERSIDE THEATRE
(Founded 1981)
213 North Gilbert St; Iowa City, IA 52245; (319) 338-7672, FAX 887-1362;
    artistic@riversidetheatre.org, www.riversidetheatre.org
Ron Clark and Jody Hovland, *Co-Artistic Directors*

Submission procedure: no unsolicited scripts; synopsis and letter of inquiry. **Types of material:** full-length plays, translations, adaptations, cabaret/revues. **Facilities:** Riverside Theatre, 118 seats, flexible stage. **Production considerations:** small cast; simple set. **Best submission time:** year-round. **Response time:** 1 month letter, if interested; 5 months script.

ROUND HOUSE THEATRE

(Founded 1978)

Box 30688; Bethesda, MD 20824; (240) 644-1099, FAX 644-1090;
productionstaff@roundhousetheatre.org, www.roundhousetheatre.org

Production Department

Submission procedure: no unsolicited scripts; agent submission only. **Types of material:** full-length plays, translations. **Special interests:** new translations of classics. **Facilities:** Round House Theatre, 400 seats, modified thrust stage; second stage, 150 seats, black box. **Best submission time:** year-round. **Response time:** varies.

SACRAMENTO THEATRE COMPANY

(Founded 1942)

1419 H St; Sacramento, CA 95814; (916) 446-7501, FAX 446-4066;
www.sactheatre.org

Peggy Shannon, *Artistic Director*

Submission procedure: no unsolicited scripts; agent submission. **Types of material:** full-length plays, adaptations, cabaret/revues. **Special interests:** contemporary social and political issues; "craftsmanship, theatricality, vital language." **Facilities:** Mainstage, 300 seats, proscenium stage; Cabaret Stage, 100 seats, cabaret; Stage 2, 90 seats, black box. **Production considerations:** cast limit of 20. **Best submission time:** Jun–Dec. **Response time:** 6 months.

THE SALT LAKE ACTING COMPANY

(Founded 1970)

168 West 500 N; Salt Lake City, UT 84103; (801) 363-0526, FAX 532-8513;
mong@saltlakeactingcompany.org

David Mong, *Literary Manager*

Submission procedure: no unsolicited scripts; professional recommendation with bio and letter of inquiry with SASE for response; accepts electronic submissions in Word format only. **Types of material:** full-length plays, translations, adaptations, musicals. **Special interests:** new plays. **Facilities:** Upstairs, 160 seats, thrust stage. **Best submission time:** year-round. **Response time:** 6 months. **Special programs:** reading series 4 times annually.

SANCTUARY: PLAYWRIGHTS THEATRE

(Founded 1997)

139 Main St; Brattleboro, VT 05301; sancplays@gmail.com,
www.sanctuarytheatre.org

Bob Jude Ferrante, *Managing Director*

Submission procedure: accepts unsolicited scripts with resume, list of current projects and letter of inquiry via email only. **Types of material:** full-length plays. **Special interests:** works from NY-area writers only; plays with "unusual structure, radical core ideas, epic form, work that's off the map or otherwise seen as impractical";

no "kitchen sink" or "TV sitcom–style" plays; no "worthy social issue earnestly told in realistic mien" plays. **Facilities:** year-round retreat space in VT; regular production season in New York City. **Production considerations:** playwright controls resources of company for duration of project. **Best submission time:** year-round. **Response time:** 6 months.

THE SANDRA FEINSTEIN–GAMM THEATRE
(Founded 1984)
172 Exchange St; Pawtucket, RI 02860; (401) 723-4266, FAX 723-0440;
    info@gammtheatre.org, www.gammtheatre.org
Tony Estrella, *Artistic Director*

Submission procedure: no unsolicited scripts; synopsis and letter of inquiry. **Types of material:** full-length plays, translations, adaptations. **Facilities:** The Sandra Feinstein–Gamm Theatre, 137 seats, thrust stage. **Best submission time:** summer. **Response time:** varies, if interested.

SAN JOSE REPERTORY THEATRE
(Founded 1980)
101 Paseo de San Antonio; San Jose, CA 95113; (408) 367-7206,
    FAX 367-7237; www.sjrep.com
Literary Department

Submission procedure: no unsolicited scripts; professional recommendation. **Types of material:** full-length plays, translations, adaptations, musicals. **Special interests:** plays by and about traditionally underrepresented voices. **Facilities:** San Jose Repertory Theatre, 525 seats, proscenium stage. **Best submission time:** Aug–Nov. **Response time:** 6 months.

SANTA MONICA PLAYHOUSE
(Founded 1960)
1211 4th St; Santa Monica, CA 90401-1391; (310) 394-9779,
    FAX 393-5573; www.santamonicaplayhouse.com
Chris DeCarlo and Evelyn Rudie, *Co-Artistic Directors*

Submission procedure: no unsolicited scripts; synopsis and letter of inquiry. **Types of material:** full-length plays, one-acts, translations, adaptations, plays for young audiences, musicals. **Facilities:** The Main Stage, 88 seats, arena/thrust stage; The Other Space, 70 seats, black box. **Production considerations:** cast limit of 8; simple production demands. **Best submission time:** year-round. **Response time:** 6 months letter; 9 months script.

SEATTLE CHILDREN'S THEATRE

(Founded 1975)

201 Thomas St; Seattle, WA 98109; (206) 443-0807, FAX 443-0442;
   torriem@sct.org, www.sct.org

Torrie McDonald, *Literary and Publications Manager*

Submission procedure: accepts unsolicited scripts for Drama School Summer Season only; professional recommendation for Mainstage. **Types of material:** full-length plays for family audiences, translations, adaptations, musicals, solo pieces. **Special interests:** sophisticated works for young audiences that also appeal to adults. **Facilities:** Charlotte Martin Theatre, 485 seats, proscenium stage; Eve Alvord Theatre, 280 seats, modified proscenium. **Best submission time:** year-round. **Response time:** 8 months. **Special programs:** Drama School Summer Season: one-act plays, 30–60 minutes in length for student performance, must have roles for 12–18 actors, ages 8–19; submit script to Don Fleming, Summer Season Producer; response if insterested.

SECOND STAGE THEATRE

(Founded 1979)

307 West 43rd St; New York, NY 10036; (212) 787-8302, FAX 397-7066;
   literary@2st.com, www.secondstagetheatre.com

Literary Department

Submission procedure: no unsolicited scripts; synopsis, 5–10-page dialogue sample, resume, production history and letter of inquiry. **Types of material:** full-length plays, adaptations, musicals. **Special interests:** new and previously produced American plays; "heightened" realism; sociopolitical issues; plays by women and minority writers. **Facilities:** Midtown Theatre, 296 seats, proscenium stage; McGinn/Cazale Theatre, 108 seats, endstage. **Best submission time:** year-round. **Response time:** 1 month letter; 6 months script. **Special programs:** annual series of readings of new and previously produced plays.

SHAKESPEARE & COMPANY

(Founded 1978)

70 Kemble St; Lenox, MA 01240; (413) 637-1199, FAX 637-4274;
   mhammond@shakespeare.org, www.shakespeare.org

Michael Hammond, *Associate Artistic Director*

Submission procedure: no unsolicited scripts; 1-page synopsis, 10-page dialogue sample and letter of inquiry with SASE or SASP for response. **Types of material:** full-length plays. **Special interests:** plays of social and political significance; no musicals. **Facilities:** Founders' Theatre, 420 seats, Elizabethan stage; Elayne P. Bernstein Theatre, 180 seats, flexible stage. **Production considerations:** small casts; minimal set pieces. **Best submission time:** winter–spring. **Response time:** 3 months.

THE SHAKESPEARE FESTIVAL AT TULANE

(Founded 1993)

Department of Theatre and Dance; Tulane University;
New Orleans, LA 70118; (504) 865-5105, FAX 865-5205;
www.neworleansshakespeare.com

Ron Gural, *Artistic Director*

Submission procedure: no unsolicited scripts; synopsis, dialogue sample, resume and letter of inquiry with SASE for response. **Types of material:** full-length plays, one-acts, adaptations. **Special interests:** LA playwrights only. **Facilities:** Lupin theatre, 150 seats, black box; Lagniappe Stage, 100 seats, black box. **Production considerations:** unit set preferred; no fly space. **Best submission time:** Aug–Nov only. **Response time:** 2 months letter; 3 months script.

THE SHAKESPEARE THEATRE COMPANY

(Founded 1986)

516 8th St SE; Washington, DC 20003-2834; (202) 547-3230,
FAX 547-0226; afox@shakespearetheatre.org,
www.shakespearetheatre.org

Akiva Fox, *Literary Associate*

Submission procedure: no unsolicited scripts; professional recommendation. **Types of material:** translations, adaptations. **Special interests:** translations and adaptations of classics only. **Facilities:** Sidney Harman Hall, 775 seats, flexible stage; The Lansburgh Theatre, 449 seats, proscenium stage. **Best submission time:** summer. **Response time:** 4 months.

SHATTERED GLOBE THEATRE

(Founded 1991)

2936 North Southport Ave, Suite 210; Chicago, IL 60657;
tcarter@shatteredglobe.org, www.shatteredglobe.org

Tiffany Carter, *Managing Director*

Submission procedure: accepts unsolicited scripts. **Types of material:** full-length plays, translations, adaptations. **Special interests:** ensemble pieces. **Facilities:** Victory Gardens Greenhouse, 60 seats, black box. **Production considerations:** cast limit of 12; no fly space. **Best submission time:** year-round. **Response time:** 6 months.

SHOTGUN PLAYERS

(Founded 1992)

1901 Ashby Ave; Berkeley, CA 94703; (510) 841-6500, FAX 841-7468;
liz@shotgunplayers.org, www.shotgunplayers.org

Liz Lisle, *Managing Director*

Submission procedure: no unsolicited scripts; professional recommendation or agent submission. **Types of material:** full-length plays, translations, adaptations, musicals. **Facilities:** The Ashby Stage, 99 seats, proscenium stage. **Best submission time:** year-round. **Response time:** 6 months.

SILK ROAD THEATRE PROJECT

(Founded 2002)

680 South Federal St, Suite 301; Chicago, IL 60605; (312) 857-1234,
    FAX 577-0849; litmanage@srtp.org, www.srtp.org.

Jennifer Shook, *Literary Manager*

Submission procedure: accepts unsolicited scripts. **Types of material:** full-length plays, one-acts, translations, adaptations, musicals, solo pieces. **Special interests:** plays by writers of Asian, Mediterranean and Middle Eastern backgrounds (or countries on the Silk Road) with protagonists of said backgrounds only. **Facilities:** Pierce Hall, 55–80 seats, flexible proscenium/thrust stage. **Production considerations:** cast limit of 12; limited backstage, no fly space, limited height. **Best submission time:** year-round. **Response time:** 6 months.

THE SKYLIGHT

(formerly Skylight Opera Theatre)

(Founded 1959)

158 North Broadway; Milwaukee, WI 53202; (414) 291-7811, FAX 291-7815;
    www.skylightopera.com

Bill Theisen, *Artistic Director*

Submission procedure: no unsolicited scripts; synopsis and letter of inquiry; include cassette or CD for musicals. **Types of material:** musicals, cabaret/revues. **Special interests:** small-scale musicals and operas. **Facilities:** Cabot Theatre, 358 seats, proscenium stage. **Production considerations:** cast limit of 22, orchestra limit of 18, prefers smaller casts. **Best submission time:** summer. **Response time:** 2 months letter; 12 months script.

SOHO REPERTORY THEATRE

(Founded 1975)

86 Franklin St, 4th Floor; New York, NY 10013; (212) 941-8632,
    FAX 941-7148; www.sohorep.org

Sarah Benson, *Artistic Director*

Submission procedure: accepts unsolicited scripts for Writer/Director Lab only (see below); direct solicitation to playwright or agent for all other plays. **Types of material:** full-length plays, one-acts, solo pieces. **Facilities:** Soho Rep, 70 seats, black box. **Special programs:** Writer/Director Lab: 6 writers, paired with directors, spend 6 months developing new play, culminating in reading series; see website for application; *deadline:* May (exact date TBA); *notification:* Sep.

SOUTH COAST REPERTORY

(Founded 1964)

Box 2197; Costa Mesa, CA 92628-2197; (714) 708-5500; www.scr.org

Literary Department

Submission procedure: no unsolicited scripts; synopsis, dialogue sample and letter of inquiry. **Types of material:** full-length plays, translations, adaptations, musicals, plays for young audiences; no solo pieces. **Facilities:** Segerstrom Stage, 507 seats, modified thrust stage; Julianne Argyros Stage, 336 seats, proscenium stage; Nicholas studio, 94 seats, black box. **Best submission time:** year-round. **Response time:** 1 month letter; 9 months script. **Special programs:** COLAB (Collaboration Laboratory) New Play Program: development program of readings, staged readings, workshop productions and full productions; playwright receives grant, commission and/or royalties depending on nature of project. Pacific Playwrights Festival: annual development program for playwrights writing in English culminating in staged readings, workshop productions and full productions performed for the public and theatre colleagues; plays selected through theatre's normal submission procedure and by invitation; not-for-profit theatres are also welcome to submit work; *dates:* May.

SPRINGER OPERA HOUSE

(Founded 1871)

103 10th St; Columbus, GA 31901; (706) 324-5714, FAX 324-4461;
    p_pierce@springeroperahouse.org, www.springeroperahouse.org

Paul Pierce, *Producing Artistic Director*

Submission procedure: no unsolicited scripts; synopsis and letter of inquiry only. **Types of material:** full-length plays, plays for young audiences, musicals, cabaret/revues. **Special Interests:** musicals, comedies. **Facilities:** mainstage, 700 seats, proscenium stage; studio II, 170 seats, flexible stage. **Production considerations:** small cast; unit set. **Best submission time:** Nov–Feb. **Response time:** 2 months letter; 6 months script.

STAGE ONE: THE LOUISVILLE CHILDREN'S THEATRE

(Founded 1946)

323 W Broadway, 6th Floor; Louisville, KY 40202; (502) 589-4060,
    FAX 589-4344; stageone@stageone.org, www.stageone.org

Peter Holloway, *Producing Artistic Director*

Submission procedure: no unsolicited scripts; synopsis and letter of inquiry. **Types of material:** plays for young audiences. **Special interests:** plays about young people in the real world; good, honest treatments of familiar titles. **Facilities:** Moritz von Bomard Theater, 610 seats, thrust stage; Todd Hall, 300 seats, flexible stage. **Production considerations:** prefers cast limit of 12; some productions tour. **Best submission time:** Oct–Dec. **Response time:** 3 months.

STAGES THEATRE COMPANY

(Founded 1984)

1111 Mainstreet; Hopkins, MN 55343; (952) 979-1123, FAX 979-1124;
    email@stagestheatre.org, www.stagestheatre.org

Sandy Boren-Barrett, *Artistic Director*

Submission procedure: no unsolicited scripts; synopsis, character breakdown, resume and letter of inquiry. **Types of material:** plays for young audiences. **Facilities:** mainstage, 723 seats, proscenium stage; FAIR, 300 seats, proscenium stage; studio, 150 seats, black box. **Best submission time:** year-round. **Response time:** varies; scripts will not be returned.

STAGE WEST

(Founded 1979)

821 West Vickery Blvd; Fort Worth, TX 76104-1144; (817) 338-1777,
    FAX 348-8392; boxoffice@stagewest.org, www.stagewest.org

Jim Covault, *Artistic Director*

Submission procedure: no unsolicited scripts; synopsis and letter of inquiry. **Types of material:** full-length plays, translations, adaptations. **Special interests:** plays by TX and Southwest playwrights; Hispanic plays; contemporary issues; TX and Southwest themes. **Facilities:** Scott Theatre, 580 seats, thrust stage; Sanders Theatre, 100 seats, flexible stage. **Production considerations:** prefers cast limit of 9. **Best submission time:** Jan–Mar. **Response time:** 1 month letter; 3 months script.

STAGEWORKS

(Founded 1983)

Box 3428; Tampa, FL 33601; (813) 251-8984;
    anna.brennen@stageworkstheatre.org, www.stageworkstheatre.org

Anna Brennen, *Producing Artistic Director*

Submission procedure: accepts unsolicited scripts. **Types of material:** full-length plays by Florida playwrights only. **Special interests:** multi-ethnic casts. **Facilities:** Mainstage, 99 seats, black box. **Production considerations:** cast limit of 8; unit set. **Best submission time:** 1 Apr–15 May. **Response time:** 30 Jun.

STAGEWORKS/HUDSON

(Founded 1993)

41-A Cross St; Hudson, NY 12534-3118; (518) 828-7843; FAX 828-4026;
    contact@stageworkshudson.org, www.stageworkshudson.org

Laura Margolis, *Executive Artistic Director*

Submission procedure: no unsolicted scripts; synopsis and letter of inquiry. **Types of material:** full-length plays, translations, adaptations, musicals, solo pieces. **Facilities:** Max and Lillian Katzman Theater, 100 seats, proscenium/thrust stage. **Production considerations:** cast limit of 10; unit set, no fly space. **Best submission time:** year-round. **Response time:** 8 months letter; 12 months script. **Special programs:** Play by Play: annual festival of new short plays; participation by invitation only.

STAMFORD THEATRE WORKS

(Founded 1988)
307 Atlantic St; Stamford, CT 06901-2403; (203) 359-4414, FAX 353-8018;
    stwct@aol.com, www.stamfordtheatreworks.org
Steve Karp, *Producing Director*

Submission procedure: no unsolicited scripts; professional recommendation. **Types of material:** full-length plays, translations, adaptations, musicals. **Special interests:** plays that are contemporary, innovative and thought-provoking; socially and culturally relevant; challenging and entertaining. **Facilities:** Center Stage, 150 seats, modified thrust stage. **Production considerations:** prefers small cast; unit set. **Best submission time:** year-round. **Response time:** 2 months letter; 6 months script.

STEPPENWOLF THEATRE COMPANY

(Founded 1976)
758 West North Ave, 4th Floor; Chicago, IL 60610; (312) 335-1888,
    FAX 335-0808; theatre@steppenwolf.org, www.steppenwolf.org
Edward Sobel, *Director of New Play Development*

Submission procedure: no unsolicited scripts; synopsis, 10-page dialogue sample, short bio or resume and letter of inquiry. **Types of material:** full-length plays. **Special interests:** ensemble pieces with dynamic acting roles. **Facilities:** Downstairs, 510 seats, proscenium stage; Upstairs, 299 seats, proscenium stage; Garage, 80 seats, flexible stage. **Best submission time:** year-round. **Response time:** 1 month letter; 8 months script.

SUNDOG THEATRE

Box 10183; Staten Island, NY 10301-0183; (718) 816-5453;
    sfenley@sundogtheatre.org, www.sundogtheatre.org
Catherine Lamm, *Literary Manager*

Submission procedure: accepts unsolicited scripts; send 2 copies of bound script. **Types of material:** one-acts. **Special interests:** plays about Staten Island. **Facilities:** multiple, 75-800 seats, blackbox and proscenium stages. **Production considerations:** prefers small cast. **Best submission time:** year-round. **Reponse time:** 6 months. **Special programs:** Scenes from the Staten Island Ferry (see Development).

SYNCHRONICITY PERFORMANCE GROUP

(Founded 1997)
Box 6012; Atlanta, GA 31107; (404) 523-1009, FAX 523-1009;
    info@synchrotheatre.com, www.synchrotheatre.com
Rachel May, *Producing Artistic Director*

Submission procedure: no unsolicited scripts; synopsis, dialogue sample, resume and letter of inquiry with SASE for response. **Types of material:** full-length plays, translations, plays for young audiences, cabaret/revues. **Special interests:** plays by or about women; social issues. **Facilities:** Actor's Express, 140 seats, black box; 7 Stages, 70 seats, black box. **Production considerations:** prefers cast limit of 12; no fly space. **Best submission time:** Jan–Jun. **Response time:** 1 month letter; 3 months script.

SYRACUSE STAGE
(Founded 1973)
820 East Genesee St; Syracuse, NY 13210-1508; (315) 443-4008,
    FAX 443-9846; www.syracusestage.org
Literary Department

Submission procedure: no unsolicited scripts; synopsis, 10-page dialogue sample, character description, resume and letter of inquiry with SASE for response. **Types of material:** full-length plays only. **Facilities:** John D. Archbold Theatre, 499 seats, proscenium stage. **Production considerations:** prefers small cast. **Best submission time:** year-round. **Response time:** 6 months letter; 12 months script.

TADA! YOUTH THEATER
(Founded 1984)
15 West 28th St, 3rd Floor; New York, NY 10001; (212) 252-1619,
    FAX 252-8763; www.tadatheater.com

Submission procedure: accepts unsolicited scripts. **Types of material:** one-acts, plays for young audiences, musicals. **Special interests:** work to be performed by children and teenagers. **Facilities:** mainstage, 98 seats, black box. **Production considerations:** modest production demands. **Best submission time:** year-round. **Response time:** 6 months.

TEATRO VISIÓN
(Founded 1984)
1700 Alum Rock Ave, Suite 265; San Jose, CA 95116; (408) 928-5582;
    elisamarina@teatrovision.org, www.teatrovision.org
Elisa Marina Alvarado, *Artistic Director*

Submission procedure: no unsolicited scripts; letter of inquiry only. **Types of material:** full-length plays, one-acts, translations. **Special interests:** new works that explore the Chicano/Latino experience; accepts bilingual and Spanish-language plays as well as translations. **Facilities:** Mexican Heritage Plaza Theater, 500 seats, proscenium stage. **Best submission time:** summer. **Response time:** 1 month. **Special programs:** Codices: annual new works program; see website for details. Instituto de Teatro: theatre training institute; includes traditional and contemporary Chicano/Latino performance forms and community-based artistic process.

TEATRO VISTA

(Founded 1989)

3712 North Broadway, #275; Chicago, IL 60613; (312) 666-4659;
    lwurz@teatrovista.org, www.teatrovista.org

Deb Davis, *Teatro Vista Ensemble*

Submission procedure: accepts unsolicited scripts. **Types of material:** full-length plays, one-acts, translations, adaptations. **Special interests:** plays by Latino playwrights and plays for Latino actors. **Facilities:** mainstage, 500, proscenium stage; alternate stage, 50 seats, black box. **Production considerations:** cast limit of 9; unit set, no fly or wing space. **Best submission time:** year-round. **Response time:** 3 months.

TECTONIC THEATER PROJECT

(Founded 1992)

204 West 84th St; New York, NY 10024; (212) 579-6111, FAX 579-6112;
    literary@tectonictheaterproject.org, www.tectonictheaterproject.org

Beth Whitaker, *Literary Manager*

Submission procedure: no unsolicited scripts; professional recommendation or agent submission. **Types of material:** full-length plays, one-acts, translations, adaptations, musicals. **Facilities:** no permanent facility. **Best submission time:** year-round. **Response time:** 8 months.

TENNESSEE REPERTORY THEATRE

(Founded 1985)

161 Rains Ave; Nashville, TN 37203; (615) 244-4878; www.tennesseerep.org

René D. Copeland, *Producing Artistic Director*

Submission procedure: no unsolicited scripts; synopsis, dialogue sample, resume and letter of inquiry with SASE or SASP for response. **Types of material:** full-length plays, adaptations, solo pieces. **Facilities:** Polk Theatre, 1100 seats, proscenium stage; Johnson Theatre, 240 seats, black box. **Production considerations:** small cast; minimal technical requirements. **Best submission time:** Jun–Sep. **Response time:** 3 months letter; 12 months script.

THALIA SPANISH THEATRE

(Founded 1977)

41-17 Greenpoint Ave; Sunnyside, NY 11104; (718) 729-3880,
    FAX 729-3388; info@thaliatheatre.org, www.thaliatheatre.org

Angel Gil Orrios, *Artistic/Executive Director*

Submission procedure: accepts unsolicited scripts. **Types of material:** full-length plays, translations, adaptations. **Special interests:** plays with Hispanic themes. **Facilities:** Thalia Spanish Theatre, 74 seats, proscenium stage. **Best submission time:** year-round. **Response time:** 3 months.

THEATRE ARIEL

(Founded 1990)

Box 0334; Merion, PA 19066; (610) 667-9230; bookings@theatreariel.org,
    www.theatreariel.org

Deborah Baer Mozes, *Artistic Director*

Submission procedure: no unsolicited scripts; synopsis, 10-page dialogue sample, character breakdown, resume and letter of inquiry. **Types of material:** full-length plays, one-acts, adaptations, plays for young audiences. **Special interests:** plays with Jewish themes only. **Facilities:** no permanent facility; touring company. **Production considerations:** cast limit of 5; simple sets, sets must be able to tour. **Best submission time:** May–Oct. **Response time:** 1 month letter; 9 months script. **Special programs:** Theatre Loves Conversation: play reading series of new works held 4 times per year, stipend provided.

THE THEATRE @ BOSTON COURT

(Founded 2003)

Box 60187; Pasadena, CA 91116-6187; (626) 683-6883, FAX 683-6886;
    aaronh@bostoncourt.com, www.bostoncourt.com

Aaron Henne and Tom Jacobson, *Co-Literary Managers*

Submission procedure: accepts unsolicited scripts from Southern California playwrights only; all others submit synopsis, first 10 pages of dialogue and letter of inquiry with SASP for response. **Types of material:** full-length plays, translations, adaptations, musicals. **Facilities:** mainstage, 99 seats, thrust stage; Branson, seats vary, black box. **Best submission time:** year-round. **Response time:** 3 months. **Special programs:** winter play reading series.

THEATER BREAKING THROUGH BARRIERS

(formerly Theater By the Blind)

(Founded 1979)

306 West 18th Street; New York, NY 10011; (212) 243-4337,
    FAX 243-4337; gar@nyc.rr.com, www.tbtb.org

Ike Schambelan, *Artistic Director*

Submission procedure: accepts unsolicited scripts. **Types of material:** full-length plays, one-acts, musicals. **Special interests:** work by and about people with disabilities. **Facilities:** company performs on Theatre Row in New York City. **Best submission time:** year-round. **Response time:** 2 months.

THEATRE BUILDING CHICAGO

(Founded 1969)

1225 West Belmont; Chicago, IL 60657-3205; (773) 929-7367, ext 229,
    FAX 327-1404; allan@theatrebuildingchicago.org,
    www.theatrebuildingchicago.org

Allan Chambers, *Associate Artistic Director*

Submission procedure: varies; see website for guidelines. **Types of material:**

musicals. **Facilities:** 3 theatres, 150 seats each, black box. **Best submission time:** Oct. **Response time:** 2 months letter; 3 months script. **Special programs:** Annual STAGES Festival held every summer; musical writers' workshop; monthly reading series; studio presentation series.

THEATER BY THE BLIND
(see Theater Breaking Through Barriers)

THEATER FOR THE NEW CITY
(Founded 1970)
155-57 First Ave; New York, NY 10003-2906; (212) 254-1109,
    FAX 979-6570; literary@theaterforthenewcity.net,
    www.theaterforthenewcity.net
Michael Scott-Price, *Literary Manager*

Submission procedure: accepts unsolicited scripts with SASE for response. **Types of material:** full-length plays. **Special interests:** plays with no previous mainstage production; experimental American works; plays with poetry, music and dance; plays with social issues. **Facilities:** Joyce and Seward Johnson Theater, 200 seats, flexible stage; Cino theatre, 99 seats, flexible stage; Community Theater, 99 seats, flexible stage; Cabaret theatre, 75 seats, flexible stage. **Best submission time:** summer. **Response time:** 12 months.

THEATRE IN THE SQUARE
(Founded 1982)
11 Whitlock Ave; Marietta, GA 30064; (770) 422-8369, FAX 424-2637
Jessica West, *Artistic Associate*

Submission procedure: no unsolicited scripts; synopsis and letter of inquiry. **Types of material:** full-length plays, translations, plays for young audiences, musicals. **Special interests:** world and southeastern premieres. **Facilities:** mainstage, 225 seats, proscenium stage; Alley Stage, up to 120 seats, thrust stage. **Production considerations:** cast limit of 9 for mainstage, 5 for Alley Stage; unit set, no fly space. **Best submission time:** Jun–Dec. **Response time:** 1 month letter, if interested; 6 months script. **Special programs:** Percolating Playreading Series: for local and Southeast regional playwrights; $1000 prize; *deadline:* year-round.

THEATER J
(Founded 1991)
1529 16th St NW; Washington, DC 20036; (202) 777-3229, FAX 518-9421;
    shirleys@washingtondcjcc.org, www.theaterj.org
Ari Roth, *Artistic Director*

Submission procedure: no unsolicited scripts; brief synopsis, 10-page dialogue sample, resume and letter of inquiry with SASE for response. **Types of material:** full-length plays, translations, adaptations, musicals, solo pieces. **Special interests:** multicultural, political and Jewish themes. **Facilities:** Cecile Goldman Theater, 236 seats, proscenium stage. **Best submission time:** spring. **Response time:** 6 months letter; 12 months script.

THEATER OF THE FIRST AMENDMENT

(Founded 1990)

MS 3E6; George Mason University; Fairfax, VA 22030-4444; (703) 993-1122, FAX 993-2191; kneshati@gmu.edu

Kristin Johnsen-Neshati, *Dramaturg/Artistic Associate*

Submission procedure: no unsolicited scripts; synopsis, sample pages, resume and letter of inquiry. **Types of material:** full-length plays, translations, adaptations, plays for young audiences. **Special interests:** sophisticated plays for younger audiences; "cultural history made dramatic as opposed to history dramatized; large battles joined; hard questions asked; word and image stretched." **Facilities:** TheaterSpace, 150–200 seats, flexible space. **Production considerations:** roles for younger actors welcome. **Best submission time:** Aug–Jan. **Response time:** 2 weeks letter; 6 months script. **Special programs:** readings, workshops and other development activities.

THEATRE RHINOCEROS

(Founded 1977)

2926 16th St; San Francisco, CA 94103; (415) 552-4100, FAX 558-9044; www.therhino.org

John Fisher, *Artistic Director*

Submission procedure: no unsolicited scripts; agent submission. **Types of material:** full-length plays, one-acts, solo pieces. **Special interests:** gay and lesbian works only. **Facilities:** Theatre Rhinoceros, 117 seats, proscenium stage; The Studio at Theatre Rhinoceros, 54 seats, studio. **Best submission time:** year-round. **Response time:** 6 months.

THEATRE THREE

(Founded 1969)

Box 512; Port Jefferson, NY 11777-0512; (631) 928-9202, FAX 928-9120; www.theatrethree.com

Jeffrey Sanzel, *Executive Artistic Director*

Submission procedure: no unsolicited scripts; synopsis, resume and letter of inquiry. **Types of material:** one-acts. **Special interests:** works not previously produced only. **Facilities:** Second Stage, 80–100 seats, black box. **Production considerations:** prefers cast limit of 6; unit set, minimal production demands. **Best submission time:** year-round. **Response time:** 1 month letter; 8 months script. **Special programs:** Annual Festival of One-Act Plays: fully staged productions; send SASE to theatre for guidelines; *deadline:* 30 Sep; *notification:* 30 Dec; *dates:* Mar.

THEATRE THREE, INC.
(Founded 1961)
2800 Routh St, Suite 168; Dallas, TX 75201-1417; (214) 871-2933,
FAX 871-3139; admin@theatre3dallas.com, www.theatre3dallas.com
Jac Alder, *Executive Producer-Director*

Submission procedure: no unsolicited scripts; agent submission. **Types of material:** full-length plays, musicals. **Facilities:** Theatre Three, 242 seats, arena stage; Theatre Too, 60 seats, black box. **Best submission time:** Sep–Dec. **Response time:** 3 months.

THEATREWORKS
(Founded 1969)
Box 50458; Palo Alto, CA 94303; (650) 463-7120, FAX 463-1963;
kent@theatreworks.org, www.theatreworks.org
Kent Nicholson, *New Works Director*

Submission procedure: no unsolicited scripts; synopsis, dialogue sample and resume; for translations and adaptations, send letter of inquiry with SASP for response. **Types of material:** full-length plays, translations, adaptations, musicals. **Special interests:** works offering opportunities for multi-ethnic casting; no one-acts. **Facilities:** Mountain View Center, 625 seats, proscenium stage; Lucie Stern Theatre, 425 seats, proscenium stage. **Best submission time:** year–round. **Response time:** 2 months letter; 6 months script. **Special programs:** New Works Initiative: developmental reading series for plays, musicals and music-theatre pieces; see website for guidelines.

THEATREWORKS/USA
(Founded 1961)
151 West 26th St, 7th Floor; New York, NY 10001; (212) 647-1100,
FAX 924-5377; mkramer@twusa.org, www.twusa.org
Molly Kramer, *Assistant Artistic Director*

Submission procedure: no unsolicited scripts; synopsis, sample scene(s) and songs (for musicals) and letter of inquiry; include cassette or CD and lyric sheet for musicals. **Types of material:** plays and musicals for young audiences grades K-12. **Special interests:** literary adaptations, historical/biographical themes, fairy tales, contemporary issues. **Facilities:** Lucille Lortel Theatre, 299 seats, proscenium stage; national tours. **Production considerations:** cast limit of 6 (can play multiple roles); sets suitable for touring. **Best submission time:** year-round. **Response time:** 1 month letter; 6 months script. **Special programs:** Theatreworks/USA Commissioning Program.

THEATRICAL OUTFIT

(Founded 1976)

Box 1555; Atlanta, GA 30301; (678) 528-1490, FAX (404) 577-5259;
    jilljane.clements@theatricaloutfit.org, www.theatricaloutfit.org
Jill Jane Clements, *Artistic Associate*

Submission procedure: no unsolicited scripts; synopsis and letter of inquiry. **Types of material:** full-length plays, musicals. **Special interests:** classic and contemporary theatre with emphasis on work "indigenous to Southern culture." **Facilities:** Balzer Theatre at Herren's, 200 seats, black box with stadium seating. **Production considerations:** cast limit of 10; limited wing space, limited run crew, no fly space. **Best submission time:** year-round. **Response time:** 6 months letter; 12 months script.

TIMELINE THEATRE COMPANY

(Founded 1997)

615 West Wellington Ave; Chicago, IL 60657; (773) 281-8463,
    FAX 281-1134; ben@timelinetheatre.com, www.timelinetheatre.com
Ben Thiem, *Literary Manager*

Submission procedure: no unsolicited scripts; 10-page sample, 1-page synopsis, resume and letter of inquiry; prefers electronic submissions. **Types of material:** full-length plays, adaptations, musicals. **Special interests:** "stories inspired by history that connect with today's social and political issues." **Facilities:** TimeLine Theatre, 85 seats, flexible black box. **Production considerations:** cast limit of 10; moderate production demands; no fly space. **Best submission time:** year-round. **Response time:** 3 months letter; 9 months script.

TOUCHSTONE THEATRE

(Founded 1981)

321 East 4th St; Bethlehem, PA 18015; (610) 867-1689, FAX 867-0561;
    touchstone@touchstone.org, www.touchstone.org
Lisa Jordan, *Producing Director*

Submission procedure: no unsolicited scripts; letter of inquiry. **Types of material:** proposals for works to be created in collaboration with company's ensemble only. **Facilities:** Touchstone Theatre, 74 seats, black box. **Production considerations:** 18' x 21' playing area. **Best submission time:** year-round. **Response time:** 8 months.

TRIAD STAGE

(Founded 2002)

232 South Elm St; Greensboro, NC 27401; (336) 274-0067, FAX 235-2173;
    artisticdept@triadstage.org, www.triadstage.org
Drew Barker, *Artistic Associate*

Submission procedure: no unsolicited scripts; synopsis and letter of inquiry. **Types of material:** full-length plays, adaptations. **Special interests:** "works that reflect Southern voices and themes." **Facilities:** Mainstage, 300 seats, thrust stage; Up Stage

Cabaret, 80 seats, cabaret. **Best submission time:** late spring/early summer. **Response time:** 3 months letter; 6 months script.

TRIARTS SHARON PLAYHOUSE
(Founded 1989)
Box 1187; Sharon, CT 06069; (860) 364-7469, FAX 364-8043;
     info@triarts.net, www.triarts.net
Michael Berkeley, *Artistic Director*

Submission procedure: no unsolicited scripts; synopsis and letter of inquiry; include CD for musicals. **Types of material:** full-length plays and musicals. **Facilities:** The Sharon Playhouse, 370 seats, proscenium stage; Gallery, 120 seats, flexible stage. **Production considerations:** no fly space. **Best submission time:** Jul–Aug. **Response time:** 2 months letter; 6 months script. **Special programs:** 3 staged readings in Gallery per year, with potential development for main stage.

TRICKLOCK COMPANY
(Founded 1993)
1705 Mesa Vista NE; Albuquerque, NM 87106; (505) 254-8393;
     dodie@tricklock.com, www.tricklock.com
Dodie Montgomery, *Managing Director*

Submission procedure: accepts unsolicited scripts. **Types of material:** full-length plays, adaptations, solo pieces. **Facilities:** mainstage, 422 seats, flexible stage (thrust and proscenium); Theatre X, 120 seats, black box. **Best submission time:** year-round. **Response time:** 6 months.

TRINITY REPERTORY COMPANY
(Founded 1964)
201 Washington St; Providence, RI 02903; (401) 521-1100, FAX 521-0447;
     www.trinityrep.com
Craig Watson, *Literary Manager*

Submission procedure: no unsolicited scripts; synopsis, dialogue sample and letter of inquiry. **Types of material:** full-length plays, translations, adaptations, musicals, solo pieces. **Facilities:** Upstairs Theatre, 500 seats, thrust stage; Downstairs Theatre, 297 seats, thrust stage. **Best submission time:** Sep–May. **Response time:** 2 months letter; 4 months script.

TRUSTUS THEATRE
(Founded 1985)
Box 11721; Columbia, SC 29211-1721; (803) 254-9732, FAX 771-9153;
     trustus@aol.com, www.trustus.org
Jon Tuttle, *Literary Manager*

Submission procedure: accepts unsolicited scripts. **Types of material:** one-acts. **Special interests:** one-acts 45–75 minutes in length; experimental, "hard-hitting, off-the-wall" one-act comedies or "dramadies" for open-minded Late-Night series, "no topic taboo"; full-length plays accepted for Trustus Playwrights' Festival only (see Prizes); no musicals or plays for young audiences. **Facilities:** Mainstage, 100 seats, flexible proscenium stage; Second Stage, 50 seats, black box. **Production considerations:** small cast; moderate production demands. **Best submission time:** Aug–Dec. **Response time:** 4 months. **Special programs:** Trustus Playwrights' Festival (see Prizes).

UNICORN THEATRE
(Founded 1974)
3828 Main St; Kansas City, MO 64111; (816) 531-7529, ext 22,
    FAX 531-0421; www.unicorntheatre.org
Herman Wilson, *Literary Assistant*

Submission procedure: accepts unsolicited scripts with synopsis, character breakdown, bio or resume and cover letter with SASE for response. **Types of material:** full-length plays. **Special interests:** contemporary social issues. **Facilities:** Unicorn Theatre, 180 seats, thrust stage; Jerome Stage, 120 seats, black box. **Best submission time:** year-round. **Response time:** 8 months; scripts will not be returned. **Special programs:** Unicorn Theatre New Play Development (see Prizes).

VALLEY YOUTH THEATRE
(Founded 1989)
807 North 3rd St; Phoenix, AZ 85004; (602) 253-8188, FAX 253-8282;
    bobb@vyt.com, www.vyt.com
Bobb Cooper, *Producing Artistic Director*

Submission procedure: no unsolicited scripts; letter of inquiry; include CD for musicals. **Types of material:** plays for young audiences, musicals. **Special interests:** large-scale musicals for family audiences. **Facilities:** Herberger Theater, 750 seats, proscenium stage; Main Stage, 202 seats, proscenium stage. **Best submission time:** Aug–Dec. **Response time:** 2 weeks letter; 2 months script.

VICTORY GARDENS THEATER
(Founded 1974)
2257 North Lincoln Ave; Chicago, IL 60614; (773) 549-5788, FAX 549-2799
Aaron Carter, *Literary Manager*

Submission procedure: accepts unsolicited scripts from Chicago-area writers only; others send synopsis, first 10 pages and letter of inquiry with SASE for response. **Types of material:** full-length plays, adaptations, musicals. **Special interests:** Chicago and Midwest playwrights; plays by women and writers of color. **Facilities:** Mainstage, 300 seats, modified proscenium stage; Second Stage, 195 seats, modified thrust stage. **Production considerations:** prefers cast limit of 10, small-cast musicals only. **Best submission time:** Jan–Jun. **Response time:** 3 months letter; 9 months script. **Special programs:** Victory Gardens Playwrights Ensemble: core group of 12 resident writers. Readers Theater: staged readings of works-in-progress by area writers twice a month. Artist Development Workshop: playwriting class offered throughout the year that brings people with and without disabilities together in a creative environment.

THE VICTORY THEATRE CENTER
(Founded 1979)
3326 West Victory Blvd; Burbank, CA 91505; (818) 841-4404,
    FAX 841-6328; thevictory@mindspring.com,
    www.thevictorytheatrecenter.org
Maria Gobetti and Tom Ormeny, *Co-Artistic Directors*

Submission procedure: no unsolicited scripts; synopsis, first 15 pages of dialogue, resume and letter of inquiry. **Types of material:** full-length plays, adaptations. **Special interests:** plays involving relationships; character-driven plays; plays with social and political issues; "well-made, but cutting-edge" plays. **Facilities:** The Big Victory Theatre, 99 seats, arena stage; The Little Victory, 48 seats, arena stage. **Production considerations:** prefers cast limit of 12; maximum 2 simple sets, no fly space. **Best submission time:** year-round. **Response time:** 2 months letter; 3 months script.

VILLAGE THEATRE
(Founded 1979)
303 Front St N; Issaquah, WA 98027; (425) 392-1942, FAX 391-3242;
    www.villagetheatre.org
Robb Hunt, *Executive Producer*

Submission procedure: no unsolicited scripts; synopsis, character breakdown with vocal ranges, CD, track listing, bio, resume and letter of inquiry. **Types of material:** musicals. **Facilities:** Everett Performing Arts Center, 512 seats, proscenium/thrust stage; Francis J. Gaudette, 488 seats, proscenium stage; First Stage, 204 seats, proscenium stage. **Best submission time:** year-round. **Response time:** 1 month letter; 6 months script. **Special programs:** Village Originals: musical development program culminating in workshop production, possible full production as part of theatre's regular season.

VINEYARD THEATRE
(Founded 1981)
108 East 15th St; New York, NY 10003-9689; (212) 353-3366,
    FAX 353-3803; www.vineyardtheatre.org
Douglas Aibel, *Artistic Director*

Submission procedure: no unsolicited scripts; synopsis or project description, 10-page dialogue sample, resume and letter of inquiry; include CD for musicals. **Types of material:** full-length plays, musicals. **Facilities:** Vineyard Dimson Theatre, 120 seats, flexible stage. **Best submission time:** year-round. **Response time:** 6 months letter, if interested; 12 months script; scripts will not be returned.

VIRGINIA STAGE COMPANY
(Founded 1979)

Box 3770; Norfolk, VA 23514; (757) 627-6988, FAX 628-5958;
   www.vastage.com

Patrick Mullins, *Associate Artistic Director*

Submission procedure: no unsolicited scripts; synopsis and letter of inquiry. **Types of material:** full-length plays, musicals. **Special interests:** plays that are "artistically surprising." **Facilities:** mainstage, 700 seats, proscenium stage. **Best submission time:** year-round. **Response time:** 1 month letter; 6 months script.

VITAL THEATRE COMPANY
(Founded 1999)

2162 Broadway, 4th Floor; New York, NY 10024; (212) 579-0528,
   FAX 579-0646; office@vitaltheatre.org, www.vitaltheatre.org

Stephen Sunderlin, *Artistic Director*

Submission procedure: no unsolicited scripts; synopsis and 10-page sample. **Types of material:** full-length plays, one-acts, musicals for young audiences. **Special interests:** original work; "we commission children's musicals and arrange collaborations." **Facilities:** McGinn/Cazale, 108 seats, proscenium stage. **Best submission time:** year-round. **Response time:** varies. **Special programs:** one-act festival; *submission time:* May–Jul.

VS THEATRE COMPANY
(Founded 2003)

Box 2293; Los Angeles, CA 91610; www.vstheatre.org

Ron Klier, *Literary Manager*

Submission procedure: no unsolicited scripts; agent submission only. **Types of material:** full-length plays. **Special interests:** world premieres or pieces rarely performed; work with an emphasis on the "unique, daring and edgy." **Facilities:** The Elephant Theatre, 60 seats, black box. **Production considerations:** cast limit of 6, characters in 20s–30s; no big, elaborate sets. **Best submission time:** year-round. **Response time:** 6 months.

THE WALNUT STREET THEATRE
(Founded 1809)

825 Walnut St; Philadelphia, PA 19107-5107; (215) 574-3550,
   FAX 574-3598; www.walnutstreettheatre.org

Beverly Elliott, *Literary Manager*

Submission procedure: no unsolicited scripts; synopsis, cast list, 10–20-page dialogue sample and letter of inquiry with SASE for response; include professional-quality CD for musicals. **Types of material:** full-length plays, musicals. **Special interests:** original, socially relevant musicals with uplifting themes; commercially viable works for Main Stage; meaningful comedies and dramas with some broad social relevance; musicals with cast of 1-6 considered for Studio 3. **Facilities:** Main Stage,

1078 seats, proscenium stage; Studio 3, 79–99 seats, flexible stage. **Production considerations:** for Studio 3: cast limit of 4. **Response time:** 3 months letter; 6 months script.

WATERTOWER THEATRE, INC.

(Founded 1976)

15650 Addison Rd; Addison, TX 75001; (972) 450-6230, FAX 450-6244; www.watertowertheatre.org

Terry Martin, *Artistic Director*

Submission procedure: no unsolicited scripts; agent submission. **Types of material:** full-length plays, musicals. **Special interests:** comedies; plays that make creative use of flexible space. **Facilities:** Addison Conference & Theatre Centre, 100–300 seats, flexible stage. **Best submission time:** Apr–Aug. **Response time:** 4 months letter; 6 months script. **Special programs:** Out of the Loop Festival: readings of previously unproduced full-length plays; agent submission only.

WEISSBERGER THEATER GROUP

(Founded 1992)

551 Fifth Ave, Suite 605; New York, NY 10176; (212) 586-4700, FAX 949-6746

Richard Garmise, *Producer*

Submission procedure: no unsolicited scripts; synopsis and letter of inquiry. **Types of material:** full-length plays, musicals. **Special interests:** topical American plays. **Facilities:** no permanent facility. **Production considerations:** cast limit of 7 for plays. **Best submission time:** year-round. **Response time:** 1 month letter; 2 months script.

WELLFLEET HARBOR ACTORS THEATER

(Founded 1985)

Box 797; Wellfleet, MA 02667; (508) 349-3011, FAX 349-9082; source@what.org, www.what.org

Jeff Zinn, *Artistic Director*

Submission procedure: no unsolicited scripts; professional recommendation. **Types of material:** full-length plays, translations, adaptations, solo pieces. **Facilities:** WHAT mainstage, 210 seats, proscenium stage; 2nd Stage, 90-seat, cabaret. **Best submission time:** year-round. **Response time:** 3 months letter; 6 months script.

WEST COAST ENSEMBLE

(Founded 1982)

Box 38728; Los Angeles, CA 90038; (323) 876-9337, FAX 876-8916

Les Hanson, *Artistic Director*

Submission procedure: accepts unsolicited scripts. **Types of material:** full-length plays, one-acts, translations, adaptations, musicals. **Special interests:** plays not previously produced in Southern CA only; musicals; short plays. **Facilities:** mainstage, 99 seats, proscenium stage. **Production considerations:** simple set; no fly space. **Best submission time:** Jun–Dec. **Response time:** 6 months. **Special programs:** staged readings of new plays.

WESTPORT COUNTRY PLAYHOUSE
(Founded 1931)
25 Powers Ct; Westport, CT 06880; (203) 227-5137, FAX 221-7482;
    www.westportplayhouse.org
Anne Keefe, *Artistic Director*

Submission procedure: no unsolicited scripts; professional recommendation. **Types of material:** full-length plays, translations, adaptations, musicals. **Facilities:** Westport Country Playhouse, 580 seats, proscenium stage. **Production considerations:** cast limit of 8; small cast and orchestra for musicals. **Best submission time:** year-round. **Response time:** 8 months.

WHEELOCK FAMILY THEATRE
(Founded 1981)
200 The Riverway; Boston, MA 02215; (617) 879-2289, FAX 879-2021;
    skosoff@wheelock.edu, www.wheelock.edu/wft
Susan Kosoff, *Producer*

Submission procedure: no unsolicited scripts; professional recommendation. **Types of material:** full-length plays, adaptations, plays for young audiences, musicals. **Special interests:** "familiar stories." **Facilities:** Wheelock Family Theatre, 645 seats, proscenium/thrust stage. **Best submission time:** fall and spring. **Response time:** 2 months.

WILL GEER THEATRICUM BOTANICUM
(Founded 1973)
Box 1222; Topanga, CA 90290; (310) 455-2322, FAX 455-3724;
    info@theatricum.com, www.theatricum.com
Ellen Geer, *Artistic Director*

Submission procedure: no unsolicited scripts; synopsis, dialogue sample and letter of inquiry. **Types of material:** full-length plays. **Special interests:** work suitable for large outdoor playing space. **Facilities:** Will Geer Theatricum Botanicum, 300 seats, outdoor amphitheatre. **Production considerations:** cast limit of 10; simple sets. **Best submission time:** Sep. **Response time:** 12 months letter; 6 months script. **Special programs:** Seedlings: new play reading series; submissions accepted year-round.

WILLIAMSTOWN THEATRE FESTIVAL

(Founded 1955)

Sep–May: 229 West 42nd St, Suite 801; New York, NY 10036-7205;
   (212) 395-9090, FAX 395-9099

Jun–Aug Season: Box 517; Williamstown, MA 01267-0517; (413) 458-3200,
   FAX 458-3147; www.wtfestival.org

Nicholas Martin, *Artistic Director*

Submission procedure: no unsolicited scripts; agent submission. **Types of material:** full-length plays, adaptations, musicals. **Facilities:** Main Stage, 512 seats, proscenium stage; 2nd stage, 175 seats, thrust stage. **Best submission time:** 1 Oct–31 Mar. **Response time:** 12 months (only if further information needed). **Special programs:** New Play Staged Readings Series.

WILLOWS THEATRE COMPANY

(Founded 1977)

636 Ward St; Martinez, CA 94553; (925) 798-1824;
   rich@willowstheatre.org, www.willowstheatre.org

Richard H. Elliott, *Artistic Director*

Submission procedure: no unsolicited scripts; synopsis, resume and SASE for response. **Types of material:** full-length comedies. **Facilities:** John Muir Amphitheater, 1200 seats, outdoor amphitheatre; Willows Theatre, 210 seats, proscenium stage; Cabaret Theatre, 176 seats, cabaret. **Production considerations:** cast limit of 35. **Best submission time:** 1 Dec–1 Apr. **Response time:** 12 months letter; 12 months script. **Special programs:** staged readings and workshop development productions.

THE WILMA THEATER

(Founded 1979)

265 South Broad St; Philadelphia, PA 19107; (215) 893-9456,
   FAX 893-0895; info@wilmatheater.org, www.wilmatheater.org

Walter Bilderback, *Dramaturg & Literary Manager*

Submission procedure: no unsolicited scripts; 10-page dialogue sample with professional recommendation and letter of inquiry; electronic submission preferred. **Types of material:** full-length plays, translations, adaptations, musicals. **Special interests:** new translations and adaptations from the international repertoire with emphasis on innovative, bold staging; world premieres; ensemble works; works with poetic dimension; plays with music; multimedia works; social issues. **Facilities:** The Wilma Theater, 300 seats, flexible/proscenium stage. **Production considerations:** prefers cast limit of 10; stage 44' x 46'. **Best submission time:** year-round. **Response time:** 12 months letter; 12 months script.

WINGS THEATRE COMPANY, INC.

(Founded 1986)

154 Christopher St; New York, NY 10014; (212) 627-2960, FAX 462-0024; jcorrick@wingstheatre.com, www.wingstheatre.com

Submission procedure: accepts unsolicited scripts. **Types of material:** full-length plays, musicals. **Special interests:** new musicals and gay-themed plays only. **Facilities:** Wings Theatre, 74 seats, proscenium stage. **Best submission time:** year-round. **Response time:** plays received by 1 May receive response in Sep of that year; plays received after 1 May receive response Sep of following year.

WOMEN'S PROJECT

(Founded 1978)

55 West End Ave; New York, NY 10023; (212) 765-1706, FAX 765-2024; info@womensproject.org, www.womensproject.org

Megan Carter, *Associate Artistic Director*

Submission procedure: no unsolicited scripts; synopsis, 10-page dialogue sample and letter of inquiry; materials will not be returned. **Types of material:** full-length plays, musicals. **Special interests:** plays by women only. **Facilities:** Julia Miles Theatre, 199 seats, proscenium stage. **Best submission time:** year-round. **Response time:** 12 months letter; 12 months script. **Special programs:** lab for playwrights, directors and producers: developmental program including play readings and work-in-progress presentations; open call for applications every 2 years; see website for details.

WOODSTOCK FRINGE

(Founded 2000)

Box 157; Lake Hill, NY 12448; (845) 810-0123; info@woodstockfringe.org, www.woodstockfringe.org

Wallace Norman, *Producing Artistic Director*

Submission procedure: no unsolicited scripts; synopsis, 10–15-page dialogue sample and letter of inquiry; resume, press/publicity materials and letter of inquiry for performance artists and solo performers only. **Types of material:** full-length plays, one-acts, translations, adaptations, musicals, solo pieces, performance art. **Facilities:** Byrdcliffe Theater in Woodstock, 100 seats, flexible stage. **Production considerations:** modest production requirements. **Best submission time:** Sep–Mar. **Response time:** 3 weeks letter; 6 months script. **Special programs:** Woodstock Fringe Festival of Theatre and Song. Woodstock Fringe Playwrights Unit: readings of new plays in New York City.

WOOLLY MAMMOTH THEATRE COMPANY
(Founded 1981)
641 D St NW; Washington, DC 20004; (202) 289-2443;
   www.woollymammoth.net
Howard Shalwitz, *Artistic Director*

Submission procedure: no unsolicited scripts; professional recommendation. **Types of material:** full-length plays, translations, adaptations, solo pieces. **Special interests:** theatrical and provocative plays which combine elevated language with edgy situations and complex characters. **Facilities:** courtyard, 265 seats, flexible stage. **Production considerations:** prefers cast limit of 6. **Best submission time:** Jun. **Response time:** 12 months. **Special programs:** Playmaking: community playbuilding projects.

WORCESTER FOOTHILLS THEATRE COMPANY
(see Foothills Theatre Company)

WOW CAFÉ THEATRE
(Founded 1976)
59-61 East 4th St; New York, NY 10003; www.wowcafe.org
Submissions

Submission procedure: accepts unsolicited scripts from "women and trans artists only"; involvement in theatre collective is encouraged; see website for details. **Types of Material:** full-length plays, one-acts, translations, adaptations, plays for young audiences, musicals, cabaret/revues, solo pieces. **Special interests:** gay, lesbian and transgender issues. **Facilities:** mainstage, 60 seats, black box with flexible seating. **Best submission time:** year-round. **Response time:** 1 month.

WRITERS' THEATRE
(Founded 1992)
376 Park Ave; Glencoe, IL 60022; (847) 242-6000, FAX 242-6011;
   info@writerstheatre.org
Jimmy McDermott, *Artistic Associate*

Submission procedure: no unsolicited scripts: synopsis and 10-page dialogue sample. **Types of material:** full-length plays, translations, adaptations. **Special interests:** highly literary, language-driven plays by or about great writers and writing. **Facilities:** Tudor Court, 108 seats, thrust stage; Books On Vernon, 50 seats, flexible stage. **Production considerations:** intimate spaces, minimal production demands. **Best submission time:** year-round. **Response time:** 6 months letter; 12 months script.

YALE REPERTORY THEATRE

(Founded 1965)

Box 208244, Yale Station; New Haven, CT 06520-8244; (203) 432-1560,
    FAX 432-1070; catherine.sheehy@yale.edu

Catherine Sheehy, *Resident Dramaturg*

Submission procedure: no unsolicited scripts; synopsis, 10-page dialogue sample and letter of inquiry. **Types of material:** full-length plays, translations, adaptations. **Special interests:** new work; new translations of classics; contemporary foreign plays. **Facilities:** University Theatre, 654 seats, proscenium stage; Yale Repertory Theatre, 487 seats, modified thrust stage. **Best submission time:** year-round. **Response time:** 2 months letter; 3 months script.

THE YORK THEATRE COMPANY

(Founded 1968)

The Theatre at Saint Peter's Church; Citicorp Center; 619 Lexington Ave;
    New York, NY 10022-4610; (212) 935-5824, FAX 832-0037;
    www.yorktheatre.org

Literary Department

Submission procedure: accepts unsolicited musical theatre scripts with SASE for response; include cassette or CD. **Types of material:** musicals, revues. **Special interests:** small-cast musicals. **Facilities:** The Theatre at Saint Peter's Church, 178 seats, flexible stage. **Best submission time:** year-round. **Response time:** 12 months.

PRIZES

What competitions are included here?

All the playwriting contests we know of that offer prizes of at least $200 or, in the case of awards to playwrights 19 or under, the equivalent in production or publication. Most awards for which the playwright cannot apply—the Joseph Kesselring Award, the Pulitzer Prize—are not listed. Exceptions are made when, as with The Susan Smith Blackburn Prize, the nominating process allows playwrights to encourage nomination of their work by theatre professionals.

How can I give myself the best chance of winning?

Send your script in well before the deadline, when the readers are fresh and enthusiastic, rather than buried by an avalanche of submissions. Assume the deadline is the date your script must be received (not the postmark date, unless otherwise stated). Make sure you don't mistake a notification date for the submission deadline. If a listing specifies "write for guidelines," be sure to follow this instruction. It usually means that we don't have space in our brief listing to give you all the information you need; also, contests may change their rules or their deadlines after this book has been published. Always send an SASE with your submission if you expect your materials to be returned.

Should I enter contests that charge entry fees?

It's true that a number of listings require a fee. Many contest sponsors are unable to secure sufficient funding to cover their costs, which are considerable. We have not included those listings with unusually high fees. Some playwrights will not pay fees as a matter of principle, others consider it part of doing business. It's up to you.

How can I find out about new prizes and updates?

Write or see the web for guidelines to ensure that you have the most recent rules. Also refer to the Membership and Service Organizations, Useful Publications and Online Resources sections in this book for those groups that list current contest news.

A couple of *Sourcebook* reminders:

"Full-length play" means a full-length, original work without a score or libretto. One-acts, musicals, adaptations, translations, plays for young audiences and solo pieces are listed separately.

Sourcebook entries are alphabetized by first word (excluding "The") even if the title starts with a proper name. So, for instance, you'll find the "Harold Morton Landon Translation Award" under H. In the index, you will also find this prize cross-listed under L.

Deadlines: Some deadlines may fall outside the publication period of this book, which is biennial. All deadlines reflect the next upcoming submission deadline for an organization at press time. Deadlines for annual awards may stay the same from year to year, but this is not absolute—always obtain the latest information (an organization's website is the best place to check) before submitting. Years are not listed for annual awards. Also note that some prizes may be given every two, three or four years, so it is very important to read dates closely.

AMERICAN TRANSLATORS ASSOCIATION AWARDS

225 Reinekers Ln, Suite 590; Alexandria, VA 22314; FAX (703) 683-6122;
   ata@atanet.org
Chair, ATA Honors and Awards

GERMAN LITERARY TRANSLATION PRIZE

Types of material: translations of full-length plays and one-acts. **Frequency:** biennial. **Remuneration:** $1000, up to $500 expenses to attend ATA annual conference. **Guidelines:** translation from German published in U.S. by American publisher during 2 years before deadline as single volume or in collection. **Submission procedure:** no submission by translator; publisher nominates translation and submits 2 copies of book plus 10 consecutive pages of German original, extra jacket and any advertising copy, and bio of translator. **Deadline:** 1 May 2009. **Notification:** fall 2009.

LEWIS GALANTIÈRE LITERARY TRANSLATION PRIZE

Types of material: translations of full-length plays and one-acts. **Frequency:** biennial. **Remuneration:** $1000, up to $500 expenses to attend ATA annual conference. **Guidelines:** translation from any language except German published in U.S. by American publisher during 2 years before deadline as single volume or in collection. **Submission procedure:** no submission by translator; publisher nominates translation and submits 2 copies of book plus 10 consecutive pages of original, extra jacket and any advertising copy, and bio of translator. **Deadline:** 1 May 2010. **Notification:** fall 2010.

ANNA ZORNIO MEMORIAL CHILDREN'S THEATRE PLAYWRITING AWARD

Department of Theatre and Dance; University of New Hampshire;
   Paul Creative Arts Center; 30 Academic Way;
   Durham, NH 03824-3538; (603) 862-3038, FAX 862-0298;
   www.unh.edu/theatre-dance/zornio.html
Administrative Manager

Types of material: plays and musicals for young audiences. **Frequency:** every 4 years. **Remuneration:** $1000, production by UNH Department of Theatre and Dance in an upcoming season. **Guidelines:** U.S. or Canadian resident; unpublished work not produced professionally, maximum 60 minutes in length; 2 submission limit; prefers single or unit set. **Submission procedure:** see website or write for guidelines. **Deadline:** 2 Mar 2012. **Notification:** Nov 2012.

THE ANNUAL NATIONWIDE BLANK THEATRE COMPANY YOUNG PLAYWRIGHTS FESTIVAL

1301 Lucile Ave; Los Angeles, CA 90026-1519; (323) 662-7734;
   info@theblank.com, www.theblank.com, www.youngplaywrights.com

Types of material: full-length plays, one-acts, plays for young audiences, musicals, operas, solo pieces. **Frequency:** annual. **Remuneration:** workshop production for approximately 9-12 playwrights; some scripts receive full production. **Guidelines:**

playwright maximum 19 years of age as of deadline date; original play of any length on any subject; send SASE in late Jan for guidelines. **Submission procedure:** script with cover sheet containing name, date of birth, home address, phone number and email address; pages must be numbered and unbound; if applicable, include name of school and/or production history. **Deadline:** 15 Mar. **Notification:** May.

APPALACHIAN FESTIVAL OF PLAYS & PLAYWRIGHTS

Barter Theatre; Box 867; Abingdon, VA 24212-0867; (276) 619-3316,
   FAX 619-3335; apfestival@bartertheatre.com,
   www.bartertheatre.com/season/festival.htm
Nicholas Piper, *Festival Director*

Types of material: full-length plays, adaptations, musicals. **Frequency:** annual. **Remuneration:** $250, 6 plays chosen for staged reading; travel and housing stipend available for readings. **Guidelines:** unproduced scripts with Appalachian themes, locations and/or setting; if playwright is from Appalachian region, play may be on any subject or theme and need not be set in Appalachia; see website for guidelines. **Submission procedure:** script. **Deadline:** 31 Mar. **Notification:** 6 months.

THE ARTS & LETTERS PRIZE IN DRAMA

Georgia College & State University; Campus Box 89;
   Milledgeville, GA 31061-0490; (478) 445-1289; al@mail.gcsu.edu,
   al.gcsu.edu
David Muschell, *Drama Editor*

Types of material: one-acts. **Frequency:** annual. **Remuneration:** $1000, production, publication in *Arts & Letters* journal. **Guidelines:** unpublished one-act. **Submission procedure:** script with separate title page containing name and address of playwright and $15 fee; includes subscription to journal. **Deadline:** 1 Apr. **Notification:** Aug.

ASF TRANSLATION PRIZE

The American-Scandinavian Foundation; 58 Park Ave; New York, NY 10016;
   (212) 879-9779, FAX 686-2115; ahenkin@amscan.org
Publishing Office

Types of material: translations. **Frequency:** annual. **Remuneration:** $2000, publication of excerpt in *Scandinavian Review*; $1000 for runner-up. **Guidelines:** unpublished translation from a Scandinavian language into English of work written by a Scandinavian author after 1800; manuscript minimum 50 pages in length if prose drama, 25 pages if verse drama, and must be conceived as part of a book. **Submission procedure:** 4 copies of translation, 1 of original, permission letter from copyright holder; write for guidelines. **Deadline:** 1 Jun. **Notification:** fall.

Attic Theatre Ensemble's One-Act Marathon

Attic Theatre and Film Center; 5429 West Washington Blvd;
  Los Angeles, CA 90016; (323) 525-0600; litmanager@attictheatre.org,
  www.attictheatre.org
James Carey, *Producing Artistic Director*

Types of material: one-acts. **Frequency:** annual. **Remuneration:** $300 1st prize; $100 2nd prize; 6 finalists receive productions; possible publishing contract with online publisher Shire Books. **Guidelines:** unproduced one-act maximum 45 minutes in length; no adaptations. **Submission procedure:** send SASE or see website for guidelines and application. **Deadline:** 31 Dec. **Notification:** May. **Dates:** Jul–Aug. (See Attic Theatre and Film Center in Production.)

Aurand Harris Memorial Playwriting Award

New England Theatre Conference Inc.; 215 Knob Hill Dr; Hamden, CT 06518;
  (617) 851-8535; mail@netconline.org, www.netconline.org

Types of material: plays for young audiences. **Frequency:** annual. **Remuneration:** $1000 1st prize; $500 2nd prize. **Guidelines:** unpublished work not produced professionally; 1 submission limit. **Submission procedure:** script, synopsis, character breakdown and statement that play has not been published or professionally produced and is not under consideration for publication or production prior to 1 Sep, $10 fee (waived for NETC members); send SASP for acknowledgment of receipt; script will not be returned; see website for guidelines. **Deadline:** 1 May. **Notification:** Sep (winners only).

Baker's Plays High School Playwriting Contest

45 West 25th St; New York, NY 10010; (212) 206-8990;
  publications@bakersplays.com, www.bakersplays.com

Types of material: full-length plays, one-acts, plays for young audiences, musicals. **Frequency:** annual. **Remuneration:** monetary prize; publication and licensing contract. **Guidelines:** high school student sponsored by high school drama or English teacher; prefers play that has been produced or given public reading. **Submission procedure:** script with signature of sponsoring teacher; see website for guidelines. **Deadline:** 31 Jan. **Notification:** May. (See Baker's Plays in Publication.)

Beverly Hills Theatre Guild—
California Musical Theatre Award

Box 148; Beverly Hills, CA 90213; www.beverlyhillstheatreguild.org
Musical Competition Coordinator

Types of material: musicals. **Frequency:** annual. **Remuneration:** $4000, possible staged reading. **Guidelines:** resident of CA only; musical must be written in English and not previously published, produced, under professional option, or the winner of any other major competition. **Submission procedure:** script, cassette or CD of music selections and application; materials will not be returned; see website or send SASE for guidelines and application. **Deadline:** 15 Nov; no submission before 15 Jun. **Notification:** Dec.

BEVERLY HILLS THEATRE GUILD PLAYWRITING AWARDS

Box 148; Beverly Hills, CA 90213; www.beverlyhillstheatreguild.org
Candace Coster, *Competition Coordinator*

JULIE HARRIS PLAYWRITING AWARDS

Types of material: full-length plays. **Frequency:** annual. **Remuneration:** $3500 Maxwell and Janet Salter Award; $2500 BHTG Award; $1500 Dr. Henry and Lilian Nesburn Award; possible staged reading for all winners. **Guidelines:** U.S. citizen or legal resident; play must be written in English; 1 submission, not published, produced, optioned or winner of any other major competition; minimum 75 minutes in length; no plays for young audiences, bills of related one-acts or musicals. **Submission guidelines:** script and application; script will not be returned; see website or send SASE for guidelines and application. **Deadline:** 1 Nov; no submission before 1 Aug. **Notification:** Jun.

THE MARILYN HALL AWARDS

Types of material: adaptations, translations, plays for young audiences. **Frequency:** annual. **Remuneration:** $700 1st prize; $300 2nd prize; possible staged reading for all winners. **Guidelines:** U.S. citizen or legal resident; plays suitable for grades 6-8 or grades 9-12, must be written in English, not published, under professional option, or winner of any other major competition; approximately 45–90 minutes in length; play may have had 1 non-professional or educational theatre production; plays with songs (but not traditional musicals) accepted; 2 submission limit. **Submission procedure:** script and application; scripts will not be returned; see website or send SASE for guidelines and application. **Deadline:** postmarked by 28 Feb; no submission before 15 Jan. **Notification:** Jun.

BIENNIAL PROMISING PLAYWRIGHT AWARD

Colonial Players, Inc; Box 2167; Annapolis, MD 21404;
    artistic@cdplayers.com, www.cplayers.com
Contest Coordinator

Types of material: full-length plays, one-acts. **Frequency:** biennial. **Remuneration:** $1000, workshop; possible full production. **Guidelines:** resident of CT, DC, DE, GA, MA, MD, NC, NH, NJ, NY, PA, RI, SC, VA or WV; playwright must be available to attend rehearsals; play not produced professionally; cast limit of 10; no musicals; see website for details. **Submission procedure:** script, summary, sample pages and application form; playwright name should appear on application only; see website for details. **Deadline:** postmarked by 1 Dec 2008; no submission postmarked before 1 Sep 2008. **Notification:** 15 Jun 2009.

BUNTVILLE CREW

Box 445; Buckley, IL 60918-0445; buntville@yahoo.fr
Steven Packard, *Artistic Director*

AWARD BLUE

Types of material: one-acts. **Frequency:** annual. **Remuneration:** $200, possible full or workshop production or staged reading. **Guidelines:** IL high-school student enrolled in the recent school year; unpublished, unproduced play maximum 15 pages in length. **Submission procedure:** script with playwright's name, address, phone number, age and name of school on title page and bio. **Deadline:** postmarked by 31 May. **Notification:** fall.

DAS GOLDKIEL

Types of material: full-length plays. **Frequency:** annual. **Remuneration:** $250, possible full or workshop production or staged reading. **Guidelines:** unpublished, unproduced play; scripts may be in English, French, German or Spanish; no translations or adaptations. **Submission procedure:** script, bio and $8 fee. **Deadline:** postmarked by 31 May. **Notification:** fall.

PRIX HORS PAIR

Types of material: one-acts. **Frequency:** annual. **Remuneration:** $200, possible full or workshop production or staged reading. **Guidelines:** unpublished, unproduced play maximum 15 pages in length; scripts may be in English, French, German or Spanish; no translations or adaptations. **Submission procedure:** script, bio and $8 fee. **Deadline:** postmarked by 31 May. **Notification:** fall.

CALIFORNIA YOUNG PLAYWRIGHTS CONTEST

Playwrights Project; 450 B St, Suite 1020; San Diego, CA 92101-8093;
  (619) 239-8222, FAX 239-8225; write@playwrightsproject.com,
  www.playwrightsproject.com
Deborah Salzer, *Executive Director*

Types of material: full-length plays, one-acts. **Frequency:** annual. **Remuneration:** 3-5 awards of $100, full production, travel, housing and board; all entrants receive written evaluation of work. **Guidelines:** resident of CA; playwright under 19 years of age as of 1 Jun; work minimum 10 pages in length; previous submissions ineligible. **Submission procedure:** 2 copies of script with playwright's date of birth on title page and cover letter. **Deadline:** 1 Jun. **Notification:** Sep; script will not be returned.

CASA 0101

2009 East First St; Los Angeles, CA 90033; (323) 263-7684;
  www.casa0101.org
José Casas, *Literary Manager*

JOSEFINA LOPEZ PLAYWRITING COMPETITION

Types of material: full-length plays, one-act plays, translations, adaptations, plays for young audiences. **Frequency:** annual. **Remuneration:** $500, staged reading, possible future production. **Guidelines:** unpublished play with no previous professional productions; play dealing with Chicano/Latino culture. **Submission procedure:** one copy of script; script will not be returned. **Deadline:** 31 May. **Notification:** Aug.

JOSEFINA LOPEZ YOUTH PLAYWRITING COMPETITION

Types of material: one-acts. **Frequency:** annual. **Remuneration:** $500, staged reading, possible future production. **Guidelines:** playwright maximum 21 years of age as of deadline; unpublished play with no previous professional productions; play dealing with Chicano/Latino culture. **Submission procedure:** one copy of script; script will not be returned. **Deadline:** 31 May. **Notification:** Aug.

CHICANO/LATINO LITERARY PRIZE CONTEST

Department of Spanish & Portuguese; University of California, Irvine;
    322 Humanities Hall; Irvine, CA 92697-5276; (949) 824-6901,
    FAX 824-2808; cllp@uci.edu;
    www.hnet.uci.edu/spanishandportuguese/contest.html
Evelyn Flores, *Prize Coordinator*

Types of material: full-length plays. **Frequency:** every 4 years. **Remuneration:** $1000 1st prize, publication by Arte Público Press, travel to attend award ceremony; $500 2nd prize; $250 3rd prize. **Guidelines:** U.S. citizen or resident; unpublished play written in Spanish or English; 1 submission limit. **Submission procedure:** 3 copies of script, minimum 90 typed, double-spaced pages; see website for details. **Deadline:** next deadline in 2010; exact date TBA.

CLAUDER COMPETITION

Portland Stage Company; Box1458; Portland, ME 04104; (207) 774-1043,
    FAX 774-0576; dburson@portlandstage.com, www.portlandstage.com
Daniel Burson, *Literary Manager*

Types of material: full-length plays. **Frequency:** biennial. **Remuneration:** $2,000 1st prize, production; 2 $500 runners-up receive workshop. **Guidelines:** New England residents only; play not previously published or produced; 1 submission per playwright; cast limit of 8. **Submission procedure:** script. **Deadline:** 1 Mar 2009. **Notification:** 20 Nov 2009.

COE COLLEGE NEW WORKS FOR THE STAGE COMPETITION

Department of Theatre Arts; 1220 First Ave NE; Cedar Rapids, IA 52402;
    (319) 399-8624, FAX 399-8557; swolvert@coe.edu,
    www.theatre.coe.edu
Susan Wolverton, *Chair, Playwriting Festival*

Types of material: full-length plays. **Frequency:** biennial, contingent on funding. **Remuneration:** $500, staged reading, travel, room and board for 1-week residency during spring term. **Guidelines:** unpublished, unproduced play; festival includes workshops and public discussions; no translations, adaptations or musicals; send SASE for guidelines. **Submission procedure:** script and resume. **Deadline:** Nov of even years. **Notification:** Jan of odd years. **Dates:** late Mar of odd years.

THE CUNNINGHAM COMMISSION FOR YOUTH THEATRE

The Theatre School; DePaul University; 2135 North Kenmore;
    Chicago, IL 60614-4111; (773) 325-7938, FAX 325-7920;
    aables@depaul.edu
Anna Ables, *Director of Marketing and Public Relations*

Types of material: plays for young audiences. **Frequency:** annual. **Remuneration:** up to $6000, possible production. **Guidelines:** Chicago-area playwright; winner commissioned to write a play for young audiences that "affirms the centrality of religion, broadly defined, and the human quest for meaning, truth and community." **Submission procedure:** 20-page dialogue sample, brief statement about interest in commission and resume; write for guidelines. **Deadline:** 1 Dec.

DAYTON PLAYHOUSE FUTUREFEST

1301 East Siebenthaler Ave; Dayton, OH 45414; (937) 424-8477,
    FAX 424-0062; www.daytonplayhouse.org
Amy Brown, *Executive Director*

Types of material: full-length plays. **Frequency:** annual. **Remuneration:** $1000 1st prize; 5 $100 runners-up; 3 plays receive full productions, 3 plays receive reading during FutureFest weekend in late Jul; travel and housing to attend weekend. **Guidelines:** unproduced, unpublished play not under consideration for publication or production prior to FutureFest weekend. **Submission procedure:** script and resume; send SASE or fax number or see website for guidelines. **Deadline:** postmarked by 31 Oct. **Notification:** May.

DOROTHY SILVER PLAYWRITING COMPETITION

Mandel Jewish Community Center of Cleveland; 26001 South Woodland;
    Beechwood, OH 44122; (216) 831-0700, FAX 831-7796;
    dbobrow@clevejcc.org, www.clevejcc.org
Deborah Bobrow, *Coordinator*

Types of material: full-length plays. **Frequency:** annual. **Remuneration:** $1000 (including $500 to cover residency expenses), staged reading. **Guidelines:** unproduced play that provides "fresh and significant perspective on the range of Jewish experience." **Submission procedure:** script. **Deadline:** 31 Dec. **Notification:** spring.

DRURY UNIVERSITY ONE-ACT PLAY COMPETITION

900 North Benton Ave; Springfield, MO 65802; (417) 873-6821;
    msokol@drury.edu
Mick Sokol, *Associate Professor of Theatre*

Types of material: one-acts. **Frequency:** biennial. **Remuneration:** $300 1st prize, possible production; 2 $150 runners-up. **Guidelines:** unproduced, unpublished play

20–45 minutes in length; prefers small cast, 1 set; 1 submission limit. **Submission procedure:** script; send SASE or email for guidelines. **Deadline:** 1 Dec 2008. **Notification:** 1 Apr 2009.

DUBUQUE FINE ARTS PLAYERS NATIONAL ONE-ACT PLAYWRITING CONTEST

1686 Lawndale Dr; Dubuque, IA 52001-4200; gary.arms@clarke.edu
Gary Arms, *Coordinator*

Types of material: one-acts. **Frequency:** annual. **Remuneration:** $600 1st prize; $300 2nd prize; $200 3rd prize; possible production for all 3 plays. **Guidelines:** unproduced, unpublished play maximum 35 pages and 40 minutes in length; adaptations of material in public domain accepted; prefers cast limit of 5, 1 set; no submission limit. **Submission procedure:** 2 copies of script, 1-paragraph synopsis, application and $10 fee per submission; optional SASE for critique and optional SASP for acknowledgment of receipt; send SASE for guidelines and application or email coordinator. **Deadline:** 31 Jan; no submission before 1 Nov. **Notification:** 30 Jun.

ECODRAMA PLAYWRIGHTS FESTIVAL

Theatre Arts, VIL 216; University of Oregon; Eugene, OR 97403;
    www.uoregon.edu/~ecodrama/play-submissions/
Theresa May, *Festival Director*

Types of material: full-length plays. **Frequency:** biennial. **Remuneration:** $2000 1st prize, workshop; $500 2nd prize, workshop; honorable mentions, staged reading. **Guidelines:** "ecological issue or environmental event must be at center of the drama"; play must be mininum 30 minutes in length; write or email for extensive and specific guidelines. **Submission procedure:** 2 copies of script, synopsis, character breakdown; playwright name on title page of script only. **Deadline:** postmarked by 1 Nov 2008. **Notification:** 15 Dec 2008.

ESSENTIAL THEATRE PLAYWRITING AWARD

Box 8172; Atlanta, GA 30306; (404) 212-0815; pmhardy@aol.com,
    www.essentialtheatre.com
Peter Hardy, *Producing Artistic Director*

Types of material: full-length plays. **Frequency:** annual. **Remuneration:** $500, production in Power Plays Festival; runners-up given staged readings and workshops. **Guidelines:** resident of GA; unproduced play. **Submission procedure:** script with SASE for response; submissions also accepted via email; see website for details. **Deadline:** 23 Apr. **Notification:** Oct. **Dates:** Jul.

FIREHOUSE THEATRE PROJECT FESTIVAL OF NEW AMERICAN PLAYS

1609 West Broad St; Richmond, VA 23220; (804) 355-2001;
  carol@firehousetheatre.org, www.firehousetheatre.org
Artistic Director

Types of material: full-length plays, solo pieces. **Frequency:** annual. **Remuneration:** $1000 1st prize, staged reading, possible production; $500 2nd prize. **Guidelines:** U.S. resident; unpublished, unproduced play; no translations or adaptations; 1 submission limit. **Submission procedure:** agent submission or script with professional letter of recommendation by director, literary manager or dramaturg; see website for guidelines. **Deadline:** 30 Jun.

FREMONT CENTRE THEATRE NEW PLAYWRIGHT CONTEST

California Performing Arts Centre (CPAC); 1000 Fremont Ave;
  South Pasadena, CA 91030; (626) 441-5977, FAX 441-5976;
  fct@fremontcentretheatre.com, www.fremontcentretheatre.com
Carol Doehring, *Contest Manager*

Types of material: full-length plays, one-acts, plays for young audiences (suitable for grades 6–12). **Frequency:** annual. **Remuneration:** $350 1st prize, staged reading; $250 2nd prize, rehearsed reading; $100 3rd prize, rehearsed reading. **Guidelines:** unpublished plays not produced professionally; all genres and age groups, especially plays based on historical events, persons or moments; plays about the African-American experience, modern or historical; comedies; maximum 10 characters. **Submission procedure:** script, 1-page synopsis, character breakdown, resume and $15 fee. **Deadline:** 30 Apr. **Notification:** 31 Oct.

GEORGE R. KERNODLE PLAYWRITING CONTEST

(see Kernodle Playwriting Contest)

GOSHEN COLLEGE PEACE PLAYWRITING CONTEST

1700 South Main St; Goshen, IN 46526; (574) 535-7393, FAX 535-7660;
  douglc@goshen.edu
Doug L. Caskey, *Director of Theater*

Types of material: one-acts. **Frequency:** biennial. **Remuneration:** $500 1st prize, production, room and board to attend rehearsals and/or performance; $100 2nd prize, possible production. **Guidelines:** 1 unproduced submission per writer, 15–50 minutes in length, exploring a "contemporary peace theme broadly defined." **Submission procedure:** script, 1-paragraph synopsis and resume; see website for details. **Deadline:** 31 Dec 2009. **Notification:** 31 May 2010.

HAROLD MORTON LANDON TRANSLATION AWARD

The Academy of American Poets; 584 Broadway, Suite 604;
New York, NY 10012; (212) 274-0343, ext 18; cevans@poets.org,
www.poets.org
CJ Evans, *Awards Coordinator*

Types of material: translations. **Frequency:** annual. **Remuneration:** $1000. **Guidelines:** U.S. citizen; published translation of verse, including verse drama, from any language into English verse; book must have been published in deadline year. **Submission procedure:** 3 copies of book (no manuscripts). **Deadline:** 31 Dec.

HELFORD PRIZE CONTEST

Jacksonville University; 2800 University Blvd N; Jacksonville, FL 32211;
(904) 256-7345, FAX 256-7375; whill@ju.edu, www.ju.edu
Bill Hill, *Dean*

Types of material: full-length plays. **Frequency:** annual. **Remuneration:** $10,000 first prize, full production, possible travel to see performances if play is produced within 2 years of prize. **Guidelines:** U.S. resident; play 90-120 minutes in length not previously published or performed; cast size 5-10. **Submission procedure:** script and application. **Deadline:** 15 May.

HENRICO THEATRE COMPANY ONE-ACT
PLAYWRITING COMPETITION

The County of Henrico; Division of Recreation and Parks; Box 27032;
Richmond, VA 23273-7032; (804) 501-5138, FAX 501-5284;
per22@co.henrico.va.us
Amy A. Perdue, *Cultural Arts Coordinator*

Types of material: one-acts, musicals. **Frequency:** annual. **Remuneration:** $300 1st prize, production; $200 2nd prize, possible production and video. **Guidelines:** unproduced, unpublished work; no controversial themes or "excessive language"; prefers small cast, simple set. **Submission procedure:** 2 copies of script; write for guidelines. **Deadline:** 1 Jul. **Notification:** 31 Dec.

HRC'S ANNUAL PLAYWRITING CONTEST

Hudson River Classics, Inc; Box 940; Hudson, NY 12534; (518) 851-7244
Jan M. Grice, *President*

Types of material: full-length plays. **Frequency:** annual. **Remuneration:** $500, staged reading. **Guidelines:** Northeast playwright; unpublished play 60–90 minutes in length. **Submission procedure:** script, bio and $5 fee. **Deadline:** 1 May; no submission before 1 Feb. **Notification:** Sep.

JACKIE WHITE MEMORIAL NATIONAL CHILDREN'S PLAYWRITING CONTEST

309 Parkade Blvd; Columbia, MO 65202; (573) 874-5628;
    bybestsy@yahoo.com
Betsy Phillips, *Director*

Types of material: plays and musicals for family audiences. **Frequency:** annual. **Remuneration:** $500, possible production by Columbia Entertainment Company; all entrants receive written evaluation. **Guidelines:** unpublished original work, 60–90 minutes in length, with minimum 7 speaking characters of all ages, at least 7 developed in some detail. **Submission procedure:** script, character breakdown, act/scene synopsis, resume, application and $20 fee; include cassette or CD and score for musical; send SASE for guidelines. **Deadline:** 1 Jun. **Notification:** 30 Aug.

JAMES D. PHELAN AWARD IN LITERATURE

Intersection for the Arts/The San Francisco Foundation; 446 Valencia St;
    San Francisco, CA 94103; (415) 626-2787, FAX 626-1636;
    www.theintersection.org
Awards Coordinator

Types of material: full-length plays, one-acts, plays for young audiences. **Frequency:** annual. **Remuneration:** $2000. **Guidelines:** CA-born author 20–35 years of age as of deadline; unpublished play-in-progress. **Submission procedure:** script and application; send SASE for guidelines and application. **Deadline:** 31 Mar; no submission before 1 Jan. **Notification:** Sep.

JANE CHAMBERS PLAYWRITING AWARD

Women & Theatre Program, ATHE; Department of Theater, Fine Arts Center
    112; University of Massachusetts Amherst; 151 Presidents Drive;
    Amherst, MA 01003; www.athe.org/wtp
Priscilla Page, *Award Submissions*

Types of material: full-length plays, one-acts, solo pieces, performance-art pieces. **Frequency:** annual. **Remuneration:** $1000, free registration and rehearsed reading at the Association for Theatre in Higher Education Conference in early Aug; student submissions eligible for $250 Student Award and staged reading at the Women & Theatre Conference in Jul. **Guidelines:** work by a woman that reflects a feminist perspective and contains a majority of roles for women; special interest in work by and about women from a diversity of positions in respect to race, class, sexual preference, physical ability, age and geographical region; experimentation with dramatic form encouraged; 1 submission limit; award administered by the Association for Theatre in Higher Education (see Membership and Service Organizations) and Women & Theatre Program. **Submission procedure:** 3 copies of script, synopsis, resume, application and $15 fee ($10 fee for students and under-employed); no electronic submissions; see website for guidelines and application. **Deadline:** 15 Feb; 1 Mar for student submission. **Notification:** 30 Jun.

JEWEL BOX THEATRE PLAYWRIGHTING AWARD

3700 North Walker; Oklahoma City, OK 73118-7031; (405) 521-1786,
    FAX 525-6562

Charles Tweed, *Production Director*

Types of material: full-length plays. **Frequency:** annual. **Remuneration:** $500, possible production. **Guidelines:** unproduced ensemble play "with emphasis on character rather than spectacle." **Submission procedure:** 2 copies of script, entry form, application and $10 fee; send SASE in Oct for guidelines and forms. **Deadline:** 15 Jan. **Notification:** Apr.

JOHN GASSNER MEMORIAL PLAYWRITING AWARD

New England Theatre Conference Inc.; 215 Knob Hill Dr; Hamden, NJ 06518;
    (617) 851-8535; mail@netconline.org, www.netconline.org

Types of material: full-length plays. **Frequency:** annual. **Remuneration:** $1000 1st prize; $500 2nd prize; staged reading, possible publication. **Guidelines:** unpublished play that has not had professional full production and is not under consideration for publication or professional production; 1 submission limit. **Submission procedure:** script with cover page, character breakdown, brief synopsis and statement that play has not been published or professionally produced and is not under consideration; $10 fee (waived for NETC members); SASP for acknowledgment of receipt; see website for guidelines. **Deadline:** 15 Apr. **Notification:** 1 Sep (winners only); script will not be returned. (See New England Theatre Conference in Membership and Service Organizations.)

KENNEDY CENTER AMERICAN COLLEGE THEATER FESTIVAL: MICHAEL KANIN PLAYWRITING AWARDS PROGRAM

The John F. Kennedy Center for the Performing Arts;
    Washington, DC 20566-0001; (202) 416-8857, FAX 416-8802;
    www.kcactf.org

Susan Shaffer, *Producing Director*
Gregg Henry, *Artistic Director*

THE DAVID MARK COHEN PLAYWRITING AWARD

Types of material: full-length plays, bills of related one-acts. **Frequency:** annual. **Remuneration:** $1000, up to $500 for travel, script-in-hand reading at annual Aug meeting of Association for Theatre in Higher Education (ATHE) (see Membership and Service Organizations), Dramatic Publishing Company (see Publication) contract offer to publish, license and market play. **Guidelines:** unpublished play or bill of related one-acts not produced professionally, produced by a KCACTF-participating college or university theatre program; see website for guidelines. **Submission procedure:** college or university which has entered production or staged reading of play in KCACTF registers work for awards program. **Deadline:** 1 Dec. **Dates:** Apr.

ISRAEL AND PALESTINE IN THE YOUNG AMERICAN MIND

(see The Quest for Peace and Playwriting Award below)

THE JEAN KENNEDY SMITH PLAYWRITING AWARD

Types of material: full-length plays, one-acts, adaptations, musicals. **Frequency:** annual. **Remuneration:** $2500, Dramatists Guild membership (see Membership and Service Organizations) and fellowship to attend prestigious playwriting program. **Guidelines:** writer enrolled as full-time student at college or university during year of production; play that explores the human experience of living with disabilities, produced by a KCACTF-participating college or university; see website for guidelines. **Submission procedure:** college or university that has entered production or staged reading of work in KCACTF registers work for awards program. **Deadline:** 1 Dec. **Dates:** Apr.

THE JOHN CAUBLE SHORT PLAY AWARDS PROGRAM

Types of material: one-acts, one-act adaptations. **Frequency:** annual. **Remuneration:** $1000; Dramatists Guild membership (see Membership and Service Organizations). **Guidelines:** writer enrolled as full-time student at college or university during year of production or during either of 2 years preceding production; one-act must be produced by a KCACTF-participating college or university; see website for guidelines. **Submission procedure:** college or university that has entered production or staged reading of work in KCACTF registers work for awards program. **Deadline:** 1 Dec. **Dates:** Apr.

THE KCACTF LATINO PLAYWRITING AWARD

Types of material: full-length plays, one-acts. **Frequency:** annual. **Remuneration:** $2500, internship to a prestigious playwriting retreat program; possible contract from Dramatic Publishing Company (see Publication) to publish, license and market winning play; $500 to the theatre department for producing the award-winning play. **Guidelines:** Latino writer enrolled as full-time student at KCACTF-participating college or university during year of production or during either of 2 years preceding production; see website for guidelines. **Submission procedure:** college or university that has entered production or staged reading of work in KCACTF registers work for awards program. **Deadline:** 1 Dec. **Dates:** Apr.

THE KCACTF MUSICAL THEATER AWARD

Types of material: musicals. **Frequency:** annual. **Remuneration:** $1000 for lyrics; $1000 for music; $1000 for book to producing college or university. **Guidelines:** at least 50% of writing team must be enrolled as full-time student(s) at college or university during year of production or during either of 2 years preceding production; original and copyrighted work produced by a KCACTF-participating college or university; see website for guidelines. **Submission procedure:** college or university that has entered production or staged reading of work in KCACTF registers work for awards program. **Deadline:** 1 Dec. **Dates:** Apr.

THE KCACTF NATIONAL SCIENCE PLAYWRITING AWARD

Types of material: full-length plays. **Frequency:** biennial. **Remuneration:** $3000, fellowship to attend Underground Railway Theater Company's professional staged reading of play in Cambridge, MA. **Guidelines:** writer enrolled as full-time student at college or university during year of production or during either of 2 years preceding production; new theme each award year; see website for guidelines. **Submission Procedure** college or university that has entered production or staged reading of work in KCACTF registers work for awards program. **Deadline:** 1 Dec . **Dates:** Apr.

THE KCACTF TEN-MINUTE PLAY AWARD

Types of material: one-acts. **Frequency:** annual. **Remuneration:** $1000 1st prize to best 10-minute play of 8 regional finalists, development work with director, dramaturg and actors, staged reading at KCACTF annual Apr festival. **Guidelines:** each region determines own submission criteria; see website for guidelines. **Submission procedure:** college or university that has entered production of work in KCACTF registers work for awards program; regional submissions from schools with no other entries will pay $20 fee per submission. **Deadline:** Nov. **Notification:** Dec. **Dates:** Jan and Feb regional festival; Apr national festival.

THE KCACTF THEATER FOR YOUTH PLAYWRITING AWARD

Types of material: full-length plays, adaptations, musicals. **Frequency:** annual. **Remuneration:** $1000, $1250 fellowship to attend the Kennedy Center's New Visions/New Voices festival (see Development). **Guidelines:** writer enrolled as full-time student at college or university during year of production or during either of the 2 years preceding production; play on theme appealing to young people from kindergarten–12th grade produced by a KCACTF-participating college or university; see website for guidelines. **Submission procedure:** college or university that has entered production or staged reading of work in KCACTF registers work for awards program. **Deadline:** 1 Dec. **Dates:** Apr.

THE LORRAINE HANSBERRY PLAYWRITING AWARD

Types of material: full-length plays, one-acts. **Frequency:** annual. **Remuneration:** $2500 1st prize for playwright, internship at the National Playwrights Conference (see Development), possible publication of play by Dramatic Publishing Company (see Publication), $750 to producing college or university; $1000 2nd prize to playwright, $500 to producing college or university. **Guidelines:** writer enrolled as full-time student at college or university during year of production or during either of 2 years preceding production; play dealing with the black experience produced by KCACTF-participating college or university; see website for guidelines. **Submission procedure:** college or university that has entered production or stated reading of work in KCACTF registers work for awards program. **Deadline:** 1 Dec. **Dates:** Apr.

THE NATIONAL STUDENT PLAYWRITING AWARD

Types of material: full-length plays, adaptations, musicals. **Frequency:** annual. **Remuneration:** $2500 for playwright, production at Kennedy Center during festival, publication by Samuel French (see Publication) with royalties, fellowship to attend Sundance Theatre Lab (see Development), Dramatists Guild membership (see Membership and Service Organizations), $1000 to producing college or university. **Guidelines:** writer enrolled as full-time student at college or university during year of production or during either of 2 years preceding production; work produced by KCACTF-participating college or university; see website for guidelines. **Submission procedure:** college or university that has entered production of work in KCACTF registers work for awards program. **Deadline:** 1 Dec. **Dates:** Apr.

THE PAULA VOGEL AWARD IN PLAYWRITING

Types of material: full-length plays. **Frequency:** annual. **Remuneration:** $2500, all expenses paid weeklong residency at Manhattan Theatre Source in Jun, where work will receive staged reading, producing department receives $500 for its support of the work; $1000 second prize, $250 to producing department for its support of the work. **Guidelines:** writer enrolled as full-time student at college or university during year of production or during either of 2 years preceding production; work produced by KCACTF-participating college or university; see website for guidelines; award given to play that "celebrates diversity and encourages tolerance while exploring issues of disempowered voices not traditionally considered mainstream." **Submission procedure:** college or university that has entered production or staged reading of work in KCACTF registers work for awards program. **Deadline:** 1 Dec. **Dates:** Apr.

THE QUEST FOR PEACE PLAYWRITING AWARD
(formerly Israel and Palestine in the Young American Mind)

Types of material: full-length plays, one-acts. **Frequency:** annual. **Remuneration:** $2500 full-length or $1000 one-act, fellowship to attend KCACTF Summer Playwriting Intensive. **Guidelines:** playwright enrolled as full-time student at college or university during year of production or during either of 2 years preceding production; work should "grapple with the complicated issues facing the Middle East, particularly Palestine and Israel"; see website for guidelines. **Submission procedure:** college or university that has entered production or staged reading of work in KCACTF registers work for awards program. **Deadline:** 1 Dec. **Dates:** Apr (residency in Jul).

THE ROSA PARKS PLAYWRITING AWARD

Types of material: full-length plays, one-acts. **Frequency:** annual. **Remuneration:** $2500 full-length, or $1000 one-act; fellowship to attend play development program. **Guidelines:** playwright must be student or faculty member in a U.S. college or university during year of production or during either of 2 years preceding production; award "recognizes the best student or faculty-written full-length or one-act play on the subject of social injustice and/or civil rights"; see website for guidelines. **Submission procedure:** college or university that has entered production or staged reading of work in KCACTF registers work for awards program. **Deadline:** 1 Dec. **Dates:** Apr.

KERNODLE PLAYWRITING CONTEST

(formerly George R. Kernodle Playwriting Contest)
Department of Drama; 619 Kimpel Hall; University of Arkansas;
    Fayetteville, AR 72701; (479) 575-2953, FAX 575-7602;
    rdgross@uark.edu
Roger Gross, *Director*

Types of material: one-acts. **Frequency:** annual. **Remuneration:** $300 1st prize; $200 2nd prize; $100 3rd prize; possible staged reading or production. **Guidelines:** unproduced, unpublished play, maximum 60 minutes in length; no restriction on style or subject matter; 3 submission limit. **Submission procedure:** script with letter stating script has not received full production; $3 fee per submission; SASE or SASP for return of script or acknowledgement of receipt. **Deadline:** 1 Jun; no submission before 1 Jan. **Notification:** 1 Nov.

KUMU KAHUA THEATRE/UHM DEPARTMENT OF THEATRE & DANCE PLAYWRITING CONTEST

46 Merchant St; Honolulu, HI 96813; (808) 536-4222, FAX 536-4226;
    kumukahuatheatre@hawaiiantel.net; kumukahua.org
Harry Wong III, *Artistic Director, Kumu Kahua Theatre*

HAWAI'I PRIZE

Types of material: full-length plays. **Frequency:** annual. **Remuneration:** $500. **Guidelines:** unproduced play set in HI or dealing with some aspect of HI experience; previous entries ineligible. **Submission procedure:** write for application and guidelines. **Deadline:** 2 Jan. **Notification:** May.

PACIFIC RIM PRIZE

Types of material: full-length plays. **Frequency:** annual. **Remuneration:** $400. **Guidelines:** unproduced play set in or dealing with Pacific Islands, Pacific Rim or Pacific Asian-American experience; previous entries ineligible. **Submission procedure:** write for application and guidelines. **Deadline:** 2 Jan. **Notification:** May.

RESIDENT PRIZE

Types of material: full-length plays, one-acts. **Frequency:** annual. **Remuneration:** $200. **Guidelines:** resident of HI at time of submission; previous entries ineligible. **Submission procedure:** write for application and guidelines. **Deadline:** 2 Jan. **Notification:** May.

LAMIA INK! INTERNATIONAL ONE-PAGE PLAY COMPETITION

Box 202; Prince St Station; New York, NY 10012; cjlamia@aol.com,
    www.lamiaink.org/opp.shtml
(Ms.) Cortland Jessup, *Artistic Director*

Types of material: 1-page plays. **Frequency:** annual. **Remuneration:** $200, publication in *Lamia Ink!* magazine for winner and all finalist plays. **Guidelines:** submission must be 1 page only; 3 submission limit; send SASE for guidelines or email (type "OPP" in subject line). **Submission procedure:** script, SASE for response and $2 fee per submission or $5 for 3 submissions. **Deadline:** postmarked by 15 Mar. **Notification:** 15 May.

L. ARNOLD WEISSBERGER AWARD

Box 428; Williamstown, MA 01267-0428;
Jun–Aug: (413) 458-3200, FAX 458-3147;
Sep–May (New York): (212) 395-9090, FAX 395-9099;
    www.wtfestival.org
Justin Waldman, *Artistic Associate*

Types of material: full-length plays. **Frequency:** annual. **Remuneration:** $10,000, publication by Samuel French (see Publication). **Guidelines:** 1 unpublished script not professionally produced or scheduled for production prior to 31 Dec; award administered by the Williamstown Theatre Festival (see Production and Development). **Submission procedure:** agent submission or script with nomination from TCG member theatre only. **Deadline:** postmarked by 10 Jun. **Notification:** winter.

LOS ANGELES DESIGNERS' THEATRE

Box 1883; Studio City, CA 91614-0883; (323) 650-9600,
    654-2700 (TDD), FAX 654-3210; ladesigners@juno.com
Richard Niederberg, *Artistic Director*

Types of material: full-length plays, bills of related one-acts, translations, adaptations, plays for young audiences, musicals, operas, solo pieces. **Frequency:** year-round. **Remuneration:** negotiable commissioning fee, possible travel to attend rehearsals if developmental work is needed. **Guidelines:** commissioning program for work with commercial potential that has not received professional full production, is not under option and is free of commitment to specific director, actors or other personnel; large casts and multiple sets welcome; prefers controversial material. **Submission procedure:** proposal or synopsis and resume; include cassette or CD for musical; materials will not be returned. **Deadline:** year-round. **Notification:** 4 months minimum.

MAXIM MAZUMDAR NEW PLAY COMPETITION

Alleyway Theatre; 1 Curtain Up Alley; Buffalo, NY 14202-1911;
    (716) 852-2600, FAX 852-2266; email@alleyway.com
Literary Manager

Types of material: full-length plays, one-acts, musicals. **Frequency:** annual. **Remuneration:** $400, production for full-length play or musical; $100 and production for one-act play or musical. **Guidelines:** unproduced full-length work minimum 90 minutes in length with cast limit of 10 and unit set or simple set, or unproduced one-act maximum 20 minutes in length with cast limit of 6 and simple set; prefers work with "unconventional setting that explores the boundaries of theatricality"; 1 submission limit in each category. **Submission procedure:** script, character breakdown and resume; include CD of complete score for musicals; $25 fee per playwright. **Deadline:** 1 Jul. **Notification:** 1 Oct for finalists; 1 Nov for winners.

McLaren Memorial Comedy Play Writing Competition

Midland Community Theatre; 2000 West Wadley Ave; Midland, TX 79705;
(432) 682-2544, FAX 682-6136; www.mctmidland.org
Coordinator

Types of material: full-length plays, one-acts, plays for young audiences. **Frequency:** annual. **Remuneration:** $400 for full-length play; $200 for one-act; finalists in each category receive staged reading. **Guidelines:** play not produced professionally; comedies only; see website for guidelines. **Submission procedure:** script, character breakdown and $15 fee per play. **Deadline:** 28 Feb; no submission before 1 Jan. **Notification:** summer. **Dates:** Sep.

Met Life Foundation Nuestras Voces
National Playwriting Competition

Repertorio Español; 138 East 27th St; New York, NY 10016;
aav@repertorio.org, www.repertorio.org
Allison Astor-Vargas, *Special Projects Manager*

Types of material: full-length plays. **Frequency:** annual. **Remuneration:** $3000 1st prize, production and royalties; $2000 2nd prize; $1000 3rd prize; 2 runners-up receive $500; finalists receive staged reading. **Guidelines:** unpublished work not produced professionally; Hispanic themes, characters and subjects; written in Spanish or English; see website for application. **Submission procedure:** 2 copies of script and application. **Deadline:** Jun. (See Repertorio Español in Production.)

The Mickey Kaplan New American Play Prize

Cincinnati Playhouse in the Park; Box 6537; Cincinnati, OH 45206-0537;
(513) 345-2242; www.cincyplay.com
Literary Associate

Types of material: full-length plays, adaptations, musicals. **Frequency:** annual. **Remuneration:** $20,000, production, travel and housing to attend rehearsals. **Guidelines:** U.S. citizen; 1 submission that has not received full professional production (previous readings/workshops allowed); no translations; special interest in plays that take linguistic and/or stylistic risks; see website for guidelines. **Submission procedure:** agent submission of full script or 10-page dialogue sample, 2-page maximum abstract including synopsis, character breakdown, bio or resume; include cassette or CD for musicals. **Deadline:** postmarked by 31 Dec; no submission before 1 Jun. Notification: 8 months.

MILDRED AND ALBERT PANOWSKI PLAYWRITING AWARD

Forest Roberts Theatre; Northern Michigan University;
   1401 Presque Isle Ave; Marquette, MI 49855-5634;
   (906) 227-2553, FAX 227-2567; www.nmu.edu/theatre
Playwriting Coordinator

Types of material: full-length plays, adaptations. **Frequency:** annual. **Remuneration:** $2000, production, travel, room and board for 1-week residency; summer workshop with dramaturg. **Guidelines:** 1 unpublished, unproduced submission; rewrites of previous entries ineligible. **Submission procedure:** script and SASE; write or see website for guidelines. **Deadline:** 31 Oct; no submission before 1 Aug. **Notification:** Apr.

MOUNTAIN PLAYHOUSE PLAYWRITING CONTEST

Box 205; Jennerstown, PA 15547; (814) 629-9201, ext 118, FAX 629-9201;
   info@mountainplayhouse.org, www.mountainplayhouse.org
Teresa Marafino, *Producer*

Types of material: full-length plays, adaptations. **Frequency:** annual. **Remuneration:** $3000, staged reading, consideration for full production in theatre's regular season. **Guidelines:** comedies only; cast limit of 8; see website for complete guidelines. **Submission procedure:** script. **Deadline:** 31 Dec. **Notification:** Jun.

MOVING ARTS PREMIERE ONE-ACT COMPETITION

Box 481145; Los Angeles, CA 90048; (323) 666-3259;
   info@movingarts.org, www.movingarts.org
Steve Lozier, *Managing Director*

Types of material: one-acts. **Frequency:** annual. **Remuneration:** $200, production in annual fall one-act festival. **Guidelines:** play not previously produced in L.A. area; 50-page maximum, single set, modest technical requirements. **Submission procedure:** script without author's name or address, cover letter, no fee for 1st submission ($10 per additional submission payable to Moving Arts); no submission before 1 Nov. **Deadline:** 31 Jan. **Notification:** summer/fall; scripts will not be returned.

NANTUCKET SHORT PLAY FESTIVAL AND COMPETITION

Box 48002; Ft. Lauderdale, FL 33348; nantucketshortplay@comcast.net
Jim Patrick, *Literary Manager*

Types of material: one-acts. **Frequency:** annual. **Remuneration:** $200; 1 or more staged readings for winning play and selected additional plays as part of Nantucket Theatrical Productions' 3 annual festivals. **Guidelines:** play that has not received Equity production, maximum 40 pages in length, minimal production demands. **Submission procedure:** email or send SASE for guidelines. **Deadline:** 1 Aug. **Notification:** 2 months.

NATF, INC. ANNUAL SCRIPT COMPETITION

The National Audio Theatre Festivals Inc.; Box 3535; Damascus, OR 97030;
(503) 465-5081; www.natf.org
A. Nannette Taylor, *Executive Director*

Types of material: radio plays. **Frequency:** annual. **Remuneration:** $800 split among top 3 winners, workshop production, published in *NATF Annual Script Book.* **Guidelines:** original radio plays only maximum 25 minutes in length; "dialogue that demonstrates how sound can color content"; strong female roles and multicultural viewpoints encouraged; 1 submission limit. **Submission procedure:** 4 copies of script in radio format, CD in PDF format, cover letter stating authorship and $25 fee. **Deadline:** 15 Nov. **Notification:** Apr. (See The National Audio Theatre Festivals in Membership and Service Organizations.)

NATHAN MILLER HISTORY PLAY CONTEST

Tribute Productions; Sprenger-Lang Foundation; 1614 20th St NW;
Washington, DC 20009; (202) 518-2023, FAX 518-0228;
lvandruff@sprengerandlang.com

Types of material: full-length plays. **Frequency:** annual. **Remuneration:** $2000 1st prize, staged reading, travel and housing; $1000 2nd prize. **Guidelines:** play not previously produced and not under option; play must "elucidate a significant event, movement or era in American social, intellectual or political history"; maximum 120 pages, cast limit of 10; special interest in plays with multicultural themes or plays that incorporate music; prior readings, workshops or school productions must be disclosed. **Submission procedure:** 1 script with full contact information, 3 blind script copies, 4 copies of 1-paragraph synopsis. **Deadline:** 31 Dec. **Notification:** mid-summer.

NATIONAL CHILDREN'S THEATRE FESTIVAL

Actors' Playhouse at the Miracle Theatre; 280 Miracle Mile;
Coral Gables, FL 33134; (305) 444-9293, ext 615, FAX 444-4181;
maulding@actorsplayhouse.org, www.actorsplayhouse.org
Earl Maulding, *Director of Theatre for Young Audiences*

Types of material: musicals for young audiences. **Frequency:** annual. **Remuneration:** $500 prize, production, travel and housing to attend festival (based on availability). **Guidelines:** unpublished musical 45–60 minutes in length for young people ages 5–12 with cast limit of 8 (may play multiple roles) and minimal sets suitable for touring; translations and adaptations eligible only if writer owns copyright to material; special interest in bilingual (Spanish/English) musicals and work dealing with social issues, including multiculturalism in today's society. **Submission procedure:** script, application and $10 fee; include score and vocal cassette or CD; write or see website for guidelines. **Deadline:** 1 Apr. **Notification:** Nov. **Dates:** Apr.

NATIONAL LATINO PLAYWRITING AWARD

Arizona Theatre Company; 40 East 14th St; Tucson, AZ 85701;
    (520) 884-8210, ext 5510, FAX 628-9129
Elaine Romero, *Playwright-in-Residence*

Types of material: full-length plays, adaptations. **Frequency:** annual. **Remuneration:** $1000. **Guidelines:** playwright of Latino heritage residing in U.S. or U.S. territories or Mexico; 1 unproduced, unpublished submission written in English, Spanish or both languages, minimum 50 pages. **Submission procedure:** script (with English translation if original is in Spanish), 1 page cover letter including development history, synopsis and bio. **Deadline:** 31 Dec. **Notification:** summer. (See Arizona Theatre Company in Production.)

NATIONAL TEN-MINUTE PLAY CONTEST

Actors Theatre of Louisville; 316 West Main St; Louisville, KY 40202-4218;
    (502) 584-1265, FAX 584-1265; www.actorstheatre.org
Amy Wegener, *Literary Manager*

Types of material: one-acts. **Frequency:** annual. **Remuneration:** $1000 Heideman Award; possible production with royalty. **Guidelines:** U.S. citizen or resident; play maximum 10 pages in length that has not had Equity production; 1 submission limit; previous entries ineligible. **Submission procedure:** script; script will not be returned; write for guidelines. **Deadline:** postmarked by 1 Nov. **Notification:** Jun. (See Humana Festival in Development.)

NATIONAL TRANSLATION AWARD

American Literary Translators Association; The University of Texas at Dallas;
    Box 830688 (JO 51); Richardson, TX 75083-0688; (972) 883-2093,
    FAX 883-6303; linda.jolly@utdallas.edu, www.utdallas.edu/alta
Linda Jolly, *Administrative Assistant*

Types of material: translations. **Frequency:** annual. **Remuneration:** $2500. **Guidelines:** book-length translation from any language into English published in U.S. or Canada during year preceding deadline. **Submission procedure:** no submission by translator; publisher nominates translation and submits 4 copies of book, cover letter and $25 fee. **Deadline:** 31 Mar. **Notification:** fall.

NEW AMERICAN COMEDY (NAC) WORKSHOP

Ukiah Players Theatre; 1041 Low Gap Rd; Ukiah, CA 95482;
    (707) 462-1210, FAX 462-1790; nac@ukiahplayerstheatre.org

Types of material: full-length plays. **Frequency:** biennial. **Remuneration:** $50 per performance for play selected for full production (6–8 performances); $25 each per performance for 2 plays chosen as staged readings; up to $500 travel, housing to attend 1-week workshop and $25 per diem if selected for developmental workshop. **Guidelines:** unproduced, unpublished comedies only; playwright must be available to participate in 1-week developmental workshop; prefers small cast, simple set. **Submission procedure:** script, 1-page plot summary, scenic requirements, character breakdown, estimated running time, resume and application; email or write for guidelines. **Deadline:** 30 Nov 2009. **Notification:** May 2010. **Dates:** Jun 2010.

NEW PROFESSIONAL THEATRE WRITERS FESTIVAL

229 West 42nd St, Suite 501; New York, NY 10036; newprof@aol.com,
    www.newprofessionaltheatre.com
Literary Manager

Types of material: full-length plays, musicals. **Frequency:** annual. **Remuneration:** $1000, 2-week residency with dramaturg, staged reading, possible production. **Guidelines:** African-American writer. **Submission procedure:** script, resume and SASP for acknowledgment of receipt; include cassette for musical. **Deadline:** 1 Jun. **Notification:** Sep.

NEW ROCKY MOUNTAIN VOICES

Westcliffe Center for the Performing Arts; Box 790; Westcliffe, CO 81252;
    (719) 783-3004, FAX (949) 499-3614; wcpa@ris.net,
    www.westcliffecenter.org
Anne Kimbell Relph, *President*

Types of material: one-acts, 10-minute plays, plays for family audiences. **Frequency:** annual. **Remuneration:** $200 1st place, workshop production by Westcliffe Center Players; $200 2nd place; 3 honorable mentions. **Guidelines:** playwright must live or attend school in AZ, CO, NM or UT; one-acts, 10-minute plays; cast limit of 6–8; 1 set; multigenerational cast preferred. **Submission procedure:** 4 copies of script, 1-page synopsis and bio; SASE if script is to be returned; $5 fee. **Deadline:** 1 Apr. **Notification:** 30 Jun.

NEW YORK CITY 15 MINUTE PLAY FESTIVAL

Turnip Theatre Company; c/o AGT; 145 West 46th St; New York, NY 10036;
    (212) 869-9808, FAX 869-9807; liz@americanglobe.org
Liz Keefe, *Executive Director*

Types of material: one-acts. **Frequency:** annual. **Remuneration:** $100–$300 for festival winner, production; $25 royalty for all plays presented. **Guidelines:** one-acts maximum 15 pages; prefers work not produced in New York City; 1 submission limit. **Submission procedure:** send SASE or email for guidelines before submitting. **Deadline:** 15 Dec. **Notification:** mid-Feb. **Dates:** Apr.

OGLEBAY INSTITUTE TOWNGATE PLAYWRITING CONTEST

Stifel Fine Arts Center; 1330 National Rd; Wheeling, WV 26003;
    (304) 242-7700, FAX 242-7767
Performing Arts Department

Types of material: full-length plays. **Frequency:** annual. **Remuneration:** $300, production, partial travel to attend performances. **Guidelines:** unpublished, unproduced play, simple set. **Submission procedure:** script and resume. **Deadline:** 30 Dec. **Notification:** 1 May.

PEN/BOOK OF THE MONTH CLUB TRANSLATION PRIZE
(see PEN Translation Prize)

PEN CENTER USA LITERARY AWARDS
c/o Antioch University Los Angeles; 400 Corporate Pointe;
  Culver City, CA 90230; (310) 862-1555, ext 362, FAX 862-1556;
  awards@penusa.org, www.penusa.org

Types of material: full-length plays, screenplays, teleplays. **Frequency:** annual. **Remuneration:** $1000 award in each of 10 categories, including drama, screenwriting and television writing. **Guidelines:** writer residing west of Mississippi River; screenplays and teleplays must be full-length; script first produced during calendar year preceding deadline. **Submission procedure:** 4 copies of script, playbill or press materials verifying eligibility, application and $35 fee. **Deadline:** 29 Jan.

THE PEN IS A MIGHTY SWORD NEW PLAY COMPETITION
The Virtual Theatre Project; Box 29340; Los Angeles, CA 90029-0340;
  (323) 377-8077; info@virtualtheatreproject.org,
  www.virtualtheatreproject.org
Whit Andrews, *Literary Manager*

Types of material: full-length plays. **Frequency:** biennial. **Remuneration:** $2000 1st prize, reading; $1000 2nd prize, reading; $500 3rd prize, reading; $100 each to 7 runners-up. **Guidelines:** unproduced play; prefers scripts 90–120 pages in length. **Submission procedure:** 1 copy of script; write, call or see website for details. **Deadline:** postmarked by 28 Feb 2009. **Notification:** 30 Jun 2009.

PEN/LAURA PELS FOUNDATION AWARD FOR DRAMA
PEN American Center; 588 Broadway, Suite 303; New York, NY 10012;
  (212) 334-1660, FAX 334-2181; nick@pen.org, www.pen.org
Nick Burd, *Coordinator*

Types of material: full-length plays. **Frequency:** annual. **Remuneration:** $5000. **Guidelines:** mid-career English-language playwright who has had at least 2 full-length plays professionally produced in theatres 299 seats or larger; translations ineligible. **Submission procedure:** playwright must be nominated by professional colleague through letter of support accompanied by list of candidate's produced work; see website for nomination guidelines. **Deadline:** 16 Jan; no submission before 1 Sep. **Notification:** spring.

PEN TRANSLATION PRIZE
(formerly PEN/Book of the Month Club Translation Prize)
PEN American Center; 588 Broadway, Suite 303; New York, NY 10012;
  (212) 334-1660, FAX 334-2181; nick@pen.org, www.pen.org
Nick Burd, *Coordinator*

Types of material: translations. **Frequency:** annual. **Remuneration:** $3000. **Guidelines:** book-length translation from any language into English published in U.S.

in 2008; no self-published books. **Submission procedure:** 3 copies of book; may be submitted by publisher, agent or translator; see website for details. **Deadline:** 16 Dec; no submission before 1 Sep. **Notification:** spring.

PERISHABLE THEATRE INTERNATIONAL WOMEN'S PLAYWRITING FESTIVAL

Perishable Theatre; Box 23132; Providence, RI 02903; (401) 331-2695,
    FAX 331-7811; wpf@perishable.org, www.perishable.org

Types of material: one-acts, musicals, solo pieces. **Frequency:** biennial. **Remuneration:** 3 writers receive $500, production, travel plus room and board to see production; possible publication in anthology. **Guidelines:** women writers only; plays that have not received a full professional production; prefers plays 10–60 minutes long. **Submission procedure:** script and $10 fee. **Deadline:** 15 Jan 2010. **Notification:** May 2010.

PLAYS FOR THE 21ST CENTURY

The Playwrights Theater; 6732 Orangewood Dr; Dallas, TX 75220;
    (469) 374-9639; alberto_rubio@sbcglobal.net,
    www.playwrightstheater.org

Types of material: full-length plays, one-acts, bills of related one-acts. **Frequency:** annual. **Remuneration:** $750 1st prize; $500 2nd prize; $250 3rd prize; $250 prize for one-act; 1st prize may receive reading, funding permitting. **Guidelines:** unpublished play not produced professionally at time of submission; see website for details. **Submission procedure:** script, application and $20 fee; electronic submission only; see website for application and guidelines. **Deadline:** varies; see website.

PLAYWRIGHTS FIRST AWARD

c/o The National Arts Club; 15 Gramercy Park S; New York, NY 10003;
    (212) 744-1312

Types of material: full-length plays. **Frequency:** annual. **Remuneration:** $1000 1st prize; reading for selected plays. **Guidelines:** 1 unproduced play; no translations, adaptations, musicals or co-written work. **Submission procedure:** script and resume; script will not be returned. **Deadline:** 15 Oct. **Notification:** May.

REVA SHINER FULL-LENGTH PLAY CONTEST

Bloomington Playwrights Project; 107 West 9th Street;
    Bloomington, IN 47404; (812) 334-1188; bppwrite@newplays.org,
    www.newplays.org
Richard Perez, *Artistic Director*

Types of material: full-length plays, musicals. **Frequency:** annual. **Remuneration:** $500, staged reading and full production. **Guidelines:** unpublished, unproduced work 75-150 minutes in length suitable for production in small 92-seat theatre; special interest in innovative work, small-scale musicals; prefers simple set; write or see website for guidelines. **Submission procedure:** script, cover letter and $10 fee; include cassette for musical; scripts will not be returned. **Deadline:** 31 Oct. **Notification:** Mar. (See Bloomington Playwrights Project in Production.)

REVERIE PRODUCTIONS NEXT GENERATION PLAYWRITING CONTEST

Reverie Productions; 520 8th Ave, Suite 317; New York, NY 10018;
(212) 244-7803; info@reverieproductions.org,
www.reverieproductions.org

Types of material: full-length plays, radio plays. **Frequency:** annual. **Remuneration:** $300 and workshop or production. **Guidelines:** work not produced in New York City area; special interest in plays that deal with social and political issues; see website for guidelines. **Submission procedure:** script and application; see website for entry fee. **Deadline:** 15 Dec. **Notification:** 1 May.

ROBERT J. PICKERING AWARD FOR PLAYWRITING EXCELLENCE

Coldwater Community Theater; 89 Division St; Coldwater, MI 49036;
(517) 278-2389, FAX 279-8095
J. Richard Colbeck, *Award Chairman*

Types of material: full-length plays, one-acts, adaptations, plays for young audiences, musicals. **Frequency:** annual. **Remuneration:** $300 1st place, full production; $100 2nd place; $50 3rd place. **Guidelines:** unproduced play. **Submission procedure:** script. **Deadline:** 31 Dec. **Notification:** 28 Feb.

THE RUBY LLOYD APSEY AWARD

University of Alabama at Birmingham Theatre Department; ASC 255;
1530 3rd Ave S; Birmingham, AL 35294-1263; (205) 934-3236,
FAX 934-8076; leeshack@uab.edu, theatre.hum.uab.edu
Will York, *Department Chair*

Types of material: full-length plays, bills of related one-acts, translations. **Frequency:** biennial. **Remuneration:** $1000, staged reading, possible full production; travel and housing if play is produced. **Guidelines:** plays confronting racial or ethnic issues, especially those calling for ethnically diverse or multiracial casting. **Submission procedure:** script and character/scene breakdown. **Deadline:** postmarked by 5 Dec 2008. **Notification:** 10 Apr 2009 (via website).

SANTA CRUZ ACTORS' THEATRE FULL-LENGTH PLAY CONTEST

1001 Center St, Suite 12; Santa Cruz, CA 95060; (831) 425-1003,
FAX 425-7560; actors@sbcglobal.net, www.sccat.org
Wendy Adler, *Office Manager*

Types of material: full-length plays. **Frequency:** annual. **Remuneration:** $200, staged reading, possible full production. **Guidelines:** unpublished play not produced professionally. **Submission procedure:** 3 copies of script and $15 fee; see website for guidelines. **Deadline:** 1 Oct. **Notification:** Mar.

SANTA FE PERFORMING ARTS NEW PLAYWRIGHTS COMPETITION

Box 22372; Santa Fe, NM 87502; (505) 982-7992, FAX 982-7993;
   office@sfperformingarts.org, www.sfperformingarts.org
W. Nicholas Sabato, *Executive Artistic Director*

Types of material: full-length plays, one-acts. **Frequency:** annual. **Remuneration:** $1000, full production. **Guidelines:** American playwright; play not previously produced; prefers small casts. **Submission procedure:** brief synopsis and character breakdown. **Deadline:** 1 Sep. **Notification:** spring.

THE SCHOLASTIC WRITING AWARDS

557 Broadway; New York, NY 10012; (212) 343-6892, FAX 389-3939;
   a&wgeneralinfo@scholastic.com, www.artandwriting.org,
   www2.scholastic.com/browse/home.jsp

Types of material: all genres, including full-length and one-act dramatic scripts, screenplays teleplays and radio plays. **Frequency:** annual. **Remuneration:** $10,000 scholarship toward college tuition for author of each of 5 best senior portfolios. **Guidelines:** 2 categories: for high school seniors only, portfolios of 3–8 pieces (fiction, poetry, drama, etc.); for students grades 7–12, individual pieces in various categories, including drama, film, television and radio scripts; unpublished script maximum 50 pages in length. **Submission procedure:** script and application. **Deadline:** varies from state to state; Nov through mid-Jan; exact date TBA. **Notification:** Apr.

SHORT GRAIN CONTEST

Grain Magazine; Box 67; Saskatoon, SK S7K 3K1; Canada; (306) 244-2828,
   FAX 244-0255; grainmag@sasktel.net, www.grainmagazine.ca
Kent Bruyneel, *Editor*

Types of material: monologues. **Frequency:** annual. **Remuneration:** 3 prizes of $500. **Guidelines:** unpublished, unproduced monologue not submitted elsewhere; 500-word maximum. **Submission procedure:** U.S. and international entries: application and $30 fee plus $6 U.S. postage for subscription mailing cost; Canadian entries: entry form and $30 fee for first 2 entries ($8 fee for 3 additional entries); fee includes 1-year subscription; write or email for guidelines. **Deadline:** 31 Jan. **Notification:** 30 Apr.

SHUBERT FENDRICH MEMORIAL PLAYWRITING CONTEST

Pioneer Drama Service; Box 4267; Englewood, CO 80155-4267;
   (303) 779-4035, FAX 779-4315; submissions@pioneerdrama.com,
   www.pioneerdrama.com
Lori Conary, *Editor*

Types of material: full-length plays, one-acts, translations, adaptations, plays for young audiences, musicals. **Frequency:** annual. **Remuneration:** publication with $1000 advance on royalties (10% book royalty, 50% performance royalty); all entries considered for publication. **Guidelines:** produced, unpublished work maximum 90 minutes in length, subject matter and language appropriate for schools and community theatres; prefers work with majority of female roles; minimal set requirements; authors currently published by Pioneer Drama Service (see Publication) are not eligible. **Submission procedure:** script with proof of production (e.g., program, reviews); include score or cassette for musical; send SASE for guidelines. **Deadline:** year-round; 1 winner selected per calendar year. **Notification:** 1 Jun.

SOUTHEASTERN THEATRE CONFERENCE NEW PLAY PROJECT

Box 9868; Greensboro, NC 27429-0868; (336) 272-3645;
   setc@setc.org, setc.org
Submissions

Types of material: full-length plays, bill of related one-acts. **Frequency:** annual. **Remuneration:** $1000, staged reading at SETC Annual Convention, travel, room and board to attend convention. **Guidelines:** resident of state in SETC region (AL, FL, GA, KY, MS, NC, SC, TN, VA, WV); unproduced work; limit of 1 full-length submission or collection of one-acts. **Submission procedure:** script and application. **Deadline:** 1 Jun. **Notification:** Nov.

SOUTHERN PLAYWRIGHTS COMPETITION

228 Stone Center; Jacksonville State University; Jacksonville, AL 36265;
   (256) 782-5414, FAX 782-5441; swhitton@jsu.edu,
   www.jsu.edu/depart/english/southpla.htm
Steven J. Whitton, *Coordinator*

Types of material: full-length plays, solo pieces. **Frequency:** annual. **Remuneration:** $1000, production, housing to attend rehearsals. **Guidelines:** native or resident of AL, AR, FL, GA, KY, LA, MS, NC, SC, TN, TX, VA or WV; 1 unpublished, original submission that focuses on Southern experience and has not received Equity production. **Submission procedure:** script, synopsis and application; write for guidelines after Sep. **Deadline:** 15 Jan. **Notification:** 31 May.

STAGE INTERNATIONAL SCRIPT COMPETITION

Professional Artists Lab; CNSI-MC 6105; University of California;
   Santa Barbara, CA 93106-6105; stage@cnsi.ucsb.edu,
   www.cnsi.ucsb.edu/stage

Types of material: full-length plays, adaptations, multimedia works. **Frequency:** biennial. **Remuneration:** $10,000, staged reading or other developmental opportunity. **Guidelines:** unpublished works not produced or reviewed professionally (prior readings and workshops are acceptable) that explore scientific and/or technological stories, themes, issues and/or events; works in English only; no science fiction; guidelines change each cycle; see website for complete information. **Submission procedure:** 3 copies of script, 1-page synopsis, bio or resume, artistic statement; online application form, printed confirmation page and cover letter; author name(s) or identification must not appear anywhere on the script, synopsis or artistic statement; see website for checklist. **Deadline:** 15 Dec 2009. **Notification:** 15 Jun 2010.

THE STANLEY DRAMA AWARD

Wagner College Theatre; 1 Campus Rd; Staten Island, NY 10301;
(718) 390-3157, FAX 390-3323; www.wagner.edu/stanley_drama/
Kevin Kane and Felicia J. Ruff, *Administrators*

Types of material: full-length plays, one-acts, musicals. **Frequency:** annual. **Remuneration:** $2000. **Guidelines:** unpublished, unproduced play or collection of one-acts; 1 submission limit. **Submission procedure:** script, CD or cassette for musicals, application and $20 fee; send SASE for guidelines and application. **Deadline:** 31 Oct. **Notification:** Apr.

SUMMERFIELD G. ROBERTS AWARD

Sons of the Republic of Texas; 1717 8th St; Bay City, TX 77414;
(979) 245-6644, FAX 244-3819; srttexas@srttexas.org,
www.srttexas.org
Janet Hickl, *Award Submissions*

Types of material: full-length plays. **Frequency:** annual. **Remuneration:** $2500. **Guidelines:** published or unplublished plays about the Republic of TX (1836–1846), completed during calendar year preceding deadline; see website for details. **Submission procedure:** 5 copies of script. **Deadline:** 15 Jan. **Notification:** Apr; scripts will not be returned.

THE SUSAN SMITH BLACKBURN PRIZE

3239 Avalon Pl; Houston, TX 77019; (713) 308-2842;
plays@blackburnprize.com, www.blackburnprize.org
Emilie S. Kilgore, *Founder and President*

Types of material: full-length plays. **Frequency:** annual. **Remuneration:** $20,000 1st prize plus signed Willem de Kooning print, made especially for Blackburn Prize; $5000 special commendation at the discretion of the judges; $1000 to each of the other finalists. **Guidelines:** woman playwright of any nationality writing in English; unproduced play or play professionally produced within 1 year of deadline; previous winners are not eligible. **Submission procedure:** no submission by playwright; professional artistic directors and literary managers of specified theatres are invited to nominate play and submit 2 copies of script; playwright may bring script to attention of eligible nominator; see website or send 63¢-postage SASE for guidelines, brochure and list of theatres eligible to nominate. **Deadline:** 20 Sep. **Notification:** Jan for finalists; Feb for winner.

TENNESSEE WILLIAMS/NEW ORLEANS LITERARY FESTIVAL ONE-ACT PLAY CONTEST

938 Lafayette St, Suite 514; New Orleans, LA 70113; (504) 234-0090;
info@tennesseewilliams.net, www.tennesseewilliams.net
Submissions

Types of material: one-acts. **Frequency:** annual. **Remuneration:** $1000, staged reading in Mar festival, full production in Mar festival the following year. **Guidelines:**

unpublished play maximum 60 minutes in length, not produced professionally; prefers minimal technical requirements and small casts with ages ranging from 20–40. **Submission procedure:** script, application and $25 fee (payable to Tennessee Williams/New Orleans Literary Festival); script will not be returned; send SASP for acknowledgment of receipt; see website ("Contests") for guidelines and application. **Deadline:** postmarked by 1 Nov; no submission before 15 Jul. **Notification:** winter. **Dates:** late Mar–1 Apr.

THEATRE CONSPIRACY ANNUAL NEW PLAY CONTEST

2711 Park Windsor Dr, #302; Ft. Myers, FL 33901; (239) 936-3239;
    www.theatreconspiracy.org
Bill Taylor, *Artistic Director*

Types of material: full-length plays. **Frequency:** annual. **Remuneration:** $700, production. **Guidelines:** play with no more than 3 previous productions, cast limit of 6, simple to moderate production demands. **Submission procedure:** script, 1-page synopsis, character breakdown, technical requirements, bio and $5 fee. **Deadline:** 30 Mar. **Notification:** Aug. **Dates:** late May–early Jun.

THEATRE OXFORD'S 10 MINUTE PLAY CONTEST

Box 1321; Oxford, MS 38655; www.10minuteplays.com
Submissions

Types of material: 10-minute plays. **Frequency:** annual. **Remuneration:** $1000 1st prize, full production; 4 finalists receive staged reading. **Guidelines:** play not previously produced, maximum 10 pages in length; no translations, adaptations, musicals or plays for young audiences; 1 submission limit; see website for guidelines. **Submission procedure:** script, character breakdown and $10 fee; author name should appear on the title page of script only; enclose SASP for acknowledgment of receipt; script will not be returned. **Deadline:** postmarked by 15 Feb. **Notification:** spring.

THEODORE WARD PRIZE FOR AFRICAN-AMERICAN PLAYWRIGHTS

Columbia College Chicago Theater/Music Center; 72 East 11th St;
    Chicago, IL 60605; (312) 344-6136, FAX 344-8077;
    chigochuck@aol.com
Chuck Smith, *Facilitator*

Types of material: full-length plays, translations, adaptations, solo pieces. **Frequency:** annual. **Remuneration:** $2000 1st prize, production, travel and housing to attend rehearsals; $500 2nd prize, staged reading. **Guidelines:** African-American U.S. resident; 1 full-length submission not produced professionally; translations and adaptations must be of material in public domain. **Submission procedure:** script, short synopsis, production history and brief resume; write for guidelines. **Deadline:** 1 Jul; no submission before 1 Apr. **Notification:** Nov.

TOWSON UNIVERSITY PRIZE FOR LITERATURE

Department of English; Towson University; Towson, MD 21252;
(410) 704-2871
Edwin Duncan, *Chair, Department of English*

Types of material: book or book-length manuscript; all literary genres eligible, including plays. **Frequency:** annual. **Remuneration:** $1000. **Guidelines:** resident of MD for 3 years at time of award; work published within 3 years prior to submission or scheduled for publication within the year. **Submission procedure:** publisher or playwright submits application and 5 copies of work; write for guidelines. **Deadline:** 15 Jun. **Notification:** 1 Dec.

TRUSTUS PLAYWRIGHTS' FESTIVAL

Trustus Theatre; Box 11721; Columbia, SC 29211-1721; (803) 254-9732,
FAX 771-9153; trustus88@aol.com, www.trustus.org
Jon Tuttle, *Literary Manager*

Types of material: full-length plays. **Frequency:** annual. **Remuneration:** $250, staged reading, 1-year development period followed by additional $500 and full production with travel and housing to attend opening. **Guidelines:** play not produced professionally; cast limit of 8; prefers challenging, innovative dramas and comedies; no musicals or plays for young audiences. **Submission procedure:** application, synopsis and resume; send SASE for guidelines and application. **Deadline:** 1 Feb; no submission before 1 Dec. **Notification:** 1 Jun. (See Trustus Theatre in Production.)

UNICORN THEATRE NEW PLAY DEVELOPMENT

3828 Main St; Kansas City, MO 64111; (816) 531-7529, ext 22,
FAX 531-0421
Herman Wilson, *Literary Assistant*

Types of material: full-length plays. **Frequency:** annual. **Remuneration:** $1000, production, possible travel and residency. **Guidelines:** unpublished play not produced professionally; contemporary (post-1950) themes and settings only; no musicals; special interest in social issues; cast limit of 10. **Submission procedure:** script, synopsis, character breakdown, resume, cover letter and SASP for response; SASE for contest results. **Deadline:** year-round. **Notification:** 8 months; scripts will not be returned.

UNIVERSITY OF LOUISVILLE GRAWEMEYER AWARD FOR MUSIC COMPOSITION

Grawemeyer Music Award Committee; School of Music;
University of Louisville; Louisville, KY 40292; (502) 852-1787,
FAX 852-0520; grawmus@louisville.edu,
www.grawemeyer.org/music/index.html

Types of material: music-theatre works, operas. **Frequency:** annual. **Remuneration:** $200,000 (paid in 5 annual installments of $40,000). **Guidelines:** works premiered between 2004–2008; entry must be sponsored by professional music organization or individual. **Submission procedure:** application, score, CD, supporting materials and $40 fee submitted jointly by composer and sponsor; see website for application and guidelines. **Deadline:** 12 Jan. **Dates:** spring (the year following award).

VERMONT PLAYWRIGHTS AWARD

The Valley Players; Box 441; Waitsfield, VT 05673-0441; (802) 583-6767; www.valleyplayers.com

Sharon Kellerman, *Coordinator*

Types of material: full-length plays. **Frequency:** annual. **Remuneration:** $1000, possible production. **Guidelines:** resident of ME, NH or VT; unproduced, unpublished play that has not won playwriting competition and is suitable for community group. **Submission procedure:** 2 copies of script and application; send SASE or see website for guidelines. **Deadline:** 1 Feb.

VSA ARTS PLAYWRIGHT DISCOVERY AWARD

818 Connecticut Ave NW, Suite 600; Washington, DC 20006; (800) 933-8721, (202) 737-0645 (TTY), FAX 429-0868; info@vsarts.org, www.vsarts.org

Types of material: one-acts. **Frequency:** annual. **Remuneration:** scholarship money; travel, room and board to attend production at The John F. Kennedy Center for the Performing Arts in Washington, DC. **Guidelines:** U.S. citizen in grades 6–12; unproduced, unpublished play maximum 40 pages in length for family audience that deals with experience of living with a disability; previous submission ineligible; 1 submission limit. **Submission procedure:** 2 copies of script and application; scripts will not be returned; write or see website for guidelines and application. **Deadline:** mid Apr.

THE WALDO AND GRACE C. BONDERMAN AWARDS

The Bonderman Playwriting for Youth at the Indiana Rep; 140 West Washington St; Indianapolis, IN 46204-3465; (317) 272-9322; dwebb@iupui.edu, www.indianarep.com/bonderman

Dorothy Webb, *Artistic Director*

Types of material: plays for young audiences. **Frequency:** biennial. **Remuneration:** 4 writers receive $1,000, rehearsed reading, travel and housing for rehearsals. **Guidelines:** play not currently in development at another theatre. **Submission procedure:** script and application. **Deadline:** 1 Aug. **Notification:** 15 Jan.

WILLIAM SAROYAN PRIZE FOR PLAYWRITING

Armenian Dramatic Arts Alliance (ADAA); 20 Concord Lane;
Cambridge, MA 02138; (617) 871-6764, FAX 491-1011;
    adaa@armeniandrama.org, www.armeniandrama.org
Lisa Kirazian, *Contest Administrator*

Types of material: full-length plays, adaptations. **Frequency:** biennial.
Remuneration: 1st place $10,000, production, travel for rehearsals and performance;
2nd and 3rd place win writing software. **Guidelines:** play written in English (no
translations) based on Armenian subject matter; play must have had professional
production or reading within 3 years of submission; 1 submission limit. **Application
procedure:** electronic submission preferred (PDF, Final Draft or MS Word); otherwise,
mail 4 copies of script, plus synopsis, character breakdown, resume and $20 fee.
Deadline: 15 Feb 2010. **Notification:** 31 Aug 2010.

WRITE A PLAY! NYC CONTEST

Box 5134; New York, NY 10185; (212) 594-5440;
    literary@youngplaywrights.org, youngplaywrights.org
Literary Associate

Types of material: full-length plays, one-acts, monologues (submissions from
elementary school students only). **Frequency:** annual. **Remuneration:** varies.
Guidelines: New York City students in grades K-12; writers 18 years of age or younger
automatically entered in Young Playwrights Festival National Playwriting Contest (see
listing this section); plays accepted in 3 categories: elementary school (K-5), junior high
school (6-8) and high school (9-12). **Submission procedure:** script with playwright's
name, date of birth, home address, phone number, school and grade on title page;
write or email for guidelines. **Deadline:** 1 Apr. **Notification:** 1 Jun.

WRITER'S DIGEST WRITING COMPETITION

700 East State St; Iola, WI 54990; (715) 445-4612, ext 13430;
    competition@fwpubs.com, www.writersdigest.com
Competition Coordinator

Types of material: full-length plays, screenplays, teleplays. **Frequency:** annual.
Remuneration: $3000 Grand Prize, travel expenses paid to New York City to meet
with editors and agents; $1000 1st prize; $500 2nd prize; $250 3rd prize (1st, 2nd and
3rd prize winners receive $100 worth of *Writer's Digest* books); $100 4th prize; $50 5th
prize; $25 6th-10th prize; all winners receive *Writer's Market Deluxe Edition* and 1-year
subscription to *Writer's Digest* magazine. **Guidelines:** unpublished, unproduced work,
not accepted by publisher or producer at time of submission; previous entries
ineligible. **Submission procedure:** 1-page synopsis, first 15 pages of script, entry
form and $15 fee; send SASE for guidelines. **Deadline:** 15 May. **Notification:** fall.
Dates: spring.

YALE DRAMA SERIES, DAVID C. HORN PRIZE

Yale University Press; Box 209040; New Haven, CT 06520; (203) 432-0960, FAX 436-1064; www.yalebooks.com

Types of material: full-length plays. **Frequency:** annual. **Remuneration:** $10,000, staged reading by Yale Repertory Theatre, travel, room and board for rehearsals and performance, possible publication by Yale University Press. **Guidelines:** unpublished, unproduced play in English by emerging writer. **Submission procedure:** contact or see website for details. **Deadline:** from 1 Jun to 15 Aug. **Notification:** Jun of the following year.

YEAR-END-SERIES (Y.E.S.) NEW PLAY FESTIVAL

Department of Theatre; Northern Kentucky University;
    Highland Heights, KY 41099; (859) 572-6303, FAX 572-6057;
    forman@nku.edu
Sandra Forman, *Project Director*

Types of material: full-length plays, adaptations, musicals. **Frequency:** biennial. **Remuneration:** 3 awards of $500, production, travel and expenses to attend final rehearsals and performance. **Guidelines:** unproduced work in which majority of roles can be handled by students; small orchestra for musicals; 1 submission limit. **Submission procedure:** script and application. **Deadline:** 30 Sep 2008. **Notification:** Dec 2008. **Dates:** 16–26 Apr 2009.

YOUNG CONNECTICUT PLAYWRIGHTS FESTIVAL

Maxwell Anderson Playwrights Series; Box 671; West Redding, CT 06896;
    (203) 270-2951
Bruce Post, *Dramaturg*

Types of material: full-length plays, one-acts, musicals, translations, adaptations, plays for young audiences, solo pieces. **Frequency:** annual. **Remuneration:** staged reading in May festival, certificate. **Guidelines:** CT resident ages 12–19 only; script maximum 60 pages in length. **Submission procedure:** script with playwright's name, date of birth, home address, phone number and name of school on title page; send SASE for guidelines. **Deadline:** 27 Mar. **Notification:** May. **Dates:** May.

YOUNG PLAYWRIGHTS FESTIVAL
NATIONAL PLAYWRITING CONTEST

Young Playwrights Inc; Box 5734; New York, NY 10185; (212) 594-5440;
    literary@youngplaywrights.org, youngplaywrights.org
Literary Associate

Types of material: full-length plays, one-acts. **Frequency:** annual. **Remuneration:** staged reading, travel and residency, consideration for full production, 1-year Dramatists Guild membership (see Membership and Service Organizations). **Guidelines:** playwright maximum 18 years of age as of deadline; submissions from playwrights of all backgrounds encouraged. **Submission procedure:** script with playwright's name, date of birth, home address, phone number and email on title page; write for guidelines. **Deadline:** 1 Dec. (See Young Playwrights Inc in Membership and Service Organizations.)

PUBLICATION

What is listed in this section?

Those who are primarily or exclusively play publishers, and literary magazines and small presses, all of whom accept work of unpublished writers.

How can I determine the best places to submit my play?

Think of these publishers as highly individual people looking for very particular kinds of material, which means you should find out as much as possible about their operations before submitting scripts. One of the best sources is the Council of Literary Magazines and Presses (154 Christopher St, Suite 3C; New York, NY 10014-9110; 212-741-9110; info@clmp.org, www.clmp.org), and their *Directory of Literary Magazines and Presses* (2008–09 edition; $15.00 plus $4.00 shipping and handling), a descriptive listing of hundreds of magazines, including many that publish plays. Other leads may be found in *The International Directory of Little Magazines and Small Presses: 2007–2008* (Dustbooks; Box 100; Paradise, CA 95967; 530-877-6110, orders 800-477-6110; info@dustbooks.com, www.dustbooks.com; $37.95 paper, $55.00 cloth, plus shipping and handling). You should also write to individual publishers listed here and ask for style sheets, catalogs, sample copies, etc. Don't forget that when publishers say they accept unsolicited scripts, they *always* require you to enclose an SASE for return of the manuscript.

ALASKA QUARTERLY REVIEW

University of Alaska Anchorage; 3211 Providence Dr; Anchorage, AK 99508;
(907) 786-6916, FAX 786-6916; ayaqr@uaa.alaska.edu,
www.uaa.alaska.edu/aqr
Ronald Spatz, *Editor*

Types of material: short full-length plays, one-acts, translations. **Remuneration:** 1 complimentary copy; 1-year subscription; payment when grant money is available. **Guidelines:** semi-annual literary magazine publishing up to 2 short plays a year in addition to fiction, poetry and nonfiction; interested in new voices; traditional and experimental work; prefers maximum 50 pages in length. **Submission procedure:** accepts unsolicited scripts with SASE; submissions read 15 Aug–15 May. **Response time:** 6 months.

ANCHORAGE PRESS PLAYS

617 Baxter Ave; Louisville, KY 40204-1105; (502) 583-2288,
FAX 583-2288; review@applays.com, www.applays.com
Marilee Hebert Miller, *Publisher*

Types of material: works for young audiences, including full-length plays, one-acts, translations, adaptations and musicals. **Remuneration:** negotiated royalty. **Guidelines:** specialty house publishing works for young audiences only; see website for submission guidelines. **Submission procedure:** accepts unsolicited scripts with proof of production. **Response time:** 12 months.

ARTE PÚBLICO PRESS

University of Houston; 452 Cullen Performance Hall;
Houston, TX 77204-2004; submapp@mail.uh.edu,
www.artepublicopress.com
Submissions

Types of material: full-length plays, one-acts, adaptations, plays for young audiences, musicals. **Remuneration:** negotiated royalty; complimentary copies. **Guidelines:** unpublished works in English or Spanish by Hispanic writers only. **Submission procedure:** accepts unsolicited scripts. **Response time:** 6 months.

BAKER'S PLAYS

45 West 25th St; New York, NY 10010; (212) 206- 8990;
publications@bakersplays.com, www.bakersplays.com
Roxane Heinze-Bradshaw, *Managing Editor*

Types of material: full-length plays, one-acts, plays for young audiences, musicals. **Remuneration:** negotiated book and production royalty. **Guidelines:** prefers produced plays; prefers plays suitable for high school, community and regional theatres; "Plays from Young Authors" division features plays by high school playwrights. **Submission procedure:** accepts unsolicited scripts with resume via email; include press clippings if play has been produced; include CD for musicals; include SASE with priority postage for return of script; see website for details.

Response time: 8 months. **Special programs:** Baker's Plays High School Playwriting Contest (see Prizes).

BROADWAY PLAY PUBLISHING, INC.

56 East 81st St; New York, NY 10028-0202; (212) 772-8334,
    FAX 772-8358; broadwaypl@aol.com, www.broadwayplaypubl.com
Christopher Gould, *Publisher*

Types of material: full-length plays, adaptations. **Remuneration:** 10% book royalty, 80% amateur royalty, 90% stock royalty; 10 complimentary copies. **Guidelines:** major interest is in produced, unpublished, original, innovative work by American playwrights; contemporary subject matter, no historical or autobiographical plays; no one-acts or solo pieces. **Submission procedure:** no unsolicited scripts; email inquiry only; see website for guidelines. **Response time:** 2 months letter; 4 months script.

BROOKLYN PUBLISHERS

1841 Cord St; Odessa, TX 79762; (432) 550-5532, FAX 368-0340;
    brookpublishing@aol.com, www.brookpub.com
Joe Burton, *President*

Types of material: full-length plays, one-acts, adaptations, plays for young audiences, solo pieces, monologues, sketches. **Remuneration:** purchase and royalties; 8 complimentary copies. **Guidelines:** plays for the teen market; works suitable for performers in grades 6–12; special interest in comedies, mysteries and 10-minute, 2-person plays. **Submission procedure:** accepts unsolicited scripts. **Response time:** 2 months.

THE CAPILANO REVIEW

2055 Purcell Way; North Vancouver, BC V7J 3H5; (604) 984-1712;
    tcr@capcollege.bc.ca, www.thecapilanoreview.ca
Jenny Penberthy, *Editor*

Types of material: one-acts, solo pieces, screenplays. **Remuneration:** $50 per page, maximum $200; 2 complimentary copies; 1-year subscription. **Guidelines:** triannual literary and visual arts journal; publishes 1–2 plays a year; special interest in short, experimental theatre pieces with an "excellent use of language"; unpublished works, maximum 20 pages in length. **Submission procedure:** accepts unsolicited scripts; enclose SASE with Canadian postage or international reply coupons. **Response time:** 4 months.

CONFRONTATION MAGAZINE

English Department; C. W. Post College of Long Island University;
Brookville, NY 11548; (516) 299-2720, FAX 299-2735;
martin.tucker@liu.edu
Martin Tucker, *Editor*

Types of material: one-acts. **Remuneration:** $50–$200; 1 complimentary copy.
Guidelines: general magazine for "literate" audience; unpublished plays maximum 40
pages in length. **Submission procedure:** accepts unsolicited scripts; no electronic
submissions. **Response time:** 3 months.

CONTEMPORARY DRAMA SERVICE

Meriwether Publishing, Ltd; 885 Elkton Dr;   Colorado Springs, CO 80907;
(719) 594-4422, FAX 594-9916;
www.meriwether.com, www.contemporarydrama.com
Arthur and Theodore Zapel, *Associate Editors*

Types of material: full-length plays, one-acts, adaptations, plays for young audiences,
musicals. **Remuneration:** book royalties and/or payment for amateur and
professional performance rights. **Guidelines:** publishes works suitable for teenage,
high school and college market, as well as collections of monologues and practical
books on theatre arts; prefers comedies. **Submission procedure:** send letter of
inquiry and $2 for sample catalog and guidelines. **Response time:** 1 month letter; 6
months script.

THE DRAMATIC PUBLISHING COMPANY

311 Washington St; Box 129; Woodstock, IL 60098; (815) 338-7170,
FAX 338-8981; plays@dramaticpublishing.com,
www.dramaticpublishing.com
Linda Habjan, *Editor*

Types of material: full-length plays, one-acts, translations, adaptations, plays for
young audiences, musicals. **Remuneration:** standard royalty; 10 complimentary copies
(33% discount on additional copies). **Guidelines:** works for professional, stock and
amateur markets; prefers produced plays. **Submission procedure:** accepts unsolicited
scripts. **Response time:** 6 months.

DRAMATICS MAGAZINE

Educational Theatre Association; 2343 Auburn Ave;
Cincinnati, OH 45219-2815; (513) 421-3900, FAX 421-7077;
dcorathers@edta.org,
www.edta.org/publications/dramatics/default.aspx
Don Corathers, *Editor*

Types of material: full-length plays, one-acts and solo pieces for young performers.
Remuneration: payment for 1-time serial rights; complimentary copies. **Guidelines:**
educational theatre magazine; plays suitable for high school production; prefers
produced plays; special interest in plays maximum 10 minutes in length. **Submission**

procedure: accepts unsolicited scripts. **Response time:** 5 months. (See Educational Theatre Association in Membership and Service Organizations.)

DRAMATISTS PLAY SERVICE, INC.

440 Park Avenue S; New York, NY 10016; (212) 683-8960,
    FAX 213-1539; postmaster@dramatists.com, www.dramatists.com
Stephen Sultan, *President*

Types of material: full-length plays, musicals. **Remuneration:** possible advance against royalties; 10% book royalty, 80% amateur royalty, 90% stock royalty; 10 complimentary copies (40% discount on additional copies). **Guidelines:** works for stock and amateur market; prefers works produced in New York City. **Submission procedure:** no unsolicited scripts; 1-page synopsis and letter of inquiry. **Response time:** 6 months letter; 6 months script.

ELDRIDGE PUBLISHING COMPANY

Box 14367; Tallahassee, FL 32317; (850) 385-2463; editorial@histage.com,
    www.histage.com
Nancy Vorhis, *Senior Editor*

Types of material: full-length plays, one-acts, adaptations, plays for young audiences, musicals. **Remuneration:** outright purchase of religious titles; 10% book royalty, 50% performance royalty; 12 complimentary copies (discount on additional copies). **Guidelines:** publishes 40 plays and musicals per year. **Submission procedure:** accepts unsolicited scripts. **Response time:** 3 months.

ENCORE PERFORMANCE PUBLISHING

Box 14367; Tallahassee, FL 32317; (850) 385-2463; editor@encoreplay.com,
    www.encoreplay.com
Meredith Edwards, *Senior Editor*

Types of material: full-length plays, one-acts, translations, adaptations, plays for young audiences, musicals. **Remuneration:** 10% book royalty, 50% performance royalty; 10 complimentary copies (discount on additional copies). **Guidelines:** publishes 10–30 plays and musicals a year; special interest in works with strong family message. **Submission procedure:** accepts unsolicited scripts. **Response time:** 3 months script.

FREELANCE PRESS

670 Centre St, Suite 8; Jamaica Plains, MA 02130; (617) 524-7045,
    FAX 524-7005; www.freelancepress.org
Jesse Olson, *Office Manager*

Types of material: musicals. **Remuneration:** 10% book royalty, 70% performance royalty. **Guidelines:** unpublished issue-oriented musicals and musical adaptations of classics approximately 1 hour long; suitable for performance by young people only; large casts with flexible male/female roles. **Submission procedure:** accepts unsolicited scripts. **Response time:** 3 months.

GREEN INTEGER

6022 Wilshire Blvd, Suite 202C; Los Angeles, CA 90036; (323) 857-1115;
   info@greeninteger.com, www.greeninteger.com
Douglas Messerli, *Publisher*

Types of material: full-length plays, translations. **Remuneration:** royalty; 10 complimentary copies. **Guidelines:** press publishing average of 10 single-play volumes per year; unpublished plays; special interest in translations. **Submission procedure:** no unsolicited scripts; letter of inquiry. **Response time:** 1 month letter; 6 months script.

HEUER PUBLISHING LLC

Box 248; Cedar Rapids, IA 52406; (319) 368-8008, FAX 368-8011;
   editor@hitplays.com, www.hitplays.com
Geri Albrecht, *Editor in Chief*

Types of material: full-length plays, one-acts, adaptations, plays for young audiences, musicals. **Remuneration:** performance royalties; complimentary copies. **Guidelines:** dramatic works suitable for educational, college and community theatres; special interest in 10-minute plays, satires, comedies, "interactive plays" and "plays of social/cultural relevance." **Submission procedure:** accepts unsolicited scripts via email or website upload. **Response time:** 3 months.

THE KENYON REVIEW

104 College Dr; Gambier, OH 43022-9623; (740) 427-5208,
   FAX 427-5417; kenyonreview@kenyon.edu, www.kenyonreview.org
David H. Lynn, *Editor*

Types of material: one-acts, solo pieces, excerpts from full-length plays. **Remuneration:** cash payment; 2 complimentary copies. **Guidelines:** literary journal publishing an average of 2 plays a year; unproduced, unpublished works maximum 30 pages in length; no simultaneous submissions. **Submission procedure:** accepts unsolicited scripts via website submission program only; see website for details. **Response time:** 4 months.

LILLENAS DRAMA RESOURCES

Lillenas Publishing Company; Box 419527; Kansas City, MO 64141;
   (800) 363-2122, FAX (816) 412-8390; drama@lillenas.com,
   www.lillenasdrama.com
George Baldwin, *Creative Director*

Types of material: full-length plays, one-acts, collections of sketches, playlets, children's recitations. **Remuneration:** outright purchase or royalty. **Guidelines:** unpublished "creatively conceived and practically producible scripts and outlines that provide church and school with an opportunity to glorify God and his creation in drama"; scripts available for download from website. **Submission procedure:** accepts unsolicited scripts; send SASE for guidelines. **Response time:** 6 months.

NEW PLAYS

Box 5074; Charlottesville, VA 22905; (434) 823-7555; patwhitton@aol.com,
    www.newplaysforchildren.com
Patricia Whitton Forrest, *Publisher*

Types of material: plays for young audiences. **Remuneration:** 10% book royalty,
50% performance royalty. **Guidelines:** innovative material not duplicated by other
sources of plays for young audiences; plays with productions directed by someone
other than author; see website for guidelines. **Submission procedure:** accepts
unsolicited scripts. **Response time:** 2 months minimum.

ORIGINAL WORKS PUBLISHING

info@originalworksonline.com, www.originalworksonline.com
Jason Aaron Goldberg, *President*

Types of material: full-length plays, one-acts, solo pieces. **Remuneration:**
negotiated book and performance royalties; 2 complimentary copies. **Guidelines:**
"bold and original plays" that have received at least 1 production; also publishes
compilations of 10-minute plays. **Submission procedure:** accepts unsolicited scripts;
see website for specific guidelines. **Response time:** 1 month.

PAJ: A JOURNAL OF PERFORMANCE AND ART

Box 532; Village Station; New York, NY 10014-0260; (212) 243-3885,
    FAX 243-3885; pajpub@mac.com, mitpress.mit.edu/paj
Bonnie Marranca and Gautam Dasgupta, *Co-Publishers and Editors*

Types of material: one-acts, translations, solo pieces. **Remuneration:** payment
varies. **Guidelines:** publishes plays and critical essays on international performance,
drama, video, music, film and photography; special interest in translations; prefers
plays less than 40 pages in length. **Submission procedure:** no unsolicited scripts;
synopsis and letter of inquiry. **Response time:** 2 months letter; 2 months script.

PIONEER DRAMA SERVICE

Box 4267; Englewood, CO 80155-4267; (303) 779-4035, FAX 779-4315;
    submissions@pioneerdrama.com, www.pioneerdrama.com
Lori Conary, *Submissions Editor*

Types of material: full-length plays, one-acts, plays for young audiences, musicals.
Remuneration: royalty. **Guidelines:** produced work suitable for educational theatre,
including melodramas and Christmas plays; prefers large, ensemble casts with majority
of female roles or flexible casting. **Submission procedure:** accepts unsolicited
scripts; prefers synopsis and letter of inquiry. **Response time:** 2 weeks letter; 4
months script. **Special programs:** Shubert Fendrich Memorial Playwriting Contest (see
Prizes).

PLAYERS PRESS
Box 1132; Studio City, CA 91614-0132; (818) 789-4980
Robert W. Gordon, *Senior Editor*

Types of material: full-length plays, one-acts, translations, adaptations, plays for young audiences, musicals, solo pieces, monologues, scenes, teleplays, screenplays. **Remuneration:** cash option and/or outright purchase or royalty; complimentary copies (20% discount on additional copies). **Guidelines:** theatre press publishing technical and reference books and scripts; produced works for professional, amateur and educational markets. **Submission procedure:** accepts unsolicited scripts with proof of production, resume and 2 business-size SASEs; prefers synopsis, proof of production, resume and letter of inquiry with SASE for response. **Response time:** 3 weeks letter; 9 months script.

PLAYSCRIPTS, INC.
325 West 38th St, Suite 305; New York, NY 10018; (866) 639-7529,
    FAX (888) 203-4519; submissions@playscripts.com,
    www.playscripts.com

Types of material: full-length plays, one-acts. **Remuneration:** royalties from amateur and professional performance licenses and book sales. **Guidelines:** unpublished plays (prior non-exclusive publications in magazines or anthologies permitted). **Submission procedure:** accepts unsolicited, unpublished scripts; electronic submissions preferred; see website for guidelines. **Response time:** 6 months.

PLAYS, THE DRAMA MAGAZINE FOR YOUNG PEOPLE
Sterling Partners, Inc; Box 600160; Newton, MA 02460; (617) 630-9100;
    www.playsmag.com
Elizabeth Preston, *Editor*

Types of material: one-act plays for young audiences, including adaptations of material in the public domain. **Remuneration:** $75-$175 depending on length of play. **Guidelines:** publishes 70 plays a year; prefers work 20-30 minutes in length for junior and senior high school, 15-20 minutes for middle grades, 8-15 minutes for lower grades; no religious plays; magazine acquires all rights. **Submission procedure:** accepts unsolicited original scripts; letter of inquiry for adaptations; prefers format used in magazine; send SASE for guidelines. **Response time:** 2 weeks letter; 1 month script.

POEMS & PLAYS
English Department; Middle Tennessee State University;
    Murfreesboro, TN 37132; (615) 898-2712, FAX 898-5098;
    gbrewer@mtsu.edu, www.mtsu.edu/~english/poemplay.html
Gaylord Brewer, *Editor*

Types of material: one-acts. **Remuneration:** 1 complimentary copy. **Guidelines:** annual magazine of poetry and short plays published each Mar, includes an average of 2-3 plays in each issue; unpublished works; prefers produced works maximum 10-15 pages in length. **Submission procedure:** accepts unsolicited scripts Oct–Nov only. **Response time:** 2 months. **Special programs:** Tennessee Chapbook Prize: annual award for either a one-act play or collection of short plays or poetry, maximum manuscript length 24–30 pages; winning script published as interior chapbook in magazine; playwright receives 50 complimentary copies; submit script, SASE and $10 fee; deadline: 30 Nov 2008; no submission before 1 Oct.

PRISM INTERNATIONAL

Creative Writing Program; University of British Columbia;
>   Buch E462-1866 Main Mall; Vancouver, BC; Canada V6T 1Z1;
>   (604) 822-2514, FAX 822-3616; prism@interchange.ubc.ca,
>   prism.arts.ubc.ca

Types of material: one-acts (including translations and solo pieces), excerpts from full-length plays. **Remuneration:** $20 per printed page; 1-year subscription. **Guidelines:** quarterly literary magazine; unpublished plays, maximum 25 pages in length; send SASE or see website for guidelines. **Submission procedure:** accepts unsolicited scripts, include copy of original with translations. **Response time:** 6 months.

RESOURCE PUBLICATIONS, INC.

160 East Virginia St, #290; San Jose, CA 95112-5876; (408) 286-8505,
>   FAX 287-8748; editor@rpinet.com, www.resourcepublications.com
William Burns, *Editor*

Types of material: plays 7-15 minutes in length. **Remuneration:** royalty. **Guidelines:** collection of skits suitable for adults, middle school or high school students; no one-acts. **Submission procedure:** accepts unsolicited scripts. **Response time:** 2 months.

ROCKFORD REVIEW

Box 858; Rockford, IL 61105; daveconnieross@aol.com,
>   writersguild1.tripod.com
David Ross, *Editor*

Types of material: one-acts, solo pieces. **Remuneration:** 1 complimentary copy; eligibility for $25 editor's choice award and invitation to perform at annual summer gala banquet. **Guidelines:** biannual journal publishing poetry, fiction, satire, artwork and an average of 2–3 plays a year; one-acts maximum 1300 words; prefers work that provides "new insight into the human dilemma." **Submission procedure:** accepts unsolicited scripts with SASE. **Response time:** 2 months.

SAMUEL FRENCH, INC.

45 West 25th St; New York, NY 10010-2751; (212) 206-8990,
>   FAX 206-1429; publications@samuelfrench.com, www.samuelfrench.com
Roxane Heinze-Bradshaw, *Managing Editor*

Types of material: full-length plays, one-acts, plays for young audiences, musicals.

Remuneration: 10% book royalty; 10 complimentary copies (40% discount on additional copies); pays production royalties, agency commissions vary. **Guidelines:** "We publish a wide variety of plays and musicals, from Broadway hits to regional gems, and we recommend that all playwrights attempt to obtain a production of their plays before submitting for publication. We are much more likely to publish an anthology or collection of one-acts, rather than individual one-act plays. Check our website for up-to-date submission information." **Submission procedure:** letter of inquiry and 10 page sample of script. **Response time:** 2 months minimum letter; 12 months script.

SINISTER WISDOM

Box 1180; Sebastopol, CA 95473; fran@sonic.net, www.sinisterwisdom.org
Fran Day, *Editor*

Types of material: one-acts, excerpts from full-length plays. **Remuneration:** 2 complimentary copies. **Guidelines:** lesbian journal of art and literature published 2–3 times a year; works by lesbians reflecting the diversity of lesbians; no heterosexual themes; full-length play excerpts maximum 2500 words. **Submission procedure:** accepts unsolicited scripts with SASE; see website for current themes and guidelines. **Response time:** 9 months.

SMITH AND KRAUS PUBLISHERS, INC.

Box 127; Lyme, NH 03768; (603) 669-7032, FAX 669-7945;
   sandk@sover.net, www.smithandkraus.com
Marisa Smith, *Publisher*

Types of material: full-length plays, one-acts, translations, adaptations, plays for young audiences, solo pieces, monologues. **Remuneration:** payment or royalty. **Guidelines:** theatre press publishing works of interest to theatrical community, especially to actors, including collections of monologues and an average of 50 full-length plays per year; prefers produced plays. **Submission procedure:** no unsolicited scripts; synopsis and letter of inquiry. **Response time:** 3 weeks letter; 4 months script.

SPEERT PUBLISHING

(212) 979-7656; espeert@speertpublishing.com, www.speertpublishing.com
Eleanore Speert, *President*

Types of material: full-length plays, one-acts, translations, adaptations, plays for young audiences, solo pieces. **Remuneration:** author establishes fee on per-project basis. **Guidelines:** self-publishing company producing industry-standard acting editions for stock, regional theatre, nonprofessional and professional markets; no musicals. **Submission procedure:** call or email for information. **Response time:** 1 week. **Special programs:** supports the Dayton Playhouse FutureFest (see Prizes).

THEATREFORUM

Theatre & Dance Department 0344; University of California–San Diego;
  9500 Gilman Dr; La Jolla, CA 92093-0344; (858) 481-1384,
  FAX 534-1080; theatreforum@ucsd.edu, www.theatreforum.org
Jim Carmody, John Rouse, Adele Edling Shank and Theodore Shank, *Editors*

Types of material: full-length plays, translations, adaptations. **Remuneration:** $200; 10 complimentary copies (discount on additional copies). **Guidelines:** biannual international journal focusing on innovative work, publishing 2 professionally produced, unpublished plays in each issue, plus articles, interviews and photographs. **Submission procedure:** no unsolicited scripts; professional recommendation. **Response time:** 3 months.

THEATER MAGAZINE

Yale School of Drama, Box 208244; New Haven, CT 06520-8244;
  (203) 432-1568; theater.magazine@yale.edu, www.theatermagazine.org
Tom Sellar, *Editor*

Types of material: full-length plays, translations, adaptations, solo pieces. **Remuneration:** varies. **Guidelines:** triquarterly theatre journal publishing an average of 3 plays in each volume, plus articles and essays; special interest in innovative work; "no standard psychological realism or TV-script clones." **Submission procedure:** no unsolicited scripts; letter of inquiry only. **Response time:** 6 months letter.

DEVELOPMENT

What's in this section?

Conferences, festivals, workshops and programs whose primary purpose is to develop plays and playwrights. Also listed are some playwright groups and membership organizations whose main activity is play development. Developmental organizations such as New Dramatists, whose many programs cannot be adequately described in the brief format used in this section, are listed in Membership and Service Organizations. Some programs listed in Prizes also include a developmental element. Note: some programs provide writers with stipends or living situations, etc. Others require a small fee. Read the "financial arrangement" section carefully.

How can I get into these programs?

Keep applying to those programs for which you are convinced your work is suited. If you're turned down one year, you may be accepted the next on the strength of your latest piece. Remember: All deadlines reflect the next upcoming submission deadline at press time (years for annual deadlines are not included). Deadlines for annual awards may stay the same from year to year but this is not an absolute—always obtain the latest information (an organization's website is the best place to check) before submitting. And if you're required to submit a script with your application, don't forget your SASE!

ABINGDON THEATRE COMPANY

312 West 36th St, 6th Floor; New York, NY 10018; (212) 868-2055,
FAX 868-2056; literary@abingdontheatre.org, www.abingdontheatre.org
Kim T. Sharp, *Literary Manager*

Open to: playwrights. **Description:** 4 plays receive readings each month; 10-12 plays receive 12 hours of rehearsal and staged readings each year; of those, 2-3 plays selected for studio production and 2-3 plays selected for mainstage production; 1 playwright annually receives $1000 Christopher Brian Wolk Award and staged reading for best script submitted. **Financial arrangement:** stipend for production. **Guidelines:** play unproduced in New York; full-length play only. **Application procedure:** script, character breakdown, bio; see website for updated guidelines. **Deadline:** year-round for developmental programs; 1 Jun for Wolk Award. **Notification:** 6 months. **Dates:** year-round.

THE ACADEMY FOR NEW MUSICAL THEATRE

5628 Vineland Ave; North Hollywood, CA 91601; (818) 506-8500;
academy@anmt.org, www.anmt.org
John Sparks, *Artistic Director*

Open to: composers, librettists, lyricists. **Description:** Sep-Jun workshop; in-house staged readings; some developmental projects with professional theatre companies and producers. **Financial arrangement:** 1st-year workshop members pay dues of $895, plus $495 for lab sessions in either book, music or lyrics; in subsequent years, members pay dues of $200-$800, depending on level. **Application procedure:** application; resume; CD of 3 songs or equivalent for composer; lyrics for 3 songs for lyricist; short scene for librettist; refundable $60 fee; application available from website. **Deadline:** 1 Aug for new members workshop. **Notification:** 1 Sep. **Dates:** Sep-Jun.

ARTWORK ENTERPRISES, INC.

Box 453; Ashland, OR 97520; (541) 482-4357; info@ashlandnewplays.org,
www.ashlandnewplays.org

ASHLAND NEW PLAYS FESTIVAL

Open to: playwrights. **Description:** 4 new works given brief rehearsal culminating in 2 public readings; beginning 2009, reading committee will provide feedback to writers. **Financial arrangement:** $500 stipend and housing. **Guidelines:** unproduced full-length play; cast limit of 6; 1 submission limit; author's name and contact information on script cover sheet only. **Application procedure:** coversheet, script, brief synopsis, bio, application and nonrefundable $15 fee; electronic submission only beginning with 2009 season. **Deadline:** 15 Jan; no submission before 15 Oct. **Notification:** Aug. **Dates:** Oct.

ROGUE VALLEY TEN-MINUTE PLAYS FESTIVAL

Amanda Berkeley

Open to: playwrights, translators. **Description:** 6-10 short plays receive staged readings at benefit performance after 3 hours rehearsal; a committee of readers rates the entries and a small group of professional actors and directors makes the final selection; the festival benefits a selected local not-for-profit and all net proceeds go to that organization. **Financial arrangement:** $20 royalty. **Guidelines:** "submissions should consider the year's beneficiary, although it's not necessary to speak directly to it"; works must not have been submitted to the RV-TMPF within 3 years. **Application procedure:** electronic submissions only; see website for details. **Deadline:** 1 Mar–15 Jun. **Notification:** Aug. **Dates:** Sep.

ASCAP MUSICAL THEATRE WORKSHOPS
1 Lincoln Plaza; New York, NY 10023; (212) 621-6234, FAX 621-6558;
   www.ascap.com
Michael A. Kerker, *Director of Musical Theatre*

ASCAP/DISNEY MUSICAL THEATRE WORKSHOP (LOS ANGELES)
Open to: composers, librettists, lyricists. **Description:** 10-session workshop in CA under the direction of Stephen Schwartz; works presented to panels of musical theatre professionals. **Financial arrangement:** free. **Guidelines:** write or see website for guidelines. **Application procedure:** synopsis, resume and CD of 4 theatrical songs. **Deadline:** see website for details.

ASCAP MUSICAL THEATRE WORKSHOP (NEW YORK)
Open to: composers, lyricists. **Description:** 10-session workshop in NY under the direction of Stephen Schwartz; works presented to panels of musical theatre professionals. **Financial arrangement:** free. **Guidelines:** see website for details. **Application procedure:** synopsis, resume and CD of 4 theatrical songs (no pop songs). **Deadline:** see website for details.

ASHLAND NEW PLAYS FESTIVAL
(see ArtWork Enterprises, Inc)

ASIAN AMERICAN THEATER COMPANY
NEWWORKS INCUBATOR PROJECT
(see Asian American Theater Company in Production)

BALTIMORE PLAYWRIGHTS FESTIVAL
251 South Ann St; Baltimore, MD 21231; (410) 276-2153;
   www.baltplayfest.com
Rich Espey, *Chairman*

Open to: playwrights, composers, librettists, lyricists. **Description:** selected plays receive public readings throughout the year; from these, participating theatres choose up to 10 scripts for full production in summer festival. **Financial arrangement:** honorarium of up to $100 and Festival Awards up to $250 for produced scripts. **Guidelines:** past or current resident of MD; unproduced and unpublished play or musical; see website for guidelines. **Application procedure:** 3 copies of script, synopsis and letter of inquiry with $10 fee. **Deadline:** 30 Sep. **Notification:** Mar. **Dates:** summer.

BAY AREA PLAYWRIGHTS FESTIVAL

Playwrights Foundation; 131 10th St; San Francisco, CA 94103;
(415) 626-0453, ext 110; info@playwrightsfoundation.org,
www.playwrightsfoundation.org
Amy Mueller, *Artistic Director*

Open to: playwrights. **Description:** 2-week festival of staged readings with professional actors; each script receives 20 hours rehearsal with director/dramaturg team plus pre-festival weekend retreat for initial collaborative activities. **Financial arrangement:** stipend, travel and housing (if needed). **Guidelines:** unproduced full-length plays; local writers, emerging writers, and writers of color are encouraged to apply. **Application procedure:** script, resume and $20 submission fee; students may include letter of recommendation from professional artist. **Deadline:** postmarked by 1 Nov. **Notification:** early May. **Dates:** late Jul or early Aug. (See Playwrights Foundation in Membership and Service Organizations.)

BMI-LEHMAN ENGEL MUSICAL THEATRE WORKSHOP

Broadcast Music, Inc; 320 West 57th St; New York, NY 10019;
(212) 830-2508, FAX 262-2824; jbanks@bmi.com
Jean Banks, *Senior Director, Musical Theatre*

Open to: composers, librettists, lyricists. **Description:** 2-year program of weekly workshop meetings; ongoing advanced group for invited alums of Workshop; showcase presentations to invited members of entertainment industry; members eligible for annual Jerry Harrington Musical Theatre Awards, cash prizes for outstanding achievement in workshop. **Financial arrangement:** free. **Application procedure:** application and work samples. **Deadline:** 1 May 2009 for librettists; 1 Aug 2009 for composers and lyricists. **Notification:** Sep 2009. (See BMI in Membership and Service Organizations.)

BROADWAY TOMORROW

191 Claremont Ave, Suite 53; New York, NY 10027; (212) 531-2447,
FAX 531-2447
Elyse Curtis, *Artistic Director*

Open to: composers, librettists, lyricists. **Description:** new musicals presented in concert with writers' involvement. **Guidelines:** resident of NY metropolitan area only. **Application procedure:** synopsis, resume, cassette or CD of 3 songs with description of scenes in which they occur, reviews if available and SASE for response. **Deadline:** year-round. **Notification:** 6 months. **Dates:** year-round.

CREATIVE EVOLUTION
21-70 Crescent St, #A1; Astoria, NY 11105; (718) 821-2682;
cevolution@mindspring.com, creative-evolution.org
Michelle Colletti, *Co-Artistic Director*

Open to: playwrights, composers, librettists, lyricists, solo performers, screenwriters. **Description:** year-round series of readings with 1 annual production. **Financial arrangement:** free; with stipend for production. **Guidelines:** women only. **Application procedure:** see website for upcoming deadlines and requirements. **Deadline:** year-round. **Dates:** year-round.

DAVID HENRY HWANG WRITERS INSTITUTE
East West Players; 120 North Judge John Aiso St; Los Angeles, CA 90012;
(213) 625-7000, FAX 625-7111; info@eastwestplayers.org,
www.eastwestplayers.org
Jeff Liu, *Literary Manager*

Open to: playwrights. **Description:** 2 10-session playwriting workshops held each year culminating in public staged readings. **Financial arrangement:** $375 fee for playwriting workshop; 2 scholarships available. **Application procedure:** application, 5-page writing sample, bio, statement of intent describing expectations and goals for workshop; see website for application. **Deadline:** see website. (See East West Players in Production.)

DRAMA LEAGUE DIRECTORS PROJECT— NEW DIRECTORS–NEW WORKS SERIES
The Drama League of New York; 520 8th Ave, Suite 320;
New York, NY 10018; (212) 244-9494, FAX 244-9191;
directorsproject@dramaleague.org, www.dramaleague.org

Open to: collaborative teams composed of director and playwright, translator, composer, librettist or lyricist. **Description:** 3 projects per year receive up to 4 weeks of rehearsal space in New York City; writer or composer applies as part of collaborative team with director; development ranges from exploratory rehearsals to workshop production according to needs of collaborative team. **Financial arrangement:** maximum $2000 stipend depending on needs of project. **Guidelines:** application submitted by director only. **Application procedure:** see website for application and guidelines. **Deadline:** 1 Feb. **Notification:** 1 Jun.

EMERGING WRITERS GROUP
The Public Theater; 425 Lafayette St; New York, NY 10003; (212) 539-8530,
FAX 539-8505; ewquestions@publictheater.org, www.publictheater.org
Liz Frankel, *Literary Associate*

Open to: playwrights. **Description:** 12 diverse and exceptionally talented writers at the earliest stage of their careers selected for a year-long program that will include 1 staged reading, bi-weekly meetings, master classes, complimentary tickets to shows at the Public and career development advice. **Financial arrangement:** $3,000 stipend, plus $500 for theater tickets. **Guidelines:** see website for eligibility requirements. **Application procedure:** application, 2 copies of script, resume, artistic statement and 2 references; see website for application and details. **Deadline:** end of Aug; see website. **Notification:** mid-Dec. **Dates:** Jan–Dec.

FIRST STAGE

Box 38280; Los Angeles, CA 90038; (323) 850-6271, FAX 850-6295;
firststagela@aol.com, www.firststagela.org
Dennis Safren, *Literary Manager*

Open to: playwrights, solo performers, screenwriters. **Description:** organization providing year-round developmental services using professional actors, directors and dramaturgs; weekly staged readings of plays and screenplays followed by discussion; bimonthly playwriting and screenwriting workshops; periodic dramaturgy workshops; annual short-play marathon; annual One-Act Play Contest with $300 first prize, $100 second and third prizes and videotaped staged reading for all winners, *deadline:* 1 Nov (send SASE for guidelines), *notification:* Dec. **Financial arrangement:** subscription of $200 per year or $60 per quarter for resident of Los Angeles, Orange or Ventura counties; $68 annual subscription for nonresident; nonmember may submit script for reading. **Application procedure:** script. **Deadline:** year-round. **Notification:** 6 months. **Dates:** year-round.

FLYING SOLO FESTIVAL

(formerly WomenSpeak Festival)
Open Stage of Harrisburg; 223 Walnut St; Harrisburg, PA 17101-1711;
(717) 232-6736, FAX 214-3247; ostagepaige@yahoo.com,
www.openstagehbg.com
Paige Pavlishin, *Administrative Assistant*

Open to: solo performers. **Description:** 4 artists chosen to give 3 performances each during 4 weekends of festival; technical crew and rehearsal time provided. **Financial arrangement:** varies; artist normally receives stipend plus expenses. **Guidelines:** solo artist; work minimum 70 minutes in length. **Application procedure:** work sample (include video if available), press clippings and resume. **Deadline:** 1 Dec. **Notification:** 1 Feb. **Dates:** 4 Jun–27 Jun 2009; 3 Jun–26 Jun 2010

THE FRANK SILVERA WRITERS' WORKSHOP

Box 1791; Manhattanville Station; New York, NY 10027; (212) 281-8832,
FAX 281-8839 (call first); playrite@earthlink.net, www.fsww.org
Garland Lee Thompson, *Founding Executive Director*

Open to: playwrights. **Description:** upper Manhattan- and Harlem-based program that includes Monday reading series of new plays by new and established writers, followed by critiques; Saturday seminars conducted by master playwrights; staged readings; 2–3 showcases and readers' theatre productions per year. **Financial arrangement:** $35 annual fee plus $10 per Saturday class; Monday night readings free. **Guidelines:** interested in new plays by writers of all colors and backgrounds. **Application**

procedure: attend Sep open house; submitting script and attending Monday night session encouraged; call for information. **Deadline:** year-round.

FREDERICK DOUGLASS CREATIVE ARTS CENTER WRITING WORKSHOPS

270 West 96th St; New York, NY 10025; (212) 864-3375,
    FAX 864-3474 (call first); fdcac@aol.com, www.fdcac.org
Raymond Gaspard, *Acting President*

Open to: playwrights, screenwriters, television writers. **Description:** 4 cycles per year of 8-week beginning and advanced playwriting workshops; advanced workshops include readings; film and television writing workshops; weekly meetings. **Financial arrangement:** $200 fee per workshop; author of play given staged reading receives $50. **Application procedure:** contact FDCAC for information. **Deadline:** Sep for 1st cycle; Jan for 2nd cycle; Apr for 3rd cycle; Jun for 4th cycle; call for exact dates.

FUSIONFEST

(formerly The Next Stage Festival of New Plays)
The Cleveland Play House; 8500 Euclid Ave; Cleveland, OH 44106-0189;
    (216) 795-7010, ext 207, FAX 795-7005
Seth Gordon, *Associate Artistic Director*

Open to: playwrights. **Description:** annual spring festival of 4–8 rehearsed readings over 1-month period; plays receive 1–3 rehearsal days with director, dramaturg and professional cast and 1–2 public readings with audience discussion; at least 1 play fully produced in following theatre season. **Financial arrangement:** stipend, travel and housing. **Guidelines:** unproduced full-length play or musical; must give theatre 90-day option on future production. **Application procedure:** letter of inquiry, brief synopsis, 10-page dialogue sample, resume, reviews and SASP for acknowledgment of receipt; include cassette for musicals. **Deadline:** year-round. **Notification:** 6 months. (See The Cleveland Play House in Production.)

GENESIUS THEATRE GUILD

(see ReVision Theatre)

GLOBAL AGE PROJECT

Aurora Theatre Company; 2081 Addison; Berkeley, CA 94704;
    www.auroratheatre.org
Literary Manager

Open to: playwrights. **Description:** 4 plays selected for staged reading; each playwright is paired with a professional director and receives 8 hours of rehearsal with professional actors. **Financial arrangement:** $1,000 stipend; out of town playwrights receive a travel stipend and housing. **Guidelines:** resident of U.S., Mexico or Canada; play not previously produced (staged readings okay); play must address life in the 21st century. **Application procedure:** script, resume and application. **Deadline:** 1 Jul. **Notification:** Dec. **Dates:** Feb.

THE HARRIET LAKE FESTIVAL OF NEW PLAYS—PLAYFEST!
(see PlayFest—The Harriet Lake Festival of New Plays)

HEDGEROW HORIZONS
Hedgerow Theatre; 64 Rose Valley Road; Rose Valley, PA 19063;
   (610) 565-4211, FAX 565-1672; www.hedgerowtheatre.org
Submissions

Open to: playwrights. **Description:** 5 full-length plays and 2 one-acts each given 1 rehearsal and 1 public reading. **Financial arrangement:** free. **Guidelines:** playwright must be resident of DE, NJ or PA; play not produced professionally. **Application procedure:** send SASE for guidelines. **Deadline:** 28 Feb. **Notification:** 30 Apr. (See Hedgerow Theatre in Production.)

HUMANA FESTIVAL OF NEW AMERICAN PLAYS
Actors Theatre of Louisville; 316 West Main St; Louisville, KY 40202-4218;
   (502) 584-1265, FAX 561-3300; www.actorstheatre.org
Amy Wegener, *Literary Manager*

Open to: playwrights. **Description:** several plays are selected for an annual presentation of new American works in rotating rep performed for members of the community and theatre professionals from around the world. **Financial arrangement:** free. **Guidelines:** full-length plays written in English by American writers. **Application procedure:** no unsolicited scripts; accepts synopsis and dialogue sample; prefers agent submissions. **Deadline:** Apr–Aug. **Notification:** late summer/early fall. **Dates:** Feb–Mar.

THE LARK PLAY DEVELOPMENT CENTER
939 Eighth Ave, Suite 301; New York, NY 10019; (212) 246-2676,
   FAX 246-2609; submissions@larktheatre.org, www.larktheatre.org
Submissions

PLAYWRIGHTS WEEK FESTIVAL

Open to: playwrights. **Description:** 8–10 plays receive 10-15 hours of rehearsal and dramaturgical support with actors, director and artistic staff, culminating in staged reading. **Financial arrangement:** stipend, travel and housing. **Guidelines:** see website. **Deadline:** early fall. **Dates:** Sep.

PONY (PLAYWRIGHTS OF NEW YORK) FELLOWSHIP
www.playwrightsofnewyork.org

Open to: recent graduates of graduate playwriting programs. **Description:** The Lark administers this annual fellowship that provides participation in core Lark programs. **Financial arrangement:** $24,000 stipend, 1-bedroom apartment in New York City for duration of fellowship. **Guidelines:** see website. **Deadline:** see website.

LITTLE FESTIVAL OF THE UNEXPECTED

Portland Stage Company; Box 1458; Portland, ME 04104; (207) 774-1043,
FAX 774-0576; dburson@portlandstage.com, www.portlandstage.com
Daniel Burson, *Literary Manager*

Open to: playwrights. **Description:** 3–5 scripts given week of rehearsal and staged reading; some years reserved specifically for finalists of the Clauder Competition (see listing in Prizes). **Financial arrangement:** $500 stipend; housing and some travel support. **Guidelines:** see website for complete guidelines. **Application procedure:** synopsis, 10-page dialogue sample and cast breakdown. **Deadline:** year-round. **Notification:** Jan–Feb. **Dates:** May.

LONG BEACH PLAYHOUSE NEW WORKS FESTIVAL

5021 East Anaheim St; Long Beach, CA 90804; (562) 494-1014,
FAX 961-8616; lbph75@aol.com, www.lbph.com
Jo Black-Jacob, *Literary Manager*

Open to: playwrights. **Description:** 4 plays chosen for annual staged reading attended by public and professional critics who provide written and oral feedback; playwright receives videotape of reading; plays may receive subsequent full production. **Financial arrangement:** $100 honorarium. **Guidelines:** unpublished full-length plays not previously produced. **Application procedure:** script, synopsis, character breakdown, application and $10 fee; see website for application. **Deadline:** 30 Sep. **Notification:** Feb. **Dates:** Mar–Jun.

LORNA LITTLEWAY'S JUNETEENTH JAMBOREE OF NEW PLAYS

Box 3463; Louisville, KY 40201-3463; (502) 636-4200;
juneteenthlegacy@aol.com, www.juneteenthlegacytheatre.com
Lorna Littleway, *Founder/Producing Director*

Open to: playwrights. **Description:** 6 plays given professional staged reading during 3-week festival. **Financial arrangement:** free. **Guidelines:** plays that address the African-American experience and explore any of 5 themes: 19th-century African-American experience, pre and Harlem Renaissance era, Caribbean/Native American influence on African-Americans, African-American youth and contemporary issues, and new images of women; young writers encouraged to apply. **Application procedure:** 4 copies of script and $15 fee (3 scripts to Louisville address and 1 script and fee to: 605 Water St, #21B; New York, NY 10002). **Deadline:** 15 Mar; no submission before 15 Dec. **Notification:** 30 Apr. **Dates:** Jun 5–20.

LOVE CREEK SHORT PLAY FESTIVAL

Love Creek Productions; c/o 21-44 45 Avenue, #4;
Long Island City, NY 11101
Cynthia Granville-Callahan, *Festival Literary Manager*

Open to: playwrights. **Description:** minimum of 60 finalists receive mini-showcase production in New York City during year-round festival. **Financial Arrangement:** free.

Guidelines: unpublished one-act not produced in New York City area within past year, maximum 40 minutes in length, minimum cast of 2, simple sets and costumes; 2 submission limit; strongly prefers women in major roles and predominantly female cast. **Application procedure:** script with letter giving theatre permission to produce play if chosen and specifying whether Equity showcase is acceptable; send SASE for themes and deadlines. **Deadline:** year-round. **Dates:** year-round.

MANHATTAN PLAYWRIGHTS UNIT

338 West 19th St, #6B; New York, NY 10011-3982; (212) 989-0948
Saul Zachary, *Artistic Director*

Open to: playwrights, screenwriters. **Description:** developmental workshop meeting weekly for in-house readings and discussions of members' works-in-progress; end-of-season series of staged readings of new plays. **Financial arrangement:** free. **Guidelines:** produced or published writer. **Application procedure:** letter of inquiry, resume and SASE for response. **Deadline:** year-round.

MILL MOUNTAIN THEATRE'S NORFOLK SOUTHERN FESTIVAL OF NEW WORKS

1 Market Square SE; Roanoke, VA 24011-1437; (540) 342-5730;
        FAX 342-5745; tristau@millmountain.org, www.millmountain.org
Literary Associate/Festival Coordinator

Open to: playwrights, composers, librettists, lyricists, solo performers. **Description:** 2 plays chosen for full production during spring festival. **Financial arrangement:** travel stipend and housing for limited residency; writer receives royalties (minimum $200). **Guidelines:** U.S. resident; 1 unproduced, unpublished submission; no 10-minute plays; prefers small cast, minimal production requirements and unit set. **Submission procedure:** script with letter of recommendation; include cassette or CD for musicals; send SASE for guidelines. **Deadline:** 1 Jan. **Dates:** Apr.

NATIONAL MUSIC THEATER CONFERENCE

(formerly O'Neill Music Theater Conference)
Eugene O'Neill Theater Center; 305 Great Neck Rd; Waterford, CT 06385;
        (860) 443-5378, ext 227; litoffice@theoneill.org, www.theoneill.org
Martin Kettling, *Literary Manager*

Open to: composers, librettists, lyricists. **Description:** developmental period of 2–3 weeks each summer at the O'Neill for new music-theatre works of all genres, daily rehearsals and several public readings (Equity contract). **Financial arrangement:** stipend, travel, room and board. **Guidelines:** unproduced works-in-progress; commissioned and optioned work acceptable; adaptations acceptable if rights have been obtained. **Application procedure:** send SASE or see website for guidelines and application. **Deadline:** 1 Dec. **Notification:** Apr. **Dates:** Jun–Jul.

NATIONAL PLAYWRIGHTS CONFERENCE

(formerly O'Neill Playwrights Conference)
Eugene O'Neill Theater Center; 305 Great Neck Rd; Waterford, CT 06385;
(860) 443-5378, ext 227; litoffice@theoneill.org, www.theoneill.org
Martin Kettling, *Literary Manager*

Open to: playwrights. **Description:** 4-week conference at the O'Neill; 8–10 plays developed and presented as staged readings. **Financial arrangement:** stipend, travel, room and board. **Application procedure:** 3 copies of script, synopsis, character breakdown, bio and $35 fee; include CD with copy of all materials; see website for details and application. **Deadline:** 17 Oct; no submission before 15 Sep. **Notification:** Apr. **Dates:** Jun–Jul.

THE NEW HARMONY PROJECT

Box 441062; Indianapolis, IN 46244; (317) 464-1103;
scripts@newharmonyproject.org, www.newharmonyproject.org
Joel Grynheim, *Project Director*

Open to: playwrights, composers, librettists, screenwriters. **Description:** 4 scripts given 2 weeks of intensive development with professional community of directors, actors, producers, dramaturgs and musical directors. **Financial arrangement:** travel, room and board. **Guidelines:** narrative works that "emphasize the dignity of the human spirit and the worth of the human experience." **Application procedure:** email PDF or Word document (as a single file) containing, in this order, 1) resume, 2) proposal and statement of artistic purpose, 3) 10-page dialogue sample from script and 4) 1 copy of proposed script; for musicals submit 10 CDs. **Deadline:** 1 Oct. **Notification:** 1 Apr. **Dates:** see website.

NEW VISIONS/NEW VOICES

The Kennedy Center Theater for Young Audiences; 2700 F Street NW;
Washington, DC 20566; (202) 416-8880, FAX 416-8297;
kctya@kennedy-center.org,
www.kennedy-center.org/education/nvnv.html
Kim Peter Kovac, *Director of Theater for Young Audiences*

Open to: playwrights. **Description:** biennial program; up to 8 plays given rehearsals and staged readings. **Guidelines:** playwright must be sponsored by theatre; unproduced plays for young and family audiences; call for information and application. **Financial arrangement:** travel and small stipend. **Application procedure:** sponsoring theatre submits completed application and supporting materials. **Deadline:** 1 Oct. **Notification:** 1 Feb. **Dates:** Apr or May.

NEW VOICES, NEW WORKS, NEW YORK

Broad Horizons Theatre Company; 7415 Ridge Oak Court;
Springfield, VA 22153; (917) 670-0830; lmagruder6@yahoo.com,
www.bhorizons.org

Lewis Magruder, *Artistic Director*

Open to: playwrights, translators, composers, librettists, lyricists, solo performers. **Description:** selected new works go through collaborative developmental process in New York City, including feedback and rewrites as suggested by director and dramaturg; staged reading for invited audience and post-mortem; writer must be available to participate in entire process. **Financial arrangement:** small stipend and per diem. **Guidelines:** unpublished script of any length, topic, style or format. **Application procedure:** script and $15 fee (check payable to Broad Horizons Theatre Company); note mailing address is in VA. **Deadline:** year-round. **Notification:** year-round. **Dates:** year-round.

NEW YORK FOUNDATION FOR THE ARTS
FISCAL SPONSORSHIP PROGRAM

155 Avenue of the Americas, 6th Floor; New York, NY 10013-1507;
(212) 366-6900, ext 223, FAX 366-1778; sponsor@nyfa.org,
www.nyfa.org/fs

Mary Six Rupert, *Managing Officer*

Open to: playwrights, translators, composers, librettists, lyricists, solo performers, screenwriters, television and radio writers. **Description:** program provides fiscal sponsorship, financial services and technical assistance to individuals or organizations without not-for-profit status so that they can seek funds from foundations, corporations and individuals that require not-for-profit status in order to contribute funds. The program has two categories: Artists' Projects (individual artists or collaborating artists); and Emerging Organizations (emerging arts organizations in the process of obtaining not-for-profit status). Program does not offer grants or provide funding. **Financial arrangement:** NYFA retains a small percentage of grants and contributions it receives on behalf of a project. **Guidelines:** selection based on artistic excellence, uniqueness and fundability of project, and on artist's previous work and proven ability to complete proposed work. **Application procedure:** write or see website for application and guidelines. **Deadline:** Nov and May; contact NYFA for exact dates. **Notification:** 3 months.

THE NEXT LINK PROJECT

The New York Musical Theatre Festival; 242 West 38th St, Suite 1102;
New York, NY 10018; info@nymf.org, www.nymf.org

Isaac Robert Hurwitz, *Executive Director and Producer*

Open to: composers, librettists, lyricists. **Description:** 12-15 musicals presented during annual 3-week fall festival attended by industry professionals; chosen participants receive dramaturgical support, production subsidies, educational seminars focused on entrepreneurial skills, promotional support and networking opportunities. **Financial arrangement:** $450 participation fee; remuneration varies depending on individual producers. **Guidelines:** "production-ready" musical that has not received major New York production, although further script development during pre-production is expected and encouraged. **Application procedure:** 15-page script sample, synopsis, CD, application and $65 fee. **Deadline:** 1 Mar. **Notification:** spring. **Dates:** Sep–Oct.

NYC PLAYWRIGHTS LAB

Box 171; Peck Slip Station; New York, NY 10272; (212) 732-1020
Dina von Zweck, *Director of New Plays*

Open to: playwrights. **Description:** 10-session annual developmental workshop; writers meet weekly for readings of work-in-progress and critiques. **Financial arrangement:** $350 fee. **Guidelines:** playwrights must attend all 10 sessions. **Application procedure:** send SASE for guidelines and application. **Deadline:** postmarked by 30 May; no submission before 1 Apr. **Notification:** 1 Aug. **Dates:** Oct–Dec.

OLD PUEBLO PLAYWRIGHTS

Box 64914; Tucson, AZ 85728; (520) 297-3317; brit4@mindspring.com,
   www.oldpuebloplaywrights.org
Gavin Kayner, *Vice President/Treasurer*

Open to: playwrights, librettists, screenwriters. **Description:** Tucson-based members meet weekly to develop scripts; staged readings at annual festival. **Financial arrangement:** $36 membership fee per year (may be waived). **Guidelines:** see website. **Application procedure:** see website for details. **Deadline:** year-round. **Dates:** year-round.

O'NEILL MUSIC THEATER CONFERENCE

(see National Music Theater Conference)

O'NEILL PLAYWRIGHTS CONFERENCE

(see National Playwrights Conference)

ORANGE COUNTY PLAYWRIGHTS ALLIANCE

412 Emerald Place; Seal Beach, CA 90740-6223; (714) 962-7686;
   firenbones@aol.com, www.ocplaywrights.org
Eric Eberwein, *Director*

Open to: playwrights. **Description:** year-round developmental workshop meeting bimonthly; up to 12 scripts each year receive staged reading or possible production. **Financial arrangement:** $80 annual membership fee. **Guidelines:** resident of Orange County/greater Los Angeles area only. **Application procedure:** work sample and resume. **Deadline:** year-round. **Notification:** 2 months.

PAGE 73 PRODUCTIONS, INC.

138 South Oxford Street, #5C; Brooklyn, NY 11217; (718)398-2099,
   FAX (718) 398-2794; info@p73.org, www.p73.org
Liz Jones and Asher Richelli, *Directors*

Open to: playwrights, composers, librettists, lyricists. **Description:** organization providing year-round developmental services; scripts may receive staged reading, workshop or equity professional production; 1 playwright selected for fellowship. **Financial arrangement:** royalty payment for work given full production; $5000 for fellowship. **Guidelines:** playwright whose work has not received major New York production; musicals accepted only if complete. **Application procedure:** open submission for fellowship, see website for guidelines; all others, see website for details. **Deadline:** spring; exact date TBA; year-round for fellowship. **Dates:** year-round.

PENN STATE NEW MUSICAL THEATRE FESTIVAL

c/o PSU School of Theatre; 103 Arts Building; University Park, PA 16801;
   raysage@psunewmusicals.org, www.psunewmusicals.org
Raymond Sage, *Artistic Director*

Open to: composers, librettists, lyricists. **Description:** 2-4 pieces receive workshops each school year with student performers and faculty directors; pieces selected for the fall will be developed throughout the semester; pieces selected for spring will receive one week of rehearsals culminating in a staged reading; one show will be chosen to be presented at the York Theatre in New York City; writers share their expertise with students via lectures, master classes or personal interactions. **Financial arrangement:** travel, housing and small stipend (varies with project). **Guidelines:** musical of any subject and any length that has not been professionally produced; small-scale opera is okay. **Application procedure:** script and demo recording. **Deadline:** year-round. **Notification:** 6 months. **Dates:** fall through spring (during the school year).

PITTSBURGH NEW WORKS FESTIVAL

Box 42419; Pittsburgh, PA 15203; (412) 881-6888;
   info@pittsburghnewworks.org, www.pittsburghnewworks.org
Play Selection Manager

Open to: playwrights. **Description:** 12 one-acts given full production by 12 collaborating theatre companies during annual 4-week fall festival; and 6 one-acts given staged readings by 6 additional companies during 2 weeks prior to festival. **Financial arrangement:** $500 award for best play. **Guidelines:** unproduced one-act, maximum 40 minutes in length; cast limit of 8; no musicals; 1 submission limit. **Application procedure:** 1 hard copy and 1 electronic copy of script, $15 fee and SASE for response; call or see website for guidelines. **Deadline:** varies; see website. **Notification:** mid-Jun. **Dates:** Sep.

PLAYFEST: THE HARRIETT LAKE FESTIVAL OF NEW PLAYS

(formerly The Harriett Lake Festival of New Plays—PlayFest!)
Orlando Shakespeare Theater; 812 East Rollins St, Suite 100;
    Orlando, FL 32803; (407) 447-1700, ext 212;
    patrickf@orlandoshakes.org, www.orlandoshakes.org
Patrick Flick, *Director of New Play Development and Casting*

Open to: playwrights, composers, librettists, lyricists, solo performers. **Description:** 10 plays chosen for readings or workshops during winter festival. **Financial arrangement:** stipend, travel and housing. **Guidelines:** new, unpublished play or musical based on or inspired by classic literature or historically significant persons or events; special interest in one-acts, solo pieces and works by Hispanic authors; prefers cast limit of 6 for plays. **Application procedure:** 5-page dialogue sample, 250 word synopsis, character breakdown, bio/resume and title page including mail address, email address and phone number; no electronic submissions. **Deadline:** 30 Jun.

PLAYFORMERS

20 Waterside Plaza, # 11G; New York, NY 10010; (917) 825-2663
Suzanne Kistler, *Submissions*

Open to: playwrights. **Description:** playwrights' support group meets once a month for readings of new work, read by professional actors, followed by discussion and critiques. **Financial arrangement:** $75 annual dues. **Guidelines:** playwright invited to attend meetings as guest before applying for membership. **Application procedure:** script and resume. **Deadline:** year-round. **Dates:** Sep–Jun.

PLAY GROUP

Ars Nova; 511 West 54th St; New York, NY 10019; (212) 489-9800;
    artistic@arsnovanyc.com, www.arsnovanyc.com.
Emily Shooltz, *Director of Artistic Development*

Open to: playwrights. **Description:** a bi-weekly meeting for members to present new work and receive peer feedback; membership is for a two-year cycle. **Financial arrangement:** free. **Guidelines:** emerging writer must attend meetings in New York City. **Application procedure:** script, resume, 2 professional references and application. **Deadline:** Sep; exact date TBA; see website. **Notification:** mid-Dec. **Dates:** Jan–Dec.

PLAYWRIGHT'S CAFÉ

980 Middlefield Rd; Berkeley, CA 94708; (570) 704-8855;
    salyons@playcafe.org, www.playcafe.org
Steve Lyons, *Founder*

Open to: playwrights. **Description:** Bay Area writers' group that hosts monthly meetings, guest speakers and 3–4 readings of members' scripts per year. **Financial arrangement:** $10 fee per meeting. **Guidelines:** Bay Area playwrights only. **Application procedure:** see website. **Deadline:** year-round.

PLAYWRIGHTS' CENTER OF SAN FRANCISCO
DEVELOPMENTAL PROGRAMS

588 Sutter St, #430; San Francisco, CA 94102; (415) 820-3206;
  submission@playwrightscentersf.org, playwrightscentersf.org
Sara Staley, *Producing Director, Staged Readings*
Jan Carty Marsh, *Director, Developmental Readings*
Andy Black, *Director, Scene Nights*

Open to: playwrights. **Description:** developmental programs meeting weekly, including Scene Nights for partial readings of work in progress, with 2 sessions of Developmental Readings per year; unrehearsed table readings of works-in-progress; and rehearsed Staged Readings of completed works. **Financial arrangement:** $40–$60 annual membership fee; membership required for Developmental or Staged Readings. **Application procedure:** no submission required for Scene Nights; for other programs, submit script, cast list and brief bio (50 words maximum) via email; see website for guidelines. **Deadline:** spring and fall; see website for exact dates. (See Playwrights' Center of San Francisco in Membership and Service Organizations.)

PLAYWRIGHTS FORUM

Box 5322; Rockville, MD 20848; (301) 816-0569; pforum@erols.com,
  users.erols.com/pforum
Ernest Joselovitz, *President*

Open to: playwrights. **Description:** developmental program including 3-tier range of membership options: Forum 1, workshop program offering sessions of 6 bi-weekly meetings 3 times a year; Forum 2, professional playwriting group meeting biweekly; and Associate Membership offering participation in many of Forum's auxiliary programs but not in workshops; depending on type of membership, members variously eligible for in-house and public readings, mentorships, special classes, production observerships, free theatre tickets, internet activities, semiannual conference, organization's newsletter and handbook, and a commissioning program. **Financial arrangement:** Forum 1, $120 per 15-week session; Forum 2, $120 every 4 months; Associate Membership, $30 fee per year; financial aid available. **Guidelines:** resident of mid-Atlantic area only; Forum 2 prefers produced playwright or former Forum 1 participant willing to make long-term commitment; send SASE or see website for information. **Application procedure:** send SASE or call for information. **Deadline:** see website. **Notification:** 1 month.

PLAYWRIGHTS GALLERY

119 West 72nd St, Box 2700; New York, NY 10023; (212) 595-2582;
  playwrightsglry@gmail.com, www.playwrightsgallery.com
Deborah Savadge, *Director*

Open to: playwrights. **Description:** developmental workshop meeting bimonthly Sep–Jun; includes work-in-progress readings by resident actors; plays receive staged readings at 3-day festivals in fall and spring. **Financial arrangement:** playwrights share cost of space rental. **Application procedure:** 15–20-page work sample. **Deadline:** 15 Mar. **Notification:** 15 Sep.

PLAYWRIGHTS LAB

Pulse Ensemble Theatre; 266 West 37th St, 22nd Floor; New York, NY 10018;
(212) 695-1596; brian@pulseensembletheatre.org,
www.pulseensembletheatre.org
Brian Richardson, *Company Manager*

Open to: playwrights, solo performers, screenwriters. **Description:** 4-month workshop meeting weekly, culminating in public staged reading; possible production. **Financial arrangement:** $100 monthly fee. **Application procedure:** writing sample and application. **Deadline:** year-round. **Notification:** year-round. **Dates:** year-round.

PLAYWRIGHTS' PLATFORM

298 Columbus Ave, #604; Boston, MA 02116-6008;
elram@comcast.net, www.playwrightsplatform.org
Regina Eliot-Ramsay, *Board Member*

Open to: playwrights. **Description:** year-round playwrights' coopertive with bi-monthly public meetings on Sundays to develop new works through informal readings and feedback sessions; hosts summer festival of short works selected from members' submissions. **Financial arrangement:** participant encouraged to become member of organization ($35 annual dues). **Guidelines:** writer near Boston available for regular meetings; unpublished, unproduced play; one-acts preferred. **Application procedure:** attend 2 readings; pay dues; submit script for upcoming reading. **Deadline:** year-round. **Notification:** year-round. **Dates:** year-round.

PLAYWRIGHTS THEATRE OF NEW JERSEY
NEW PLAY DEVELOPMENT PROGRAM

Box 1295; Madison, NJ 07940; (973) 514-1787, ext 18; www.ptnj.org
John Pietrowski, *Artistic Director*

Open to: playwrights. **Description:** new plays developed through table readings, staged readings and workshop productions; liaison with other producing theatres. **Financial arrangement:** playwright receives royalty. **Guidelines:** American playwright; unproduced play; see website for complete guidelines. **Application procedure:** agent submission; see website for guidelines. **Deadline:** year-round. **Notification:** 12 months. **Dates:** year-round.

PREMIERE STAGES PLAY FESTIVAL

Kean University; 1000 Morris Ave; Union, NJ 07083; (908) 737-4092,
FAX 737-4636; premiere@kean.edu, www.kean.edu/premierestages
Elizabeth Coen, *Producing Associate*

Open to: playwrights. **Description:** 3 plays receive reading with 4 hours of rehearsal; 1 of these selected for Equity staged reading with 4 weeks of rehearsal; another selected for full Equity production with 3 weeks of rehearsal. **Financial arrangement:** $2000 to play selected for production; $750 for staged reading; $500 for 3rd place. **Guidelines:** playwright born or residing in CT, NJ, NY or PA; unpublished, full-length play not produced professionally; cast limit of 8; see website for guidelines.

Application procedure: script through agent submission; synopsis, 8-page dialogue sample, character breakdown, development history and bio through playwright. Deadline: 31 Jan. Notification: May. Dates: May–Jul.

PUERTO RICAN TRAVELING THEATRE PLAYWRIGHTS' UNIT

304 West 47th St; New York, NY 10036; (212) 354-1293, FAX 307-6769;
    allen@prtt.org
Allen Davis III, *Director*

Open to: playwrights, solo performers. Description: 7-9-month workshops comprised of 2 units, 1 for professional playwrights, 1 for beginners; weekly meetings; spring staged reading series; City "In Sight" showcase production series. Financial arrangement: $150 fee per workshop cycle. Guidelines: resident of New York City area; Latino or other minority playwright or playwright interested in multicultural theatre. Application procedure: for professional unit, submit full-length play; beginners contact director. Deadline: 15 Sep. Notification: 1 month. Dates: Oct-Jul.

REMEMBRANCE THROUGH THE PERFORMING ARTS
NEW PLAY DEVELOPMENT

Box 162446; Austin, TX 78716; (512) 329-9118; remperarts@aol.com
Rosalyn Rosen, *Artistic Director*

Open to: playwrights. Description: 8 playwrights chosen annually for developmental workshops, culminating in staged readings or work-in-progress productions; plays subsequently given referral to nationally recognized theatres for world premieres. Financial arrangement: $500 fee per workshop. Guidelines: U.S. resident; concept or full-length play that has not received Equity production. Application procedure: email synopsis, 5-page dialogue sample and resume. Deadline: year-round.

ReVISION THEATRE

(formerly Genesius Theatre Guild)
P.O. Box 973; Asbury Park, NJ 07712; info@revisiontheatre.org,
    www.revisiontheatre.org
Lou Liberatore, *Literary Director*

Open to: playwrights, translators, composers, librettists, lyricists, solo performers. Description: operates as a regional theatre offering programs in the development of new plays and musicals including in-house readings, staged readings and workshop and showcase productions; development process varies according to needs of script. Financial arrangement: royalty paid for mainstage productions. Application procedure: agent submission or professional recommendation only. Deadline: year-round. Dates: year-round.

THE RICHARD RODGERS AWARDS

American Academy of Arts and Letters; 633 West 155th St;
New York, NY 10032-7599; (212) 368-5900, FAX 491-4615;
www.artsandletters.org

Open to: playwrights, composers, librettists, lyricists. **Description:** 1 or more works per year given full production, studio/lab production or staged readings by not-for-profit theatre in New York City; writer(s) participate in rehearsal process. **Financial arrangement:** free. **Guidelines:** U.S. citizen or permanent resident; new work by writer/composer not already established in musical theatre; innovative, experimental material encouraged; 1 submission limit; previous submissions ineligible. **Application procedure:** see website or send SASE for application and information. **Deadline:** 3 Nov. **Notification:** Mar.

RISK IS THIS...THE CUTTING BALL NEW PLAYS FESTIVAL

The Cutting Ball Theater; 131 10th St; San Francisco, CA 94103;
(415) 419-3584; literary@cuttingball.com, www.cuttingball.com
Meg O'Connor, *Literary Manager*

Open to: playwrights. **Description:** 3 plays given 1 week of rehearsal with resident company of actors and directors, culminating in staged reading; plays considered for subsequent full production. **Financial arrangement:** $200 honorarium, travel and housing. **Guidelines:** playwright available for 1 week of rehearsal in Bay Area during Nov or Dec; non-naturalistic plays with attention to language. **Application procedure:** script, resume and SASE for notification. **Deadline:** 1 Feb. **Notification:** 1 Oct. **Dates:** Nov–Dec.

ROSELILY PRODUCTIONS PLAYWRIGHTS DEVELOPMENT

862-49th St; Brooklyn, NY 11220-2442
Laura Cosentino, *Founder and Artistic Director*

Open to: playwrights. **Description:** plays selected for reading series; possible publication. **Financial arrangement:** $100 honorarium to play chosen best of reading series. **Guidelines:** prefers intergenerational and multicultural casts; send SASE for guidelines. **Application procedure:** 1 act of a full-length or short play and SASE for response. **Deadline:** year-round. **Notification:** varies. **Dates:** year-round.

THE SAMUEL FRENCH OFF-OFF BROADWAY
SHORT PLAY FESTIVAL

45 West 25th St; New York, NY 10010-2751; (212) 206-8990,
FAX 206-1429; oobfestival@samuelfrench.com, www.samuelfrench.com
Kenneth Dingledine, *Festival Coordinator*

Open to: playwrights. **Description:** festival production adjudicated by established playwrights, agents, our editorial staff and other NY-area industry professionals; winners published by Samuel French (see Publication). **Financial arrangement:** free. **Guidelines:** one-acts less than 30 minutes in length only; play must be sponsored by a producing organization. **Application procedure:** script and application submitted by playwright and producing organization; see website for application. **Deadline:** spring; exact date TBA. **Notification:** 2 months. **Dates:** summer.

SCENES FROM THE STATEN ISLAND FERRY

Sundog Theatre; Box 10183; Staten Island, NY 10301-0183;
(718) 816-5453; sfenley@sundogtheatre.org, www.sundogtheatre.org
Catherine Lamm, *Literary Manager*

Open to: playwrights. **Description:** annual festival of short plays set on the Staten Island Ferry; 6 selected plays receive a short rehearsal period and 5 performances viewed primarily by Staten Island residents. **Financial arrangement:** $100 stipend. **Guidelines:** short plays 10–20 minutes in length that are set on the Staten Island Ferry; cast limit of 3; minimal production requirements; no musicals. **Application procedure:** 2 bound and blind scripts, synopsis, cast breakdown, play history, 100-word bio and resume. **Deadline:** 1 Dec.

THE SCRIPTEASERS

3404 Hawk St; San Diego, CA 92103-3862; (619) 295-4040;
thescripteasers@msn.com, www.thescripteasers.org
Jonathan Dunn-Rankin, *Corresponding Secretary*

Open to: playwrights, screenwriters, television writers. **Description:** writers, directors and actors meet every other Friday evening in private home for cold readings of new scripts, followed by constructive criticism; 1 or 2 rehearsed staged readings a year presented at local theatres as showcases. **Financial arrangement:** donations of $1 accepted at each reading. **Guidelines:** unproduced script by new or established writer who is resident of San Diego County; guest writer must attend at least 2 readings before submitting script. **Application procedure:** write or call for guidelines. **Deadline:** year-round.

SOUTHERN APPALACHIAN PLAYWRIGHTS' CONFERENCE— SCRIPTFEST

Southern Appalachian Repertory Theatre; Box 1720; Mars Hill, NC 28754;
(828) 689-1384, FAX 689-1272; sart@mhc.edu, www.sartplays.org
William Gregg, *Artistic Director*

Open to: playwrights, composers, librettists, lyricists. **Description:** up to 5 writers selected to participate in annual fall weekend conference at which 1 work by each writer is given reading and discussion; 1 work may be selected for production as part of following summer season. **Financial arrangement:** room and board; writer of work selected for production receives $1000 honorarium. **Guidelines:** unproduced, unpublished full-length play or musical on any subject. **Application procedure:** script with author's name on title page only, synopsis, character breakdown and resume. **Deadline:** 30 Sep.

SUMMERNITE

School of Theatre and Dance; Northern Illinois University;
DeKalb, IL 60115; (815) 753-1334, FAX 753-8415; cmarkle@niv.edu,
www.niv.edu/summernite
Christopher Markle, *Artistic Director*

Open to: playwrights. **Description:** play chosen for full production; some plays chosen for periodic staged readings. **Financial arrangement:** royalties for play chosen for production. **Guidelines:** world, U.S. or Chicago-area premiere; "innovative and intellectual stimulating works"; special interest in large-cast full-length plays and translations. **Application procedure:** agent submission only. **Deadline:** year-round. **Notification:** 2 months. **Dates:** year-round.

SUMMER PLAY FESTIVAL (SPF)

The Living Room for Artists; Box 778; New York, NY 10108; (212) 279-4040,
FAX 279-4041; info@spfnyc.com, www.spfnyc.com
Thom Clay, *Managing Director*

Open to: playwrights. **Description:** each summer 8-16 plays receive 2 weeks of rehearsal and 1 week of performance in New York City; critics do not review the productions. **Financial arrangement:** stipend; writers from outside NY receive housing and travel. **Guidelines:** playwright cannot have had a NY production in a theatre larger than 99 seats; see website for details. **Application procedure:** script and application form. **Deadline:** see website. **Notification:** Apr. **Dates:** Jul.

THE SUNDANCE THEATRE LAB

8530 Wilshire Blvd, 3rd Floor; Beverly Hills, CA 90211; (310) 360-1981,
FAX 360-1975; theatre@sundance.org, www.sundance.org
Philip Himberg, *Producing Artistic Director,*
Sundance Institute Theatre Program

Open to: playwrights, solo performers. **Description:** 7-8 scripts workshopped for 20 days. **Financial arrangement:** travel, room and board. **Guidelines:** full-length play, new adaptation and/or translation of classic material, musical, play for young audiences, solo piece. **Application procedure:** see website for application and guidelines. **Deadline:** 15 Dec. **Notification:** Apr. **Dates:** Jul.

THE TEN-MINUTE MUSICALS PROJECT

Box 461194; West Hollywood, CA 90046; www.tenminutemusical.org
Michael Koppy, *Producer*

Open to: composers, librettists, lyricists. **Description:** up to 10 brief pieces selected during annual cycle for possible inclusion in full-length anthology; musicals to be produced at Equity theatres in U.S. and Canada; occasionally some pieces workshopped using professional actors and director. **Financial arrangement:** $250 royalty advance with equal share of licensing royalties when produced. **Guidelines:** complete work "with definite beginning, middle and end," 7-14 minutes in length, in any musical style or genre; adaptations of well-structured material in the public domain or for which rights have been obtained are encouraged; cast of 2-10, prefers 6-10; write for guidelines. **Application procedure:** script, lead sheets and cassette or CD of sung material. **Deadline:** 31 Aug. **Notification:** 30 Nov.

THEATRE WEST WRITERS WORKSHOP
3333 Cahuenga Blvd W; Los Angeles, CA 90068; (323) 851-4839,
    FAX 851-5286; www.theatrewest.org
Doug Haverty and Chris DiGiovanni, *Moderators*

Open to: playwrights, translators, librettists, lyricists. **Description:** weekly development workshop, utilizing professional actor members, presenting 2 staged readings per year, limited-run workshop productions with juried cash prize and possible main stage production. **Financial arrangement:** $50 monthly fee. **Guidelines:** full-length plays, translations, adaptations and plays for young audiences; large-casts encouraged. **Application procedure:** script and resume with SASE for response. **Deadline:** year-round. **Notification:** 4 months. **Dates:** year-round.

UTAH SHAKESPEAREAN FESTIVAL
NEW AMERICAN PLAYWRIGHTS PROJECT
351 West Center St; Cedar City, UT 84720-2498; (435) 586-7880,
    FAX 865-8003; metten@bard.org, www.bard.org
Charles Metten, *Director, USFNAPP*

Open to: playwrights. **Description:** 3 plays receive up to 5 rehearsals with director and Festival actors, culminating in 3 staged readings. **Financial arrangement:** travel, housing and complimentary theatre tickets provided. **Guidelines:** plays with no previous mainstage production only; 90-page limit; classical and western U.S. themes encouraged. **Application procedure:** script only. **Deadline:** Dec 1; no submission before 1 Jul. **Notification:** 15 Mar. **Dates:** Aug for staged readings.

VOICE & VISION ENVISION RETREAT
FOR WOMEN THEATER ARTISTS
Voice & Vision; 520 8th Ave, #316; New York, NY 10018; (212) 268-3717,
    FAX 268-5462; vandv@vandv.org, www.vandv.org
Jean Wagner, *Artistic Director*

Open to: playwrights, solo performers, multidisciplinary artists, collaborative teams. **Description:** 6-8 female initiating artists and their collaborators spend up to 2 weeks at Bard College working on projects in various stages of development, with opportunities for informal presentations of works-in-progress; possible further development through ENVISION Lab in New York City. **Financial arrangement:** small stipend, housing, rehearsal space, production support, transportation from New York City and most meals. **Guidelines:** women theatre artists only; see website for complete guidelines. **Application procedure:** script, 1-page project description, 3 professional references, resumes of participants, list of special needs and $15 application fee; provide video if applicable; see website for complete guidelines. **Deadline:** early Mar. **Notification:** late Apr. **Dates:** summer.

THE WATERFRONT ENSEMBLE AND NEW JERSEY DRAMATISTS

Box 1486; Hoboken, NJ 07030; (201) 708-6535;
  njdramatists@hotmail.com, www.njdramatists.org
Henry Meyerson, *Co-Artistic Director*

Open to: playwrights, translators, solo performers. **Description:** playwright-driven company of actors, directors and playwrights that meets weekly to work on new plays in preparation for productions in NY and NJ; 15 one-acts and 2 full-length plays produced each year. **Financial arrangement:** suggested donation for lab; no fee for selected programs; call or write for information. **Guidelines:** NY/NJ-area playwright. **Application procedure:** up to 30-page writing sample and resume. **Deadline:** year-round. **Notification:** 12 months. **Dates:** year-round.

WILLIAMSTOWN THEATRE FESTIVAL

229 West 42nd St, Suite 801; New York, NY 10036-7299; (212) 395-9090,
  FAX 395-9099; www.wtfestival.org
Nicholas Martin, *Artistic Director*

Open to: playwrights. **Description:** 6 plays each season given public reading. **Financial arrangement:** travel and housing. **Guidelines:** play not professionally produced. **Application procedure:** agent submission only. **Deadline:** 15 Feb; no submission before 1 Oct. **Notification:** 12 months.

WOMEN PLAYWRIGHTS SERIES

Centenary Stage Company; 400 Jefferson St; Hackettstown, NJ 07840;
  (908) 979-0900, FAX 979-4297; rustc@centenarycollege.edu,
  www.centenarystageco.org
Catherine Rust, *Program Director*

Open to: playwrights. **Description:** 1 play given 1 week of rehearsal with professional actors and director, followed by staged reading and possible mainstage production. **Financial arrangement:** $200 honorarium; room and board; 1 playwright each session receives travel. **Guidelines:** woman playwright; full-length play. **Application procedure:** 10–20-page writing sample, synopsis, letter of recommendation from field. **Deadline:** 1 Nov. **Notification:** 30 Jan. **Dates:** Apr.

WOMENSPEAK FESTIVAL

(see Flying Solo Festival)

YOUNG PLAYWRIGHTS INC.

Box 5134; New York, NY 10185; (212) 594-5440;
  admin@youngplaywrights.org, youngplaywrights.org

ADVANCED PLAYWRITING WORKSHOP

Advanced Playwriting Coordinator

Open to: playwrights. **Description:** weekly classes; guest lectures by prominent

American playwrights; viewing of Broadway and Off-Broadway plays; development of new short play for public performance with professional actors and director. **Financial arrangement:** playwright must work minimal office hours in lieu of tuition. **Guidelines:** New York City metropolitan area high school student. **Submission procedure:** 3–5-page writing sample, recommendation from teacher or mentor and application; call or email for application. **Deadline:** Sep; exact date TBA; see website. **Dates:** year-round.

URBAN RETREAT
Urban Retreat Coordinator

Open to: playwrights. **Description:** 1-week New York City retreat for writers ages 14–21; guest lectures by prominent American playwrights; one-on-one sessions with teaching artists; 3 intensive daily writing workshops; viewing of Broadway and Off-Broadway plays; development of new short play for public performance with professional actors and director. **Financial arrangement:** $1650 tuition includes meals, transportation in New York City, supervised housing and theatre tickets; limited financial aid available. **Guidelines:** playwright ages 14–21. **Application procedure:** 3–5-page writing sample, recommendation from teacher or mentor, application and $100 fee (applied to tuition; refundable if applicant does not attend); call or email for application. **Deadline:** 1 May. **Dates:** Jul.

PART 2
CAREER
OPPORTUNITIES

Agents

Fellowships and Grants

Emergency Funds

State Arts Agencies

Colonies and Residencies

Membership and Service Organizations

AGENTS

I'm wondering whether or not I should have an agent. Where can I get information to help me decide?

See the Association of Authors' Representatives website (www.aar-online.org) to view their publications on the role of the literary agent, the canon of ethics, and their membership list. Also, see Useful Publications for sources you may consult on the subject, ask your fellow playwrights, look at copies of scripts for the names of agents and make an intelligent guess as to whether they would be interested in representing your work.

How do I select the names of appropriate agents to contact?

All of the agents listed here represent playwrights. The Dramatists Guild also has a list of agents available to its members, and provides advice on relationships with agents (see Membership and Service Organizations). You may come across names that appear on none of these lists, but be wary, especially if someone tries to charge you a fee to read your script.

How do I approach an agent?

Do not telephone, do not drop in, do not send manuscripts. Write a brief letter describing your work and asking if the agent would like to see a script. Enclose your professional resume; it should show that you have had work produced or published, and make clear that you look at writing as an ongoing career, not an occasional hobby. If you're a beginning writer who's just finished your first play, you'd probably do better to work on getting a production rather than an agent.

ABRAMS ARTISTS AGENCY

275 7th Ave, 26th Floor; New York, NY 10001; (646) 486-4600
Sarah Douglas, Charles Kopelman, *Co-Directors, Literary Division*
Beth Blickers, Ron Gwiazda, Morgan Jenness, Kate Navin, Maura Teitelbaum, *Agents*

ANN ELMO AGENCY

60 East 42nd St; New York, NY 10165; (212) 661-2880
Mari Cronin, Letti Lee, *Agents*

THE BARBARA HOGENSON AGENCY, INC.

165 West End Ave, Suite 19C; New York, NY 10023; (212) 874-8084
Barbara Hogenson, *Agent*
Nicole Verity, *Contracts Manager*

BRET ADAMS LTD/ROSENSTONE ADAMS LLC

448 West 44th St; New York, NY 10036; (212) 765-5630; www.bretadamsltd.net
Bruce Ostler, *Co-Owner, President Literary*
Mark Orsini, *Agent*
Marie Darden, Natasha Sinha, *Agent Trainees*

THE DRAMATIC PUBLISHING COMPANY

311 Washington St; Woodstock, IL 60098; (815) 338-7170;
plays@dramaticpublishing.com, www.dramaticpublishing.com
Linda Habjan, *Agent*

FARBER LITERARY AGENCY

14 East 75th St, 2E; New York, NY 10021; (212) 861-7075
Ann Farber, Seth Farber, *Agents*

FIFI OSCARD AGENCY, INC.

110 West 40th St, 21st Floor; New York, NY 10018; (212) 764-1100
Carolyn French, Carmen LaVia, Peter Sawyer, *Agents*

GAGE GROUP

14724 Ventura Blvd, Suite 505; Sherman Oaks, CA 91403; (818) 905-3800
Martin Gage, *Agent*

THE GERSH AGENCY

41 Madison Ave, 33rd Floor; New York, NY 10010; (212) 997-1818
John Buzzetti, Seth Glewen, Peter Hagan, Joyce Ketay, Carl Mulert, Sonia Pabley, Phyllis
Wender, Scott Yoselow, *Agents*

GRAHAM AGENCY

311 West 43rd St; New York, NY 10036; (212) 489-7730
Earl Graham, *Agent*

GRANT, SAVIC, KOPALOFF & ASSOCIATES
6399 Wilshire Blvd, Suite 414; Los Angeles, CA 90048; (323) 782-1854
Larry Metzger, *Agent*

HARDEN-CURTIS ASSOCIATES
850 Seventh Ave, Suite 903; New York, NY 10019; (212) 977-8502
Scott Edwards, Mary Harden, *Agents*

INTERNATIONAL CREATIVE MANAGEMENT (ICM)
825 Eigth Ave; New York, NY 10019; (212) 556-5600
Patrick Herold, Thomas Pearson, Buddy Thomas, *Agents*

JUDY BOALS, INC.
307 West 38th St, #812; New York, NY 10018; (212) 500-1424; info@judyboals.com
Judy Boals, *Agent*

MARK CHRISTIAN SUBIAS AGENCY
331 West 57th St, #462; New York, NY 10019; (212) 445-1091
Mark Christian Subias, *Agent*

THE MARTON AGENCY, INC.
1 Union Square West, Suite 815; New York, NY 10003-3303; (212) 255-1908;
info@martonagency.com
Tonda Marton, Anne Reingold, *Agents*

PARADIGM
360 Park Avenue South, 16th Floor; New York, NY 10010; (212) 897-6400
William Craver, Jack Tantleff, Michael Moore, *Agents*

PEREGRINE WHITTLESEY AGENCY
279 Central Park West, #23; New York, NY 10024; (212) 787-1802
Peregrine Whittlesey, *Agent*

PINDER LANE & GARON-BROOKE ASSOCIATES
159 West 53rd St; New York, NY 10019; (212) 489-0880
Dick Duane, Robert Thixton, *Agents*

ROBERT A. FREEDMAN DRAMATIC AGENCY, INC.
1501 Broadway, Suite 2310; New York, NY 10036; (212) 840-5760
Robert A. Freedman, Selma Luttinger, Marta Praeger, *Agents*

STEPHEN PEVNER, INC.
382 Lafayette St, 8th Floor; New York, NY 10003; (212) 674-8403
Stephen Pevner, *Producer*

THE SUSAN GURMAN AGENCY, LLC

245 West 99th St, 24th Floor; New York, NY 10025; (212) 749-4618;
www.gurmanagency.com
Susan Gurman, *Agent*

SUSAN SCHULMAN, A LITERARY AGENCY

454 West 44th St; New York, NY 10036; (212) 713-1633
Susan Schulman, *Agent*

WILLIAM MORRIS AGENCY

1325 Ave of the Americas; New York, NY 10019; (212) 586-5100
Val Day, Peter Franklin, David Kalodner, Biff Liff, Elsa Neuwald, Roland Scahill,
Susan Weaving, Derek Zarky, *Agents*

FELLOWSHIPS AND GRANTS

Can I apply directly to all the programs listed in this section?

No. A number of the grant programs we list must be applied to by a producing or presenting organization. However, you should be aware that these programs exist so that you can bring them to the attention of organizations with which you have a working relationship. All or most of the funds disbursed benefit the individual artist by covering commissioning fees, residencies and other expenses related to the creation of new works.

How can I enhance my chances of winning an award?

Apply for as many awards as you qualify for; once you have written the first grant proposal, you can often, with little additional work, adapt it to fit other guidelines. Some deadlines will fall outside the publication period of this biennial sourcebook. All deadlines reflect the next upcoming submission deadline for an organization at press time (years for annual deadlines are not included). Dates may stay the same from year to year, but this is not an absolute—always obtain the latest information (an organization's website is the best place to check) before submitting. Use the Submission Calendar in the back of this book to help you plan your campaign. Start early. In the case of all programs for which you can apply directly, obtain the guidelines and application forms months ahead. Study the guidelines carefully and follow them meticulously. Don't hesitate to ask for advice and assistance from the organization to which you are applying. Submit a well-thought-out, clearly written, neatly typed application—and make sure it arrives in the organization's office by the deadline. (Never assume, without checking, that the deadline is the postmark date.)

THE ALRED HODDER FELLOWSHIP
(see The Hodder Fellowship)

AMERICAN ANTIQUARIAN SOCIETY FELLOWSHIPS
185 Salisbury St; Worcester, MA 01609; (508) 471-2131, FAX 754-9069;
cmcrell@mwa.org, www.americanantiquarian.org
James David Moran, *Director of Outreach*

Open to: playwrights, translators, composers, librettists, lyricists, solo performers, screenwriters. **Frequency:** annual. **Remuneration:** $1200 grant; up to $400 in travel reimbursement. **Guidelines:** fellowships to support historical research that will lead to production of imaginative, nonformulaic works dealing with pre-20th-century American history; prefers work for general public rather than for academic or educational audiences. **Application procedure:** work sample, letter of recommendation, resume, 5-page narrative describing project and application. **Deadline:** 5 Oct. **Notification:** 15 Dec.

THE AMERICAN-SCANDINAVIAN FOUNDATION
58 Park Ave; New York, NY 10016; (212) 879-9779, FAX 249-3444;
grants@amscan.org, www.amscan.org
Fellowship Program

Open to: playwrights, translators, composers, librettists, lyricists. **Frequency:** annual. **Remuneration:** $4000–$20,000 grant. **Guidelines:** U.S. citizen or permanent resident with undergraduate degree; grants and fellowships for research and study in Scandinavian countries. **Application procedure:** supplementary materials, application and $10 fee; see website for application and guidelines. **Deadline:** 1 Nov. **Notification:** 15 Mar.

THE ARCH AND BRUCE BROWN FOUNDATION
31855 Date Palm Dr, PMB 503; Cathedral City, CA 92234;
archwrite@aol.com, www.aabbfoundation.org
Arch Brown, *President*

Open to: playwrights, composers, librettists, lyricists, screenwriters. **Frequency:** award rotates triennially among fiction, short fiction, one-act plays, full-length plays and screenplays. **Remuneration:** $1000 grant. **Guidelines:** work that presents gay and lesbian lifestyle in positive way, and is inspired by historical person, culture, event or work of art; see website for guidelines. **Application procedure:** script and short note describing "historical inspiration" for the work; materials will not be returned. **Deadline:** postmarked by 30 Nov 2008. **Notification:** May 2009.

ARTISTS-IN-BERLIN RESIDENCY PROGRAM (BERLINER KÜNSTLERPROGRAMM)

To obtain application only:

German Academic Exchange Service (DAAD); 871 United Nations Plaza; New York, NY 10017; (212) 758-3223, FAX 755-5780; daadny@daad.org, www.daad.org, www.berliner-kuenstlerprogramm.de

All applications and inquiries to:

Deutscher Akademischer Austauschdienst (DAAD); Markgrafenstrasse 37; D-10117 Berlin, Germany; 49-30-20-22-08-20, FAX 49-30-204-12-67; bkp.berlin@daad.de, www.berliner-kuenstlerprogramm.de

Open to: playwrights, composers, screenwriters. **Frequency:** annual. **Remuneration:** monthly grant to cover living costs and rent during 1-year residency in Berlin (6 months for screenwriters); workspace provided or paid for; travel for artist and any members of immediate family who will be staying in Berlin for period of residency; in some cases specific projects such as readings or publications can be subsidized. **Guidelines:** assistance to enable 15–20 internationally known and qualified young artists to pursue own work while participating in city's cultural life and making contact with local artists; must reside in Berlin for period of grant; German nationals and international writers residing in Germany ineligible; write or see website for guidelines. **Application procedure:** samples of published work (no manuscripts), preferably in German, otherwise in English or French, and application for playwrites; scores, records, tapes or published work for composers; films with synopsis for screenwriters. **Deadline:** 1 Jan. **Notification:** spring. **Dates:** residency begins between 1 Jan and 30 Jun.

ARTIST TRUST

1835 12th Ave; Seattle, WA 98122; (206) 467-8734, FAX 467-9633; info@artisttrust.org, www.artisttrust.org

Monica Miller, *Director of Programs*

FELLOWSHIPS

Open to: playwrights, composers, librettists, lyricists, screenwriters, radio and television writers. **Frequency:** biennial for theatre artists (award rotates among disciplines). **Remuneration:** $7500 grant. **Guidelines:** WA resident only; practicing professional artist of exceptional talent and demonstrated ability; award based on creative excellence and continuing dedication to artistic discipline; send SASE for guidelines (application available mid–Apr 2009). **Application procedure:** work sample and application. **Deadline:** Jun 2010.

GAP (GRANTS FOR ARTIST PROJECTS)

Open to: playwrights, composers, librettists, lyricists, screenwriters, radio and television writers. **Frequency:** annual. **Remuneration:** grant up to $1500. **Guidelines:** WA resident only; grant provides support for artist-generated projects, which can include (but are not limited to) the development, presentation or completion of new work; award based on quality of work and on creativity and feasibility of proposed project; send SASE for guidelines (application available Dec). **Application procedure:** work sample and application. **Deadline:** Feb 20.

AURAND HARRIS CHILDREN'S THEATRE GRANTS AND FELLOWSHIPS
The Children's Theatre Foundation of America; 1114 Red Oak Dr;
　　Avon, IN 46123; (317) 272-9322; www.childrenstheatrefoundation.org
Dorothy Webb, *President*

FELLOWSHIPS

Open to: playwrights. **Frequency:** annual. **Remuneration:** $5000 maximum award. **Guidelines:** U.S. resident; funds to be used for specific projects or professional development of theatre artists who work in theatre for young audiences. **Application procedure:** see website for information and application. **Deadline:** 1 Apr. **Notification:** 1 Sep.

GRANTS

Open to: not-for-profit theatres and theatre artists serving young people. **Frequency:** annual. **Remuneration:** grant up to $5000. **Guidelines:** grant to assist in production costs of premiere of new play for children, including expenses to enable playwright to participate in rehearsals and attend performances. **Application procedure:** write for guidelines. **Deadline:** 1 Apr. **Notification:** 1 Sep. (See The Children's Theatre Foundation of America in Membership and Service Organizations.)

BUSH ARTIST PROGRAM
Bush Foundation; 332 Minnesota St, Suite E-900; St. Paul, MN 55101;
　　(651) 227-5222; bafinfo@bushfoundation.org, www.bushfoundation.org

Open to: playwrights, composers, screenwriters. **Frequency:** award rotates biennially among disciplines. **Remuneration:** $48,000 grant in equal monthly installments for 12–24 months. **Guidelines:** U.S. citizen or permanent resident minimum 25 years of age who is not a student; playwright must have had at least 1 play given full production or workshop production; screenwriter must have had 1 public staged reading or workshop production, or screenplay sale or option. **Application procedure:** see website for details. **Deadline:** fall 2008; exact date TBA. **Notification:** Apr 2009.

CINTAS FELLOWSHIPS
The Patricia and Philip Frost Art Museum, Florida International University;
　　University Park; 10975 Southwest 17th St; Miami, FL 33199;
　　(305) 348-2890, FAX 348-2762; artinfo@fiu.edu,
　　www.cintasfoundation.org/fellowships.htm
Program Manager

Open to: playwrights. **Frequency:** biennial; award rotates among artistic disciplines. **Remuneration:** $15,000 stipend. **Guidelines:** artist of Cuban decent or citizenship living outside of Cuba. **Application procedure:** up to 2 work samples no longer than 25 pages combined, artistic statement, project statement, 2 letters of recommendation and application; call or see website for guidelines; next creative writing fellowship in 2010. **Notification:** exact date TBA (May in 2008). **Deadline:** exact date TBA (14 Jan in 2008).

CREATIVE CAPITAL GRANTS

Creative Capital Foundation, Grants & Services; 65 Bleecker St, 7th Floor;
New York, NY 10012; grants@creative-capital.org,
www.creative-capital.org
Kemi Ilesanmi, *Associate Director, Grants and Services*

Open to: playwrights, composers, solo performers. **Frequency:** triennial. **Remuneration:** $10,000 grant; additional follow-up and strategic funding; technical assistance and general career advice. **Guidelines:** U.S. citizen or permanent resident, minimum 25 years of age, with minimum 5 years experience as an artist. **Application procedure:** letter of inquiry only; work sample, resume and application upon notification of advance to application stage. **Deadline:** Mar 2010; exact date TBA. **Notification:** Jan 2011.

DOBIE-PAISANO FELLOWSHIP

The University of Texas at Austin; The Graduate School; 1 University Station,
G0400; Austin, TX 78712; (512) 471-8528, FAX 471-7620;
adameve@mail.utexas.edu, www.utexas.edu/ogs/paisano
Michael Adams, *Director*

Open to: playwrights. **Frequency:** annual. **Remuneration:** living allowance to cover 6-month residency at 265-acre ranch; housing; families welcome; 2 writers selected each year. **Guidelines:** native Texan, or playwright who has lived in TX for at least 3 years or has published work about TX. **Application procedure:** see website. **Deadline:** 15 Jan. **Notification:** May.

THE DON AND GEE NICHOLL FELLOWSHIPS IN SCREENWRITING

Academy of Motion Picture Arts and Sciences; 1313 Vine St;
Los Angeles, CA 90028; (310) 247-3010; www.oscars.org/nicholl
Greg Beal, *Program Coordinator*

Open to: playwrights, screenwriters. **Frequency:** annual. **Remuneration:** up to 5 fellowships of $30,000. **Guidelines:** playwright or screenwriter who has not worked as a professional screenwriter for theatrical films or television or sold screen or television rights for any original story, treatment, screenplay or teleplay; 1st-round selection based on submission of original screenplay or screen adaptation of own original work by writer or two collaborators; 100–130 pages, written in standard screenplay format; write for guidelines after 1 Jan. **Application procedure:** screenplay, application and $30 fee; application available from website. **Deadline:** 1 May. **Notification:** Aug for 1st-round selection; late Oct for winners.

ELECTRONIC ARTS GRANT PROGRAM

Experimental Television Center; 109 Lower Fairfield Rd;
    Newark Valley, NY 13811; (607) 687-4341, FAX 687-4341;
    etc@experimentaltvcenter.org, www.experimentaltvcenter.org
Sherry Miller Hocking, *Program Director*

FINISHING FUNDS

Open to: media artists, including writers and composers, involved in creation of film, audio, video, new media, sonic arts or computer-generated time-based works. **Frequency:** annual. **Remuneration:** up to $2500 grant. **Guidelines:** resident of NY state; funds to be used to assist completion of work that is time-based in conception and execution; work must be presented as installation performance, on video, as website production or must utilize new technologies; write or see website for guidelines. **Application procedure:** project description, work sample, resume and 3 copies of application; application available from website. **Deadline:** 15 Mar. **Notification:** 3 months.

PRESENTATION FUNDS

Open to: not-for-profit organizations presenting audio, film, video or computer-generated time-based works. **Frequency:** year-round. **Remuneration:** grant up to $1000 for artist's fees for in-person appearances by cinema or sonic artists. **Guidelines:** NY state organization; event must be open to public; write or see website for guidelines. **Application procedure:** individual may not apply; application and supporting materials submitted by organization well in advance of event; application available from website. **Deadline:** year-round. **Notification:** 15th of month following month of submission.

FULBRIGHT SCHOLAR AWARDS FOR FACULTY AND PROFESSIONALS

Council for International Exchange of Scholars (CIES);
    3007 Tilden St NW, Suite 5L; Washington, DC 20008-3009;
    (202) 686-7877, FAX 362-3442; apprequest@cies.iie.org, www.cies.org

Open to: scholars and professionals in all areas of theatre and the arts, including playwrights, translators, composers, librettists and lyricists. **Frequency:** annual. **Remuneration:** grant for lecturing at university or research in one of more than 150 countries for 3–9 months; amount varies with country of award; travel; maintenance allowance for living costs of grantee and possibly family. **Guidelines:** U.S. citizen; Ph.D., MFA or comparable professional qualifications; university or college teaching experience for lecturing award. **Application procedure:** application available from website. **Deadline:** 1 Aug; no submission before 1 Mar. **Notification:** up to 11 months, depending on country.

GEORGE BENNETT FELLOWSHIP

Phillips Exeter Academy; 20 Main St; Exeter, NH 03833-2460;
    www.exeter.edu
Charles Pratt, *Coordinator, Selection Committee*

Open to: playwrights. **Frequency:** annual. **Remuneration:** academic-year stipend of $12,000; room and board for fellow and family. **Guidelines:** individual who is seriously contemplating or pursuing a career as a writer (in any genre) and who needs time and freedom from material considerations to complete a project in progress; committee favors playwrights who have not yet been produced commercially or at a major not-for-profit theatre; fellow expected to make self and talents available in informal and unofficial way to students interested in writing; see website for guidelines and application (no phone inquiries). **Application procedure:** work sample, statement concerning work-in-progress, names of 2 references, application and $10 fee to Phillips Exeter Academy; work samples will not be returned. **Deadline:** 1 Dec. **Notification:** 15 Mar. **Dates:** Sep–Jun.

HARVARD UNIVERSITY RADCLIFFE INSTITUTE FOR ADVANCED STUDY FELLOWSHIPS

The Radcliffe Institute for Advanced Study; Fellowships Office;
    8 Garden Street; Cambridge, MA 02138; (617) 496-1324,
    FAX 495-8136; fellowships@radcliffe.edu, www.radcliffe.edu/fellowships

Open to: playwrights, composers, librettists. **Frequency:** annual. **Remuneration:** up to $70,000 1-year fellowship. **Guidelines:** professionals of "demonstrated accomplishment and exceptional promise" to complete substantial project in their field; full-time appointment; fellow required to reside in Boston area and expected to present work-in-progress in scheduled event during year; office or studio space, auditing privileges and access to libraries and other resources at Harvard provided; call, write or see website for guidelines and application. **Application Procedure:** see website. **Deadline:** postmarked by 1 Oct. **Notification:** Mar. **Dates:** Sep–Jun.

THE HODDER FELLOWSHIP

(formerly The Alfred Hodder Fellowship)
Princeton University; Lewis Center for the Arts; Program in Creative Writing;
    185 Nassau Street; Princeton, NJ 08542; (609) 258-4096;
    jbraude@princeton.edu, www.princeton.edu/arts/fellows

Open to: playwrights, translators. **Frequency:** annual. **Remuneration:** $60,000 fellowship. **Guidelines:** "typical fellows have published 1 highly acclaimed work and are undertaking a significant new project that might not be possible without the fellowship"; prefers individual outside of academia; send SASE or see website for guidelines. **Application procedure:** maximum 10-page work sample (materials will not be returned), 2–3 page project proposal and resume. **Deadline:** postmarked by 1 Nov.

JAPAN-UNITED STATES ART PROGRAM

Asian Cultural Council; 437 Madison Ave, 37th Floor;
New York, NY 10022-7001; (212) 812-4300, FAX 812-4299;
acc@accny.org, www.asianculturalcouncil.org

Open to: playwrights, composers, librettists, lyricists. **Frequency:** annual.
Remuneration: amount varies. **Guidelines:** support of residencies in Japan for
American artists for a variety of purposes, including creative activities (other than
performances), research projects, professional observation tours and specialized
training. **Application procedure:** application form and project description. **Deadline:**
1 Feb.

JOHN SIMON GUGGENHEIM MEMORIAL FOUNDATION

90 Park Ave; New York, NY 10016; (212) 687-4470, FAX 697-3248;
fellowships@gf.org, www.gf.org

Open to: playwrights, composers. **Frequency:** annual. **Remuneration:** 1-year
fellowship (in 2008, 190 fellowships with average grant of $43,200). **Guidelines:**
citizen or permanent resident of U.S. or Canada; recipient "must demonstrate
exceptional creative ability"; grant to support research in any field of knowledge or
creation in any of the arts under the freest possible conditions. **Application
procedure:** write for guidelines. **Deadline:** 15 Sep. **Notification:** Apr.

THE KLEBAN AWARD

c/o New Dramatists; 424 West 44th St; New York, NY 10036;
(212) 757-6960, FAX 609-5901; newdramatists@newdramatists.org,
www.newdramatists.org
Jocelyn Sawyer, *Kleban Award Administrator*

Open to: librettists and/or lyricists. **Frequency:** annual. **Remuneration:** $100,000
award each to lyricist and librettist, paid in installments of $50,000 per year.
Guidelines: applicant whose work has received a full or workshop production, or who
has been a member or associate of a professional musical workshop or theatre group
(e.g., ASCAP or BMI workshops; see Development); writer whose work has been
performed on the Broadway stage for a cumulative period of 2 years ineligible; write or
see website for guidelines. **Application procedure:** work sample and application.
Deadline: postmarked by 15 Sep. (See New Dramatists in Membership and Service
Organizations.)

LUDWIG VOGELSTEIN FOUNDATION, INC.

4001 Inglewood Ave, # 101-309; Redondo Beach, CA 90278;
lvf@earthlink.net
Diana Braunschweig, *Executive Director*

Open to: playwrights. **Frequency:** annual. **Remuneration:** grants of $1000–$3000.
Guidelines: individual grants for writers of merit who have no source of funding.
Application procedure: work sample, resume, project proposal (include name,
address, age and social security number in upper right corner), copy of last IRS return

and proposed budget; all materials should include writer's name on each page; email for guidelines. **Deadline:** spring (Mar in 2008); email for exact date.

MARIN ARTS COUNCIL PROGRAMS

555 Northgate Dr, Suite 270; San Rafael, CA 94903; (415) 499-8350,
   FAX 499-8537; lance@marinarts.org, www.marinarts.org
Lance Walker, *Grants Program Director*

CAREER GRANTS

Open to: playwrights, solo performers, screenwriters. **Frequency:** biannual. **Remuneration:** grant of up to $1500. **Guidelines:** resident of Marin County, CA; grants intended to help individual artists "take steps to enhance professional development." **Application procedure:** 4 copies of work sample, narrative of proposed project, simple budget and application; see website for application and guidelines. **Deadline:** fall 2008; spring 2009; see website for exact dates.

COMMUNITY ARTS PARTNERSHIP GRANTS

Open to: artists in all fields in partnership with community organizations. **Frequency:** annual. **Remuneration:** grant up to $5000. **Guidelines:** resident of Marin County, CA; grant supports project that engages the community in the arts; programs for youth encouraged; project must take place within 1 year of grant. **Application procedure:** project description, budget breakdown, overview of participants, letters of recommendation, supporting materials and application; see website for application and guidelines. **Deadline:** fall; exact date TBA.

MEET THE COMPOSER PROGRAMS

90 John Street, #312; New York, NY 10038; (212) 645-6949,
   FAX 645-9669; eficklin@meetthecomposer.org,
   www.meetthecomposer.org
Edward Ficklin, *Senior Program Manager*

COMMISSIONING MUSIC/USA

Open to: theatre and music-theatre companies. **Frequency:** categories rotate annually. **Remuneration:** commissioning grant up to $30,000 to cover composer and librettist fees and copying costs. **Guidelines:** organizations that have been producing or presenting for at least 3 years; plans must involve full production of new work and a minimum of 4 performances for a single organization or a minimum of 6 for a consortium; see website for guidelines and application. **Application procedure:** individuals may not apply; 1 host organization submits application and supporting materials; application may be from a single organization for grants up to $15,000 or from consortium of organizations for grants up to $30,000. **Deadline:** Mar 2010 for theatre; exact date TBA.

CREATIVE CONNECTIONS

Open to: theatre and music-theatre companies. **Frequency:** quarterly. **Remuneration:** up to $5000 appearance fee for composer actively participating in events featuring the performance of their music. **Guidelines:** awards based on the overall quality of application, level of composer participation and level of audience/community involvement; see website for guidelines and application. **Application procedure:** individuals may not apply; performing organizations apply on behalf of composer. **Deadline:** 1 Oct; 5 Jan; 1 Apr; 1 Jun.

GLOBAL CONNECTIONS

Open to: not-for-profit organizations. **Frequency:** biannual. **Remuneration:** $500–$5000 grant. **Guidelines:** provides financial assistance to composers traveling to another country to engage in a variety of activities surrounding the live performance of their music or traveling to another country for research and development of a new project or work; grants are based on the overall strength of the application and the level of the composer's participation in the proposed event. **Application procedure:** applications are submitted jointly by a composer and a hosting organization; composer and organization may not be based in the same country and 1 must be based in the U.S.; see website for guidelines and application. **Deadline:** 1 Nov; 1 May.

NATIONAL ENDOWMENT FOR THE ARTS INTERNATIONAL PARTNERSHIPS/ARTSLINK PROJECTS

CEC ArtsLink, Inc.; 435 Hudson St, 8th Floor; New York, NY 10014;
(212) 643-1985, ext 22, FAX 643-1996; al@cecartslink.org,
www.cecartslink.org

Open to: playwrights, translators, composers, librettists, lyricists, solo performers. **Frequency:** biennial; award rotates among disciplines. **Remuneration:** grant up to $10,000 (average grant $4500). **Guidelines:** U.S. citizen or permanent resident; enables individual artist or groups of artists and arts organizations to work with their counterparts in Eastern and Central Europe, Russia, Central Asia and the Caucasus on mutually beneficial collaborative project that will enrich artist's work and/or create new work that draws inspiration from knowledge and experience gained in country visited; write for guidelines. **Application procedure:** application and supporting materials. **Deadline:** next deadline for playwrights: Jan 2010; exact date TBA. **Notification:** Apr 2010.

NATIONAL ENDOWMENT FOR THE ARTS LITERATURE FELLOWSHIPS FOR TRANSLATORS

1100 Pennsylvania Ave NW, Washington, DC 20506;
(202) 682-5034; www.arts.gov

Open to: translators. **Frequency:** annual. **Remuneration:** $10,000–$20,000 fellowship. **Guidelines:** previously published drama, verse, prose and poetry by translator of exceptional talent. **Application procedure:** see website for guidelines and application. **Deadline:** Jan; exact date TBA.

NATIONAL ENDOWMENT FOR THE HUMANITIES DIVISION OF PUBLIC PROGRAMS/AMERICA'S MEDIA MAKERS

1100 Pennsylvania Ave NW; Washington, DC 20506; (202) 606-8269,
    FAX 606-8557; publicpgms@neh.gov, www.neh.gov
Margaret Scrymser, *Lead Program Analyst*

Open to: U.S. not-for-profit organizations with IRS 501(c)(3) tax exempt status, state and local governmental agencies; individuals are not eligible to apply but may seek an eligible organization to sponsor the project and submit the application to NEH. **Frequency:** annual. **Remuneration:** varies. **Guidelines:** support for development, planning, writing or production of television and radio projects that "substantially draw their content from scholarship in the humanities and are aimed at a national or broad regional audience"; no adaptations of literary works. **Application procedure:** option to submit draft proposal before making formal application; call or see website for guidelines. **Deadline:** Aug; Jan. **Notification:** Mar for Aug deadline; Aug for Jan deadline; exact dates TBA.

NATIONAL ENDOWMENT FOR THE HUMANITIES DIVISION OF RESEARCH PROGRAMS/COLLABORATIVE RESEARCH

1100 Pennsylvania Ave NW; Washington, DC 20506; (202) 606-8461;
    FAX 606-8204; mhall@neh.gov, www.neh.gov
Joel Schwartz, *Program Officer*

Open to: translators. **Frequency:** annual. **Remuneration:** amount varies according to project. **Guidelines:** U.S. citizen or resident for 3 years; money to support collaborative projects to translate into English works that provide insight into the history, literature, philosophy and artistic achievements of U.S. or other cultures and that make available to scholars, students, teachers and the public the thought and learning of those civilizations; write or see website for guidelines. **Application procedure:** application and supporting materials. **Deadline:** 5 Nov. **Notification:** Jun.

NATIVE ARTS PROGRAM VISITING ARTIST APPOINTMENTS

National Museum of the American Indian; Smithsonian Institution;
    Cultural Resources Center; 4220 Silver Hill Rd; Suitland, MD 20746;
    (301) 238-1540, FAX 238-3200; nap@si.edu,
    www.americanindian.si.edu
Community Services Outreach Program Specialist

Open to: playwrights, translators, composers, librettists, lyricists, solo performers, screenwriters. **Frequency:** annual. **Remuneration:** $6000 award, travel, housing, 14–21-day visit to New York City, Boston, Philadelphia and Washington, DC. **Guidelines:** Native American of the Western Hemisphere and Hawaii; professional artist; no students; see website for guidelines. **Application procedure:** work sample, 2 letters of recommendation, resume, 1-page artist statement, budget proposal, tribal identification and application. **Deadline:** 1st Monday in May. **Notification:** Sep.

NEW JEWISH THEATRE PROJECTS

(formerly New Play Commissions in Jewish Theatre)

Foundation for Jewish Culture; 330 7th Ave, 21st Floor;
 New York, NY 10001; (212) 629-0500, ext 215, FAX 629-0508;
 grants@jewishculture.org, www.jewishculture.org

Kristen L. Runk, *Associate Operations Director*

Open to: U.S. not-for-profit theatres that have completed at least 2 seasons of public performance. **Frequency:** annual. **Remuneration:** grant of $1000–$5000. **Guidelines:** grant for the commissioning of new plays, musicals or multimedia works of Jewish significance; grant is meant to support play or performance development, which can include commissioning fees, playwright's residency expenses and research or worshop costs; award is distributed directly to the organization unless special arrangements are made in advance. (See Foundation for Jewish Culture in Membership and Service Organizations.) **Application procedure:** see website. **Deadline:** see website.

NEW PLAY COMMISSIONS IN JEWISH THEATRE

(see New Jewish Theatre Projects)

NEW YORK FOUNDATION FOR THE ARTS (NYFA) ARTISTS' FELLOWSHIPS

155 Avenue of the Americas, 14th Floor; New York, NY 10013-1507;
 (212) 366-6900, ext 217, FAX 366-1778; nyfaafp@nyfa.org,
 www.nyfa.org

Penelope Dannenberg, *Director of Programs*

Open to: playwrights, composers, librettists, screenwriters. **Frequency:** award alternates biennially between disciplines. **Remuneration:** $7000 fellowship. **Guidelines:** NY state resident for 2 years prior to deadline; students ineligible. **Application procedure:** application and supporting materials; application seminars held each Sep. **Deadline:** next deadline for playwrights, composers, librettists and screenwriters postmarked early Oct; see website for exact deadline.

NEW YORK THEATRE WORKSHOP PLAYWRITING FELLOWSHIP

New York Theatre Workshop; 83 East 4th St; New York, NY 10003;
 (212) 780-9037, FAX 460-8996; fellowshipinfo@nytw.org,
 www.nytw.org

Ruben Polendo, *Artistic Associate*

Open to: playwrights. **Frequency:** annual. **Remuneration:** stipend of approximately $3000. **Guidelines:** writer of color with minimal professional experience; resident of New York City; must be available to attend monthly group meetings and 1-week summer retreat; writer must make 1-year commitment. **Application procedure:** 20-page writing sample, artistic statement, resume and 2 letters of recommendation. **Deadline:** see website. (See New York Theatre Workshop in Production.)

PEW FELLOWSHIPS IN THE ARTS

1608 Walnut St, 18th Floor; Philadelphia, PA 19103; (267) 350-4920,
    FAX 350-4997; www.pewarts.org
Melissa Franklin, *Director*

Open to: playwrights, composers. **Frequency:** annual; award rotates among various disciplines. **Remuneration:** up to 12 $60,000 fellowships. **Guidelines:** fellowship to give artists living in Southeastern PA the opportunity to dedicate themselves wholly to the development of their work for up to 2 years; call, write or see website for application and guidelines. **Application procedure:** work sample and application. **Deadline:** Dec; exact date TBA.

PILGRIM PROJECT

156 Fifth Ave, Suite 400; New York, NY 10010; (212) 627-2288,
    FAX 627-2184
Davida Goldman, *Secretary*

Open to: playwrights, solo performers, individual producers and theatre companies. **Frequency:** year-round. **Remuneration:** grant of $1000–$7000. **Guidelines:** grant toward cost of reading, workshop production or full production of play that deals with questions of moral significance. **Application procedure:** script only; write for information. **Deadline:** year-round.

THE PLAYWRIGHTS' CENTER GRANT PROGRAMS

2301 Franklin Ave E; Minneapolis, MN 55406-1099; (612) 332-7481;
    info@pwcenter.org, www.pwcenter.org
Polly K. Carl, *Producing Artistic Director*

JEROME FELLOWSHIPS IN PLAYWRITING

Open to: playwrights, solo performers. **Frequency:** annual. **Remuneration:** 5 1-year fellowships of $10,000. **Guidelines:** U.S. citizen or permanent resident; emerging playwright whose work has not received more than 2 professional full productions; fellow must spend year in residence at Center where fellow has access to developmental workshops, readings and other services; see website for guidelines. **Application procedure:** application and supporting materials. **Deadline:** mid-Sep. **Notification:** Feb. **Dates:** 1 Jul–30 Jun.

McKNIGHT ADVANCEMENT GRANTS

Open to: playwrights, solo performers. **Frequency:** annual. **Remuneration:** 2 grants of $25,000; up to $2000 per fellow for workshops and staged readings using Center's developmental program, or for allocation to partner organization for joint development and/or production. **Guidelines:** U.S. citizen or permanent resident and legal MN resident since 1 Jul 2007; playwright of exceptional merit and potential who has had at least 1 play fully produced by a professional theatre; funds are intended to significantly advance fellow's art and/or career and may be used to cover a variety of expenses, including writing time, residency at theatre or other arts organization, travel/study, production or presentation; recipients are required to participate actively in Center's programs during grant year; see website for more information. **Application procedure:** application and supporting materials. **Deadline:** Feb. **Notification:** Apr. **Dates:** 1 Jul–30 Jun.

McKnight National Playwriting Residency and Commission

Open to: playwrights, solo performers. **Frequency:** annual. **Remuneration:** $12,500 commission; $2500 to support the creation of a new work during 4-week residency; housing; and round-trip travel to Minneapolis. **Guidelines:** U.S. citizen or permanent resident, not MN resident; playwright must have had at least 2 works fully produced by professional theatres; work must have made a significant impact on contemporary theatre; must spend 4 weeks (not necessarily consecutive) in residency at the Center where playwright has access to developmental readings, workshops and other services; send SASE for guidelines. **Application procedure:** agent submission of project description, writing sample and supporting materials. **Deadline:** Dec. **Notification:** Feb. **Dates:** 1 Jul–30 Jun.

Princess Grace Awards: Playwright Fellowship

Princess Grace Foundation-USA; 150 East 58th St, 25th Floor;
    New York, NY 10155; (212) 317-1470, FAX 317-1473;
    grants@pgfusa.org, www.pgfusa.com
Kathleen Richards, Program Manager

Open to: playwrights. **Frequency:** annual. **Remuneration:** $7500 grant; residency at New Dramatists (see Membership and Service Organizations) in New York City; inclusion of submitted script in New Dramatists' lending library and in its ScriptShare national script-distribution program for 1 year; representation and publication by Samuel French, Inc. (see Publication). **Guidelines:** U.S. citizen or permanent resident; emerging artist at onset of career; award based primarily on artistic quality of submitted play and potential of fellowship to assist writer's growth; unproduced, unpublished play (no adaptations); see website for guidelines. **Application procedure:** script, letter of recommendation, resume and application; application available from website. **Deadline:** 31 Mar.

TCG Artistic Programs

Theatre Communications Group; 520 8th Ave, 24th Floor;
    New York, NY 10018-4156; (212) 609-5900, FAX 609-5901;
    grants@tcg.org, www.tcg.org

The New Generations Program: Future Leaders

Michael Francis, *Artistic Programs Associate*

Open to: not-for-profit professional theatres in association with theatre practitioners (including playwrights). **Frequency:** annual. **Remuneration:** individual receives mentorship from professional theatre artist for period of 2 years (8 awarded in 2008). **Guidelines:** program's focus is "cultivating and strengthening a new generation of theatre leadership"; see website for guidelines. **Application procedure:** intent to apply card followed by preliminary proposal;

only those selected by panel submit full application. **Deadline:** Oct (application deadline); exact date TBA.

TCG/ITI Travel Grants

Michael Shatara, *Artistic Programs Associate*

Open to: theatre practitioners (including playwrights) and educators. **Frequency:** biannual. **Remuneration:** $3000 grant (15 awarded in 2007). **Guidelines:** program supports cultural exchange and artistic partnerships between professionals in U.S. and their counterparts in Russia and Eastern and Central Europe; grant covers transportation and living expenses essential to collaborative project, including research materials, communication costs, theatre tickets and/or services of interpreter. **Application procedure:** completed application. **Deadline:** 2 deadlines; exact dates TBA.

Theatre Bay Area Grant Programs

Theatre Bay Area; 870 Market St, Suite 375; San Francisco, CA 94102;
(415) 430-1140, FAX 420-1145; members@theatrebayarea.org,
www.theatrebayarea.org

CA$H Workshops

Open to: playwrights, solo performers, small theatre companies. **Frequency:** annual. **Remuneration:** grants of $1500 to individual artists or $2500 to companies. **Guidelines:** Northern CA theatre artists or small companies with budgets less than $100,000; grants awarded to support "innovative projects resulting in a tangible creative activity." **Application procedure:** send SASE for guidelines. **Deadline:** spring and fall; see website for exact dates.

New Works Fund

Open to: playwrights, composers, lyricists and performance artists, in conjunction with theatre companies. **Frequency:** annual. **Remuneration:** 2 grants of $10,000 ($5000 each to artist and company) to be used by artist and theatre company to develop and fully produce a new work. **Guidelines:** open to Theatre Bay Area members (see Theatre Bay Area in Membership and Service Organizations) with operating budgets between $50,000–$750,000; playwright must reside in greater San Francisco Bay Area. **Application procedure:** see website for application and guidelines. **Deadline:** fall; see website for exact dates.

Travel and Study Grant Program

c/o Jerome Foundation; 400 Sibley St, Suite 125; St. Paul, MN 55101;
(651) 224-9431, FAX 224-3439; www.jeromefdn.org
Cynthia Gehrig, *President*

Open to: playwrights, composers. **Frequency:** biennial. **Remuneration:** grant up to $5000 for foreign or domestic travel. **Guidelines:** resident of MN or New York City; program supports periods of significant professional development through travel and study for independent professional artist; see website for guidelines. **Application**

procedure: work sample, resume and application. **Deadline:** TBA; see website for exact dates.

U.S. DEPARTMENT OF STATE FULBRIGHT U.S. STUDENT PROGRAM AT THE INSTITUTE OF INTERNATIONAL EDUCATION
809 United Nations Plaza; New York, NY 10017-3580; (212) 984-5330;
   www.fulbrightonline.org

Open to: playwrights, translators, composers, librettists, lyricists. **Frequency:** annual. **Remuneration:** grant amount varies with country of award. **Guidelines:** specific opportunities for study abroad in the arts; write for brochure. **Application procedure:** application and supporting materials. **Deadline:** 20 Oct. **Notification:** Jan.

WISCONSIN ARTS BOARD ARTIST FELLOWSHIP AWARDS
101 East Wilson St, 1st Floor; Madison, WI 53702; (608) 264-8191,
   FAX 267-0380; mark.fraire@wisconsin.gov
Mark Fraire, *Grant Programs and Services Specialist*

Open to: playwrights, composers. **Frequency:** biennial. **Remuneration:** $8000 fellowship. **Guidelines:** WI resident for at least 1 year at time of application; artist must produce 1 public presentation of work as part of fellowship; see website for guidelines and application. **Application procedure:** application and work sample. **Deadline:** 15 Sep 2010. **Notification:** Jan 2011.

EMERGENCY FUNDS

How do emergency funds differ from other sources of financial aid?

Emergency funds aid writers in severe temporary financial difficulties. Some funds give outright grants, others make interest-free loans. For support for anything other than a genuine emergency, turn to Fellowships and Grants.

THE AUTHOR'S LEAGUE FUND

31 East 32nd St, 7th Floor; New York, NY 10016; (212) 268-1208,
   FAX 564-8363; staff@authorsleaguefund.org
Sarah Heller, *Administrator*

Open to: playwrights. **Type of assistance:** interest-free loan; request should be limited to immmediate needs. **Guidelines:** published or produced working professional; must demonstrate real need. **Application procedure:** application and supporting materials. **Notification:** 1 month.

CARNEGIE FUND FOR AUTHORS

1 Old Country Rd, Suite 113; Carle Place, NY 11514

Open to: playwrights. **Type of assistance:** emergency grant. **Guidelines:** playwright who has had at least 1 play or collection of plays published commercially in book form (anthologies excluded); emergency that has placed applicant in substantial verifiable financial need. **Application procedure:** write for application.

THE DRAMATISTS GUILD FUND

1501 Broadway, Suite 701; New York, NY 10036; (212) 391-8384,
   FAX 944-0420
Susan Drury, *Administrator*

Open to: playwrights, composers, librettists, lyricists. **Type of assistance:** interest-free grant; grants to not-for-profit theatres producing contemporary American work; request should be limited to immediate needs. **Guidelines:** published or produced working professional; must demonstrate real need. **Application procedure:** application and supporting materials. **Notification:** 1 month.

MARY MASON MEMORIAL LEMONADE FUND

Theatre Bay Area; 870 Market St, Suite 375; San Francisco, CA 94102;
   (415) 430-1140, FAX 430-1145; dale@theatrebayarea.org,
   www.theatrebayarea.org/programs/lemonade.jsp
Dale Albright, *Individual Services Director*

Open to: playwrights, translators, lyricists, librettists, composers. **Type of assistance:** grants up to $1000. **Guidelines:** resident of San Francisco Bay Area who has worked professionally or vocationally in theatre with minimum 2 years experience within the last 5 years who is diagnosed with terminal or life-threatening illness; monies cannot be used for hospital expenses. **Application procedure:** call or email for application. **Notification:** 1 month. (See Theatre Bay Area in Membership and Service Organizations.)

PEN FUND FOR WRITERS & EDITORS WITH AIDS

PEN American Center; 588 Broadway, Suite 303; New York, NY 10012;
(212) 334-1660, FAX 334-2181; www.pen.org

Open to: professional playwrights, translators, librettists, screenwriters, radio writers. **Type of assistance:** grant up to $2000. **Guidelines:** emergency assistance for published and/or produced writer who is HIV-positive and having financial difficulties. **Application procedure:** documentation of financial emergency, resume and application; see website for information and application. **Notification:** 2 months.

PEN WRITERS FUND

PEN American Center; 588 Broadway, Suite 303; New York, NY 10012;
(212) 334-1660, ext 101, FAX 334-2181; www.pen.org

Open to: professional playwrights, translators, librettists, screenwriters, radio writers. **Type of assistance:** grant up to $2000. **Guidelines:** emergency assistance for published and/or produced writer having financial difficulties. **Application procedure:** work sample, documentation of financial emergency, resume and application; see website for information and application. **Notification:** 2 months.

State Arts Agencies

What can my state arts agency do for me?

Possibly quite a bit—ask your agency for guidelines and study them carefully. State programs vary greatly and change frequently. Most have some sort of residency requirement, but eligibility is not always restricted to current residents, and may include people who were born or raised in, attended school in or had some other association with the state in question.

What if my state doesn't give grants to individual artists?

A number of state arts agencies are restricted in this way. However, those with such restrictions, by and large, are eager to help artists locate not-for-profit organizations that channel funds to individuals. The New York State Council on the Arts, for example, is prohibited from funding individuals directly, and must contract with a sponsoring not-for-profit organization when it awards grants to individual artists. Yet NYSCA has a number of ways of supporting the work of theatre writers. The Literature Program funds translations and a number of other activities of interest to playwrights. The Individual Artists Program assists not-for-profit organizations in commissioning new theatre works. NYSCA also subgrants funds to the New York Foundation for the Arts (see Fellowships and Grants, and Development), which provides funds and project development assistance for individual artists.

At the least, every state has some kind of artist-in-education program; if you are able and willing to function in an educational setting you should certainly investigate this possibility.

ALABAMA STATE COUNCIL ON THE ARTS
201 Monroe St; Montgomery, AL 36130-1800; (334) 242-4076,
FAX 240-3269; staff@arts.alabama.gov, www.arts.state.al.us
Al Head, *Executive Director*

ALASKA STATE COUNCIL ON THE ARTS
411 West 4th Ave, Suite 1E; Anchorage, AK 99501-2343;
(907) 269-6610, (888) 278-7424, (800) 770-8973 (TTY),
FAX (907) 269-6601; charlotte.fox@alaska.gov, www.eed.state.ak.us/aksca
Charlotte Fox, *Executive Director*

AMERICAN SAMOA COUNCIL ON CULTURE, ARTS AND HUMANITIES
Box 1540; Office of the Governor; Pago Pago, AS 96799;
(684) 633-4347, FAX 633-2059

ARIZONA COMMISSION ON THE ARTS
417 West Roosevelt St; Phoenix, AZ 85003; (602) 771-6501,
FAX 256-0282; info@azarts.gov, www.azarts.gov
Robert C. Booker, *Executive Director*

ARKANSAS ARTS COUNCIL
1500 Tower Bldg; 323 Center St; Little Rock, AR 72201; (501) 324-9766,
324-9150 (TTD), FAX 324-9207; info@arkansasarts.com, www.arkansasarts.com
Joy Pennington, *Executive Director*

CALIFORNIA ARTS COUNCIL
1300 I St, Suite 930; Sacramento, CA 95814; (916) 322-6555,
(800) 201-6201, FAX (916) 322-6575; info@caartscouncil.com,
www.cac.ca.gov
Muriel Johnson, *Director*

COLORADO COUNCIL ON THE ARTS
1625 Broadway, Suite 2700; Denver, CO 80204; (303) 892-3802,
FAX 892-3848; coloarts@state.co.us, www.coloarts.org
Elaine Mariner, *Executive Director*

COMMONWEALTH COUNCIL FOR ARTS AND CULTURE (NORTHERN MARIANA ISLANDS)
Box 5553, CHRB; Saipan, MP 96950; (670) 322-9982, 322-9983,
FAX 322-9028; galaidi@vzpacifica.net,
www.geocities.com/ccacarts/ccacwebsite.html
Robert H. Hunter, *Executive Director*

CONNECTICUT COMMISSION ON CULTURE AND TOURISM, ARTS DIVISION

1 Constitution Plaza, 2nd Floor; Hartford, CT 06103; (860) 256-2800, FAX (860) 256-2811; artsinfo@ctarts.org, www.cultureandtourism.org
An-Ming Truxes, *Division Director*

DELAWARE DIVISION OF THE ARTS

Carvel State Office Bldg, 4th Floor; 820 North French St; Wilmington, DE 19801; (302) 577-8278, FAX 577-6561; delarts@state.de.us, www.artsdel.org
Paul Weagraff, *Director*

DISTRICT OF COLUMBIA (DC) COMMISSION ON THE ARTS AND HUMANITIES

1371 Harvard Street, NW; Washington, DC 20009; (202) 724-5613, 727-4493 (TTY/TTD), FAX 727-4135; cah@dc.gov, dcarts.dc.gov

FLORIDA DIVISION OF CULTURAL AFFAIRS

R.A. Gray Bldg, 3rd Floor; 500 South Bronough St; Tallahassee, FL 32399-0250; (850) 245-6470, FAX 245-6497; infd@florida-arts.org, www.florida-arts.org
Sandy Shaughnessy, *Division Director*

GEORGIA COUNCIL FOR THE ARTS

260 14th St NW, Suite 401; Atlanta, GA 30318; (404) 685-2787, 685-2799 (TTY), FAX 685-2788; gaarts@gaarts.org, www.gaarts.org
Susan S. Weiner, *Executive Director*

GUAM COUNCIL ON THE ARTS & HUMANITIES AGENCY

Box 2950; Hagatna, Guam 96932; (671) 646-2781, FAX 648-2787; www.guamcaha.com
Sylvia Flores, *Executive Director*

HAWAII STATE FOUNDATION ON CULTURE AND THE ARTS

250 South Hotel St, 2nd Floor; Honolulu, HI 96813; (808) 586-0300, 586-0740 (TTY), FAX 586-0308; ken.hamilton@hawaii.gov, www.state.hi.us/sfca
Ronald K. Yamakawa, *Executive Director*

Idaho Commission on the Arts

Box 83720; Boise, ID 83720-0008; (208) 334-2119, (800) 278-3863,
FAX (208) 334-2488; info@arts.idaho.gov, www.arts.idaho.gov
Michael Faison, *Executive Director*

Illinois Arts Council

James R. Thompson Center; 100 West Randolph, Suite 10-500;
Chicago, IL 60601; (312) 814-6750, (888) 261-7957 (TTY), (800) 237-6994,
FAX (312) 814-1471; info@arts.state.il.us, www.state.il.us/agency/iac
Terry A. Scrogum, *Executive Director*

Indiana Arts Commission

150 West Market St, Suite 618; Indianapolis, IN 46204; (317) 232-1268,
FAX 232-5595; indianaartscommission@iac.in.gov, www.in.gov/arts
Lewis Ricci, *Executive Director*

Institute of Puerto Rican Culture

Box 9024184; San Juan, PR 00902-4184; (787) 724-0700, FAX 724-8393;
www@icp.gobierno.pr, www.icp.gobierno.pr
Dr. José Luis Vega, *Executive Director*

Iowa Arts Council

600 East Locust; Des Moines, IA 50319-0290; (515) 281-6412,
242-5147 (TDD), FAX 242-6498; www.iowaartscouncil.org
Cyndi Pederson, *Executive Director*

Kansas Arts Commission

700 Southwest Jackson, Suite 1004; Topeka, KS 66603-3761;
(785) 296-3335, FAX (785) 296-4989; kac@arts.state.ks.us, arts.state.ks.us
(Ms.) Llwellyn Crain, *Executive Director*

Kentucky Arts Council

Capital/Plaza Tower, 21st Floor; 500 Mero St; Frankfort, KY 40601-1987;
(502) 564-3757, (888) 833-2787, FAX (502) 564-2839;
kyarts@ky.gov, artscouncil.ky.gov
Lori Meadows, *Executive Director*

Louisiana Division of the Arts

Box 44247; Baton Rouge, LA 70804-4247; (225) 342-8180,
FAX 342-8173; arts@crt.state.la.us, www.crt.state.la.us/arts
Danny Belanger, *Interim Director*

MAINE ARTS COMMISSION
193 State St; 25 State House Station; Augusta, ME 04333-0025;
(207) 287-2724, (877) 887-3878 (TTY), FAX (207) 287-2725;
mainearts.info@maine.gov, www.mainearts.com
Donna McNeil, *Director*

MARYLAND STATE ARTS COUNCIL
175 West Ostend St, Suite E; Baltimore, MD 21230; (410) 767-6555,
333-4519 (TTY), FAX 333-1062; msac@msac.org, www.msac.org
Theresa M. Colvin, *Executive Director*

MASSACHUSETTS CULTURAL COUNCIL
10 St. James Ave, 3rd Floor; Boston, MA 02116-3803; (617) 727-3668,
338-9153 (TTY), FAX 727-0044; mcc@art.state.ma.us,
www.massculturalcouncil.org
Anita Walker, *Executive Director*

MICHIGAN COUNCIL FOR THE ARTS & CULTURAL AFFAIRS
702 West Kalamazoo St; Box 30705; Lansing, MI 48909-8205;
(517) 241-4011, 373-1592 (TTY), FAX 241-3979;
artsinfo@michigan.gov, www.michigan.gov/hal
John Bracey, *Executive Director*

MINNESOTA STATE ARTS BOARD
Park Square Court, Suite 200; 400 Sibley St; St. Paul, MN 55101-1928;
(651) 215-1600, 215-6235 (TTY), (800) 866-2787, FAX (651) 215-1602;
msab@arts.state.mn.us, www.arts.state.mn.us
Sue Gens, *Interim Executive Director*

MISSISSIPPI ARTS COMMISSION
501 North West St, Suite 1101A; Woolfolk Building; Jackson, MS 39201;
(601) 359-6030, (800) 582-2233 (TTY), FAX (601) 359-6008;
www.arts.state.ms.us
Malcolm White, *Executive Director*

MISSOURI ARTS COUNCIL
815 Olive Street, Suite 16; St. Louis, MO 63101-1503; (314) 340-6845,
(866) 407-4752, (800) 735-2966 (TTY), FAX (314) 340-7215;
moarts@ded.mo.gov, www.missouriartscouncil.org
Beverly Strohmeyer, *Executive Director*

MONTANA ARTS COUNCIL

Box 202201; Helena, MT 59620; (406) 444-6430, FAX 444-6548;
mac@mt.gov, www.art.state.mt.us
Arlynn Fishbaugh, *Executive Director*

NEBRASKA ARTS COUNCIL

1004 Farnam St, Plaza Level of the Burlington Building; Omaha, NE 68102;
(402) 595-2122, 595-2122 (TTY), (800) 341-4067, FAX (402) 595-2334;
swise@nebraskaartscouncil.org, www.nebraskaartscouncil.org
Suzanne Wise, *Executive Director*

NEVADA ARTS COUNCIL

716 North Carson St, Suite A; Carson City, NV 89701;
(775) 687-6680, FAX 687-6688; nevadaculture.org/docs/arts
Susan Boskoff, *Executive Director*

NEW HAMPSHIRE STATE COUNCIL ON THE ARTS

2 1/2 Beacon St, 2nd Floor, Suite 225; Concord, NH 03301-4447;
(603) 271-2789, (800) 735-2964 (TTY/TDD), FAX (603) 271-3584;
www.nh.gov/nharts
Rebecca L. Lawrence, *Director*

NEW JERSEY STATE COUNCIL ON THE ARTS

Box 306; 225 West State St; Trenton, NJ 08625; (609) 292-6130,
633-1186 (TTY), FAX 989-1440; njsca@arts.sos.state.nj.us,
www.njartscouncil.org
Steve Runk, *Executive Director*

NEW MEXICO ARTS

Box 1450; Santa Fe, NM 87504-1450; (505) 827-6490,
(800) 879-4278, FAX (505) 827-6043; www.nmarts.org
Loie Fecteau, *Executive Director*

NEW YORK STATE COUNCIL ON THE ARTS

175 Varick St; New York, NY 10014-4604; (212) 627-4455,
(800) 895-9838 (TDD), FAX (212) 620-5911; www.nysca.org
Heather Hitchens, *Executive Director*

NORTH CAROLINA ARTS COUNCIL

MSC #4632, Department of Cultural Resources; Raleigh, NC 27699-4632;
(919) 807-6500, FAX 807-6532; ncarts@ncmail.net, www.ncarts.org
Mary B. Regan, *Executive Director*

NORTH DAKOTA COUNCIL ON THE ARTS
1600 East Century Ave, Suite 6; Bismarck, ND 58503; (701) 328-7590,
FAX 328-7595; comserv@state.nd.us, www.state.nd.us/arts
Jan Webb, *Executive Director*

NORTHERN MARIANA ISLANDS
(see Commonwealth Council for Arts and Culture [Northern Mariana Islands])

OHIO ARTS COUNCIL
727 East Main St; Columbus, OH 43205-1796; (614) 466-2613,
FAX 466-4494; www.oac.state.oh.us
Julie S. Henahan, *Executive Director*

OKLAHOMA ARTS COUNCIL
Box 52001-2001; Oklahoma City, OK 73152-2001; (405) 521-2931,
FAX 521-6418; okarts@arts.ok.gov, www.oklaosf.state.ok.us/~arts
Suzanne Tate, *Executive Director*

OREGON ARTS COMMISSION
775 Summer St NE, Suite 200; Salem, OR 97301-1280;
(503) 986-0082, (800) 735-2900 (TDD), FAX 986-0260;
oregon.artscomm@state.or.us, www.oregonartscommission.org
Christine T. D'Arcy, *Executive Director*

PENNSYLVANIA COUNCIL ON THE ARTS
Finance Bldg, Room 216; Harrisburg, PA 17120; (717) 787-6883,
(800) 654-5984 (TTY), FAX (717) 783-2538; www.pacouncilonthearts.org
Philip Horn, *Executive Director*

PUERTO RICO
(see Institute of Puerto Rican Culture)

RHODE ISLAND STATE COUNCIL ON THE ARTS
1 Capitol Hill, 3rd Floor; Providence, RI 02908; (401) 222-3880,
222-7808 (TTY), FAX 422-3018; info@arts.ri.gov, www.arts.ri.gov
Randall Rosenbaum, *Executive Director*

SOUTH CAROLINA ARTS COMMISSION
1800 Gervais St; Columbia, SC 29201; (803) 734-8696, FAX 734-8526;
www.state.sc.us/arts
Suzette M. Surkamer, *Executive Director*

SOUTH DAKOTA ARTS COUNCIL
711 East Wells Ave; Pierre, SD 57501-3369; (605) 773-3301,
FAX 773-5657; sdac@state.sd.us, artscouncil.sd.gov
Dennis Holub, *Executive Director*

TENNESSEE ARTS COMMISSION
401 Charlotte Ave; Nashville, TN 37243-0780;
(615) 741-1701, 532-5940 (TDD), FAX 741-8559; www.arts.state.tn.us
Rich Boyd, *Executive Director*

TEXAS COMMISSION ON THE ARTS
Box 13406; Austin, TX 78711-3406; (512) 463-5535, 475-3327 (TTY),
(800) 252-9415, FAX (512) 475-2699; front.desk@arts.state.tx.us,
www.arts.state.tx.us
Gary Gibbs, *Executive Director*

UTAH ARTS COUNCIL
617 East South Temple; Salt Lake City, UT 84102-1177; (801) 236-7555,
(800) 346-4128 (TTY), FAX (801) 236-7556; arts.utah.gov
Margaret Hunt, *Director*

VERMONT ARTS COUNCIL
136 State St, Drawer 33; Montpelier, VT 05633-6001; (802) 828-3291,
FAX (802) 828-3363; info@vermontartscouncil.org, www.vermontartscouncil.org
Alexander L. Aldrich, *Executive Director*

VIRGINIA COMMISSION FOR THE ARTS
Lewis House; 223 Governor St; Richmond, VA 23219; (804) 225-3132,
225-3132 (TTY), FAX 225-4327; arts@arts.virginia.gov, www.arts.state.va.us
Peggy J. Baggett, *Executive Director*

VIRGIN ISLANDS COUNCIL ON THE ARTS
5070 Norre Gade; St. Thomas, VI 00802-6876; (340) 774-5984,
FAX 774-6206; blmahoney@vica.gocomtek.com, www.vicouncilonarts.org
Betty Mahoney, *Executive Director*

WASHINGTON, DC
(see District of Columbia [DC] Commission on the Arts and Humanities)

WASHINGTON STATE ARTS COMMISSION
711 Capitol Way S, Suite 600; Box 42675; Olympia, WA 98504-2675;
(360) 753-3860, FAX 586-5351; info@arts.wa.gov, www.arts.wa.gov
Kris Tucker, *Executive Director*

WEST VIRGINIA COMMISSION ON THE ARTS
West Virginia Division of Culture and History; The Cultural Center,
Capitol Complex; 1900 Kanawha Blvd E; Charleston, WV 25305-0300;
(304) 558-0240, 558-3562 (TTY), FAX 558-2779;
jeff.pierson@wvculture.org, www.wvculture.org/arts
Jeff Pierson, *Director*

WISCONSIN ARTS BOARD
101 East Wilson St, 1st Floor; Madison, WI 53702; (608) 266-0190,
267-9629 (TDD), FAX 267-0380; artsboard@arts.state.wi.us,
arts.state.wi.us/static
George Tzougros, *Executive Director*

WYOMING ARTS COUNCIL
2320 Capitol Ave; Cheyenne, WY 82002; (307) 777-7742, 777-5964 (TDD),
FAX 777-5499; rbasom@state.wy.us, wyoarts.state.wy.us
Rita Basom, *Arts Council Manager*

COLONIES AND RESIDENCIES

What entries make up this section?

Though artist colonies that admit theatre writers constitute the majority of the listings here, there are other kinds of residencies, such as artist-in-residence positions at universities, listed here as well. You can also find listings in the Development and Fellowships and Grants sections that could be considered residencies. We have chosen to limit our listings to those places that are set up as retreats for writers or that, in addition to reasonable lodging, provide services to benefit writers.

Note: deadlines may stay the same from year to year, but this is not an absolute—always obtain the latest information (an organization's website is the best place to check) before submitting. You should assume that each deadline listed in this section is the date application materials must be *received*, unless otherwise stated. Years for annual deadlines are not listed.

ALDEN B. DOW CREATIVITY CENTER

Northwood University; 4000 Whiting Dr; Midland, MI 48640;
    (989) 837-4478, FAX 837-4468; creativity@northwood.edu,
    www.northwood.edu/abd
Cheryl A. Smith, *Interim Director*

Open to: playwrights, translators, composers, librettists, lyricists, screenwriters. **Description:** several "Creativity Fellowships" each year for individuals working in any field, including the arts; 6–8 week summer residency at Northwood University, which provides environment for intense independent study; program includes interaction among fellows and formal presentation of work at end of program. **Financial arrangement:** travel stipend, room, board, $750 stipend for project costs. **Guidelines:** projects that are creative, innovative and unique; prefers 1 applicant per project; no accommodation for spouses, children or pets; write for brochure or see website for more information. **Application procedure:** project description, work sample, resume and $10 application fee. **Deadline:** 31 Dec. **Notification:** 1 Apr. **Dates:** Jun–Aug.

ALTOS DE CHAVON

c/o Parsons School of Design; 66 Fifth Ave, #604A; New York, NY 10011;
    (212) 229-5370, FAX 229-8988; altos@earthlink.net
Carmen Lorente, *Program Coordinator*

Open to: playwrights, composers, screenwriters. **Description:** residencies of 3 1/2 months for 8 artists per year, 1–2 of whom may be writers or composers, at not-for-profit arts center located in tropical Caribbean 8 miles from town of La Romana in the Dominican Republic; efficiency studios or apartments with kitchenettes; small individual studios nearby; small visual-arts-oriented library. **Financial arrangement:** $100 nonreturnable reservation fee; resident pays rent of $400 per month and provides own meals (estimated cost $20 per day) and transportation. **Guidelines:** prefers Spanish-speaking artists who can use talents to benefit community, and whose work relates to Dominican or Latin American context; residents may teach workshops and are expected to contribute to group exhibition/performance at end of stay; write for further information. **Application procedure:** letter explaining applicant's interest in program, work sample and resume. **Deadline:** 1 Aug. **Notification:** after 1 Sep. **Dates:** residencies start 1 Feb; 1 Sep.

ATLANTIC CENTER FOR THE ARTS

1414 Art Center Ave; New Smyrna Beach, FL 32168; (386) 427-6975,
    (800) 393-6975, FAX (386) 427-5669;
    program@atlanticcenterforthearts.org, www.atlanticcenterforthearts.org
Ann Brady, *Executive Director*
Nicholas Conroy, *Program Director*

Open to: playwrights, composers. **Description:** 6 3-week workshops each year offering writers, choreographers, media, visual and performing artists opportunity of concentrated study with internationally known Master Artists-in-Residence. **Financial arrangement:** housing, which includes private room and bath and access to communal studio; weekday meals provided. **Application procedure:** Master Artist specifies submission materials and selects participants; see website or call for more information. **Deadline:** 3 months before residency. **Notification:** 2 months before residency. **Dates:** exact dates TBA; see website.

BLUE MOUNTAIN CENTER

Box 109; Blue Mountain Lake, NY 12812; (518) 352-7391;
    bmc@bluemountaincenter.org, www.bluemountaincenter.org
Ben Strader, *Managing Director*

Open to: playwrights, composers, librettists, lyricists. **Description:** 4-week residencies for 14 writers, composers and visual artists at center in Adirondack Mountains. **Financial arrangement:** room and board. **Guidelines:** artist whose work is aimed at a general audience and reflects social concerns. **Application procedure:** send SASE or see website for information. **Deadline:** 1 Feb. **Notification:** early Apr. **Dates:** mid-Jun–Oct.

BYRDCLIFFE ART COLONY

The Woodstock Guild; 34 Tinker St; Woodstock, NY 12498-1233;
    (845) 679-2079, FAX 679-4529; wguild@ulster.net,
    www.woodstockguild.org
Artists Residency Program

Open to: playwrights, translators, librettists, lyricists, solo performers, screenwriters. **Description:** 4-week residencies for writers, composers and visual artists at historic 300-acre colony in the Catskill Mountains, 1 1/2 miles from Woodstock village center, 90 miles north of New York City; private room and separate individual studio space in Villetta Inn, spacious turn-of-the-century mountain lodge; common dining room and living room; resident provides own meals, using community kitchen. **Financial arrangement:** resident pays fee of $300 per session; inquire about Handel Playwright Fellowship. **Guidelines:** proof of serious commitment of endeavor to field is major criterion for acceptance; professional recognition helpful but not essential; send SASE for further information. **Application procedure:** work sample, project description, resume, reviews and articles if available, contact information for 2 references, application and $35 fee. **Deadline:** 2 Mar (applications received after deadline considered if space is available). **Notification:** 15 May. **Dates:** Jun–Sep.

CAMARGO FOUNDATION

1 Avenue Jermini; Cassis, France 13260; www.camargofoundation.org
Jean-Pierre Dautricourt, *Executive Director*

Open to: playwrights, translators, composers. **Description:** 13 concurrent residencies, most are given to scholars and teachers pursuing projects relative to Francophone culture, but there are 2 for writers, 2 for composers and 2 for visual artists at estate in ancient Mediterranean fishing port 30 minutes from Marseilles; furnished apartments; music studio available for composer. **Financial arrangement:** $2500 stipend; housing; resident provides own meals. **Guidelines:** resident outlines project to fellow colony members during stay and writes final report; families welcome when space available. **Application procedure:** see website for guidelines and application. **Deadline:** 12 Jan; no submission before 25 Sep. **Notification:** Apr. **Dates:** Sep–Dec; Jan–May.

CENTRUM CREATIVE RESIDENCIES PROGRAM

Fort Worden State Park; Box 1158; Port Townsend, WA 98368;
  (360) 385-3102, FAX 385-2470; info@centrum.org, www.centrum.org
Lisa Werner, *Residency Program Facilitator*

Open to: playwrights, translators, composers, librettists, lyricists, solo performers, screenwriters, television writers. **Description:** creative residencies for writers, composers, poets, visual artists and choreographers near Victorian seaport on 440-acre Fort Worden State Park; self-contained cabins near beach and hiking trails. **Financial arrangement:** resident pays $300 per week for housing. **Guidelines:** artist who has clear direction and some accomplishment in field; artist who wants to explore new style, medium or genre; see website for guidelines. **Application procedure:** project description, work sample, resume and application. **Deadline:** year-round. **Dates:** Jan–Jun; Sep–Nov.

DJERASSI RESIDENT ARTISTS PROGRAM

2325 Bear Gulch Rd; Woodside, CA 94062-4405; (650) 747-1250,
  FAX 747-0105; drap@djerassi.org, www.djerassi.org
Dennis O'Leary, *Executive Director*
Judy Freeland, *Residency Coordinator*

Open to: playwrights, translators, composers, librettists, lyricists, solo performers, screenwriters. **Description:** 4–5 week residencies for writers, choreographers, composers, media, visual and interdisciplinary artists and performers concurrently at 600-acre ranch in Santa Cruz mountains 1 hour south of San Francisco; collaborative projects considered. **Financial arrangement:** room and board. **Guidelines:** emerging or established artist whose work has clear direction. **Application procedure:** sample of published work or work-in-progress, resume, application and $30 fee; application available from website. **Deadline:** 15 Feb. **Notification:** 15 Aug. **Dates:** Mar–Nov.

DORSET COLONY FOR WRITERS

Box 221; Dorset, VT 05251; (802) 867-2223, FAX 867-0144;
  dorsetcolony@hotmail.com
John Nassivera, *Executive Director*
Paula Mann Nassivera, *Director*

Open to: playwrights, composers, librettists, lyricists. **Description:** residencies of 1 week–1 month at house located in historic village in southern VT. **Financial arrangement:** resident pays $230 per week for housing; meals not provided; large, fully equipped kitchen. **Guidelines:** artist must demonstrate seriousness of purpose and have record of professional achievement (readings or productions of works); collaborative teams may apply; work sample may be requested from less established artist. **Application procedure:** letter of inquiry with description of proposed project and desired length and dates of stay, and resume. **Deadline:** year-round. **Notification:** 1 month. **Dates:** 1 Oct–30 Nov; 1 Apr–30 May.

EDWARD F. ALBEE FOUNDATION

William Flanagan Memorial Creative Persons Center; 14 Harrison St; New York, NY 10013; (212) 226-2020; www.albeefoundation.org

Open to: playwrights, translators, composers, librettists, screenwriters. **Description:** 1-month residencies for up to 5 writers, composers and visual artists concurrently at "The Barn" in Montauk, Long Island. **Financial arrangement:** housing. **Guidelines:** admission based on talent and need; write or see website for information. **Application procedure:** script (recording for composer), supporting materials and application. **Deadline:** 1 Mar; no submission before 1 Jan. **Notification:** May. **Dates:** 1 Jun–1 Oct.

THE HAMBIDGE CENTER FOR CREATIVE ARTS AND SCIENCES

Box 339; Rabun Gap, GA 30568; (706) 746-5718, FAX 746-9933; center@hambidge.org, www.hambidge.org

Open to: playwrights, translators, composers, librettists, lyricists. **Description:** residencies of 2 weeks–2 months for professionals in all areas of arts and humanities on 600 acres in northeast GA mountains; 8 private cottages with bedroom, kitchen, bathroom and studio/work area; evening meal provided Mon–Fri. **Financial arrangement:** resident pays minimum of $150 per week toward total cost. **Guidelines:** send SASE or see website for guidelines. **Application procedure:** work sample, resume, bio, 3 letters of recommendation from professionals in applicant's field, application and $30 fee; application available from website. **Deadline:** 15 Jan for May–Aug; 15 Apr for Sep–Nov; 15 Sep for Dec–Apr (application received after deadline considered if space is available). **Notification:** 2 months. **Dates:** Feb–Dec.

HAWTHORNDEN CASTLE INTERNATIONAL RETREAT FOR WRITERS

Lasswade, Midlothian; Scotland EH18 1EG; 44-131-440-2180, FAX 44-131-440-1989
Administrator

Open to: playwrights. **Description:** 4-week residencies for playwrights, poets and novelists at medieval castle on secluded crag overlooking valley of the River Esk, 8 miles south of Edinburgh; 6 writers in residence at any one time; fully furnished study-bedroom; communal breakfast and dinner, lunch brought to writer's room; typewriter rental and use of excellent libraries in Edinburgh can be arranged. **Financial arrangement:** room and board. **Guidelines:** author of at least 1 published work. **Application procedure:** write for application and further information. **Deadline:** Sep. **Notification:** Jan. **Dates:** Feb–Dec.

HEADLANDS CENTER FOR THE ARTS
944 Fort Barry; Sausalito, CA 94965; (415) 331-2787, FAX 331-3857;
   www.headlands.org
Gary Sangster, *Executive Director*

Open to: playwrights, composers, screenwriters. **Description:** residencies of 1-3 months for artists in all disciplines at Center in national park on 13,000 acres of coastal wilderness across the bay from San Francisco; accommodation in 4-bedroom house with communal kitchen; meals provided Sun-Thur; 6-month "live-out" residencies available for Bay Area artists only, providing studio space, 2 meals per week and access to Center's facilities but no housing; all residents encouraged to interact with fellow artists in other media and with the environment. **Financial arrangement:** housing for artist from outside Bay Area; studio space for Bay Area artist. **Guidelines:** Regional, national or international artist; students ineligible. **Application procedure:** send SASE or see website for application (available Mar). **Deadline:** 5 Jun. **Dates:** Mar–Nov.

HEDGEBROOK
2197 Millman Rd; Langley, WA 98260; (360) 321-4786;
   connect@hedgebrook.org, www.hedgebrook.org

Open to: playwrights, librettists. **Description:** retreats of 2 weeks–2 months for women writers on Whidbey Island, 48 beautiful acres near Seattle; writers of diverse cultural backgrounds working in all genres; writer stays in one of six cottages and gathers in the farmhouse kitchen to share a home-cooked meal in the evening; writer furnishes own computer; Hedgebrook sponsors the annual Women Playwrights Festival; see website for details. **Financial arrangement:** room and board. **Guidelines:** women writer age 18 and up, published or unpublished; women of color encouraged to apply. **Application procedure:** project description, work sample, application and $25 fee; send SASE for application or download from website beginning Jun. **Deadline:** 25 Sep. **Notification:** 3 months. **Dates:** Feb-Nov.

HELENE WURLITZER FOUNDATION OF NEW MEXICO
Box 1891; Taos, NM 87571; (575) 758-2413, FAX 758-2559;
   hwf@taosnet.com, www.wurlitzerfoundation.org
Michael Knight, *Director*

Open to: playwrights, composers, screenwriters. **Description:** 11 studios/ apartments available to writers, composers, poets and visual artists; length of residency flexible, usually 3 months. **Financial arrangement:** housing and utilities; resident provides own meals; no financial aid. **Application procedure:** project description, work sample, resume and application; send SASE or email for application. **Deadline:** 18 Jan. **Dates:** residencies available year-round, but on limited basis in Nov–Mar.

ISLE ROYALE NATIONAL PARK ARTIST-IN-RESIDENCE
800 East Lakeshore Dr; Houghton, MI 49931;
   (906) 482-0984 (general information), 487-7152 (Greg Blust),
   FAX 482-8753; greg_blust@nps.gov, www.nps.gov/volunteer/air.htm
Greg Blust, *Supervisor*

Open to: playwrights, composers, lyricists, solo performers. **Description:** 1 artist housed for 2-3 weeks in cabin on remote island on Lake Superior; no electricity; resident must bring 2-3-week supply of food. **Financial arrangement:** housing. **Guidelines:** writer with artistic integrity; ability to live in wilderness environment and to relate to park through his/her work; must donate 1 work to park and communicate experience of residency through 1 program per week for public. **Application procedure:** project description, work sample, resume and application. **Deadline:** 16 Feb. **Notification:** 1 May. **Dates:** Jun-Sep.

JENTEL ARTIST RESIDENCY PROGRAM
130 Lower Piney Creek Rd; Banner, WY 82832; (307) 737-2311,
   FAX 737-2305; jentel@jentelarts.org, www.jentelarts.org
Mary Jane Edwards, *Executive Director*

Open to: playwrights. **Description:** 1-month residency for up to 6 writers and visual artists on working cattle ranch in foothills of the Big Horn Mountains, 20 miles from Sheridan, WY; private studio; communal kitchen, dining and living areas, library and computer/printer; internet access in writers' studios. **Financial arrangement:** $400 stipend, housing; optional community outreach during residency. **Guidelines:** U.S. citizen or international artist currently residing in U.S., minimum 25 years of age. **Application procedure:** project description, work sample, 3 letters of recommendation, resume, application and $20 fee; application available from website. **Deadline:** 15 Sep for Jan-May; 15 Jan for May-Dec. **Notification:** 2 months. **Dates:** 15 Jan-13 Dec.

KALANI OCEANSIDE RETREAT, INSTITUTE FOR CULTURE AND WELLNESS
RR2 Box 4500; Pahoa-Beach Road, HI 96778-9724; (808) 965-7828,
   FAX 965-0527; kalani@kalani.com, www.kalani.com
Richard Koob, *Director*

Open to: playwrights, translators, composers, librettists, lyricists, solo performers, screenwriters, television writers. **Description:** up to 20 artists share 4 500-1000-square-foot studio spaces for 2-week-2-month residencies at 120-acre coastal resort spa with private rooms, restaurant and shared or private baths. **Financial arrangement:** artist eligible for up to 50% discount on regular daily room rates of $105-$260; meals available at resort restaurant, artist pays per meal or $45 per day. **Guidelines:** professional artist. **Application procedure:** resume, application and $10 fee. **Deadline:** year-round. **Notification:** 1 week. **Dates:** year-round, but discounted rates more likely available May-Nov.

LANESBORO RESIDENCY PROGRAM FELLOWSHIPS

Cornucopia Arts Center; Box 152; Lanesboro, MN 55949; (507) 467-2446,
    FAX 467-4446; executive@lanesboroarts.org, www.lanesboroarts.org
Michael-jon Pease, *Executive Director*

Open to: playwrights, composers, librettists, lyricists, screenwriters, television
writers. **Description:** 4-6 residencies of 2 or 4 weeks in small MN town with
historic Main Street, 200-foot bluffs, trout river and bike trail; active arts and
cultural community; artist spends minimum 6-8 hours working in community as
part of proposed project. **Financial arrangement:** $625 stipend per week.
Guidelines: innovative and creative projects that further artist's work and
promote meaningful community experience; send SASE for application and
guidelines. **Application procedure:** work sample, 1-page community project
description, resume, artist statement, 2 letters of reference and application.
Deadline: 15 Jun. **Notification:** 2 months. **Dates:** Nov–May.

LEDIG HOUSE INTERNATIONAL WRITERS' COLONY

55 Fifth Ave, 15th Floor; New York, NY 10003; (212) 206-6060,
    FAX 206-6114; writers@artomi.org, www.artomi.org
D. W. Gibson, *Executive Director*

Open to: playwrights, translators, screenwriters, television writers. **Description:**
residencies of 3 weeks-2 months in the spring and fall for writers of all genres at 400-
acre farm in upstate NY with library and computer access; private sleeping and work
space; communal living and dining rooms; all meals provided. **Financial arrangement:**
room and board. **Guidelines:** published and unpublished writers proficient in English;
call or fax for guidelines. **Application procedure:** project description, work sample,
resume and letter of recommendation with SASE for notification. **Deadline:** 30 Nov.
Notification: 15 Jan. **Dates:** spring session mid-Mar–early Jun; fall session mid-Sep-late
Nov.

LEIGHTON ARTISTS' COLONY FOR INDEPENDENT RESIDENCIES

(formerly Leighton Studios for Independent Residencies)
The Banff Centre; Box 1020, Station 28; 107 Tunnel Mountain Dr;
    Banff, Alberta; Canada T1L 1H5; (403) 762-6180, (800) 565-9989,
    FAX (403) 762-6345; arts_info@banffcentre.ab.ca, www.banffcentre.ca
Office of the Registrar

Open to: playwrights, translators, composers, librettists, lyricists, performance artists,
screenwriters, television writers. **Description:** residencies of 1 week-3 months for
writers and composers at studios situated in mountains of Banff National Park; 8
furnished studios, each with washroom, kitchenette, Macintosh or PC with printing
capabilities, CD/cassette player and internet/email access; living accommodations
(single room with bath) on Centre's main campus; nearby access to all amenities of
Centre, including dining room, library and recreation complex. **Financial
arrangement:** resident pays approximate daily cost of $130 Canadian (about $125
U.S.) for studio, room and meals; discount on studio cost available for those who

demonstrate need. **Guidelines:** established or emerging artist who demonstrates sustained contribution to own field and shows evidence of significant achievement. **Application procedure:** write, email or see website for application and further information. **Deadline:** year-round; apply at least 6 months before desired residency. **Dates:** year-round.

THE MACDOWELL COLONY

100 High St; Peterborough, NH 03458-2485; (603) 924-3886,
    (212) 535-9690, FAX (603) 924-9142; info@macdowellcolony.org,
    www.macdowellcolony.org
Cheryl Young, *Executive Director*

Open to: playwrights, composers, screenwriters. **Description:** residencies of up to 2 months for writers, composers, visual artists, video/filmmakers, architects and interdisciplinary artists at 450-acre estate; exclusive use of studio; studios and common areas accessible for those with mobility impairments. **Financial arrangement:** room and board; travel grants available; artists in need of financial assistance are eligible for grants of up to $1000 to relieve financial burdens related to their stay at the Colony; voluntary contributions accepted. **Guidelines:** admission based on talent. **Application procedure:** work samples, project description, names of 2 professional references, application and $20 fee; collaborating artists must apply separately; call or see website for application. **Deadline:** 15 Sep for 1 Feb–31 May; 15 Jan for 1 Jun–30 Sep; 15 Apr for 1 Oct–31 Jan. **Notification:** 2 months. **Dates:** year-round.

MARY ANDERSON CENTER FOR THE ARTS

Box 12; 101 St. Francis Dr; Mount St. Francis, IN 47146; (812) 923-8602,
    FAX 923-0294; macarts@onebox.com, www.maryandersoncenter.org
Lisa Angell, *Executive Director*

Open to: playwrights, translators, composers, librettists, lyricists. **Description:** residencies of any length for up to 5 writers, musicians and visual artists concurrently on rural 400 acres of woods, meadows and lake 15 minutes from Louisville, KY; private bedroom, shared bathroom, communal kitchen and dining room. **Financial arrangement:** resident pays fee of $60 per night for room and board; $40 per night for room; email for information. **Guidelines:** formal education and production credits are not requirements but will be taken into consideration when application is reviewed. **Application procedure:** project description, work sample, resume, 2 references and application. **Deadline:** year-round. **Notification:** 2 weeks. **Dates:** year-round. (See organization's listing in Membership and Service Organizations.)

THE MILLAY COLONY FOR THE ARTS

Box 3; 454 East Hill Rd; Austerlitz, NY 12017-0003; (518) 392-3103;
residency@millaycolony.org, www.millaycolony.org
Calliope Nicholas, *Residency Director*

Open to: playwrights, composers, screenwriters. **Description:** 1-month residencies for 6 writers, composers, photographers, filmmakers and visual artists concurrently at 600-acre former estate of Edna St. Vincent Millay in upstate NY; studio space with separate bedroom; Colony accommodates artists with disabilities. **Financial arrangement:** room, board and studio space. **Application procedure:** application and supporting materials; send SASE or see website for application. **Deadline:** 1 Oct. **Notification:** 15 Feb. **Dates:** Apr–Nov.

MONTANA ARTISTS REFUGE

Box 8; Basin, MT 59631; (406) 225-3500; mar@mt.net,
www.montanarefuge.org
Debbie Sheehan, *Residency Coordinator*

Open to: playwrights, translators, composers, librettists, lyricists, solo performers, screenwriters, television writers. **Description:** 1-6 month residencies (preference given to 6-month residents) for up to 5 artists of all disciplines, located in a former gold camp in the midst of the Rocky Mountains, approximately 12 miles from the Continental Divide (Basin has 250 residents, post office and town park); artist housed in fully equipped apartment with kitchen, private phone and broadband wireless internet access. **Financial arrangement:** resident pays $550-$1225 per month; meals not provided; very limited financial aid available. **Guidelines:** send SASE or see website for guidelines. **Application procedure:** work sample, project description, resume and application. **Deadline:** 30 Jul for Oct–Mar; 15 Dec for Apr–Sep.

NEW YORK MILLS ARTS RETREAT

24 North Main Ave, Box 246; New York Mills, MN 56567; (218) 385-3339;
nymills@kulcher.org, www.kulcher.org
Arts Retreat Coordinator

Open to: playwrights, composers, librettists, lyricists, solo performers, screenwriters. **Description:** 1 artist at a time housed for 2-4 weeks in small farming community in north central MN; housing in small 1-bedroom home; resident provides own meals. **Financial arrangement:** Jerome Foundation Fellowships stipend of $1500 for 4-week residency or $750 for 2-week residency; special emphasis on opportunities for artists of color. **Guidelines:** emerging artist of demonstrated ability; must donate minimum 8–15 hours during residency to community outreach, most often teaching in area schools. **Application procedure:** project description, work sample, resume, 2 letters of recommendation and application. **Deadline:** 1 Oct for Jan–Jun; 1 Apr for Jul–Dec. **Notification:** 2 months. **Dates:** Jan–Jun; Jul–Dec.

RAGDALE FOUNDATION

1260 North Green Bay Rd; Lake Forest, IL 60045; (847) 234-1063, ext 206;
admissions@ragdale.org, www.ragdale.org
Regin Igloria, *Director of Admissions*

Open to: playwrights, composers, librettists, performance artists. **Description:** residencies of 2 weeks–2 months for writers, composers and visual artists from the U.S. and abroad on edge of 55-acre prairie, 1 mile from town center. **Financial arrangement:** resident pays $25 per day for room and board; partial or full fee waivers awarded on basis of financial need. **Guidelines:** admission based on quality of work submitted. **Application procedure:** description of work-in-progress, work sample, resume, 2 references, application and $30 fee; call, email, send SASE or see website for guidelines. **Deadline:** 15 Jan for Jun–Dec; 1 Jun for Jan–May. **Notification:** 15 Apr for Jan deadline; 1 Sep for Jun deadline. **Dates:** year-round except for 2 weeks in Jun, 2 weeks in Oct and 2 weeks in Dec.

ROCKY MOUNTAIN NATIONAL PARK
ARTIST-IN-RESIDENCE PROGRAM

1000 Highway 36; Estes Park, CO 80517; (970) 586-1206;
www.nps.gov/romo
Information Office

Open to: playwrights, composers, lyricists, solo performers. **Description:** 2-week residencies for 1 artist at a time in renovated historic furnished cabin overlooking meadow and stream with Rocky Mountains in distance; 1 bedroom, kitchen, living/dining room, bathroom and porch; artist gives 2 45-minute public presentations. **Financial arrangement:** housing; resident provides own meals; must donate 1 appropriate work within 1 year of residency. **Guidelines:** professional artist. **Application procedure:** submit 6 copies of all materials including 1-page statement of purpose (detailing focus of project, relevance to national parks and potential for personal growth), work sample, resume with list of professional works, application and $35 fee; write or call for application. **Deadline:** postmarked by 1 Dec; no submission before Oct. **Notification:** Apr; exact date TBA. **Dates:** Jun–Sep.

STUDIO FOR CREATIVE INQUIRY

Carnegie Mellon University; College of Fine Arts, Room 111; Forbes Ave;
Pittsburgh, PA 15213-3890; (412) 268-3454, FAX 268-2829;
studio-info@andrew.cmu.edu, www.cmu.edu/studio
Margaret Myers, *Associate Director*

Open to: playwrights, translators, composers, librettists, lyricists, solo performers, screenwriters, television writers. **Description:** residencies of 1 year concurrently for artists in all disciplines; residency provides studio facility located in Carnegie Mellon's College of Fine Arts building, including office and meeting space, work area, computers, sound and video editing equipment; fellow may also use resources of university, including library. **Financial arrangement:** stipend; assistance in finding housing in community. **Guidelines:** writer able to use science and technology in work, interested in taking leadership role in collaborative projects and able to relate work to larger community. **Application procedure:** concept proposal, work sample, resume and references; admission based on quality of work, clear statement of intention, experience with collaboration and project feasibility; send application 6 months prior to desired residency period; see website for guidelines. **Deadline:** year-round. **Notification:** 2 months. **Dates:** year-round.

THE TYRONE GUTHRIE CENTRE

Annaghmakerrig; Newbliss; County Monaghan; Ireland; 353-47-54003,
  FAX 353-47-54380; info@tyroneguthrie.ie, www.tyroneguthrie.ie
Resident Director

Open to: playwrights, composers, librettists, lyricists, screenwriters, television writers. **Description:** residencies of 1 week–6 months for artists in all disciplines at former country home of Tyrone Guthrie, set amid 450 acres of forested estate overlooking large lake; private apartments; music room, rehearsal/performance space and extensive library. **Financial arrangement:** non-Irish artists pay about $540 per week for housing and meals; self-catering houses also available at less expensive rents (about $270 per week); fees may be negotiable depending on factors such as length of stay, nature of project, involvement with Irish artists or institutions, etc. **Guidelines:** artist must show evidence of sustained dedication and a significant level of achievement; prefers artist with clearly defined project; artist teams (e.g., writer/director, composer/librettist) welcome. **Application procedure:** write for application and further information. **Deadline:** year-round. **Dates:** year-round.

UCROSS FOUNDATION RESIDENCY PROGRAM

30 Big Red Lane; Clearmont, WY 82835; (307) 737-2291, FAX 737-2322;
  info@ucross.org, www.ucrossfoundation.org
Sharon Dynak, *Executive Director*

Open to: playwrights, translators, composers, librettists, lyricists. **Description:** residency of 2–6 weeks at "Big Red," restored historic site in foothills of the Big Horn Mountains; 8 concurrent residencies for writers, composers and visual artists; opportunity to concentrate on own work without distraction and to present work to local communities, if desired. **Financial arrangement:** room, board and studio space. **Guidelines:** admission based on quality of work and commitment; send SASE for application and further information. **Application procedure:** project description, work sample and application. **Deadline:** 1 Oct for Feb–Jun; 1 Mar for Aug–Dec. **Notification:** 2 months. **Dates:** year-round except Jan and Jul.

The U.S./Japan Creative Artists' Program

Japan-U.S. Friendship Commission; 1201 15th St, #330;
    Washington, DC 20005; (202) 653-9800, FAX 653-9802;
    jusfc@jusfc.gov, www.jusfc.gov
Eric J. Gangloff, *Executive Director*

Open to: playwrights, composers, librettists, lyricists, solo performers, screenwriters, television writers. **Description:** residencies of 5 continuous months for 3-5 artists each year; resident finds own housing in location of his/her choice in Japan. **Financial arrangement:** monthly stipend of ¥400,000 (about $4000) plus ¥100,000 (about $1000) for housing and ¥100,000 (about $1000) for professional expenses; travel and predeparture Japanese language instruction. **Guidelines:** U.S. citizen or permanent resident; mid-career professional artist with compelling reason to work in Japan whose work "exemplifies the best in U.S. art"; see website for application and information. **Application procedure:** work sample, resume and application. **Deadline:** 1 Feb. **Notification:** by 31 May. **Dates:** year-round.

Virginia Center for the Creative Arts

154 San Angelo Dr; Amherst, VA 24521; (434) 946-7236, FAX 946-7239;
    vcca@vcca.com, www.vcca.com
Director

Open to: playwrights, composers, librettists, lyricists, screenwriters. **Description:** residencies of 2 weeks-2 months for writers, composers and visual and performance artists on 450-acre estate in Blue Ridge Mountains; separate studios and bedrooms; all meals provided. **Financial arrangement:** suggested daily contribution of $30 for room and board or as means allow; financial status not a factor in selection process. **Guidelines:** admission based on achievement or promise of achievement. **Application procedure:** work sample, resume, 2 recommendations and application. **Deadline:** 15 Sep for Feb–May; 15 Jan for Jun–Sep; 15 May for Oct–Jan. **Notification:** 3 months. **Dates:** year-round.

William Inge Center for the Arts

Box 708; Independence, KS 67301; (620) 331-7768, ext 4216;
    FAX 331-9022; bpeterson@ingecenter.org, www.ingecenter.org
Peter Ellenstein, *Artistic Director*

Open to: playwrights. **Description:** residencies of 8-9 weeks for 2 writers at a time at William Inge's family home in small midwestern town; private bedroom in historic 1920s-era home, shared bath; shared modern kitchen; playwrights share teaching of 1 college class and 1 high-school class 10-12 hours a week; resident receives at least 1 rehearsed reading of work. **Financial arrangement:** $4000 stipend plus travel; meals not provided. **Guidelines:** playwright with teaching experience whose work has had several professional productions. **Application procedure:** writing sample, project description, resume (with references and teaching experience), 1-page bio, 3 letters of recommendation from professional theatres or play development centers, availability over next 2 years and letter of inquiry. **Deadline:** year-round. **Notification:** 6 months.

WRITERS & BOOKS GELL CENTER OF THE FINGER LAKES

c/o Writers & Books; 740 University Ave; Rochester, NY 14607;
(585) 473-2590, ext 103, FAX 442-9333; www.wab.org
Kathy Pottetti, *Gell Center Director of Operations and Programming*

Open to: playwrights, translators, librettists, lyricists, solo performers, screenwriters, television writers. **Description:** private bedroom and bath plus shared living, dining and kitchen area available in house surrounded by 23 acres of woodlands; resident provides own meals. **Financial arrangement:** resident pays $35 per day. **Application procedure:** write or call for application. **Deadline:** year-round. **Notification:** 1 week. **Dates:** year-round.

THE WRITERS ROOM

740 Broadway, 12th Floor; New York, NY 10003; (212) 254-6995,
FAX 533-6059; www.writersroom.org
Donna Brodie, *Executive Director*

Open to: playwrights, translators, composers, librettists, lyricists. **Description:** 6-month term for 400 writers of all genres; large room with 43 desks separated by partitions; kitchen, lounge, bathrooms, storage for files and laptops, small reference library; open 24 hours a day year-round; monthly readings. **Financial arrangement:** $75 application fee; $450–$650 semiannual fee (6-month period). **Guidelines:** emerging or established writer, must show seriousness of intent; write or email for guidelines and further information (no visits without appointment). **Application procedure:** references and application. **Deadline:** year-round.

THE WRITERS' STUDIO

Mercantile Library Center for Fiction; 17 East 47th St; New York, NY 10017;
(212) 755-6710, FAX 758-1387; info@mercantilelibrary.org,
www.mercantilelibrary.org/studio.html

Open to: playwrights. **Description:** carrel space for writers in not-for-profit, private lending library; wireless internet access, storage for personal computers, locker; library membership; discounted admission to programs. **Financial arrangement:** $100–$130 monthly fee, plus $75 administrative fee; 3-month minimum, renewal possible for up to 1 year. **Guidelines:** open to all writers (priority given to fiction writers); must submit proof of publication or correspondence with publisher; see website for guidelines. **Application procedure:** work sample or project outline, possible interview with selection committee and application; application available from website. **Deadline:** year-round. **Notification:** 1 month.

YADDO

Box 395; Saratoga Springs, NY 12866; (518) 584-0746,
    FAX 584-1312; yaddo@yaddo.org, www.yaddo.org
Admissions Committee

Open to: playwrights, composers, librettists, performance artists, screenwriters. **Description:** residencies of 2 weeks–2 months for artists in all genres, working individually or as collaborative teams up to 3 persons, at 19th-century estate on 400 acres; approximate total of 200 residents per year. **Financial arrangement:** room, board and studio space. **Guidelines:** admission based on review by panels composed of artists in each genre; quality of work submitted is major criterion; send 60¢ SASE for application and further information. **Application procedure:** work sample, resume, 2 letters of support, application and $20 fee; send SASP for acknowledgment of receipt. **Deadline:** postmarked by 1 Jan for mid-May–Feb; postmarked by 1 Aug for late Oct–May. **Notification:** 15 Mar for Jan deadline; 1 Oct for Aug deadline. **Dates:** year-round except early Sep.

MEMBERSHIP AND SERVICE ORGANIZATIONS

What's included here?

A number of organizations that exist to serve either the American playwright or a wider constituency of writers, composers and arts professionals. Some have a particular regional or special-interest orientation; some provide links to theatres in other countries. Taken together, these organizations represent an enormous range of services available to those who write for the theatre, and it is worth getting to know them.

ALLIANCE FOR INCLUSION IN THE ARTS

(formerly Non-Traditional Casting Project, Inc.)
1560 Broadway, Suite 1600; New York, NY 10036; (212) 730-4750,
    FAX 730-4820; info@inclusioninthearts.org, www.inclusioninthearts.org
Sharon Jensen, *Executive Director*

Founded in 1986, Alliance for Inclusion in the Arts is a not-for-profit advocacy organization that serves as an advocate and educational resource for full inclusion in theatre, film, television and related media. The Alliance works to advance the creative participation of artists of color and artists with disabilities by promoting the values of inclusion and diversity throughout the industry in the areas of writing, hiring, casting, directing and producing. Key Alliance programs include roundtable discussions with industry leaders, National Diversity Forum and a national Consulting and Information Program.

THE ALLIANCE OF LOS ANGELES PLAYWRIGHTS

7510 Sunset Blvd, #1050; Los Angeles, CA 90046-3418; (323) 957-4752;
    info@laplaywrights.org, www.laplaywrights.org
Dan Berkowitz and Jon Dorf, *Co-Chairs*

Founded in 1993, ALAP is a support and service organization dedicated to addressing the professional needs of the Los Angeles playwriting community. ALAP's programs and activities include the Playwrights Expo, which brings together L.A. playwrights and dozens of representatives of local and national theatres; the series In Our Own Voices, in which members read from and share their work; the annual Playreading Festival; a bimonthly New Works Lab, featuring table readings of plays in development; a website with a catalog of members' bios and scripts; the C. Bernard Jackson Award, given in recognition of individuals and organizations that nurture, develop and support L.A. playwrights; symposia and panel discussions; and networking and social events. ALAP's publications include the bimonthly *NewsFlash*, which keeps members posted on upcoming events. Annual dues are $40; lifetime membership $275.

THE ALLIANCE OF RESIDENT THEATRES/NEW YORK

520 8th Ave, 3rd Floor, Suite 319; New York, NY 10018; (212) 244-6667,
    FAX 714-1918; questions@art-newyork.org, www.art-newyork.org
Virginia P. Louloudes, *Executive Director*

The Alliance of Resident Theates/New York (A.R.T./New York), founded in 1972, is the service organization for Off-Broadway theatre, currently serving more than 300 not-for-profit theatres and related organizations throughout the 5 boroughs of New York City. In recent years, A.R.T./New York has established itself as a provider of management-related technical assistance, a grantmaker to small and emerging theatres, a provider of low-cost office and rehearsal space, a developer and producer of audience development initiatives and an advocate for the arts at the state and local levels.

ALTERNATE ROOTS

1083 Austin Ave; Atlanta, GA 30307; (404) 577-1079, FAX 577-7991;
    info@alternateroots.org, www.alternateroots.org
Carolyn Morris, *Executive Director*

Founded in 1976, Alternate ROOTS is a service organization run by and for
southeastern artists. Its mission is to support the creation and presentation of original
art that is rooted in a particular community of place, tradition or spirit. It is committed
to social and economic justice and the protection of the natural world, and addresses
these concerns through its programs and services. ROOTS now has more than 150
individual members across the country, including playwrights, directors,
choreographers, musicians, storytellers and new vaudevillians, and representatives of
diverse performing and presenting organizations. ROOTS makes artistic resources
available to its members through workshops; creates appropriate distribution networks
for the new work being generated in the region via touring, publications and liaison
activity; and provides opportunities for enhanced visibility and financial stability via
publications and periodic performance festivals. Opportunities for member playwrights
include readings and peer critiques of works-in-progress at the organization's annual
meeting. Membership is open to all artists whose work is consistent with the goals of
ROOTS; members are accepted throughout the year. The organization's meetings and
workshops are open to the public and its newsletter is available to the public for a
small fee. Annual membership dues are $50 for members, $75 for board members; $20
introductory membership available, see website.

AMERICAN INDIAN COMMUNITY HOUSE

11 Broadway, 2nd Floor; New York, NY 10004; (212) 598-0100,
    FAX 598-4909; www.aich.org
Jim Cyrus, *Performing Arts Director*

American Indian Community House was founded in 1969 to encourage the interest of
all U.S. ethnic groups in the cultural contributions of the American Indian, and to foster
intercultural exchanges. The organization now serves the Native American population
of the New York City region through a variety of social, economic and educational
programs, and through cultural programs that include theatre events, an art gallery
and a newsletter. Native Americans in the Arts, the performing arts component of the
Community House, is committed to the development and production of works by
Indian authors, and presents staged readings, workshops and full productions in The
Circle, their in-house performance space. The Community House also sponsors several
other performing groups, including Spiderwoman Theater, Coatlicue Theatre Company,
Off the Beaten Path, the Thunderbird American Indian Dancers, the Silver Cloud
Singers and the jazz-fusion and traditional singing group Ulali. A showcase for Native
American artists is presented to agents and casting directors once a year.

AMERICAN MUSIC CENTER (AMC)

30 West 26th St, Suite 1001; New York, NY 10010-2011;
   (212) 366-5260, ext 10, FAX 366-5265; info@amc.net, www.amc.net
Joanne Hubbard Cossa, *Chief Executive Officer*

Founded in 1939, the American Music Center brings together artists, organizations and audiences interested in new American music through many resources and programs. AMC advocates for new music through NewMusicBox (www.newmusicbox.org) and CounterstreamRadio, a 24-hour online station broadcasting music by a broad range of U.S. composers. AMC makes grants to composers and ensembles, and offers professional development programs for artists. AMC provides information services designed to facilitate performances, including the AMC Online Library, a searchable database of works by 5,400 American composers; Opportunity Update—a monthly listing of opportunities in new music useful to industry professionals; and benefits and services for members. Individual and organizational membership is open to the public at varying annual membership rates. See website for membership details.

AMERICAN TRANSLATORS ASSOCIATION (ATA)

225 Reinekers Lane, Suite 590; Alexandria, VA 22314-2840;
   (703) 683-6100, FAX 683-6122; ata@atanet.org, www.atanet.org
Walter W. Bacak, Jr., *Executive Director*

Founded in 1959, the ATA is a national not-for-profit association which seeks to promote recognition of the translation profession; disseminate information for the benefit of translators and those who use their services; define and maintain professional standards; foster and support the training of translators and interpreters; and provide a medium of cooperation with persons in allied professions. Members receive the monthly *ATA Chronicle* and are included in the online membership directory and *Directory of Translating and Interpreting Services*. ATA holds an annual conference and sponsors several honors and awards (see American Translators Association Awards in Prizes). Active membership is open to U.S. citizens and permanent residents who have professionally engaged in translating or closely related work and have passed an ATA certification examination or demonstrated professional attainment by other prescribed means. Those who meet these professional standards but are not U.S. citizens or residents may hold corresponding membership; other interested persons may be associate members. Interested persons should contact ATA for a membership application, or see the ATA website. Annual dues are $80 for associate-students, $145 for active, corresponding and associate members, $180 for institutions, $300 for corporations.

ASCAP (AMERICAN SOCIETY OF COMPOSERS, AUTHORS AND PUBLISHERS)

1 Lincoln Plaza; New York, NY 10023; (212) 621-6234, FAX 621-6558; www.ascap.com

Michael A. Kerker, *Director of Musical Theatre*

ASCAP is a not-for-profit organization whose members are writers and publishers of musical works. It operates as a clearinghouse for performing rights, offering licenses that authorize the public performance of all the music of its composer, lyricist and music publishing members, and collects license fees for these members. ASCAP also sponsors workshops for member and nonmember theatre writers (see ASCAP Musical Theatre Workshops in Development). Membership in ASCAP is open to any composer or lyricist who has been commercially recorded or regularly published.

ASSITEJ/USA

(see Theatre for Young Audiences/USA)

ASSOCIATION FOR JEWISH THEATRE

1330 West Fargo Ave, Suite 2A; Chicago, IL 60626; dchack@afjt.com, www.afjt.com

David Chack, *President*

Founded in 1987, the Association for Jewish Theatre is dedicated to promoting the development and production of plays relevant to Jewish life and values. AJT acts to promote the visibility and viability of those theatres and theatre artists, throughout the world, dedicated to Jewish works. Membership is open to theatres and individual artists that have shown a commitment to Jewish theatre. Services include an annual conference (reduced fee for members), new play showcases at conferences, free tickets to member theatre productions, publication of semiannual newsletter, networking opportunities and assistance in coordinating cooperatively developed projects. Annual dues are $80 for individuals ($30 rate available for students) and range from $80–$155 for theatres, depending on budget.

ASSOCIATION FOR THEATRE IN HIGHER EDUCATION (ATHE)

Box 1290; Boulder, CO 80306-1290; (888) 284-3737, (303) 530-2167, FAX 530-2168; nericksn@aol.com, www.athe.org

Nancy Erickson, *Administrative Director*

Founded in 1986, ATHE is an organization composed of individuals and institutions that provides leadership for the profession and promotes excellence in theatre education. Membership services include insurance benefits; scholarships; annual professional awards, including the Jane Chambers Playwriting Award (see Prizes); and assistance with issues such as tenure and alternate employment opportunities. The annual conference convenes theatre scholars, educators and professionals from all over the world to participate in workshops, performances, plenary sessions and group meetings. ATHE publishes several periodicals of interest to the theatre professional, including *ATHENEWS*, a newsletter that includes a list of teaching positions available at member organizations; *Theatre Topics*, a semiannual journal; *Theatre Journal*, a quarterly journal; a membership directory; and pamphlets on various topics such as assessment guidelines for higher education theatre programs and tenure. There are 5 annual membership levels: students, $65; retirees, $80; individuals, $130; 2-person households, $190; organizations, $230. Members receive all publications.

ASSOCIATION OF HISPANIC ARTS, INC.

1702 Lexington Avenue (store front); El Barrio, NY 10029; (212) 876-1242,
  (888) 876-1240, FAX (212) 876-1285; beni@latinoarts.org,
  www.latinoarts.org
Beni Matias, *Executive Director*

Founded in 1975, AHA is a not-for-profit arts organization serving the Latino arts and cultural community. AHA offers programs and services that develop audiences, enhance the management and professional skills of Latino arts organizations and individual artists, and provide a consistent and reliable source of information on all aspects of Latino arts and culture.

THE ASSOCIATION OF WRITERS & WRITING PROGRAMS (AWP)

Mail Stop 1E3; George Mason University; Fairfax, VA 22030; (703) 993-4301,
  FAX 993-4302; awp@awpwriter.org, www.awpwriter.org
David Fenza, *Executive Director*

Founded in 1967, AWP is a not-for-profit organization serving the needs of writers, college and university writing programs, and students of writing by providing information services, job placement assistance, publishing opportunities, literary arts advocacy and forums on all aspects of writing and its instruction. Writers' Conferences & Centers (WC&C), an association of 50 nonacademic conferences for writers, is now a division of AWP. Writers who are not affiliated with colleges and universities but who support collective efforts to improve opportunities are also represented by AWP. The *Writer's Chronicle,* published 6 times annually and available for $20 per year, includes listings of publishing opportunities, grants, awards and fellowships; interviews with writers; and essays on writing technique. The *AWP Official Guide to Writing Programs* (11th edition, $28.45 including shipping) offers a listing of writing programs and a section on writing conferences, colonies and centers.

AUSTIN SCRIPT WORKS (ASW)

Box 9787; Austin, TX 78766; (512) 454-9727; info@scriptworks.org,
  www.scriptworks.org
Christina J. Moore, *Executive Director*

Founded in 1997, Austin Script Works is a playwright-driven organization that provides support for playwrights at all stages in the writing process. ASW's programs include the Out of Ink 10-minute play showcase; salon readings; staged readings; workshops; one-act commissions; online services; a weekly email newsletter; "seed support" funding for member-initiated development; and the Latino Playwright Initiative, a 3-

phase commissioning and development program for Latino writers. Membership is $45 ($35 for students and senior citizens over 62).

BLACK THEATRE NETWORK (BTN)

2609 Douglass Rd SE, Unit 102; Washington, DC 20020; (202) 419-9968; lreese@udc.edu, www.blacktheatrenetwork.org

Professor LaTanya L. Reese, *Vice President*

Black Theatre Network (BTN) is a national network of professional artists, scholars and community groups founded in 1986 to provide an opportunity for the interchange of ideas within the African-American theatre community and among related institutions. BTN publishes information regarding black theatre activity; provides a national conference each summer to view and discuss black theatre (location varies); and encourages and promotes black dramatists and the production of plays about the black experience. BTN members are eligible to participate in national conferences and workshops and receive complimentary copies of all BTN publications, which include the quarterly *Black Theatre Network Newsletter*, listing conferences, contests, BTN business matters and national items of interest; *Black Theatre Directory*, which contains more than 800 listings of black theatre artists, scholars, companies, higher education programs and service organizations; *Dissertations Concerning Black Theatre from 1900–2000*, a listing of Ph.D. theses; and *Black Theatre Connections*, a quarterly listing of jobs in educational and professional theatre and other career-development opportunities. *Black Voices*, a catalog of works by black playwrights, is available from BTN for $20. Annual dues are $35 for retirees and students, $75 for individuals, $110 for organizations.

BMI (BROADCAST MUSIC INCORPORATED)

320 West 57th St; New York, NY 10019-3790; (212) 586-2000, FAX 262-2824; jbanks@bmi.com

Jean Banks, *Senior Director, Musical Theater and Jazz*

BMI, founded in 1940, is a performing rights organization which acts as a steward for the public performance of the music of its writers and publishers, offering licenses to music users. BMI monitors music performances and distributes royalties to those whose music has been used. Any writer whose songs have been published and are likely to be performed can join BMI at no cost. BMI also sponsors a musical theatre workshop (see BMI-Lehman Engel Musical Theatre Workshop in Development). The BMI Foundation was established in 1984 to provide support for individuals in furthering their musical education and to assist organizations involved in the performance of music and music training.

CENTRE FOR CREATIVE COMMUNITIES

Regent House Business Centre; 24/25 Nutford Pl, Marble Arch;
  London W1H 5YN; England; 44-20-7569-3005;
  info@creativecommunities.org.uk, www.creativecommunities.org.uk
Jennifer Williams, *Director*

Founded in 1978, the Centre for Creative Communities is an independent research and policy center that believes in working and thinking innovatively across borders, disciplines and sectors. It is dedicated to promoting inclusive community development through creativity and learning. CCC conducts research, organizes conferences and produces a free monthly electronic newsletter. The Centre maintains a website and a specialized arts, education and community-development library open to the public by appointment. CCC is not a grant-giving organization.

THE CENTRE FOR INDIGENOUS THEATRE

401 Richmond St W, Suite 205; Toronto, Ontario M5V 1X3; Canada;
  (416) 506-9436, FAX 506-9430; citmail@indigenoustheatre.com,
  www.indigenoustheatre.com
J.L. Watson, *Managing Director*
Rose Stella, *Artistic Director*

The Centre for Indigenous Theatre grew out of the Native Theatre School, established in 1974 by the late James H. Buller. It was Buller's vision to create an environment that would nourish the creative aspirations of indigenous peoples and inspire a new generation of writers, actors and directors. In 1994, The Centre for Indigenous Theatre was born, and today CIT offers a full-time program as well as two summer programs that bring together classical theatre training and traditional teachings to support and enrich artists through self-exploration, song, story and performance. CIT distributes a biannual newsletter, which describes school and student activities. Membership dues are $25 Canadian (approximately $22 U.S.).

CHICAGO ALLIANCE FOR PLAYWRIGHTS (CAP)

Theatre Building; 1225 West Belmont; Chicago, IL 60657-3205;
  (773) 929-7367, ext 60, FAX 327-1404;
  info@chicagoallianceforplaywrights.org,
  www.chicagoallianceforplaywrights.org
Joanne Koch, *President*

The Chicago Alliance for Playwrights is a service organization founded in 1990 to establish a network for Chicago-area playwrights and others committed to the development of new work for the stage. Members of the coalition include Chicago Dramatists (see listing below), Chicago Writers Bloc, Columbia College Theatre/Music Department and Theatre Building Chicago (see Production). CAP sponsors writers forums and publishes an online directory of Chicago-area playwrights and their principal works. Annual dues are $25 for individuals, $100 for groups.

CHICAGO DRAMATISTS

1105 West Chicago Ave; Chicago, IL 60622-5702; (312) 633-0630,
FAX 633-0840; newplays@chicagodramatists.org,
www.chicagodramatists.org
Russ Tutterow, *Artistic Director*

Founded in 1979, Chicago Dramatists is dedicated to the development of playwrights and new plays. It employs a variety of year-round programs to nurture the artistic and career development of both established and emerging playwrights, including play readings, productions, classes, workshops, symposia, festivals, talent coordination, marketing services, collaborative projects with other theatres and referrals to producers. The Resident Playwright program seeks to nurture the work and careers of Chicago-area dramatists who will potentially make significant contributions to the national theatre repertory. At no charge, Resident Playwrights benefit from Chicago Dramatists' fullest and longest-term support (a 3-year, renewable term), with complete access to all programs and services. Admittance to the program is selective, with emphasis on artistic and professional accomplishment or potential. Interested playwrights should contact Chicago Dramatists for full information and details of the application procedure, which includes the submission of 2 plays, a resume and letters of recommendation and intent. *Deadline:* 1 Apr annually (no submission before 1 Mar). The Playwrights' Network provides any U.S. playwright the opportunity to form an association with Chicago Dramatists. For an annual fee of $125, Network playwrights receive written script critiques, consideration for all programs and productions, class discounts, free admittance to events and other benefits. Classes and the quarterly 10-Minute Workshop are open to all playwrights. Website and quarterly flyers announce events and programs, and include application and submission procedures.

THE CHILDREN'S THEATRE FOUNDATION OF AMERICA (CTFA)

1114 Red Oak Dr; Avon, IN 46123; (317) 272-9322
Dorothy Webb, *President*

Founded in 1958, The Children's Theatre Foundation of America (CTFA) is a not-for-profit organization which seeks to advance the artistic and professional interests of theatre and theatre education for children and youth by funding proposals of artists and scholars working in those fields. In the past, CTFA has funded playwriting grants, scholarships, research, performances and lectures, theatre festivals, conferences, symposia, publications and crisis-management assistance. CTFA also administers the annual Aurand Harris Children's Theatre Grants and Fellowships (see Fellowships and Grants), as well as awarding Medallions for significant achievements in the field of children's theatre.

CORPORATION FOR PUBLIC BROADCASTING

401 9th St NW; Washington, DC 20004-2129; (202) 879-9600,
    FAX 879-9700; www.cpb.org
Patricia de Stacy Harrison, *CEO and President*

Founded in 1967, the Corporation for Public Broadcasting, a private not-for-profit organization funded by Congress, promotes and helps finance public television and radio. CPB provides grants to local public television and radio stations, and conducts research in audience development, new broadcasting technologies and other areas. The corporation helped establish the Public Broadcasting Service. It supports public radio programming through programming grants to stations and other producers, and television programming by funding proposals made by stations and independent producers.

THE DRAMATISTS GUILD OF AMERICA, INC.

1501 Broadway, Suite 701; New York, NY 10036; (212) 398-9366,
    FAX 944-0420; tstratton@dramatistsguild.com, www.dramatistsguild.com
John Weidman, *President*

The Dramatists Guild of America, founded more than 75 years ago, is the only professional association governed by and established to advance the rights of playwrights, composers and lyricists. The Guild has more than 6000 members worldwide, from beginning writers to Broadway veterans. Membership benefits include a business affairs toll-free hotline, which offers advice on all theatre-related topics, including options, commissions, copyright procedures and contract reviews; model production contracts, which provide the best protection for the writer at all levels of production; collaboration, commission and licensing agreements; seminars led by experienced professionals concerning pressing topics for today's dramatist; access to a national health insurance program and a group term life insurance plan; free/discounted tickets to Off-Broadway/Broadway performances; and a meeting room that can accommodate more than 50 people for readings and backer auditions, available for a nominal rental fee.

Members receive *The Dramatists Guild Newsletter,* issued 6 times per year, with up-to-date business affairs articles and script opportunities; *The Dramatist,* a magazine that contains interviews as well as articles on all aspects of theatre; *The Dramatists Guild Resource Directory,* an annual collection of contact information on producers, agents, contests, workshops and production companies. The periodicals are available to nonwriters on a subscription basis: Individual Subscribers ($25 per year)— individuals receive *The Dramatist* only; Institutional Subscribers ($135 per year)— educational institutions, libraries and educational theatres receive all 3 periodicals and have access to audiotapes of Guild seminars; Professional Subscribers ($200 per year)— producers and agents receive all 3 periodicals. The Guild has 4 levels of membership: (1) Active ($150 per year): writers who have been produced on Broadway, Off-Broadway or on the mainstage of a LORT theatre; (2) Associate ($95 per year): theatrical writers who have been produced in other venues or who have completed a full script; (3) Student ($35 per year): full-time students; (4) Estate ($125 per year): representatives of the estates of deceased authors.

EDUCATIONAL THEATRE ASSOCIATION

2343 Auburn Ave; Cincinnati, OH 45219-2815; (513) 421-3900;
    FAX 421-7077; info@edta.org, edta.org
Michael J. Peitz, *Executive Director*

The Educational Theatre Association (EdTA) is a professional association for theatre education founded in 1929. EdTA's mission is to create a network for theatre arts educators, students, professionals and enthusiasts to share ideas and support efforts to have theatre arts education (including film, television and other related media) recognized in all phases of education and lifelong learning. EdTA operates the International Thespian Society, an honorary organization for middle school and high school students. EdTA also publishes *Dramatics* (see Publications), a monthly magazine; and *Teaching Theatre*, a quarterly journal for theatre education professionals.

THE FIELD

161 Sixth Ave; New York, NY 10013; (212) 691-6969, FAX 255-2053;
    info@thefield.org, www.thefield.org
Tanya Calamoneri, Jennifer Wright Cook, *Co-Directors*

The Field, founded in 1986, is a not-for-profit organization dedicated to helping independent performing artists develop artistically and professionally through a variety of performance opportunities, workshops and services. The Field does not engage in curatorial activity; all artists are eligible to participate in its programs. Of special interest to New York metropolitan playwrights wishing to produce their own work are programs such as Fieldday, a performance showcase; and Fieldwork, a creative laboratory for works-in-progress, guided by trained facilitators. Writers should also note Artward Bound, free 10-day summer residencies at various rural locations on the East Coast for multidisciplinary groups of 6–10 artists with at least 3 years professional experience; transportation, room and board, rehearsal space, workshops and career guidance seminars all provided. The Field assists artists with many aspects of producing their work, including grant writing, fundraising, project management and promotional efforts. Publications include a monthly member newsletter of upcoming grants and opportunities for performing artists. All programs are available to members and nonmembers; members receive publications and discounts on programs, and may use The Field as an umbrella organization for fiscal sponsorship through its not-for-profit status. Annual membership costs $100; individual programs range from $25–$125. Field programs are also offered in many other cities; see their website for a complete list.

FIRST STAGE

Box 38280; Los Angeles, CA 90038; (323) 850-6271, FAX 850-6295;
    firststagela@aol.com, www.firststagela.org
Dennis Safren, *Literary Manager*

Founded in 1983, First Stage is a service organization for playwrights that holds staged readings, which are videotaped for the author's archival purposes; conducts workshops; provides referral services for playwrights; and publishes *First Stage Newsletter*. Services are free to nonmembers, except for workshops, which are available to members only. Membership dues are $75 per quarter or $250 per year; $68 per year for nonlocal members.

THE FOUNDATION CENTER
National Library:
79 Fifth Ave; New York, NY 10003; (212) 620-4230, FAX 807-3677;
    www.foundationcenter.org
Regional Offices:
1627 K St NW; Washington, DC 20006; (202) 331-1400;
312 Sutter St; San Francisco, CA 94108; (415) 397-0902;
Hurt Building, Suite 150, Grand Lobby; 50 Hurt Plaza; Atlanta, GA 30303;
    (404) 880-0094;
1422 Euclid, Suite 1600; Cleveland, OH 44115; (216) 861-1934
Charlotte Dion, *Director, New York Library*

Established in 1956, The Foundation Center is a service organization that maintains a comprehensive database on U.S. grantmakers and their grants, incorporating research, education and training programs designed to advance philanthropy at every level. The Center provides free and affordable resources at its web site; in its five regional library/learning centers; and through its national network of Cooperating Collections.

FOUNDATION FOR JEWISH CULTURE
(formerly The National Foundation for Jewish Culture)
330 Seventh Ave, 21st Floor; New York, NY 10001; (212) 629-0500,
    FAX 629-0508; grants@jewishculture.org, www.jewishculture.org
Elise Bernhardt, *Executive Director*

Founded in 1960, Foundation for Jewish Culture (FJC) invests in creative individuals and ideas in order to nurture a vibrant and enduring Jewish identity, culture and community. FJC provides grants, recognition awards, networking opportunities and professional development services to artists and scholars. New Jewish Theatre Projects provides grants up to $5,000 to national, not-for-profit theatre companies for the commissioning of new plays, musicals or multimedia works of Jewish significance. Such a grant supports play or performance development, which can include commissioning fees, playwright's residency expenses, and research or workshop costs. Awards are distributed directly to the venue where the work is to be presented unless special arrangements are made in advance.

THE FUND FOR WOMEN ARTISTS

3739 Balboa St, Suite 181; San Francisco, CA 94121; (415) 751-2202,
     FAX (650) 244-9136; info@womenarts.org, www.womenarts.org
Martha Richards, *Executive Director*

The Fund for Women Artists was founded in 1994 with the belief that women artists have the power to change the way women are perceived in our society. The Fund supports the creation and appreciation of art that reflects the full diversity and complexity of women's lives, and advocates to increase the employment opportunities available to women artists. The Fund also publishes free electronic newsletters: *WomenArts News*, a funding e-newsletter for theatre artists and a funding e-newsletter for film and video artists. The publications provide subscribers with information regarding new and current grant programs, calls for proposals and calls for new works. Any female artist can create a free profile page on the Women Arts Network at www.womenarts.org. The Fund also coordinates the celebrations of International Support Women Artists Day, an annual event held on the last Saturday of Mar.

GREENSBORO PLAYWRIGHTS' FORUM

c/o City Arts; 200 North Davie St, Box #2; Greensboro, NC 27401;
     (336) 335-6426, FAX 373-2659; stephen.hyers@greensboro-nc.gov,
     www.playwrightsforum.org
Stephen D. Hyers, *Director*

Greensboro Playwrights' Forum (GPF) was founded in 1993 to facilitate a monthly gathering for playwrights to discuss works in progress, share knowledge and encourage each other's artistic growth. Programs include cold and staged readings of member's plays and the annual North Carolina New Play Project, open to NC playwrights; winner receives $500 and workshop production; *deadline:* 15 Nov. GPF also provides members with studio space for play development. Membership is open to anyone. Annual dues are $25.

HATCH-BILLOPS COLLECTION

491 Broadway, 7th Floor; New York, NY 10012-4412; (212) 966-3231,
     FAX 966-3231 (call first); hatchbillops@yahoo.com,
     www.hatch-billopscollection.org
James V. Hatch, *Executive Secretary*

Founded in 1975, the Hatch-Billops Collection is a not-for-profit research library specializing in black American art and theatre history. It collects and preserves primary and secondary resource materials in the black cultural arts; provides tools and access to these materials for artists and scholars, as well as the general public; and develops programs in the arts using the Collection's resources. The library's holdings include 1800 oral-history tapes; theatre programs; approximately 800 published and unpublished plays by black American writers from 1858 to the present; files of clippings, letters, announcements and brochures on theatre, art and film; slides, photographs and posters; and more than 4000 books and 400 periodicals. The Collection also presents a number of salon interviews, which are open to the public;

and publishes transcriptions of its annual "Artist and Influence" series of salon interviews, many of which feature playwrights, actors, directors, technicians, dancers and musicians. The collection is open to artists, scholars and the public by appointment only at a rate of $5 per hour.

HISPANIC ORGANIZATION OF LATIN ACTORS (HOLA)

Clemente Soto Vélez Cultural Center; 107 Suffolk St, 3rd Floor;
New York, NY 10002; (212) 253-1015, FAX 253-9651;
holagram@hellohola.org, www.hellohola.org
Manuel Alfaro, *Executive Director*

Founded in 1975, HOLA is a not-for-profit arts service organization for Hispanic performers and theatre artists. HOLA provides information, a 24-hour hotline, casting referral services, professional seminars and workshops. The organization publishes an annual online *Directory of Hispanic Talent: HOLA Pages* and a newsletter, *La Nueva Ola*, which lists job opportunities, grants and contests of interest to Hispanic artists. Members pay annual dues of $125.

INDEPENDENT FEATURE PROJECT (IFP)

104 West 29th St, 12th Floor; New York, NY 10001-5310; (212) 465-8200,
FAX 465-8525; www.ifp.org
Michelle Byrd, *Executive Director*

The Independent Feature Project (IFP), a not-for-profit membership-supported organization, was founded in 1979 to encourage creativity and diversity in films produced outside the established studio system. The IFP produces the IFP Market, which features 300 American independent features, shorts, works-in-progress, documentaries and feature scripts, and publishes *Filmmaker*, a quarterly magazine. IFP also sponsors a series of screenings, professional seminars and industry showcases, including a conference on screenplay development. Group health insurance, production insurance, discounts, a Resource Program, publications and a series of transcripts of previous seminars and workshops are available to members. Membership dues start at $100 per year ($65 for students).

INSTITUTE OF OUTDOOR DRAMA

CB #3240; University of North Carolina; Chapel Hill, NC 27599-3240;
(919) 962-1328, FAX 962-4212; outdoor@unc.edu,
www.unc.edu/depts/outdoor
Rob Franklin Fox, *Director*

The Institute of Outdoor Drama, founded in 1963, is a research and advisory agency of the University of North Carolina. It serves as a communications link between producers of existing outdoor dramas and is a resource for groups, agencies or individuals who wish to create new outdoor dramas or who are seeking information on the field. The Institute provides professional consultation and conducts feasibility studies; holds annual auditions for summer employment in outdoor drama; sponsors conferences, lectures and symposia; and publishes a quarterly newsletter, as well as information bulletins. Writers should note that the Institute maintains a roster of available artists and production personnel, including playwrights and composers. It seeks to interest established playwrights and composers in participating in the creation of new outdoor dramas, and to encourage and advise new playwrights who wish to write for this specialized form of theatre.

INTERNATIONAL THEATRE INSTITUTE–U.S. CENTER

Theatre Communications Group; 520 8th Ave, 24th Floor;
New York, NY 10018-4156; (212) 609-5900, FAX 609-5901;
iti@tcg.org, www.tcg.org
Emilya Cachapero, *Director*

Now operating centers in 90 countries, ITI was founded in 1948 by UNESCO "to promote the exchange of knowledge and practice in the theatre arts." The U.S. Center of ITI became part of Theatre Communications Group in Nov 1999. ITI assists both foreign theatre visitors in the U.S. and American theatre representatives traveling abroad. TCG/ITI Travel Grants, funded by the Trust for Mutual Understanding, offer $3000 grants for American theatre artists to travel to Russia or Central Europe (see TCG Artistic Programs in Fellowships and Grants). The International Theatre Institute/Martha W. Coigney Collection, a reference library that documents theatrical activity in 146 countries and houses more than 12,700 plays from 97 countries, is now housed at The New York Public Library for the Performing Arts (see listing this section). American playwrights, as well as other theatre professionals, can use the collection to make international connections; to consult foreign theatre directories for names of producers, directors or companies, with a view to submitting plays abroad; and to research the programs and policies of theatres or managements.

THE INTERNATIONAL WOMEN'S WRITING GUILD

Box 810, Gracie Station; New York, NY 10028-0082; (212) 737-7536,
FAX 737-9469; iwwg@iwwg.org, www.iwwg.org
Hannelore Hahn, *Executive Director*

The International Women's Writing Guild, founded in 1976, is a network of international women writers. Playwrights, television and film writers, songwriters, producers and other women involved in the performing arts are included in its membership. Workshops are offered throughout the U.S. and annually at a week-long writing conference/retreat at Skidmore College. Members may also submit playscripts to theatres who have offered to read, critique and possibly produce IWWG members' work. *Network*, a 32-page newsletter published 6 times per year, provides a forum for members to share views and to learn about playwriting contests and awards and theatre- and TV-related opportunities. The Guild provides contacts with literary agents, dental and vision insurance and other services to its members. Annual dues are $45.

LA STAGE ALLIANCE

644 South Figueroa St; Los Angeles, CA 90017; (213) 614-0556,
 FAX 614-0561; info@lastagealliance.com, www.lastagealliance.com

Founded in 1975, LA Stage Alliance is a membership organization dedicated to building awareness, appreciation and support for the performing arts in Greater Los Angeles. LA Stage Alliance accomplishes its mission for its members through community building, collaborative marketing, advocacy, audience development, professional development and strengthening operations. It serves more than 325 organizational members annually in the counties of Los Angeles, Orange, Riverside, San Bernadino, Santa Barbara and Ventura, and individual members comprised of local, regional, national and international performing arts patrons. Organizational membership is comprised of professional, educational and community-based producing and presenting performing arts organizations.

LEAGUE OF CHICAGO THEATRES/LEAGUE OF CHICAGO THEATRES FOUNDATION

228 South Wabash, Suite 200; Chicago, IL 60604; (312) 554-9800,
 FAX 922-7202; info@chicagoplays.com, www.chicagoplays.com

Founded in 1979, the League of Chicago Theatres/League of Chicago Theatres Foundation is a member organization which advocates for the business and artistic needs of the Chicago theatre community. It operates as an information clearinghouse; offers a cooperative advertising program; offers "Play Money" Theater Gift Certificates; offers professional development workshops; implements marketing initiatives such as Theater Thursdays; and sells half-price theatre tickets through its 2 Hot Tix locations. Publications include the quarterly *Chicagoplays Theater Guide*. Theatre companies, producers and presenters incorporated for at least 2 years and located within 50 miles of Chicago are eligible to apply for membership.

LEAGUE OF PROFESSIONAL THEATRE WOMEN/NEW YORK

411 East 53rd St, #19A; New York, NY 10022; (212) 414-8048,
 FAX (212) 223-2378; www.theatrewomen.org
Lynn Rogers, *Co-President*

Founded in 1979, the League is a not-for-profit organization of theatre professionals providing programs and services that promote women in all areas of professional theatre, create industry-related opportunities for women, and highlight contributions of theatre women, past and present. Through its salons, seminars, educational programs, social events, awards and festivals, the League links professional theatres with theatre women nationally and internationally and provides an ongoing forum for ideas, methods and issues of concern to the theatrical community and its audiences. Programs include the Lee Reynolds Award, given annually to a woman or women whose work for, in, about or through the medium of theatre has helped to illuminate the possibilities for social, cultural or political change; the Oral History Project, which seeks to chronicle and document the contribution of significant theatre women; a membership directory; and panels discussing topics of interest to women theatre professionals with well-known experts in the field. Regular monthly meetings enable members to network, initiate programs and serve on committees. To be eligible for membership in the league, playwrights, composers, librettists and lyricists must have had a work presented in a professional production in the U.S. or Canada; or in a New York City theatre under Equity's Basic Minimum Contract, excluding showcases; or at least 2 productions presented in a resident theatre, as defined under Equity's Minimum Basic Contract for Resident Theatres. All other theatre professionals must meet criteria listed on website. Annual dues are $150.

LITERARY MANAGERS AND DRAMATURGS OF THE AMERICAS (LMDA)

Box 728, Village Station; New York, NY 10014; (800) 680-2148;
    lmdanyc@gmail.com, www.lmda.org
Shelley Orr, *President*

LMDA, the professional service organization for American and Canadian literary managers and dramaturgs, was founded in 1985 to affirm, examine and develop these professions. Among the programs and services it offers to members are a university caucus and a student caucus, which act as liaisons between training programs and the profession; an advocacy caucus, which examines and reports on current working conditions; an annual conference each Jun; funding opportunities for small dramaturgy projects; discussion and announcement listservs and job postings. Publications include the quarterly *LMDA Review*, the *LMDA Script Exchange*, the *Production Notebooks* (2 volumes), employment guidelines, a guide to training programs, a sourcebook for teachers of dramaturgy and an annual bibliography; most of these publications are available through the LMDA website. Voting membership is open to dramaturgs and literary managers; associate membership is open to playwrights, artistic directors, literary agents, educators and other theatre professionals. Dues are $60 for voting members ($25 for non-voting or student members), $130 for institutional members.

LUMINOUS VISIONS

134 West 87th St, Suite 1R; New York, NY 10024; (212) 724-7059,
    FAX 724-2118; carlaluminous@aol.com, www.luminousvisions.org
Carla Pinza, *Co-Founder*

Founded in 1976 by Raul Julia and Carla Pinza, Luminous Visions is a multicultural, not-for-profit volunteer organization dedicated to developing the creative skills of film and television writers, directors and actors seeking employment within the English-speaking film and television mainstream. All productions are developed and produced by Luminous Visions. Major funds are earmarked for children living below the poverty level, and children with life-threatening illnesses.

MARY ANDERSON CENTER FOR THE ARTS
Box 12; 101 St. Francis Dr; Mount Saint Francis, IN 47146; (812) 923-8602,
FAX 923-0294; macarts@onebox.com, www.maryandersoncenter.org
Lisa Angell, *Executive Director*

The Mary Anderson Center, founded in 1989, is a not-for-profit organization that offers emerging and established writers, visual artists and musicians/composers a quiet place to focus on their art. Named after the 19th-century actress from Louisville who became an international celebrity, the Center is located on 400 acres owned and tended by the Franciscan friary. The Center provides residencies for artists in many disciplines (see the organization's listing in Colonies and Residencies). As part of its arts outreach, the Center sponsors exhibits, clay classes and special events. An email newsletter featuring Center activities, fellowships and news of alumni is sent monthly to donors, alumni and area artists.

MEET THE COMPOSER
90 John St, #312; New York, NY 10038; (212) 645-6949, FAX 645-9669;
mtc@meetthecomposer.org, www.meetthecomposer.org
Ed Harsh, *President*

Founded in 1974, Meet The Composer is a national service organization whose mission is to increase opportunities for composers by fostering the creation, performance, dissemination and appreciation of their music. With support from foundations, corporations, individual patrons and government sources, Meet The Composer designs programs that support composers writing in all styles of music: classical, jazz, folk, electronic, symphonic, opera, dance, experimental, etc. Through a variety of programs, Meet The Composer provides composer fees to not-for-profit organizations that perform, present and commission original works. Applications to all Meet The Composer programs are submitted by sponsoring organizations, not individual composers. Its programs include: Commissioning Music/USA, Creative Connections and Global Connections (see Meet The Composer Programs in Fellowships and Grants).

MISSOURI ASSOCIATION OF PLAYWRIGHTS
6 Godwin Lane; St. Louis, MO 63124; igotbetter@sbcglobal.net
Joe Wegescheide, *President*

Missouri Association of Playwrights (MAP) was founded in 1978 to assist playwrights in developing their skills. The association's activities include staged readings and workshops of members' plays, as well as seminars on playwriting. A member newsletter promotes upcoming readings and events and publishes information about opportunities for playwrights, as well as articles on playwriting and stagecraft. Membership is open to all playwrights, but most members live in the greater St. Louis area (including southwest IL and out-state MO). Annual dues for playwrights are $20.

MUSE OF FIRE THEATRE COMPANY

475 West 57th St, Suite 24C2; New York, NY 10019; (212) 397-2757,
    FAX 397-2757; glenn.english2@verizon.net,
    www.museoffiretheatreco.org
Glenn English and Vivian Paxton, *Co-Artistic Directors*

Founded in 1999, Muse of Fire Theatre Company is a not-for-profit organization dedicated to developing and producing original plays by American playwrights. With a resident company of actors, directors and playwrights, Muse of Fire seeks to promote new playwriting and develop new audiences, particularly young audiences. Its programs include an ongoing readers workshop that offers staged readings of new plays, the Muse Writers Workshop (open to members only) and the Sirens One Act Festival, dedicated to promoting work by women writers. The organization publishes the quarterly *Muse of Fire Newsletter*. Writers interested in becoming a part of Muse of Fire should submit writing sample, bio and letter of inquiry.

NATIONAL ALLIANCE FOR MUSICAL THEATRE

520 8th Ave, Suite 301; New York, NY 10018; (212) 714-6668,
    FAX 714-0469; info@namt.org, www.namt.org
Kathy Evans, *Executive Director*

The National Alliance for Musical Theatre, founded in 1985, is the national service organization for musical theatre. NAMT's mission is to nurture the development and production of new musicals. Its membership includes theatres, presenting organizations, universities and individual producers. Located throughout 33 states and 6 countries, member companies vary substantially in size, structure and purpose, reflecting the increasing diversity of the field. Cumulatively, NAMT's 140-plus member organizations have 700,000 subscribers, $500 million in operating revenues and an annual attendence of more than 15 million people. As part of its services, NAMT presents 2 annual conferences, maintains a website, surveys the membership on industry issues, and publishes a weekly electronic newsletter and an annual membership directory. NAMT also produces an annual Festival of New Musicals in New York City to promote the discovery, development and advancement of the musical theatre art form. Submissions for the Festival are accepted in Jan and Feb.

THE NATIONAL AUDIO THEATRE FESTIVALS, INC. (NATF)

Box 3535; Gresham, OR 97030; (503) 465-5081; www.natf.org
A. Nanette Taylor, *Executive Director*

Founded in 1979, The National Audio Theatre Festivals, Inc. is a national resource center for audio theatre. The NAFT hosts the annual Audio Theatre Workshop, a hands-on, intensive, one-week experience at Southwest Missouri State University in West Plains, MO. NATF is a membership-based, not-for-profit arts organization that serves the advancement of audio theatre and media arts through education and presentation; NATF provides information and referral services and technical assistance to interested individuals and groups; creates and distributes educational materials; presents workshops throughout the country; and publishes a newsletter and the *Audio*

Dramatists Directory, an online guide to current audio artists, producers, programmers and professional resources. NATF also holds an annual script contest to identify and promote emerging and established audio script writers (see NATF Script Competition in Prizes). Winning scripts may be produced during one of a series of audio theatre workshops held each year. Membership fees vary.

THE NATIONAL FOUNDATION FOR JEWISH CULTURE
(see Foundation for Jewish Culture)

THE NATIONAL LEAGUE OF AMERICAN PEN WOMEN, INC. ,
1300 17th St NW; Washington, DC 20036-1973; (202) 785-1997,
    FAX 452-6868; nlapw1@verizon.net, www.nlapw.org
N. Taylor Collins, *National President*

Founded in 1897, the NLAPW is a national membership organization for professional women writers, composers and visual artists. It holds monthly local meetings, annual State Association meetings, a Mid-Administration Congress, the National Biennial Convention and a National Art Show, and sponsors the Mature Woman Scholarship Award. Members receive the bimonthly magazine *The Pen Woman* and a national roster. Annual national dues are $40; dues for individual branches are separate and vary.

THE NATIONAL THEATRE WORKSHOP OF THE HANDICAPPED
535 Greenwich St; New York, NY 10013; (212) 206-7789, FAX 206-0200;
    admissions@ntwh.org, ntwh.org
Rick Curry S. J., *Founder and Artistic Director*

The National Theatre Workshop of the Handicapped (NTWH) is a not-for-profit organization founded in 1977 to provide persons with disabilities the opportunity to learn the communication skills necessary to pursue a life in professional theatre and to enhance their opportunities in the workplace. NTWH advocates for persons with physical disabilities in the theatre and offers a forum for dramatic literature on themes of disability. NTWH also runs a Playwright's Workshop, developing new works in residence at NTWH-Crosby, a fully handicapped-accessible residential facility in Belfast, ME, with selected works produced later. NTWH also offers professional instruction in acting, singing, voice, movement and playwriting at the ME campus and at the NTWH Mary Pozycki Studio in New York City.

NEW DRAMATISTS
424 West 44th St; New York, NY 10036; (212) 757-6960, FAX 265-4738;
    newdramatists@newdramatists.org, www.newdramatists.org
Todd London, *Artistic Director*

Founded in 1949, New Dramatists is the nation's oldest playwright development center, designed to provide member playwrights with the resources they need to create plays for the American theatre. Rather than producing plays, New Dramatists supports playwrights in the development of their craft through play readings and workshops; dramaturgy; advocacy; musical-theatre development; ScriptShare (a national script distribution program); fellowships, awards and prizes; a free ticket program for Broadway and Off-Broadway productions; writing spaces and accommodations; and photocopying. All development is playwright-driven, and all services are provided free of charge to company members.

In addition, New Dramatists hosts several playwright exchanges, including the Ted Tulchin Exchange/Max Weitzenhoffer Fellowship with the Royal National Theatre of Great Britain, England; and the Sumner Locke Elliott Exchange with Playwriting Australia.

Company membership is open to playwrights living in the greater New York area, and to those living outside the area who demonstrate a willingness to regularly travel to New York and actively participate in this community of artists. Membership applications are accepted 15 Jul–15 Sep; interested playwrights should write for guidelines.

NEW ENGLAND THEATRE CONFERENCE (NETC)
215 Knob Hill Dr; Hamden, CT 06518; (617) 851-8535; mail@netconline.org, www.netconline.org

Founded in 1952, New England Theatre Conference is a membership organization including playwrights, teachers, students and theatre professionals, but not exclusively for the New England theatre community. Services include an annual conference, publication of a member directory and annual summer theatre auditions. NETC also administers both the John Gassner Memorial Playwriting Award and the Aurand Harris Memorial Playwriting Award (see Prizes). The organization publishes *New England Theatre Journal* and *NETC News*. Membership dues are $30 for students, $45 for individuals, $95 for groups.

NEW PLAYWRIGHTS FOUNDATION
c/o 608 San Vicente Blvd, #18; Santa Monica, CA 90402; (310) 393-3682; www.newplaywrights.org
Jeffrey Lee Bergquist, *Artistic Director*

Founded in 1968, New Playwrights Foundation is a service organization for writers working in theatre, film, television and video. The Foundation runs developmental workshops, holds readings, produces plays, musicals, video and film projects and assists members in furthering their careers. Membership in NPF is limited to a maximum of 15 writers who must be able to attend meetings in Santa Monica every other Thursday night. Candidates for membership attend 3 meetings before submitting copyrighted materials to be reviewed by the group. Annual membership dues are $25.

THE NEW YORK PUBLIC LIBRARY FOR THE PERFORMING ARTS

40 Lincoln Center Plaza; New York, NY 10023-7498; (212) 870-1639,
    FAX 870-1868; theatrediv@nypl.org, www.nypl.org
Bob Taylor, *Curator, The Billy Rose Theatre Division*

Founded in 1931, The Billy Rose Theatre Division of the Library for the Performing Arts is open to the public (ages 18 and over) and contains material on all aspects of theatrical art and the entertainment world, including stage, film, radio, television, circus, vaudeville, burlesque and numerous other genres. The Theatre on Film and Tape Archive (TOFT) is a special collection of moving images of theatrical productions recorded during performance, as well as informal dialogues with important theatrical personalities. Tapes are available for viewing by appointment (call 212-870-1642) to students, theatre professionals and researchers.

NON-TRADITIONAL CASTING PROJECT, INC.

(see Alliance for Inclusion in the Arts)

NORTH CAROLINA WRITERS' NETWORK

Box 954; Carrboro, NC 27510; (919) 967-9540, FAX 929-0535;
    mail@ncwriters.org, www.ncwriters.org
Cynthia Barrett, *Executive Director*

Founded in 1985, North Carolina Writers' Network is a statewide not-for-profit organization serving writers at all stages of development. The Network offers workshops, conferences, classes, competitions, editing services, a resource center and a summer residency program. Members can market books at festivals and in a catalog, can announce events in weekly email calendars, and receive a bimonthly newsletter with free classified ads and discounts on all Network programs and events. Annual dues are $75 ($55 for seniors and students).

PEN AMERICAN CENTER

588 Broadway, Suite 303; New York, NY 10012; (212) 334-1660,
    FAX 334-2181; pen@pen.org, www.pen.org
Michael Roberts, *Executive Director*

Founded in 1922, PEN American Center is the largest of the 145 centers that comprise the human rights and literary organization International PEN. The 3300 members of PEN American Center are established North American writers, translators and editors. PEN activities include defending writers in prison or in danger of imprisonment for their work, sponsoring public literary programs and forums on current issues, encouraging literacy in inner-city schools, promoting international literature and administering literary prizes and grants. Among PEN's annual prizes and awards are the PEN Translation Prize and the PEN/Laura Pels Foundation Award for Drama (see Prizes) and Writing Awards for Prisoners. The PEN Writers' Fund and the PEN Fund for Writers & Editors with AIDS assist writers (see Emergency Funds). PEN's publications include *Grants and Awards Available to American Writers*, an online directory of prizes, grants, fellowships and awards; and *PEN America*, a biannual literary journal.

THE PLAYWRIGHTS' CENTER

2301 East Franklin Ave; Minneapolis, MN 55406-1099; (612) 332-7481; info@pwcenter.org, www.pwcenter.org

Polly K. Carl, *Producing Artistic Director*

Founded in 1971, The Playwrights' Center is a service organization for playwrights. Its programs include developmental services (readings and workshops), including the Ruth Easton Playlabs Series; fellowships; exchanges with theatres and other developmental programs; and playwriting classes. The Center annually awards more than $500,000 each year in residencies, commissions, prizes and development funds, including 5 Jerome Fellowships in Playwriting, for which competition is open nationally; 1 McKnight National Residency and Commission; 2 McKnight Advancement Grants, open to MN playwrights; 3 McKnight Theater Artist Grants, open to MN artists; and Many Voices Residency opportunities for MN playwrights of color (see organization's listing in Fellowships and Grants). Benefits of membership include online columns and discussion forums, discounts on classes, access to script-development readings, workshops, dramaturgical support, access to regularly updated listings of opportunities, a bi-weekly e-bulletin. A broad-based Center membership is available to any playwright or interested person for $50 per year. Institutional membership is available to colleges and universities for $275 per year through the New Plays on Campus program.

PLAYWRIGHTS' CENTER OF SAN FRANCISCO

588 Sutter St, #430; San Francisco, CA 94102; (415) 820-3206; pcsf@playwrightscentersf.org, www.playwrightscentersf.org

Bob Hayden, *Membership Director*

The Playwrights' Center of San Francisco, founded in 1980, is a membership organization devoted to helping Bay Area playwrights develop their scripts from initial concept to staged reading with professional actors and direction. The Center provides several developmental programs (see Playwrights' Center of San Francisco Developmental Programs in Development), and "Theatre Nights," where members attend performances at a discount and participate in post-show discussions. The Center also provides its members with a weekly e-newsletter with announcements and notices of special events and current opportunities. Membership includes a personal email address, resume hosting, discounts and voting privileges. Annual dues are $40–$60 (see website for details). The Center is committed to never turning away a member for financial reasons. A limited number of "waivers" are available for those desiring membership who cannot afford the annual fee; those interested should come to a Tuesday night event.

PLAYWRIGHTS FOUNDATION

131 10th St, 3rd Floor; San Francisco, CA 94103; (415) 626-0452, ext 110;
admin@playwrightsfoundation.org, www.playwrightsfoundation.org
Amy Mueller, *Artistic Director*

Founded in 1976, Playwrights Foundation actively fosters the inception and development of new plays by diverse playwrights throughout the U.S. The Foundation produces the annual Bay Area Playwrights Festival (see Development), and has year-round programming that includes a Resident Playwrights Initiative, an In The Rough reading series of early drafts of new plays, a Studio Incubator series, a Commissioning/Producing Partnership program, and partnerships with theatres and development organizations locally and nationally. The Foundation's New Play Institute offers year-round playwriting classes. Playwrights Foundation accepts open submissions for the Bay Area Playwrights Festival, which serves as the gateway to all its programs.

PLAYWRIGHTS THEATRE OF NEW JERSEY

Box 1295; Madison, NJ 07940; (973) 514-1787, FAX 514-2060;
www.ptnj.org
John Pietrowski, *Artistic Director*

Founded in 1986, the Playwrights Theatre of New Jersey is both a service organization for playwrights of all ages and a professional developmental theatre. In addition to its New Play Development Program (see Development), PTNJ co-sponsors, with the New Jersey State Council on the Arts, the New Jersey Writers Project, a statewide program that teaches prose, poetry and dramatic writing in schools. Specialized programs include a playwriting-for-teachers project; adult playwriting classes; children's creative dramatics classes; playwriting projects with residents of housing projects, senior citizens, teenage substance abusers, court-appointed youth, persons with physical disabilities and adults in prison; and a program that teaches Spanish-language prose, poetry and dramatic writing. Young playwrights festivals are held in Madison and Newark, in addition to a statewide festival which is part of the New Jersey Young Playwrights Program. (See Playwrights Theatre of New Jersey in Production.)

PLAZA DE LA RAZA

3540 North Mission Rd; Los Angeles, CA 90031; (323) 223-2475,
FAX 223-1804; information@plazadelaraza.org, www.plazadelaraza.org
Rose Marie Cano, *Executive Director*

Founded in 1970, Plaza de la Raza is a cultural center for the arts and education, primarily serving the surrounding community of East Los Angeles. Plaza de la Raza conducts classes in drama, dance, music and the visual arts; provides resources for teachers in the community; and sponsors special events, exhibits and performances.

PROFESSIONAL ASSOCIATION OF CANADIAN THEATRES

215 Spadina Ave, Suite 555; Toronto, Ontario M5T 2C7; Canada;
    (416) 595-6455, FAX 595-6450; info@pact.ca, www.pact.ca
Lucy White, *Executive Director*

PACT is a member-driven organization that serves as the collective voice of professional Canadian theatres. For the betterment of Canadian theatre, PACT provides leadership, national representation and a variety of programs and practical assistance to member companies, enabling members to do their own creative work. PACT publishes *The Theatre Listing*, a directory of English-language Canadian theatres, rehearsal and performance spaces, government agencies and arts service organizations; *Artsboard*, a bimonthly e-bulletin of employment opportunities in the arts in Canada; *Human Resources in the Canadian Theatre*; and various studies and research papers available from PACT's website. PACT also hosts an annual theatre conference each spring.

THE PURPLE CIRCUIT

921 North Naomi St; Burbank, CA 91505; (818) 953-5096;
    purplecir@aol.com, www.buddybuddy.com/pc.html
Bill Kaiser, *Coordinator*

The Purple Circuit, founded in 1991, is a network of gay, lesbian, queer, bisexual and transsexual theatres, producers, performers and "Kindred Spirits" (theatres which are not exclusively gay or lesbian in orientation but are interested in producing gay or lesbian material on a regular basis). The Purple Circuit Hotline (818-953-5072) provides information on gay and lesbian shows currently playing in CA, advises travelers on shows around the U.S. and abroad, and provides information for playwrights, journalists and others interested in promoting gay/lesbian/ bisexual/transgender theatre and performance. The Purple Circuit publishes news, information and articles of interest to its constituency on its website. *The Purple Circuit Directory* lists theatres and producers around the world that are interested in presenting gay, lesbian, bisexual and transsexual works.

THE SCRIPTWRITERS NETWORK

6404 Wilshire Blvd, # 1640; Los Angeles, CA 90048; (888) 796-9673;
    www.scriptwritersnetwork.org
Bill Lundy, *Chairman Emeritus*

Although The Scriptwriters Network, founded in 1986, is predominantly an affiliation of film, television and corporate/industrial writers, playwrights are welcome. Bimonthly meetings feature guest speakers talking about writing craft and the industry; developmental feedback on scripts is available. The network sponsors a High School Fellowship Program, publishes a quarterly newsletter and maintains various resources for members only. Membership dues are $75 per year with a one-time $15 initiation fee for new members. Applications available on the website.

THE SONGWRITERS GUILD OF AMERICA

Administrative/Nashville Office:
209 10th Ave S, Suite 534; Nashville, TN 37212; (615) 329-1782;
   nash@songwritersguild.com, www.songwritersguild.com
Evan Shoemake, *Central Project Manager*
New York Office:
   1560 Broadway, Suite 408; New York, NY 10036; (212) 768-7902;
   ny@songwritersguild.com
Mark Saxon, *East Coast Project Manager*
Los Angeles Office:
6430 Sunset Blvd, Suite 705; Hollywood, CA 90028; (323) 462-1108;
   la@songwritersguild.com
Aaron Lynn, *West Coast Project Manager*

Founded in 1931, The Songwriters Guild is a voluntary national association run by and for songwriters; directors are unpaid. Among its many services to composers and lyricists, the Guild provides a standard songwriter's contract and reviews this and other contracts on request; collects writers' royalties from music publishers; maintains a copyright renewal service; conducts songwriting workshops and critique sessions with special rates for members; issues news bulletins with essential information for writers; and offers a group medical and life insurance plan. The Guild currently offers 3 levels of membership, with dues starting at $60; membership is open to published and unpublished songwriters. See website for details.

S.T.A.G.E. (SOCIETY FOR THEATRICAL ARTISTS' GUIDANCE AND ENHANCEMENT)

1106 Lupo Dr; Dallas, TX 75207; (214) 630-7722, FAX 630-4468;
   stage-online@sbcglobal.net, www.stage-online.org
Jeff Fenter, *Operations Manager*

Founded in 1981, S.T.A.G.E. is a not-for-profit membership organization which serves as an information clearinghouse and provides training and education for the theatre, broadcast and film industries in north central TX. The society maintains a library of plays, theatre texts and resource information; offers counseling on agents, unions, personal marketing and other career-related matters; posts job opportunities; maintains a callboard for regional auditions in theatre and film; and sponsors an actor's showcase, Noon Preview. Members of S.T.A.G.E. receive audition postings via email. Annual dues are $80, $45 for volunteers.

STAGESOURCE

88 Tremont St, Suite 714; Boston, MA 02108; (617) 720-6066,
   FAX 720-4275; info@stagesource.org, www.stagesource.org
Jeffrey Poulos, *Executive Director*

Founded in 1985, StageSource, the Greater Boston Theatre Alliance, is a not-for-profit arts service organization committed to providing leadership and resources for the advancement of theatre in the Greater Boston/New England area. Its membership includes more than 220 producing organizations and 2000 individual theatre artists. StageSource hosts annual Equity and non-Equity auditions and a biannual theatre conference. Its other programs include: health insurance for freelance theatre artists; the Professional Development Series, offering career development and master classes in art and business; a Playwrights Alliance, focusing on needs of area playwrights; an online Talent Bank of resumes and headshots; and a 2-for-1 ticket discount program to more than 60 Greater Boston area theatres. Weekly e-newsletters feature job, audition and workshop opportunities; news; and free and discount ticket offers. StageSource publishes a quarterly calendar, *The Stage Page*. Membership is open to individuals, theatres and producing organizations. Annual dues for individuals are $60 for students and renewing members, $115 for new members, $155–$490 for theatres and producing organizations, based on operating budget.

THEATRE BAY AREA (TBA)

870 Market St, Suite 375; San Francisco, CA 94102; (415) 430-1140,
    FAX 430-1145; tba@theatrebayarea.org, www.theatrebayarea.org

Founded in 1976, Theatre Bay Area is a resource organization for San Francisco Bay Area theatres and theatre workers. Its membership includes 3000 individuals and some 400 theatre and dance companies. Its programs include TIX Bay Area, San Francisco's half-price ticket booth; TIX By Mail, half-price tickets online; professional workshops; and communications and networking services. Membership includes a subscription to *Theatre Bay Area Magazine*, a monthly magazine featuring articles, interviews and essays on the northern CA theatre scene, as well as information on play contests and festivals, and listings of production activity, workshops, classes, auditions, jobs and services. TBA also publishes *Theatre Directory of the Bay Area*, which includes entries of local theatre companies; the *Performance and Rehearsal Space Directory of the Bay Area*, with listings of rehearsal and performance spaces; *Sources of Publicity*; and *Management Memo*, a monthly e-newsletter for theatre administrators and artistic directors. The website includes a playbill calendar, online tickets and sample magazine articles. Annual dues are $65.

THEATRE COMMUNICATIONS GROUP

520 8th Ave, 24th Floor; New York, NY 10018-4156; (212) 609-5900,
    FAX 609-5901; tcg@tcg.org, www.tcg.org
Teresa Eyring, *Executive Director*

Founded in 1961, Theatre Communications Group (TCG) offers a wide array of services in line with its mission: to strengthen, nurture and promote the not-for-profit professional American theatre. TCG's programs and services encompass 5 primary areas of activity: artistic programs, including grants to artists and theatres; management programs, including conferences, research and management training; international programs, including the U.S. Center of the International Theatre Institute (see listing this section); advocacy, serving as the primary national advocate for the field, in conjunction with the American Arts Alliance; and publications.

TCG has 17,000 individual members, including theatre professionals, educators and students, and a network of more than 460 member theatres nationwide, representing a wide range of institutional sizes, structures and aesthetics.

TCG's artistic programs available to playwrights include TCG/ITI Travel Grants, which provide $3000 grants to theatre professionals in the U.S. and their counterparts in Russia and Eastern and Central Europe to foster partnerships; and the New Generations Program, funded by the Doris Duke Charitable Foundation and The Andrew W. Mellon Foundation, which offers full-time mentorships in resident professional theatres and $3000 unrestricted travel grants. (See TCG Artistic Programs in Fellowships and Grants. Program guidelines are available on TCG's website.)

In addition to *American Theatre* magazine, which provides an up-to-date perspective on theatre throughout the country and includes the full texts of five new plays annually, other TCG publications of interest to theatre writers include the annual *Theatre Directory*, which provides complete contact information for more than 450 U.S. not-for-profit professional theatres and related organizations; *Stage Writers Handbook: A Complete Business Guide for Playwrights, Composers, Lyricists and Librettists*, by Dana Singer; *The Production Notebooks: Theatre in Process*, Volumes I and II, edited by Mark Bly; *Stage Directors Handbook: Opportunities for Directors and Choreographers*, edited by the SDC Foundation; and *ARTSEARCH*, a biweekly bulletin of job opportunities in the arts, available online or in print. TCG also publishes plays and musicals, theatre-related books, and resource books on the not-for-profit professional theatre. (See Publications and Useful Publications. A complete publications catalog is available from TCG and on TCG's website.)

Individual members receive a free subscription to *American Theatre* magazine, discounted tickets to performances at theatres nationwide and discounts on all TCG books, including TCG distribution titles. Other benefits include discounts on car rentals and hotels and eligibility for a no-fee affinity credit card. Individual memberships are available for $39.95 per year, $20 for students. (See TCG membership information at the back of this book.)

THEATRE FOR YOUNG AUDIENCES/USA (UNITED STATES CHAPTER OF ASSITEJ, THE INTERNATIONAL ASSOCIATION OF THEATRE FOR CHILDREN AND YOUNG PEOPLE)

(formerly ASSITEJ/USA)
2936 North Southport, 3rd Floor; Chicago, IL 60657; (703) 403-5820,
    FAX (773) 529-2693; info@tyausa.org, www.assitej.org
Caitlin Hansen, *Office Administrator*

Founded in 1965, TYA/USA is a national service organization promoting the power of professional theatre for young audiences through excellence, collaboration and innovation across cultural and international boundaries. Members include theatres, institutions and individuals concerned about the theatre, young audiences and international goodwill. Members receive *TYA Today*, published semiannually, and priority consideration for participation in national and international events. Annual membership dues are $35 for students, $40 for retirees, $60 for libraries, $75 for individuals, $150–$425 for organizations (depending on budget).

THE THEATRE MUSEUM
(see The Victoria & Albert Theatre Collections)

THEATRE PROJECT
45 West Preston St; Baltimore, MD 21201; (410) 539-3091, FAX 539-2137;
 office@theatreproject.org, www.theatreproject.org
Anne Cantler Fulwiler, *Producing Director*

Founded in 1971, the Theatre Project, also known as Baltimore Theatre Project, offers established and emerging performing artists a supportive environment to develop and present their work. Theatre Project productions provide Baltimore with a professional international center for diverse artistic voices. Artists receive visitor housing; technical, promotional and front-of-house support; and opportunities to meet with other artists. Additional services include workshops, roundtables, seminars, open auditions and a shared database of Baltimore-area affiliated artists.

THE VICTORIA & ALBERT THEATRE COLLECTIONS
Victoria & Albert South Kensington; Cromwell Rd; London SW7 2RL; England;
 44-20-7942-2000; vanda@vam.ac.uk,
 www.vam.ac.uk/collections/theatre_performance/index.html

Founded in 1987, The Collections, a branch of the Victoria & Albert Museum, is Britain's national museum of the performing arts. In addition to its regular displays, which feature 400 years of the history, technology, art and craft of theatre, and its special exhibitions, the museum houses the U.K.'s largest archive of performing arts materials, including play texts, photographic and biographical files, theatre programs and reviews, and books about the theatre. The museum's education department runs workshops and study days on theatre practice for children, students, teachers and adult groups. The museum also runs a program of celebrity interviews, seminars and events.

VOLUNTEER LAWYERS FOR THE ARTS
1 East 53rd St, 6th Floor; New York, NY 10022-4201;
 (212) 319-2787, ext 1 (administrative office and Art Law Hotline),
 FAX 752-6575; vlany@vlany.org, www.vlany.org
Elena M. Paul, *Executive Director*

Founded in 1969, VLA provides pro bono legal services, education and advocacy to the New York arts community. Through public advocacy, VLA frequently acts on issues vitally important to the arts community, with freedom of expression and the First Amendment as areas of special expertise and concern. VLA provides legal assistance to more than 6000 clients each year through a variety of programs, including pro bono case placements for low-income artists and not-for-profit arts organizations; the VLA Legal Clinic; the Edmond de Rothschild Foundation Not-for-profit Assistance Program; and the Art Law Line, a legal hotline. VLA operates a membership program for artists. Membership benefits include discounts on VLA workshops and publications, invitations to member events, access to the VLA Art Law Line, access to the members-only VLA Legal Clinic, discounts on staff consultations and mediator services, and access to VLA's Speaker's Bureau and Board Bank. Programs of special interest to playwrights include workshops on copyright and contracts. VLA can also make referrals to similar organizations nationwide.

WOMEN'S THEATRE ALLIANCE (WTA)

2936 North Southport; Chicago, IL 60657-4120; womenstheatre@lycos.com, www.wtachicago.org
Katie Carey Govier, *President*

Founded in 1992, the Women's Theatre Alliance (WTA) is dedicated to the development of dramatic works by, for and/or about women and to the promotion of women's leadership within the Chicago theatre community. Programs of special interest to playwrights include the Play Development Workshop and New Plays Festival, which unites women writers with a director and actors for a development process culminating in a 2-week festival of staged readings; Solo Voices, which facilitates the creation of one-woman shows and performance pieces; and the Salon Series, an informal presentation of new work offering social networking opportunities. WTA also publishes a monthly newsletter. Membership is open to women and men. Annual dues are $25.

WRITERS GUILD OF AMERICA, EAST (WGAE), AFL-CIO

555 West 57th St; New York, NY 10019; (212) 767-7800, FAX 582-1909; www.wgaeast.org
Lowell Peterson, *Executive Director*

WGAE is the union for writers in the fields of motion pictures, television, radio and new media who reside east of the Mississippi River (regardless of where they work). The union negotiates collective bargaining agreements for its members and represents them in grievances and arbitrations under those agreements. The Guild gives annual awards; sponsors a foundation, which offers educational programs to veterans, disadvantaged young people and others; and offers a 10-year script registration service. WGAE participates in reciprocal arrangements with the International Affiliation of Writers Guilds and with its sister union, Writers Guild of America, West.

WRITERS GUILD OF AMERICA, WEST (WGAW)

7000 West 3rd St; Los Angeles, CA 90048-4329; (323) 951-4000, FAX 782-4800; www.wga.org
David Young, *Executive Director*

WGAW is the union for writers who write entertainment and news programming in the fields of motion pictures, television, radio and new media. It represents its members in collective bargaining and other labor matters. It publishes a monthly magazine, *Written By*. The Guild registers material, including screenplays and teleplays, books, plays, poetry and songs (call 323-782-4500). The WGAW library is open to the public Mon-Fri (call 323-782-4544).

YOUNG PLAYWRIGHTS INC.

Box 5134; New York, NY 10185; (212) 594-5440;
   admin@youngplaywrights.org, www.youngplaywrights.org
Sheri M. Goldhirsch, *Artistic Director*

Young Playwrights Inc. (YPI), founded in 1981 by Stephen Sondheim, is America's only not-for-profit professional theatre devoted solely to playwrights ages 18 years and younger. The producer of the annual Young Playwrights Festival, YPI's mission is to identify and develop promising young writers, while encouraging self-expression through playwriting and its integration into the basic curriculum. YPI serves as an advocate for young writers regardless of ethnicity, physical ability, sexual orientation or economic status, and works to ensure that their voices are acknowledged by a diverse community of artists and theatregoers. Competitions include the Young Playwrights Festival National Playwriting Contest and the Write a Play! NYC Contest (see Prizes). Programs include the Young Playwrights Writers Conference; Urban Retreat, a summer playwriting program in NYC; Advanced Playwriting Workshop, a weekly after-school seminar (see organization's listing in Development); Write a Play! Workshops, which bring playwriting into the classroom; and Write a Play! Teacher Training Institute, a curriculum-based professional development program.

PART 3
RESOURCES

USEFUL PUBLICATIONS

This is a selective listing of the publications that we think most usefully supplement the information given in the *Sourcebook*. Note that publications of interest to theatre writers are also described throughout this book, particularly in the chapter introductions, in the Membership and Service Organizations listings and in the Online Resources chapter. We have purposely left out any "how to" books on the art of playwriting because we do not want to promote the concept of "writing-by-recipe." Pricing and ordering information may change after this book goes to press, so it would be wise to confirm details before ordering a publication.

AMERICAN THEATRE

Theatre Communications Group; 520 8th Ave, 24th Floor;
New York, NY 10018-4156; (212) 609-5900, FAX 609-5901;
custserv@tcg.org, www.tcg.org

1-year subscription/TCG membership $39.95; single issue $5.95. This magazine, published 10 times per year, provides comprehensive coverage of all aspects of theatre. *American Theatre* regularly features articles and interviews dealing with theatre writers and their works, and publishes the complete texts of 5 new plays per year. Schedules for more than 400 theatres are published in each issue, and a special Oct Season Preview issue prints upcoming season schedules. Selected feature articles and season schedules are posted on the website monthly.

BACK STAGE

Back Stage East:

770 Broadway, 7th Floor; New York, NY 10003;
backstage@backstage.com, www.backstage.com

1-year subscription $99, 2 years $169; single issue $2.95.

Back Stage West:

5055 Wilshire Blvd; Los Angeles, CA 90036; backstage@backstage.com,
www.backstage.com

1-year subscription $99, 2 years $169; single issue $2.95.

1-year subscription to Backstage.com $135; 1-year combination online and print subscription (specify *Back Stage East* or *West*) $195. This actor's resource weekly includes national coverage of industry news, career advice, theatre reviews, and interviews with industry professionals including playwrights. The primary focus is on casting; script solicitation, workshops and classes for playwrights are also advertised.

DIRECTORY OF THEATRE TRAINING PROGRAMS

Theatre Directories, Inc; Box 159; Dorset, VT 05251-0159; (802) 867-9333,
FAX 867-2297; info@theatredirectories.com,
www.theatredirectories.com

11th ed, 2007. 304 pp, $39.50 (plus shipping and handling) paper. Published biennially, this directory contains detailed listings of admissions, tuition, scholarships, curriculum, faculty, productions and philosophy of training for 475 theatre training programs in the U.S., Canada and the U.K. The next edition will be published in 2009.

HOLLYWOOD SCRIPTWRITER

Box 3761; Cerritos, CA 90703; (310) 283-1630;
intern@hollywoodscriptwriter.com, www.hollywoodscriptwriter.com

1-year subscription (6 issues) $36 U.S., $45.00 Canada, $55.00 all other international. This 24-page trade paper contains interviews and articles that provide advice to playwrights and screenwriters, including a "Markets for Your Work" section. A list of back issues with a summary of the contents of each issue is available; call for information.

INSIGHT FOR PLAYWRIGHTS

11309 East Petra Ave; Mesa, AZ 85212-1981;
info@insightforplaywrights.com, www.insightforplaywrights.com

1-year subscription (12 issues) $45, email subscription $35. This monthly marketing newsletter for playwrights provides submission guidelines for theatres, residencies, publishers, grants, festivals and contests, and lists special programs for women writers, and more; see website for sample issue.

LITERARY MARKET PLACE 2008

Information Today, Inc; 630 Central Ave; New Providence, NJ 07974;
(800) 409-4929, Customer Service: 300-9868, FAX (908) 219-0192;
custserv@infotoday.com, www.literarymarketplace.com

2008. 2043 pp, $299.95 (plus $25 and tax shipping and handling). Also available online at www.literarymarketplace.com (various fee options and subscription rates are provided). This directory of the North American book publishing industry gives contact information for book publishers and those in related fields, and includes 2 "Names & Numbers" indexes totaling nearly 600 pages. The 2009 LMP is due out in Oct 2008.

PROFESSIONAL PLAYSCRIPT FORMAT GUIDELINES & SAMPLE

Feedback Theatrebooks; Order Department; Box 174; Brooklin, ME 04616;
(207) 359-2781, FAX 359-5532; info@feedbacktheatrebooks.com,
www.feedbacktheatrebooks.com

2nd ed, 2001. 42 pp, $12.95 (plus $5.50 shipping via USPS and sales tax where applicable) paper. This booklet provides updated and expanded instructions for laying out a script in the professional format; includes "Margin and Tab Setting Guide" and sample pages of script.

REGIONAL THEATRE DIRECTORY

Theatre Directories, Inc; Box 159; Dorset, VT 05251-0159; (802) 867-9333,
FAX 867-2297; info@theatredirectories.com,
www.theatredirectories.com

2008-2009 ed, 2008. 167 pp, $29.50 (plus shipping and handling) paper. An employment and internship directory for professionals and students. Contains 400 listings of regional and dinner theatres in the US. The listings include productions, physical plant, hiring, internships and theatre missions. The next edition will be published in 2009.

Stage Directions Magazine

6000 S. Eastern Ave, Suite 14J; Las Vegas, NV 88119; (702) 932-5585,
    FAX 554-5340; jcoakley@stage-directions.com,
    www.stage-directions.com

1-year subscription (12 issues) offered free to qualifying theatre professionals. This magazine provides information for theatre professionals about new plays and musicals, new products, and industry-related news, as well as information regarding lighting, sound, costumes, scenery and makeup.

Stage Writers Handbook: A Complete Business Guide for Playwrights, Composers, Lyricists and Librettists

Theatre Communications Group; 520 8th Ave, 24th Floor;
    New York, NY 10018-4156; (212) 609-5900, FAX 609-5901;
    custserv@tcg.org, www.tcg.org

1997. 328 pp, $22.95 (plus $5 postage and handling for 1 book, 50¢ for each additional book) paper. This comprehensive guide, written by the former Executive Director of The Dramatists Guild, covers such topics as copyright (updated 2004), collaboration, underlying rights, marketing and self-promotion, production contracts, representation (agents and lawyers), publishers, authors' relationships with directors, and videotaping and electronic rights.

The Student's Guide to Playwriting Opportunities, 3rd Edition

Box 159; Dorset, VT 05251; (802) 867-9333; FAX 867-2297;
    info@theatredirectories.com, www.theatredirectories.com

3rd ed, 2002. 128 pp, $23.95 paper. This guide is a compendium of 79 academic (undergraduate/graduate) and 80 professional programs, which includes submission opportunities and essays on playwriting.

Summer Theatre Directory

Theatre Directories, Inc; Box 159; Dorset, VT 05251-0159; (802) 867-9333,
    FAX 867-2297; info@theatredirectories.com,
    www.theatredirectories.com

2007. 133 pp, $29.50 (plus shipping and handling) paper. An employtment guide for performers (equity and non-equity), designers, directors, staff and tech in summer theatres, theme parks, cruise ships and tours. The next edition will be published in 2009.

THEATRE DIRECTORY 2007–08

Theatre Communications Group; 520 8th Ave, 24th Floor;
New York, NY 10018-4156; (212) 609-5900, FAX 609-5901;
custserv@tcg.org, www.tcg.org

2008. 278 pp, $14.95 (plus $5 postage and handling for 1 book, 50¢ for each additional book) paper. TCG's directory provides complete contact information for more than 470 not-for-profit professional theatres and more than 60 arts resource organizations. Includes special interest, budget, personnel and state index for all theatres.

THEATRE PROFILES 12

Theatre Communications Group; 520 8th Ave, 24th Floor;
New York, NY 10018-4156; (212) 609-5900, FAX 609-5901;
custserv@tcg.org, www.tcg.org

1996. 254 pp, $22.95 (plus $5 postage and handling for 1 book, 50¢ for each additional book) paper. The 12th volume of this biennial series contains artistic profiles, production photographs, financial information and repertoire information for the 1993–95 seasons of 257 theatres. Theatre Profiles project encompassing theatre seasons 1996–2008 is available from the TCG website.

U.S. COPYRIGHT OFFICE PUBLICATIONS

Copyright Office; Library of Congress; 101 Independence Ave SE;
Washington, DC 20559-6000; (202) 707-3000, 707-6737 (TTY);
copyinfo@loc.gov, www.copyright.gov/pubs.html

There are many ways to receive free informational circulars and registration forms: copyright registration forms, informational circulars and general copyright information are available through the website; the Publications Hotline (202-707-9100) processes requests for circulars and forms (if interested in registering a dramatic work, request packet FL-119). Copyright information specialists can answer questions Monday–Friday 8:30 A.M. to 5:00 P.M. at (202) 707-3000.

THE WRITER

c/o Kalmbach Publishing Co; 21027 Crossroads Circle; Box 1612;
Waukesha, WI 53187-1612; (262) 796-8776, FAX 798-6468;
editor@writermag.com, www.writermag.com

1-year subscription (12 issues) $32.95, 2 years $61, 3 years $88. This monthly magazine publishes articles on the process of writing, feature interviews with writers, market news and announcements of prizes and events.

ONLINE RESOURCES

What's here and what's not.

Now that nearly every organization, theatre and otherwise, has established an internet presence, our goal in presenting Online Resources in *Dramatists Sourcebook* is to spotlight sites that offer useful information distinct from opportunities already included elsewhere in the book. Many local playwrights' home pages, community playwrights' forums and college playwriting courses appear in the far reaches of search engine results. In the interest of accuracy and longevity, we have opted to include a select menu of sites that are mainstays of the internet playwriting community—sites with free content and broad professional appeal. Take the time to assess the editorial merit and accuracy of each site. What we present here is a guide to the best that's currently available, which you can also use to measure the quality of new ventures.

AISLE SAY

www.aislesay.com

Description: no-frills compilation of reviews by local theatre critics of professional and community theatre productions from around the country. The writing style and quality of the reviews vary significantly, but the coverage is thorough and fair. **Site includes:** reviews, links to critics' biographies and a script consultation service, and index of additional sources for reviews.

AMERICANTHEATERWEB

www.americantheaterweb.com

Description: database where theatres around the country post their production schedules. The listings are not comprehensive but the collection of theatres is diverse. **Site includes:** theatre headlines, current production listings by region, blogs and newsletter.

ARTS JOURNAL

www.artsjournal.com

Description: chronicle of feature articles on arts and culture from more than 180 English-language newspapers, magazines and publications. Direct links to the most interesting or important stories are posted every weekday beginning at 8 A.M. EST. Stories from sites that charge for access are excluded, as are sites that require visitors to register, with the exception of the *New York Times*. **Site includes:** articles sorted by discipline and date, newsletter, weekly email updates, blogs, classifieds and related links.

ARTSLYNX INTERNATIONAL ARTS RESOURCES

www.artslynx.org

Description: a compilation of international links for a great variety of artistic disciplines. **Site includes:** multitude of links and resource pages on many topics, from mime to makeup artistry to playwriting.

ARTS RESOURCE NETWORK

www.artsresourcenetwork.net

Description: portal for Seattle arts community. **Site includes:** links to organizations and information, online community for artists, newsletter and "SPACEfinder" tool for locating rehearsal, performance and event spaces.

ASIAN AMERICAN THEATRE REVUE

www.aatrevue.com/AATR-1.html

Description: hub for Asian-American theatre. **Site includes:** news, calendar, list of Asian-American playwrights and their plays; directory of Asian-American theatre companies; reviews; library of anthologies, individual authors and critical perspectives; bulletin boards and related links.

BACKSTAGEJOBS.COM

www.backstagejobs.com

Description: free entertainment internship and job listings. **Site includes:** postings in the design, technical and administrative fields, including specific listings for playwrights; also includes Contact Sheet of directors, designers, stage managers and technicians listed by region.

BARTLEBY.COM

www.bartleby.com

Description: online version of Bartleby's bookstore, which provides searchable databases of reference materials and works of verse, fiction and nonfiction free of charge. **Site includes:** unlimited access to a variety of major contemporary and classic reference works, including *Columbia Encyclopedia*; *American Heritage Dictionary*; *Roget's II: The New Thesaurus*; *American Heritage Book of English Usage*; *Columbia World of Quotations*; *Simpson's Contemporary Quotations*; *Bartlett's Familiar Quotations*; *King James Bible*; *Oxford Shakespeare*; *Gray's Anatomy*; *Strunk's Elements of Style*; *World Factbook* and *Columbia Gazzetteer*.

BROADWAY STARS

www.broadwaystars.com

Description: index of theatre news online. **Site includes:** headlines and links to current news items from theatre news sites and major newspapers, and links to other theatre sites, news outlets, unions, service organizations and other information.

CAMBRIDGE DICTIONARIES ONLINE

dictionary.cambridge.org

Description: *Cambridge Dictionary* online. **Site includes:** full access to *Cambridge International Dictionary*; international dictionary of idiom, international dictionary of phrasal verbs, *Learner's Dictionary* of English and others.

CITYSEARCH

www.citysearch.com

Description: nationwide, city-specific entertainment guide for arts, events, restaurants, etc., by city, date or subject. **Site includes:** database of cities by neighborhood and zip code, maps, classifieds and links to local services.

THE ENCYCLOPEDIA MYTHICA

www.pantheon.org/mythica.html

Description: capsule definitions and explanations from world mythology, folklore and legend. **Site includes:** lists of more than 7000 articles, 300 illustrations, maps and genealogy tables from more than 25 cultures.

INTERNET BROADWAY DATABASE
www.ibdb.com

Description: IBDB is the official database for Broadway production information. **Site includes:** several search options including keyword search, category search (shows, people, theatre or season) or date search (date range, day or current production).

INTERNET MOVIE DATABASE
www.imdb.com

Description: comprehensive searchable database containing complete credit information for film, video, made-for-TV movies and TV series. **Site includes:** artist filmographies; movie and TV news; U.S. movie show times searchable by date, city, state and zip code; photo galleries; IMDb staff and user recommendations; independent film index; new releases and user favorites.

INTERNET OFF-BROADWAY DATABASE
www.iobdb.com

Description: searchable database of Off-Broadway production information culled from the Lortel Archives. **Site includes:** credits and production information searchable by show title, theatre, people, awards and company name.

IN TRANSLATION
www.intranslation.com.ar

Description: central database of Spanish to English theatre translations that can be downloaded in their entirety. **Site includes:** database of Spanish to English theatre translations listed by author; alphabetical listing of translators with contact information; resources section including information about conferences, workshops and deadlines.

KMC: A BRIEF GUIDE TO INTERNET RESOURCES IN THEATRE AND PERFORMANCE STUDIES
www.stetson.edu/csata/thr_guid.html

Description: selected list of theatre resources compiled by Ken McCoy, Ph.D., Associate Professor of Communication Studies and Theatre Arts at Stetson College. **Site includes:** list of McCoy's most used sites, resources searchable by theatre subject, listservs, newsgroups and other guides.

NATIVE AMERICAN AUTHORS
www.ipl.org/div/natam

Description: information about contemporary Native North American authors including playwrights. **Site includes:** searchable database of writers with bibliographies of their published works and biographical information, and links to interviews, online texts and tribal websites.

NATIVE AMERICAN WOMEN PLAYWRIGHTS ARCHIVE (NAWPA)
staff.lib.muohio.edu/nawpa

Description: catalog of writing by Native American women playwrights. **Site includes:** playwright directory, online exhibit of Spiderwoman Theater, bibliography of Native American women's theatre, author's roundtable, archive of *NAWPA* newsletters, listings of recent programs and productions, and related links.

NEW YORK THEATRE WIRE
www.nytheatre-wire.com

Description: source for what's playing on New York City stages. **Site includes:** articles, publication information; Broadway, Off-Broadway, Experimental Theater, Film, Dance, Opera and International Festival listings and reviews; museum directory and classifieds.

NYFA INTERACTIVE
www.nyfa.org

Description: official website of New York Foundation for the Arts; includes NYFA Source, a national database of grants, awards, services and publications for artists. **Site includes:** calendar of grant and award deadlines; lists of services, fellowships, organizations and publications; job listings for artists; tutorials; artist news and other services.

NYTHEATRE.COM
www.nytheatre.com

Description: source for New York theatre that gives equal attention to Broadway, Off- and Off-Off-Broadway. **Site includes:** listings, articles, reviews, interviews, free newsletter, venue information, not-for-profit theatre news and other features.

OFF-BROADWAY ONLINE
www.offbroadwayonline.com

Description: official information on Off-Broadway theatre presented by The Alliance of Resident Theatres/New York (see Membership and Service Organizations). **Site includes:** information on more than 400 Off-Broadway theatres, searchable database of current productions, career center and other information.

THE OFF-OFF BROADWAY REVIEW
www.oobr.com

Description: no-frills publication detailing the theatre of Off-Off-Broadway. **Site includes:** reviews, listings, archives and festival information.

PLAYBILL.COM
www.playbill.com

Description: expanded version of *Playbill*'s print publication including information about Broadway and Off-Broadway. **Site includes:** playbill archive, news from the U.S., Canada and international theatre communities; Broadway and Off-Broadway listings; online ticket sales; feature articles; job bank and links.

PLAYS AND PLAYWRIGHTS
groups.yahoo.com/group/playsandplaywrights

Description: discussion group for playwrights. **Site includes:** discussion comprised of monthly messages from 1000+ members on plays and playwriting, production information, submission and grant opportunities, teaching and professional development; discussion can be viewed online or emailed to participants.

PLAYWRIGHTS ON THE WEB
www.stageplays.com/writers.htm

Description: international database of playwrights and their websites. **Site includes:** plays listed alphabetically by author, nation and genre; a playwright discussion forum; newsletter; callboard and links.

STAGESPECS ONLINE
www.stagespecs.com

Description: technical information for theatre professionals. **Site includes:** theatres, listed by state, and their technical specs; glossary of technical terms, links to production resources, job listings and book store.

THEATERMANIA
theatermania.com

Description: portal featuring theatre news and information from major cities around the country and some international locations. **Site includes:** theatre ticket services, listings organized by city, feature and news articles, links to theatre festivals and awards, theatre store and membership information.

THE U.S. COPYRIGHT OFFICE
www.copyright.gov

Description: branch of the Library of Congress. **Site includes:** general copyright information; copyright records; publications, including forms in downloadable format; and legislation and copyright links.

WOMEN OF COLOR, WOMEN OF WORDS

www.scils.rutgers.edu/~cybers/home.html

Description: information site on accomplished women playwrights of color, especially African-Americans. **Site includes:** writers' bios, list of completed works, directory of libraries and research centers with an African-American focus, list of critical/biographical resources, links to theatres that produce multicultural work, directory of dissertations on featured playwrights, recommended books on African-American theatre history and an e-group for African-American women playwrights.

WRITEEXPRESS ONLINE RHYMING DICTIONARY

www.writeexpress.com/online2.html

Description: online rhyming dictionary. **Site includes:** database searchable by end, last syllable, double, beginning and first syllable rhymes.

WRITERSDIGEST.COM
THE 101 BEST WEB SITES FOR WRITERS

www.writersdigest.com/101BestSites

Description: well-indexed list of web resources for writers. **Site includes:** links to search engines, media news and reference sites, job sites, the writing life, self- and e-publishing, and writers' organizations.

THE WWW VIRTUAL LIBRARY THEATRE AND DRAMA

vl-theatre.com

Description: library of international theatre resources updated daily. **Site includes:** links to academic/training institutions, book dealers, conferences for theatre scholars, online play archives, online journals, mailing lists, monologues/plays in print, newsgroups, theatre books in print, theatre companies, and theatre image and syllabus banks.

YOURDICTIONARY.COM

www.yourdictionary.com

Description: index of online dictionaries. **Site includes:** dictionaries (of varying completion and quality) in 260 languages, multilingual dictionaries, specialty English dictionaries, thesauri and other vocabulary aids, language identifiers and guessers, index of dictionary indices and an online grammar tool.

YAHOO THEATRE INDEX

dir.yahoo.com/arts/performing_arts/theater

Description: index of theatre-related sites. **Site includes:** links to information on many topics including playwrights and plays.

SUBMISSION CALENDAR

Included here are all specified deadlines; the more general submission dates for theatres listed in Production are not included. Deadlines listed reflect upcoming submission deadlines as provided at press time. Some listing deadlines may fall outside the years covered by this book and are not included in this calendar listing. It is always important to confirm a deadline before submitting work.

NOVEMBER

1 American-Scandinavian Foundation, 182
1 Bay Area Playwrights Festival, 153
1 City Theatre, 24
1 Ecodrama Playwrights Festival, 112
1 First Stage One-Act Play Contest, 155
1 Global Connections (1st deadline), 190
1 Hodder Fellowship, 187
1 Julie Harris Playwriting Awards, 108
1 National Ten-Minute Play Contest, 125
1 Tennessee Williams/New Orleans Literary Festival One-Act Play Contest, 132
1 Women Playwrights Series, 172
3 Richard Rodgers Awards, 168
5 NEH Division of Research Programs/Collaborative Research, 191
15 Beverly Hills Theatre Guild-California Musical Theatre Award, 107
15 NATF, Inc Annual Script Competition, 124
15 North Carolina New Play Project, 236
30 Arch and Bruce Brown Foundation, 182
30 Ledig House International Writers' Colony, 216
30 New American Comedy (NAC) Workshop, 125

30 Poems & Plays Tennessee Chapbook Prize, 146
Contact for exact deadline during this month:
Coe College New Works for the Stage Competition, 110
KCACTF Ten-Minute Play Award, 118
Lost Nation Theater, 51
NYFA Sponsorship Program (1st deadline), 161

DECEMBER

1 Biennial Promising Playwright Award, 108
1 Cunningham Commission for Youth Theatre, 111
1 David Mark Cohen Playwriting Award, 116
1 Drury University One-Act Play Competition, 111
1 Flying Solo Festival, 155
1 George Bennett Fellowship, 187
1 Jean Kennedy Smith Playwriting Award, 117
1 John Cauble Short Play Awards Program, 117
1 KCACTF Latino Playwriting Award, 117
1 KCACTF Musical Theater Award, 117
1 KCACTF National Science Playwriting Award, 117
1 KCACTF Theater for Youth Playwriting Award, 118
1 Lorraine Hansberry Playwriting Award, 118
1 National Music Theater Conference, 159
1 National Student Playwriting Award, 118
1 New Stage Theatre Eudora Welty New Plays Series, 60
1 Paula Vogel Award in Playwriting, 119
1 Quest for Peace Playwriting Award, 119
1 Rocky Mountain National Park Artist-in-Residence, 219
1 Rosa Parks Playwriting Award, 119
1 Scenes from the Staten Island Ferry, 169
1 Utah Shakespearean Festival New American Playwrights Project, 171
1 Young Playwrights Festival National Playwriting Contest, 137
5 Ruby Lloyd Apsey Award, 129
15 Montana Artists Refuge (2nd deadline), 218
15 New York City 15 Minute Play Festival, 126
15 Reverie Productions Next Generation Playwriting Contest, 129
15 STAGE International Script Competition, 131
15 Sundance Theatre Lab, 170
16 PEN Translation Prize, 127
30 Oglebay Institute Towngate Playwriting Contest, 126

JANUARY

31 Moving Arts Premiere One-Act Competition, 123

31 Premiere Stages Play Festival, 166

31 Short Grain Contest, 130

Contact for exact deadline during this month:

Centre Stage-South Carolina, 21

Frederick Douglass Writing Workshops (2nd deadline), 156

National Endowment for the Arts International Partnerships/ArtsLink
    Projects, 190

National Endowment for the Arts Literature Fellowships for Translators, 190

National Endowment for the Humanities Division of Public
    Programs/America's Media Makers (1st Deadline), 191

FEBRUARY

1 Blue Mountain Center, 211

1 Drama League Directors Project-New Directors-New Works Series, 154

1 Japan-United States Arts Program, 188

1 Kitchen Dog New Works Festival, 48

1 Risk Is This...The Cutting Ball New Plays Festival, 168

1 Trustus Playwrights' Festival, 134

1 U.S./Japan Creative Artists' Program, 221

1 Vermont Playwrights Award, 135

15 Djerassi Resident Artists Program, 212

15 Jane Chambers Playwriting Award (regular submission), 115

15 Theatre Oxford's 10 Minute Play Contest, 133

15 William Saroyan Prize for Playwriting, 136

15 Williamstown Theatre Festival, 172

16 Isle Royale National Park Artist-in-Residence, 215

20 GAP (Grants for Artist Projects), 183

28 Hedgerow Horizons, 157

28 Marilyn Hall Awards, 108

28 McLaren Memorial Play Writing Competition, 122

28 Pen Is a Mighty Sword New Play Competition, 127

Contact for exact deadline during this month:

McKnight Advancement Grants, 193

MARCH

1 Clauder Competition, 110

1 Edward F. Albee Foundation, 213

1 Field Artward Bound, 234

Contact for exact deadline during this month:

APRIL

Contact for exact deadline during this month:

MAY

1 Aurand Harris Memorial Playwriting Award, 107
1 BMI Musical Theatre Workshop (librettists), 153
1 Don and Gee Nicholl Fellowships in Screenwriting, 185
1 German Literary Translation Prize, 105
1 Global Connections (2nd deadline), 190
1 HRC's Annual Playwriting Contest, 114
1 Lewis Galantière Literary Translation Prize, 105
1 Wings Theatre Company, Inc, 100
1 Young Playwrights Inc Urban Retreat, 173
15 Helford Prize Contest, 114
15 Virginia Center for the Creative Arts (3rd deadline), 221
15 Writer's Digest Writing Competition, 136
30 NYC Playwrights Lab, 162
31 Buntville Crew, 109
31 Josefina Lopez Playwriting Competition, 109
31 Josefina Lopez Youth Playwriting Competition, 110
Contact for exact deadline during this month:
Native Arts Program Visiting Artist Appointments, 191
NYFA Sponsorship Program (2nd deadline), 161
Soho Repertory Theatre Writer/Director Lab, 82

JUNE

1 Abingdon Theatre Company Wolk Award, 151
1 ASF Translation Prize, 106
1 California Young Playwrights Contest, 109
1 Creative Connections (4th deadline), 190
1 Jackie White Children's Playwriting Contest, 115
1 Kernodle Playwriting Contest, 120
1 New Professional Theatre Writers Festival, 126
1 Ragdale Foundation (2nd deadline), 219
1 Southeastern Theatre Conference New Play Project, 131
5 Headlands Center for the Arts, 214
10 L. Arnold Weissberger Award, 121
15 Lanesboro Residency Program Fellowships, 216
15 Towson University Prize for Literature, 134
30 Firehouse Theatre Project Festival, 113
30 PlayFest: The Harriett Lake Festival of New Plays, 164

20 Susan Smith Blackburn Prize, 132

25 Hedgebrook, 214

30 Baltimore Playwrights Festival, 152

30 Long Beach Playhouse New Works Festival, 158

30 Southern Appalachian Playwrights' Conference-ScriptFest, 169

30 Theatre Three Annual Festival of One-Act Plays, 90

30 Year-End-Series (Y.E.S.) New Play Festival, 137

Contact for exact deadline during this month:

Ensemble Theatre of Cincinnati, 32

Foothills Theatre Company, 34

Frederick Douglass Writing Workshops (1st deadline), 156

Hawthornden International Retreat for Writers, 213

Jerome Fellowships in Playwriting, 193

Play Group, 164

Will Geer Theatricum Botanicum, 98

Young Playwrights Inc Advanced Playwriting Workshop, 172

OCTOBER

1 Creative Connections (1st deadline), 190

1 Harvard University Radcliffe Institute for Advanced Study Fellowships, 187

1 Millay Colony for the Arts, 218

1 New Harmony Project, 160

1 New Visions/New Voices, 160

1 New York Mills Arts Retreat (1st deadline), 218

1 Santa Cruz Actors' Theatre Full-Length Play Contest, 129

1 Ucross Foundation Residency Program (1st deadline), 220

5 American Antiquarian Society Fellowships, 182

15 Playwrights First Award, 128

17 National Playwrights Conference, 160

20 U.S. Department of State Fulbright U.S. Student Program, 196

31 Dayton Playhouse FutureFest, 111

31 Mildred and Albert Panowski Playwriting Award, 123

31 Reva Shiner Full-Length Play Contest, 128

31 Stanley Drama Award, 132

Contact for exact deadline during this month:

New Generations Program, 194

New York Foundation for the Arts (NYFA) Artists' Fellowships, 192

SPECIAL INTERESTS INDEX

Here is a guide to entries that indicate a particular or exclusive interest in certain types of material, or contain an element of special interest to writers in certain categories. The Multicultural category is for those organizations expressing general interest in muticultural works; under African-American, Asian-American, Hispanic/Latin-American and Native American Theatre, we have included only those organizations specifically seeking work by or about people from these ethnic groups. The Student/College Submission category refers to college students or students in an affiliated writing program. Young Playwrights is a special interest category for playwrights 18 or under. Listings are alphabetized letter by letter (see Preface), and regardless of the way "theatre" (and "center," etc.) is spelled in a listing's name, it is alphabetized here as if it were spelled "theatre."

AFRICAN-AMERICAN THEATRE

ASIAN-AMERICAN THEATRE

COMEDY

DISABILITIES: Theatre for and by people with disabilities

EXPERIMENTAL THEATRE

GAY AND LESBIAN THEATRE

HISPANIC/LATIN AMERICAN THEATRE

JEWISH THEATRE

MEDIA (film, radio, television)

MULTICULTURAL THEATRE

MULTIMEDIA

MUSICAL THEATRE

NATIVE AMERICAN THEATRE

ONE-ACTS AND SHORT PLAYS

PERFORMANCE ART

RELIGIOUS/SPIRITUAL THEATRE

SENIOR CITIZENS

SOCIAL-POLITICAL THEATRE

SOLO PERFORMANCE

STUDENT/COLLEGE SUBMISSIONS

TRANSLATIONS

WOMEN'S THEATRE

YOUNG AUDIENCES

YOUNG PLAYWRIGHTS PROGRAMS

GENERAL INDEX

Remember the alphabetizing principles used throughout the book: entries are alphabetized letter by letter (see Preface). In listings, entries beginning with a person's name are alphabetized by the first name rather than the surname; however, in the index, you can find these entries cross-indexed under both names. Hence, in the index, you will find the Robert J. Pickering Award for Playwriting Excellence under "R" and "P." Regardless of the way "theatre" is spelled in an organization's name, it is alphabetized as if it were spelled "re."

T

ABOUT THEATRE COMMUNICATIONS GROUP

Theatre Communications Group (TCG), the national organization for the American theatre, offers a wide array of services in line with its mission: to strengthen, nurture and promote the professional not-for-profit American theatre. Artistic programs support theatres and theatre artists by awarding grants (approximately $3 million in 2008), and offer career development programs for artists. Management programs provide professional development opportunities for theatre leaders through workshops, conferences, forums and publications, as well as industry research on the finances and practices of the American not-for-profit theatre. Advocacy, conducted in conjunction with other performing arts fields, includes guiding lobbying efforts and providing theatres with timely alerts about legislative developments. The country's leading independent press specializing in dramatic literature, TCG publishes *American Theatre* magazine, the *ARTSEARCH* employment bulletin, plays, translations and theatre resource and reference books. As the U.S. Center of UNESCO's International Theatre Institute, a worldwide network, TCG supports cross-cultural exchange through travel grants and other assistance to traveling theatre professionals. Through these programs, TCG seeks to increase the organizational efficiency of its member theatres, cultivate the artistic talent and celebrate the achievements of the field, and enhance public understanding and appreciation of theatre. TCG serves nearly 500 member theatres nationwide.

TCG is proud to publish the following authors:

Jon Robin Baitz
Augusto Boal
Anne Bogart
Eric Bogosian
Lee Breuer
Peter Brook
Jo Carson
Aimé Césaire
Joseph Chaikin
Ping Chong
Caryl Churchill
Pearl Cleage
Constance Congdon
Rachel Corrie
Nilo Cruz
Culture Clash
E. L. Doctorow
Declan Donnellan
Will Eno
The Five Lesbian
    Brothers
Dario Fo
Richard Foreman
Athol Fugard
Philip Kan Gotanda
Spalding Gray
André Gregory
Adam Guettel

Jessica Hagedorn
Peter Hall
Karen Hartman
Tina Howe
David Henry Hwang
Adrienne Kennedy
Harry Kondoleon
Lisa Kron
Tony Kushner
Tina Landau
Tracy Letts
Robert Lepage
David Lindsay-Abaire
Kristin Linklater
Romulus Linney
Todd London
Craig Lucas
Charles Ludlam
Eduardo Machado
Emily Mann
Donald Margulies
Richard Maxwell
Ellen McLaughlin
Conor McPherson
Sherrill Myers
Richard Nelson
Danny Newman
Marsha Norman

Lynn Nottage
Sarah O'Connor
Robert O'Hara
John O'Keefe
Suzan-Lori Parks
Reynolds Price
Alvin H. Reiss
Ronald Ribman
José Rivera
Sarah Ruhl
Carl Hancock Rux
Steven Sater
David Savran
John Patrick Shanley
Wallace Shawn
Christopher Shinn
Nicky Silver
Dana Singer
Stephen Sondheim
Tadashi Suzuki
Alfred Uhry
Paula Vogel
Donna Walker-Kuhne
Naomi Wallace
Michael Weller
Thornton Wilder
August Wilson
George C. Wolfe

To order books, visit our website: www.tcg.org
Catalog available upon request

JOIN NOW AND SAVE

TCG MEMBERS SAVE ON ALL TCG RESOURCES AND BOOKS

Stage Writers Handbook
By Dana Singer

Singer gathers the information and ideas stage writers need to conduct their careers in a businesslike manner, with all the protections the law provides. Subjects covered include copyright, collaboration, underlying rights, marketing, self-promotion and more. **PAPER $18.95**

Stage Directors Handbook

The first and only sourcebook for theatre directors and choreographers is now available in an updated and revised second edition. This is the only guide that brings together a comprehensive list of opportunities with essays by prominent professionals in the field. An invaluable resource for directors and choreographers at every stage of their career. **PAPER $19.95**

The Production Notebooks
Theatre in Process, Volume Two
Edited with an Introduction by Mark Bly

Four of the finest dramaturgs offer comprehensive histories of the development of four major productions, *The First Picture Show* by David and Ain Gordon, *Shakespeare Rapid Eye Movement* directed by Robert Lepage, *In the Blood* by Suzan-Lori Parks and *Geography* by Ralph Lemon. **PAPER $18.95**

The Playwright's Voice
American Dramatists on Memory, Writing and the Politics of Culture
Interviews by David Savran

Interviews with fifteen of the theatre's most important artists: Edward Albee, Jon Robin Baitz, Philip Kan Gotanda, Holly Hughes, Tony Kushner, Terrence McNally, Suzan-Lori Parks, José Rivera, Ntozake Shange, Nicky Silver, Anna Deavere Smith, Paula Vogel, Wendy Wasserstein, Mac Wellman and George C. Wolfe. **PAPER $16.95**

THESE FINE BOOKS AND OTHERS ARE AVAILABLE FROM TCG.

VISIT OUR ONLINE BOOKSTORE AT WWW.TCG.ORG